"Writing with emotional honesty from the truthful depth of his soul, Frank describes his journey from the darkness of hopelessness and self-rejection to the light of healing that flows from a felt sense of God's compassionate love and from a restored capacity to embrace his wounded inner child. This fascinating memoir provides rich food for psychological and spiritual growth."

—Wilkie Au, coauthor with Noreen Cannon Au of *Aging with Wisdom and Grace*

"Frank Rogers Jr. recounts a palpable rendering of mind, body, and soul torment generated from childhood trauma and sexual abuse. Through narrative and spiritual processing, he demonstrates the vital need for pathways which can support transcendent meaning making, coherence, validation, and healthy attachments. He ultimately conveys how spiritual and reflective exercises along with creative experiential processes, compassion, and love are healing threads within the fabric of trauma recovery."

—Heather M. Boynton, PhD, RSW, HBPE,
Assistant Professor at the University of Calgary

"Frank Rogers tells us the story of his own journey of recovery from sexual abuse with tremendous honesty and sensitivity. For those who suffer from sexual abuse, the book offers great compassion, understanding, and guidance to the way toward healing. For those who are listening there is a teaching of the way of kindness, compassion, and presence that we might learn to be companions along the way of healing of others."

—Elizabeth Conde-Frazier, Director for the Association of
Hispanic Theological Education

"Frank Rogers is a spellbinding storyteller. Here he bravely narrates the tale of coming to terms with his own painful past—and how that journey can light the way for clarity, faith, and a measure of inner freedom."

—David Freudberg, host of public radio's *Humankind*

"This courageous and evocative book is a powerful testimony to the heart-breaking realities of childhood sexual abuse and the potential pathways to healing and restoration. The groundbreaking narrative reveals the despair of traumatic experience, the power of resilience, and the transformational potential of the sacred. Grounded in the challenges of complex trauma from multigenerational sexual abuse in the family and in the church, this book offers compassionate insights into the restorative journey toward connection and wholeness."

—Sheryl A. Kujawa-Holbrook, EdD, PhD, Professor of Practical Theology,
Claremont School of Theology

"Frank Rogers Jr. vulnerably shares the devastating impact of childhood sexual abuse and the intensely complex journey of healing. The courage, faith and determination of survivors is validated on every page. For any who desire to deeply understand what the healing of childhood trauma entails, *Cradled in the Arms of Compassion* is a must read that provides a seamless weaving of story, trauma-based healing modalities, and contemplative spiritual practices."

—Janyne McConnaughey, author of
Trauma in the Pews: The Impact on Faith and Spiritual Practices

"This is an amazing book that I couldn't put down once I started it. If you are a survivor of any of these: chronic sex abuse, toxic parents, psychiatric institutions—or if you've cut yourself, felt hopelessly suicidal, or plagued by inner demons, hated yourself for your symptoms and shamefully hid them from others, then this is the book for you. In Frank's brutally honest and remarkably disclosive telling of his story you will find a hope-filled model. His simple, spontaneous act of turning toward and listening to his inner tormentors rather than fighting or running from them, led him, with the help of good therapy, on a remarkable spiritual and healing journey that will inspire all who read it."

—Richard Schwartz, PhD, Founder the Internal Family Systems Institute and author of *No Bad Parts*

"Where does one find sanctuary and safety from those who have abused us, and from the shame that accompanies us like an unwelcome apparition? Rogers offers a harrowing spiritual memoir documenting childhood abuse and trauma, and at the same time, a faithful walk in search of the divine that should be read alongside Julian of Norwich, Dorothy Day, Thomas Merton, Bishop Desmund Tutu, and all the great memoirs."

—Patrick B. Reyes, PhD, Dean of Auburn Seminary, and award-winning author of *The Purpose Gap*

"For Frank Rogers spiritual practice is not an academic theory nor an additive to bourgeois religious life, but a hard-won path to staying alive. No child should ever have to suffer abuse nor any adult the resulting self-loathing; but, like Dante, Frank intuits that the way 'up' to God and life is necessarily 'down,' through sin's source where his demons are rendered in vivid personal detail, given voice by his artful writing, which turns out to be key in his healing."

—David F. White, Professor at Austin Presbyterian Theological Seminary and author of *Tending the Fire that Burns at the Center of the World: Beauty and the Art of Christian Formation*

"With the wisdom of a sage, the genius of a master storyteller, and the tender compassion of a saint, Frank Rogers Jr. offers this memoir as an invitation to dive deep into the waters of human experience and bear witness to it by the power of love. And along with radical care, courage, and candor, the pages are brimming forth with possibilities for hope and healing in a wounded world. I am confident that through this book many lives will be powerfully transformed!"

—Aizaiah G. Yong, author of *Multiracial Cosmotheandrism* and *The Pulse of Life*

Cradled in the Arms of
COMPASSION

Cradled in the Arms of
COMPASSION

A SPIRITUAL JOURNEY
from
TRAUMA TO RECOVERY

FRANK ROGERS JR.

LAKE DRIVE
lakedrivebooks.com

Lake Drive Books
6757 Cascade Road SE, 162
Grand Rapids, MI 49546

info@lakedrivebooks.com
lakedrivebooks.com
@lakedrivebooks

Publishing books that help you heal, grow, and discover.

Hardcover ISBN: 978-1-957687-20-9
eBook ISBN: 978-1-957687-21-6

Library of Congress Control Number: 2023931921

Paraphrased sections of *The God of Shattered Glass*, by Frank Rogers Jr., published by Emerald City Books, 2000, are used with permission.

Cover Design by Laura Duffy
Pietà cover photograph St. Giles' Cathedral, Prague, Czech Republic by Renáta Sedmáková/ Adobe Stock

This book is a memoir. It reflects the author's present recollections and information gathering of experiences over time. Some of the names of individuals or institutions and their characteristics have been changed, some events have been compressed, and some dialogue has been recreated.

If you are feeling suicidal, are thinking about hurting yourself, or are concerned that someone you know may be in danger of hurting himself or herself, call the National Suicide Prevention Lifeline at 1-800-273-TALK (1-800-273-8255). You can also find help in locating a mental health professional by consulting with your health-care provider.

For Linda

Pi.e.tà (pee-ay-TAH) *n.* [Ital., pity, a pietà < Lat. pietàs] 1. A representation of the Virgin Mary holding and mourning the dead body of Jesus in her arms. 2. Maternal compassion cradling with care one who is suffering. 3. A big brother holding his deceased sister's story nestled within his own.

A Word of Encouragement for the Reader

———•◆•———

THIS BOOK TELLS a painful story. And it can be a painful read. It chronicles the experience of childhood sexual abuse, its torturous aftermath, and the long, anguishing road to psychological and spiritual well-being. Some scenes are graphic. The emotions felt are raw. The perils along the way can be harrowing.

If at any point it becomes too much, take a break. Put the book down and go for a walk, bake bread, run a bath, tend a garden, sip tea, and watch the sunset. Listen to your body and care for its needs in the way that you know how. The book will still be there whenever you are ready.

And if you are a survivor yourself, and you become flooded by memories or emotions that are engulfing, lay the book aside altogether and tend to your regulation and recovery. Seek out someone to talk to. Metabolize your pain. Respect the pace of true inner healing. And go as slow as your body necessitates. Take all the time that you need before coming back to this book—ten days, ten years, or even not at all.

My primary hope in writing this book is that other survivors will know that there are people, much like them, who have also been abused, that the shames that fester in the secrets that we hide can be disclosed and faced with resilience, and that genuine healing is possible.

This book need not be read to serve that purpose.

If scanning but a few pages, or its mere appearance in a bookstore, inspires one person to claim the truth of their experience, to share their pain with a caring listener, and to step toward an emboldened recovery, then its writing will have been worth it. The unread book can become a back-seat companion. Its sheer presence in the world can bear testimony: To those on the journey, "You are not alone. There is at least one person who gets it. And healing can come through telling your story."

CONTENTS

Part I

San Mateo, CA—Age 8

Winter 1966

————◆————

"IS THERE SOMETHING in your dream world that is more important than knowing the source of your sin?"

The nearness of her voice snapped me back. Clad in black, Sister Bernard hovered so close to my desk I could feel the ire emanating from her body. My skin burned, shame oozing from every pore. Her finger stabbed the catechism splayed open on my desk.

"What is the sin called which we inherit from our first parents?" she seethed, apparently for the third or fourth time. I stared at the catechism, unable to focus. Her finger jabbed it again. She still stared at me. But she called on somebody else. "Theresa, 'What is the sin called which we inherit from our first parents?'"

Theresa recited the answer, "The sin which we inherit from our first parents is called original sin."

Sister Bernard still looked at me. "Stop your daydreaming," she scolded. "Your soul depends upon it." She lingered, then released me, returning to the front of the classroom.

I had not been daydreaming. I was wide awake to reality. As if prompted by a premonition, I had glanced out the window beside me. The road alongside the Catholic school playground led to the neighborhood where I lived. When I glanced out, I saw him driving by on his way to our house.

I knew that my grandfather was arriving that day for an extended visit. All the same, seeing him in person caused my stomach to turn. His huge body, more bullish than obese, was crammed into the tiny cab of the Chinook camper he was driving. He slouched forward, as if on a mission, two hands squeezing the wheel, eyes boring straight ahead. And I knew, with a dread as certain as the shame that already soiled me, *Here comes pure evil. And it's coming after me.*

Is there anything more important than knowing the source of our sin? No. Not when its stain causes a child to recognize evil in a grandfather.

MIDMORNING RECESS FOUND me outside, but its usual safe haven brought no reprieve. With my appetite for play dispelled, I walked the edge of the asphalt playground all but oblivious to the squeals of my classmates kicking the ball and skipping rope. The playground's merriment felt unbearable, exposing my despondency with a glare too bright to withstand. I wanted to hide. That's why I sought refuge. I wanted to find a place to get away from it all—the morning's humiliation, my classmates' cackling, the foreboding of my grandfather stalking our house. Nothing pious inspired me. I entered the sanctuary simply to disappear for a while.

I have replayed the ensuing moments so often its details are seared into my imagination. Our chapel, large enough to hold five hundred families, abutted the end of the school building. I could have walked the hall from my classroom and entered the church through a door on the side. Instead, I climbed the outside steps and entered from the front.

As soon as the door closed behind me, I was sealed off from the outside world. The looming sanctuary was silent, the cathedral quiet palpable. And dark. So dark, the scattered candles before the statues up front stood out like stars glistening in the night sky. I stepped in cautiously, only a few feet, and sat in one of the pews near the back. I had never been in the sanctuary alone before. I may well have been trespassing to be in such a holy place all by myself.

Soft streaks of colored light drifted down from the stained-glass windows along the side. The altar up front, draped by a purple cloth, held a cup and a plate. Two spiked candles stood sentry on either side. Above, a life-size crucifix was suspended. The dead body of Jesus hung askew. His eyes, drained of life, were closed.

Mary's, however, were open.

Behind the cross, perched at a height that could peer across creation, an ivory statue of the Madonna gazed out in maternal majesty. Her arms were outstretched, poised to embrace any who would weep into her shoulder. Her face was tender—sobered by the pain that all of us carry, yet all too content to companion us through it. And her eyes. Her eyes held it all—the death of her son on a cross hanging before her; the table that promised bread to endure; the rows of pews still haunted by the countless faithful longing for a place to feel safe and at home; and me, sitting alone in the back.

I cannot explain it. I can only try to describe it. Staring into those eyes, I was cradled into love. She saw me. She saw all of it—my dread, my shame, my sorrow, my depletion. And she got it. I was no longer alone. I was no longer untouchably soiled. I was swaddled in a blanket of sacred care as tender as a mother harboring her newborn. It was not cognitive; I was not thinking. It was not imaginative; I saw no visions. It was immediate. Intuitive. Visceral. And more real than reality. I just knew. Whatever numinous phenomenon that goes by "God" was as with me as if Mary herself—cloaked in invisible presence— had come down from her perch, sat in my pew, and wrapped me in her embrace. I let myself be wrapped. I sank into a warmth, a peace, a security I never knew existed.

Mystics describe being absorbed into the divine as like a drop of water dissolving into an ocean of oneness. I was not dissolved. I was fully aware while it was happening. I was still me. I was, however, fully enveloped in that ocean. For those few moments, nothing else existed. The day—what lay behind, what lay ahead—even the sanctuary I was sitting in, just melted away. Until all that was left was me, and this womb-like presence, soaking me, from within and without, in a cosmic sea of compassion. In that moment, in that eternity, embryonic as it was, I knew in my bones the birthright of every being that dwells in creation. I was welcomed. I was known. And I was loved. With a love more pure than I dared dream possible.

It did not last long.

A door clicked closed off to the side. A visiting priest, not one of our regulars, had vacated the confessional. I turned to catch him staring at me. He smiled, but I was not comforted. I only knew, all of a sudden, that I should not have been there at all.

"You looked so peaceful," he said. "So innocent."

I was not sure if he was sincere or toying with me. I felt anything but innocent. I was spotted in a place where I did not belong, an intruder inside the Holy of Holies.

"What is your name?" he asked.

I was too stricken to answer.

"Aren't you in Sister Bernard's catechism class?" I nodded, still mute with guilt. "Recess is over. Shouldn't you be there?" Of course, I should. He had me. And he knew it. He studied my traumatized stare. "Come with me," he said. "I'll take you there." I had no illusion of his benevolence. It was a command, not an offer. I was caught and being escorted to my punishment.

He placed his hand on my shoulder as he ushered me out through the side door and into the school's hallway. His touch was gentle. His hand trembled slightly, as if some resolve within him was weakening. Then he pressed down. His firmness told me to stop walking.

"I have a better idea," he said. "Why don't you study catechism with me?"

He asked it like I had a choice, like I might really want to, like a classmate suggesting we do homework together at his house after school. I had no choice.

"Wait here," he said. "I'll talk to Sister Bernard."

I watched him walk down the hall, then stop at the door to my classroom. Sister Bernard, I knew, would be livid by now—I was egregiously tardy. The priest disappeared into my classroom. Within moments, he was out. His stride was determined now. If once wavering, his resolve was back. Sister Bernard stormed out behind him, then stopped at the doorway. I was right. She was incensed.

The priest walked toward me, ignoring her presence as he left her in his wake. Behind him, I could see her. Her hands were fisted impotently at her sides. Her face was creased with controlled rage. And she was glaring. Not at him. At me.

I was so pinned to the spot, I could only stare back. Her eyes quivered with fury. They bored into me like she wanted to scorch me telepathically with the death ray of her wrath.

Pierced by her stare, however, I could see that there was something more. Something that almost seemed softer. If I ever thought her capable of feeling anything human, I would swear I saw something like pity lacing the fury in those eyes. It was as if she shared the dread of a schoolboy summoned to be disciplined, while scorning the one punishing the poor lad in the first place. I did not know if her pity was real. Perhaps it was only some trick of my mind grasping for mercy from any unlikely source. What I do know is this: I held onto that pity like a lifeline. As if her stare was all that tethered me to a shore where clemency had a chance.

Then the line gave out. The priest grabbed my arm and whisked me to his office. Once inside, he locked the door, sat me on his couch, and closed the curtains to the windows.

He was not interested, it turned out, in studying catechism. And he assured me that he was not there to punish me. He only wanted to play a game. He sat in a chair, scooted up close in front of me, and, with his hands on my knees, whispered the instructions. It was simple, really. We would take turns. Whatever he did to me, I would do to him.

He started out innocently enough. But it did not matter. The game was not fun for me. The priest did not seem to care. As the turns became less innocent, I fixed my eyes someplace else. Over his shoulders, straight across from me, a writing desk faced the wall. A handful of books were lined in a row. They were ordered by height, descending from left to right. The littlest book, the size of a pocket, was black. Its binding, shiny, looked soft and smooth to the touch. The edges of the pages on top glittered, gilded in silver. The end of a tassel strayed from the bottom as if the book had a tail, a tail that lay there limply, puny and impassive.

Next to the book, so close I need not move a muscle to see it, a glass jar held a bouquet of candy sticks. Maybe a dozen, each one was the same color— green, with yellow stripes. They were long and slender, the kind of stick you could suck to a point so sharp it could pierce somebody's flesh.

A fraction of a glance next to the candy, a postcard crucifix was propped against the wall. Though small, its features were clear. Jesus was naked to the waist. His arms were spread wide. His hands and feet were fixed in place with nails. And his eyes were open. He was watching. Without blinking once, he took in every sordid detail. I watched him watch. His face was expressionless, his disgust masked. He simply stared stoically at each turn the priest and I took. I could not tell from those relentless eyes—maybe he knew; maybe he didn't; maybe it didn't matter to him anyway. But the game was not fun for me.

When the priest was done, he got my attention. He told me to pull my pants back up and to button up my shirt. He told me it was a bad thing that I did, making him play this game. And he told me not to tell anyone—not even in order to cleanse myself in confession—at the risk of my soul and my family's souls suffering in hell forever. Then, with a flick of his wrist, he disposed of me as if I stank of excrement. "Get back to your class," he dismissed. "Sister Bernard will be waiting for you."

I retraced my steps through the deserted hallway. At the side entrance to the sanctuary, I paused. I was not ready to face Sister Bernard with whatever reception she had waiting for me. And my ache overcame any remnant of worry that another trespass could stain me any further. I opened the door and reentered the church.

I did not sit this time. I stood just inside, not daring to penetrate further. Though I surmised better, something in me still hoped. That a womb of sacred care would still be there to embrace me. Its warmth cradling me. Its waters bathing me. Its love real and restoring.

But it was gone. The place was cold. Jesus's eyes were closed again. Mary was just a statue made of stone. As quickly as it had come, the ocean of divine mercy had evaporated. I was alone again. Soiled with sin. As I had been from the beginning. Perhaps since our first parents.

From that day forward, I have been haunted by a question, a question of life or death for me.

Was that glimpse of God I had in the church, that womb of grace that swaddled me, simply some dream world? Or was it real, a cosmic sea of compassion purifying enough that its wash could cleanse the filth that I had become?

Upland, CA—Age 35

November 30, 1993

———◆———

HOW MANY OF *these would it take to kill yourself?* My eyes strained to figure it out. The fine print on the bottle of Tylenol PM was impossibly small to decipher. I could only make out the overdose warning in bold. The proper dose was two pills. No more than two pills every twenty-four hours. But how many was too much? Enough too much to end it for good? I had no idea. I had never gone this far before. Fantasies—incessantly. But I had never acted on them for real. Not until now.

I returned the bottle to the shelf and grabbed another. I faced a wall of them. From the floor to chest-high, five shelves stocked an overwhelming display of choices—the PM varieties of Tylenol, Aleve, and Advil; organic compounds rooted in various quantities of melatonin; and a dizzying array of outright nighttime sleeping aids, each one packaged from short-term doses to yearlong supplies, each one coming in soft gels, coated caplets, and tablets that melted in your mouth; and each one accompanied by the Sav-On generic option at a fraction of the cost. The deluge of possibilities paralyzed me.

I had already been mired in a foggy leadenness. My body was so devoid of energy that driving to the drugstore felt like wading through a muddy bog fevered and fatigued. It took all that I had to drag myself from my Datsun pickup, into the Sav-On Pharmacy, and over to the stupefying panel of sleeping pills. How could I begin to choose from among them?

Some distant voice within me raised an alarm even as I stood there. *Are you really going through with this? Are you really buying sleeping pills? Are you really acting out on the fantasy that has seduced you for years—making it as easy as driving to someplace secluded, opening a bottle, and swallowing a handful of tablets?* I was. But which ones? And how many?

I returned the box and grabbed another. I tried to study its tiny script. It was as indecipherable as the others. I put it back and retrieved another. Then another. And another. At some point, I ended back up with the Tylenol PM. *Okay*, I exhorted myself, trying to jump-start some spark of clarity. *Figure this out. Two tablets a night. You'd have to double that for sure. And double that again. Would ten pills do it? Twenty?* If I went through with this, I wanted no margin for error. No bringing me back from the brink. No facing a single person with the unlivable shame of failing at taking your own life. The bottle that I held contained fifty pills. Surely fifty pills would do it.

"I don't think you want to buy those," said someone next to me. I turned to find a man in a white coat at my side—a pharmacist badge on his breast. A couple of aisles behind him, two women, also clad in white coats, huddled in the plexiglass booth where the prescription medicines were stored and measured. They whispered inconspicuously to each other but cast furtive glances in my direction. Even through my dazed exhaustion, I could deduce what was happening. They had been monitoring me. Then sent the pharmacist to intervene. I looked outside and saw that it was dark. How could that be? I came in right after the day's despair bottomed out with my public disgrace at work—it was four thirty at that point, five o'clock at the latest. With the winter's early sunset, it must be after six. Could I really have been standing here for over an hour?

"Here," the pharmacist continued, "why don't I take these?" He spoke carefully, like he was taking a knife from a madman.

I sputtered into speech. "What? Oh. Yeah. Here." I handed him the bottle. "I was just looking," I added feebly.

He held onto the pills as if that particular bottle held the power over my future. "Are you okay?" he asked with cautious care.

"I'm fine," I said, obviously not. I felt the urge to flee. This was humiliating. I tried to mobilize myself, but I was too disoriented to make a move, like I was still waking up from a drugged-out slumber and wondering how I got where I was.

"Do you need someone to talk to?" he asked with genuine concern. His kindness only mortified me further.

"No," I sighed. "Really, I'm fine." Taking a breath to exert myself, I found a gear and made for the door.

"Hey," he called. I turned back. "Whatever it is, there's always a way." He still held the bottle of pills.

"Sure," I said. "Thanks." But I knew better. There was no way out of the hell of my life. No way but one.

I WAS THIRTY-FIVE years old, and by all outward appearances, I was not only well-adjusted, I was successfully launched into an adulthood brimming with promise. I was married—albeit not happily but able to conceal our biting discontent from public scrutiny. I had a child—a boy, nearly four, who adored me. I owned a home—giving me a foothold into the coveted Southern California real estate market. I had a bachelor's, a master's, and a PhD—my studies surveying the regions of Christian spirituality, depth psychology, mystical theology, and the theory and practice of religious formation. And I was three years in as a tenure-track professor at a progressive, ecumenical school of theology acclaimed worldwide. I was popular in the classroom, esteemed by my colleagues, active in my parish, and a sought-out speaker with a penchant for storytelling. I even chaired the outreach committee at the local council of churches—where during my several years of service we had founded an interfaith AIDS resource center, convened a gang-prevention task force with a cross section of civic stakeholders, and converted a litter-laden vacant lot into a meditation garden with paths of recycled concrete and plants both indigenous and drought-resistant. I exemplified my image of the model professor, person of faith, and family man. I was bright. I was upbeat. I was involved as a dad, as a teacher, as an advocate for the common good.

And I was tortured to the edge of death.

Though I concealed it with a granite tenacity, whipping squalls of malevolent chaos ravaged my interior world. I had always been plagued by a mild depression—a low-grade fever of despondency that occasionally spiked into a spell where my life's preoccupations lost such meaning that getting out of bed in the morning required a herculean effort. And as far back as I could remember, I had lulled myself to sleep with a fantasy of how I would one day kill myself. I would drive up the California coast to a beach in the redwood country outside Eureka. I would park my car facing the ocean. I would listen to the surf as the sun set into the sea. Then, once dark, I would swallow sleeping pills with gulps of wine until sleep came and took me to a place from which I would never have to wake up again.

I did not consider this nightly routine unusual. It was soothing in the way bedtime rituals can be—a glass of warm milk, a prayer to be watched over, a kiss from a loved one, and a fantasy of suicide to settle one into the depths of sleep's relief. Morning always came. And with it, the fevered weariness. I would force myself up and into the day, posing as an exemplar of piety and responsibility.

The internal malaise intensified, however, after my son was born. A disturbing visit from a relative precipitated a tailspin into an interior netherworld where malicious spirits wreaked havoc on my soul and on my sanity. I had forewarnings that this funhouse of sleaze—with its lecherous phantoms and crazy-making distortions—existed in the darkest caverns of my being. But whenever it intimated itself in the past, I was able to fight it back into the shadows, fiercely denying its reality, and dismiss it from my mind as a place too dangerous to ever entertain. Something in me knew. A descent into that sinister necropolis not only threatened my sanity; it threatened my life.

Unfortunately, one visit from my mother was all that it took to suck me into its cyclone of bedlam.

JUSTIN WAS ABOUT six months old when my mom drove down from Northern California to meet him. Not your typical grandmother, the gifts that she brought did not include baby toys or surplus supplies for a newborn. For Cathy, my wife, she brought an album of my baby pictures—a couple from the hospital, one from my baptism, then a photo shoot of several dozen snapshots from various angles of me on a bed wearing nothing but my birthday suit. For me, she brought a caricature of her and my stepdad made on a day trip to Fisherman's Wharf. When the boardwalk artist asked them what their hobbies happened to be, my mom teased flirtatiously, "Well, we have eight children between us." The artist was on it. He drew her in bed grinning with an insatiable lasciviousness as her outstretched arm grasped the back of the boxer shorts on my otherwise naked stepdad as he tried to flee the bed from exhaustion. My mom thought it was a hoot. And for some reason, she thought I should have it.

During her overnight stay, she had no interest in feeding Justin at mealtimes, or burping him after a bottle, or rocking him to sleep in her arms while humming him a lullaby. After eight of them, birthing five, babies seemed to have sucked her maternal instincts dry. Yet on the afternoon that she was leaving, she did ask me if she could change him. We were sitting in my living room, Justin strapped contentedly in his Baby Bouncer between us. Since Justin showed no signs of having soiled himself, the question caught me off guard.

"I'm not sure he needs changing, Mom," I replied.

"Well," she said, "why don't I just check?"

A tremor of alarm rumbled in my belly, a primal red alert that something was not right. And yet, a grandmother changing her grandson's diaper seemed innocent enough. "Okay," I consented guardedly.

She laid his powder-blue blanket on the floor, knelt before it, and placed Justin upon it. He wiggled, smiling up at her, as she paused to gaze at him.

"Couldn't you just eat him up?" she mused mistily.

She slipped him free from his footed pajamas and unpinned his diaper. He was dry. She set the diaper aside anyway, then stared at him again, his naked body still wiggling with happy abandon.

"You are so delicious," she said. She bent down and kissed him on his bare chest. As she rose, she paused midway and lingered. She was lost in a look of sensuous delight. Then she started to lean back down, her head toward his groin, her mouth preparing to kiss his tiny infant penis.

Something in me came uncorked. "*Get away from him!*" I yelled, loud enough that Cathy came rushing in from the kitchen. My mom looked at me with stunned innocence. "*What're you doing?*" I demanded.

"What?" she said. "I was just giving him a little lovin'."

"He doesn't need it," I yelled. "He doesn't need that kind of lovin'." I leapt down, wrapped him in his blanket, and hauled him to his bedroom.

Shortly thereafter, my mom left. She was no longer perplexed at my outburst. She stroked my cheek, saying goodbye as if the incident had never happened.

I, however, could not shake it off so quickly. In fact, it unleashed in me a torrent of rage. For days, I fumed in fury, beseeching Cathy, "*Can you believe it? Right in front of my eyes!*" Cathy, equally incensed, and harboring her own suspicions about the sleaze within the funhouse of my family's dysfunction, demanded that my mom never touch him again, that she never *see* him again unless one of us was on her like a hawk. Whatever my mom was up to, Justin would be protected with a she-bear ferocity.

Though the months progressed, my fury did not dissipate. It only escalated and morphed. I returned to my routine where I kept my composure by sheer force of will, but something had ruptured within me, and my inner world became a madhouse mayhem of lurid hallucinations. I would be sitting at my desk, or driving to work, or watching Justin sleep, or drifting into sleep myself, when images, both grotesque and obscene, would flash before me like shards piercing my façade of sanity—my mom actually kissing my son's penis; my mom kissing my own infant penis; lying naked as a boy in her bed tinged with the scent of her pleasure; a penis in my mouth too big for my hands; being raped from behind by some bullish brute.

It sickened me. What kind of twisted pervert would conceive of such pornographic disgust? But the fantasies were unstoppable. They invaded my consciousness with inescapable force. I could not will them away, wish them away, or whisk them away through some form of distraction. They stabbed my mind like knife wounds.

They even invaded my sleep. Once a refuge, my slumber was now assaulted by nightmares: bullies forcing fellatio; bullish beasts storming into my bedroom; a faceless brute seducing me into a truck's camper; and fire, fire everywhere—torching my mother, torching the beasts, torching my boyhood house, even torching myself in a pyre of self-immolation. I came to dread the night.

And I dreaded the day almost as much. For the truth is, as unnerving as these invasive fantasies were, they paled before the gale-force passions that now ripped within me like crosscurrents in a tempest. My rage became near insuppressible, erupting with a volcanic fury at the slightest provocation—a streetlight turning red, a dawdling salesclerk, my wife requesting that I hang up my jacket, a smirk at my attire from one of my in-laws. Revulsion turned me rancid—at being touched, at being looked at, at being eyed by my wife and found desirable either sexually or simply out of a liking to be close. Despair sucked me into a black hole so dark it squeezed to death every sense of purpose, every sliver of hope, every soul-sustaining delight at the simple pleasures of life to the point of leaving me unmoved and hollow even before the smile from my own baby boy. And lust consumed me—a desire, carnal and debased, that I dared only satiate in the privacy of my own shower, followed by a self-disgust that instantly swallowed any gasp of satisfaction.

I felt possessed by demons, unfettered from their underworld and taking their turns inhabiting me. Not literally, of course, but emotionally. These passions came with such force I was gripped by their power and held at their mercy—no longer in my right mind, no longer even my real self. I strained for dear life to keep them contained and to minimize the damage they sought to unleash in my life. I was kin with the pitiable man from the Gospels, the Gerasene demoniac, the one possessed by so many unclean spirits he named himself Legion and writhed, outcast, beyond the city walls. If I had lived in New Testament times, I too would have been banished to the tombs, far from town, wailing in despair, spewing profanity, and thrashing with a rage so severe it would shatter the shackles that bound us. And like him, I also cut myself with stones.

For me, the most insidious demon, the most soul-crushing and psychically crippling, was shame. I loathed myself. *My God*, I would castigate in a hateful tirade of self-accusation, *look at you. What kind of a depraved person are you? Who would imagine things so lewd? Who would feel things so vile? Who would let such filth into their soul at all? You are supposed to be a Christian, for God's sake, not some degenerate. You're a professor of spirituality, of all things! If your students, your colleagues, your fellow churchgoers had any clue about who you really are, they wouldn't just be disappointed in you, they would be downright repulsed. They would turn their backs with disgust and forsake you as the cesspool you really are. You would make them vomit. You are sick. And sickening. From the inside out, you reek like shit.*

It is true. I despised myself with a disdain so venomous that I would get lost in the fantasy of lacerating myself with sword blades, or riddling myself with bullets, or dousing myself with gasoline and leaping headlong into an inferno. I detested myself. And the demon of self-loathing is as lethal as it is sinister.

I DID SEEK a way out. My life's work, after all, was devoted to exploring spiritual practices that fostered psychological well-being and deepened one's connection to a vivifying divine. My vocation was rooted in my existential quest. I wanted both. I craved to find some peace within—to be emotionally stable and mentally sane enough to find contentment in simply being alive. And I ached to know the Source of true spiritual vitality, that sacred reality that the mystics describe whose benevolent presence stills the storms within, renews life, and roots us in such a sense of belovedness we become vessels of love for ourselves and for others. My soul's deepest desire was simple. I longed to see the face of God—and for that face to be both loving and restorative.

So I plunged into the practices that I studied and taught. With the discipline of a Trappist monk hell-bent on spiritual perfection, I started each day attending daily Mass, practicing some form of contemplative prayer, then recording my experience in my journals. I extended mindful awareness to my breath, my body, my passing thoughts. I meditated, *lectio*-style, on the words of the daily scriptures. I recited a sacred word and used it to return my intention to God through twenty-minute sits of Centering Prayer. I even entered the Gospel stories imaginatively, guided by Ignatius's *Spiritual Exercises* through several weekend retreats at the Jesuit Center.

To be sure, these contemplative forays yielded some moments of relief from my internal maelstrom. They offered the occasional sense of something sacred close to our world—not the face of God per se, but a glimpse, perhaps, of the shadow cast by a presence still hidden in the depths. They were not, however, able to quell my demons for long.

More often than not, my meditation time felt like an extended internal battle. I would try to settle into the quiet prayer chamber within my soul, but intruding passions and fantasies would invade like a battalion of ghouls whose sole charge was to wreak havoc upon the quiet at all costs. I muscled them behind the doors of my awareness and strained to keep them at bay by focusing on my breath, or my sacred word, or the phrase of scripture that I was meditating upon, but they pounded through anyway and flanked from behind. I battled these furies with every weapon at my disposal—suppressing, ignoring, scolding, beseeching, drowning them out with the drone of a mantra—but they hounded and harassed with relentless tenacity until my timer brought the contemplative bout to a close.

Which, of course, did not discourage the demons. They merely bullied their way into the rest of my day. No, my contemplative practice did not coax any coming of the benevolent face of God. Which, really, was no surprise. Why would God's face come to one so vile? Unless to sneer at me with contempt. Which was not necessary. God's disgusted absence was enough. I wasn't worth the time even to condemn.

At some point, I conceded to the indignities of therapy. I was self-aware enough to know that my turmoil had roots in the mysteries of my past. Both my wife and my friends suspected sexual abuse in my history despite my insistent denials. And I knew, in theory at least, that psychological counseling could be a path of healing and self-restoration. But at the time, exposing the haunted-house horrors of my inner world to the scrutiny of another felt like submission to certain humiliation. My torment, however, was just too much. So I sought the curative promise of a mental health professional.

Perhaps to be expected, finding the right professional proved to be a challenge. The first therapist I visited asked me to complete a battery of tests, then meet for an initial consultation. He studied the results from behind his desk, then looked up and said that I seemed to be struggling with anger. That he would presume insight into my psyche on the sole basis of some standardized test score so enraged me that I stormed out of his office midsession never to return again. Several others, consulting similar tests, suggested antidepressants. After getting over feeling like a cliché—another poster boy for the Prozac nation—I conceded to a prescription or two, but the meds only dulled my awareness of my demons. They did not make them torment me with any less tenacity. I endured a session of therapeutic massage—unwittingly uncorking a primal scream at the gentle pass through a suspected pressure point—but my aversion to touch would not allow the masseuse to press any deeper. A psychologist suggested pounding her couch with foam bats, but the contrivance could not ignite my rage, only a tepid annoyance at the charade. The hypnotherapist proved unable to bypass some sentry part of me not about to open Pandora's box. A family-systems therapist suggested that I lie in my mother's arms like a newborn baby. A Christian therapist recommended more time in the Bible. And the marriage therapists—all three in succession—threw up their hands and counseled divorce.

Finally, I found Helen. A Jungian analyst and quintessential listener with an all-embracing warmth that was worth the fee alone, she was the first therapeutic companion I trusted to help me decipher my past.

Unfortunately, we quickly encountered a near-impassable obstacle. I had no past to decipher. I could not conjure a single reliable memory before the age of thirteen, when my parents split up the day before I began high school. My entire childhood until then was blank. I could recall biographical information. I knew that I had lived in South San Francisco until I was five. I knew that I had played baseball throughout my school years. I knew that we had lived those years further down the peninsula in Foster City. I knew that we had attended St. Timothy's Roman Catholic Church. But I could not retrieve the memory of any of it.

I could look at a photograph, say, of the kindergarten play in which I had frozen when I was supposed to bear-hug my mother on stage. I could recognize it as an event in my past—but the memory itself, with that self-authenticating internal imprint that rings from within that the event really happened, was altogether missing. I was like the Vietnam vet who knew that he had completed a tour of duty but had no recollection of having been in a battle—the whistle of gunfire, the burn of napalm, the screams of the corpsmen with blown tissue for legs, the terror in the eyes of the young men he had killed, all completely erased from his remembrance of his time in the service.

And that is what made all the turmoil within me so infuriating. The rages, the revulsions, the lurid fantasies—they made no sense. Nothing in my past could explain them. The images that pierced like flashbacks of trauma were not memories in any form that I could identify. They were fictions and fragments. They were set in locales from my childhood and peopled with players from my past, but the events themselves felt like unconscious fabrications. Week after week, Helen would insist that my feelings and fantasies came from somewhere, that the body does not make up this kind of thing. But I would stare back in impenetrable disbelief, knowing better, certain that I was simply sick and perverted, inexplicably soiled in my very cells, goods so damaged in my DNA that no years of therapy, no spiritual practice, no self-help regimen could ever wash away my inherent depravity. And Helen would nod knowingly, ever the exemplar of compassion, then reaffirm with eyes that seemed so certain: I was not inherently depraved; my feelings and fantasies came from somewhere.

Thus commenced my search for my past. I became a detective of my own experience. I constructed timelines of my childhood and filled in details as they came to me. I studied old pictures and made notes of the stories that I had been told. I made inconspicuous phone calls to my mom, my dad, and my siblings, slipping in the occasional question about some piece of my history. And throughout, I journaled all my feelings, drew pictures to discern their texture, and plumbed the images that assailed me, sifting through the clues to separate nightmare from memory, fact from fiction, fantasy from flashbacks of real events. It was tortuous. It was exhausting. And at first, it was more crazy-making than sanity-restoring.

And all of it was in secret. My outer world was a façade, as I was role-playing the part of the spiritually insightful professor by day, a devoted and blissful family man by night. My inner world, on the other hand, was a subterranean cauldron of volcanic activity—boiling, fuming, rumbling, blistering—ever on the verge of a catastrophic eruption.

Until I could no longer contain it.

MY WIFE AND I had been struggling throughout. As my turmoil intensified, the strain on our marriage became unbearable. Our bickering escalated into bouts of yelling—flinging at each other complaints and accusations, insults and ultimatums, in verbal free-for-alls that wailed into the wee hours of the morning. One finally cut to the bone. We had been shouting at each other in our kitchen when words failed my rage and indignation. I screamed my fury and stormed out of the room. I realized that Justin—now three and a half—was no longer watching videos in the living room. I went upstairs and found him in our bedroom, lying on the floor between our bed and the wall, clutching his blankie while sucking his thumb. I lay down next to him and asked him what he was doing. The anguish in his eyes pierced me as much as his words.

"Please, Daddy," he said. "Make all the screaming go away."

Too raw to keep from screaming at my partner and too tortured to quiet the screaming in my head, I honored his request in the only way that I was able. I moved out. It was the first crack in the well-polished persona that I presented to the world. The clean-cut suburban couple was splitting up.

THE SUMMER BEFORE I found myself staring at a drugstore's shelf of sleeping pills, I rented a cabin in the mountains above the town where I worked and had lived. The rustic single-room bungalow had just a stove and counter on one side, a bed in a nook on the other, and a sofa and stone fireplace in the living space between them. It was only a twenty-minute drive from my office—a straight shot, really—two turns, then stay on Mount Baldy Road until the second switchback past the Icehouse Canyon trailhead. But that twenty minutes climbed five thousand feet on a twisting two-lane road with mountain wall on one side and cliffs on the other. By the time I navigated the ascent each evening, I was as isolated as a misanthropic loner. And just as mad.

The silence of the alpine barrenness, the desolation of my aloneness, and the public humiliation of marital separation conspired to erode any remaining constraints that could contain the passions that afflicted me. I plunged into a crippling depression, isolating myself entirely except for twice-a-week sessions with Helen, and limiting my appearances in town to faking my way through classes and filling a chair at faculty meetings. I lost my appetite altogether, becoming so gaunt my colleagues feared that I was terminally ill. I stalked the woods with a baseball bat, consumed by a rage, insane and homicidal, pummeling trees while screaming obscenities. When that was not enough, and the night was black, I sped down the mountain road at terrifying speeds, one time tearing through a stop sign without slowing, just daring a car to appear that I could smash through into oblivion. Then, back at the cabin, I would cut myself with razor blades, slicing dozens of tiny gouges up the insides of my arms, feeling the pull of the blade along my skin not in any effort to kill myself—the cuts themselves barely drew blood—but to punish my skin for some betrayal that soiled it, and to feel on my body physically the pain that I felt in my soul so acutely.

And at night, in bed, I rehearsed my fantasy of suicide with detailed specificity. I composed what I would write in a letter to my son. I scripted the message that I would leave for my dean. I visualized the route that I would drive up north. I pictured the beach where I would park, the crash of the waves against the rocks, the redwood trees standing watch, the setting sun sliding into the sea. I tasted the wine from the bottle, saw the pills poured into my hand, felt the capsules poised in my mouth, then swallowed them down, surrendering into the slow descent of drowsiness as it slipped me into the peaceful sleep for which I so desperately longed. Then I writhed in the anguish of knowing that I could never do this to my boy, some insane logic calculating that I could never live with myself if I killed myself. But I wanted to. As sure as the breakdown toward which I was plunging headlong, I wanted to.

Then Thanksgiving happened.

AS I SPIRALED through that autumn of tortured isolation, one of the beasts appearing in my lurid hallucinations took on a recognizable form. Like a sinister ancestral presence rising out of the mists of the past, my mother's stepfather, my grandpa Harold, came to haunt me with a bedeviling persistence. It was odd. I had no memory of ever being with him. In fact, I came to realize that I knew next to nothing about him at all. Somewhere along the way, I had absorbed that he had lived in Southern California with my grandmother when my mom met my dad in high school; that he and my grandmother had moved to the central coast for a while when I was a child; and that they later moved to rural western Oregon where they had lived in a trailer, miles off the grid, deep in the Cascade Forest. That was it. And I didn't know how I knew that much. As if we had made some unwritten pact, our family never acknowledged his presence. We never mentioned his name in casual conversation. We never called him up on the telephone. We never sent him a package at Christmas. We never so much as mentioned that it happened to be his birthday. Our muteness about him was militant, as if the violence of our silence could void his existence altogether.

And yet, I had a visceral impression of him. I knew exactly what he looked like—a large bull of a man with a prison guard crew cut and a wartime tattoo inside his left forearm. And I knew how I felt if I were around him—the very sight of him chilled me with dread. As if his reach could stretch from the darkness of an Oregon forest a thousand miles away—or even, years later, from the other side of the grave—I could feel his menacing hulk always looming in the shadows of my childhood recollections, ever staring, ever brooding, ever poised to prey upon us in sadistic violation.

His nefarious reach even stretched into my lonely mountain cabin. Slipping through my defenses with sociopathic malevolence, he penetrated my nightmares on a near nightly basis—sometimes assaulting my mother; sometimes assaulting girls that I could not see; sometimes sending apish beasts to break into my childhood home, snatch me from our living room, and abduct me into a camper where he assaulted me alone. Then he trespassed into my waking hours through the fantasies that invaded me by day. I saw his face on the one fellating me, his face raping me from behind, his face lying with my mom and me in a tangle of erotic intimacy. The images repulsed me. My body would convulse in an attempt to flick them out of my being. But they persisted, assaulting me with their filth until they crystalized into a storyline that played out with such Technicolor clarity I could not keep from imagining it, time and time again, with sickened fascination.

I am staring out of my living room window, three years old, at a green truck with a full-sized camper mounted on the bed. I hear the music of the ice cream man driving onto our street. Somehow knowing it is forbidden, I walk toward my mother's bedroom, the desire for ice cream overcoming my trepidation. I stop at the door. My mother and grandfather are naked in her bed, my mother ashen, my grandfather grunting on top of her. She sees me. Her eyes are vacant and resigned. He turns and sees me too. He sneers, then smiles malignantly. He makes my mother undress me and set me on the bed. She looks at him as he stares at me, his eyes diabolical and scheming.

Before he makes a move, she turns back to me. As my grandfather watches, she caresses my chest, her middle finger sliding down toward my privates, which she then fondles, kisses, and mouths. With a snort, he pushes her away, glares at me with contempt, and with the snap of his middle finger, flicks my stiffened penis. Through with us both, he dresses and leaves the room. My mom rolls over and cups me under the covers like two nude lovers escaping into the sanctity of their own bed. I stare out the window. The music from the ice cream truck fades in the distance.

The fantasy nauseated me. What kind of a deviant would conjure up such abhorrent filth? Yet, for all its lewdness, I could not refrain from replaying it with painful precision, my body recognizing each sensation as if it had experienced it all for real. But I hadn't! The entire daydream was a lurid lie.

Helen, when I poured it all out during therapy, trusted my body's memory more than my amnesic insistence that I was making it all up. She was sure that my nightmares and fantasies were at least symbolic of some actual experience of abuse, sure that I must have had some encounter with this man who was so haunting me. But I insisted that he had never come to our house, that I had never seen him in person, that I had no reason whatsoever to think that he was anything but a reclusive relative who lived in the woods hundreds of miles away.

"How do you know for sure?" she would query. "You may have blocked it out with everything else."

"I don't know for sure," I would counter. "But I don't know anything different."

"How do you explain the visceral sensations?" she asked.

"Like I've been telling you," I came back with desperate exasperation, "I'm either sordidly depraved, or I'm going insane."

"Well," she continued undeterred, "it is well worth looking into. Is there any way to find out more about your grandfather?"

So it was that I made my Thanksgiving pilgrimage to pay a visit to my parents. It was not a social call. It was a fact-finding mission. It was time to learn more about this mysterious man shrouded in shadows and secrecy. It was time to find out if I simply was just inexplicably depraved—or, at least, if I had lost my toehold on sanity.

THOUGH MY MOM lived on the San Francisco Peninsula near where I had grown up, my dad lived in the country just south of Sacramento. An hour or so apart from each other, they were both about a seven-hour drive from Southern California. I decided to take Justin and drive up to my dad's for Thanksgiving Day with the intention of finding some private time to ask him a few questions, then drive to my mom's Friday afternoon to do the same with her. I hoped one or the other could offer some clues that either confirmed or discredited my grandfather's influence on my childhood. I should have been careful what I hoped for.

With a house full of relatives—playing pool, watching football, and cooking and cleaning while the children ran about in round after round of foxtail tag—Thanksgiving Day yielded no time for an intimate conversation with my dad. Friday morning, however, I found him starting a fire in the family room downstairs while the others were all still sleeping. I had told him before I came up that I hoped for a few moments to talk with him, that I had been thinking about my childhood and was curious about a few things. Conversation was not my father's forte—he was a carpenter who measured the value of work by the callouses it left on one's hands. If not talkative, though, he was always reflective any time that you asked him a question. We sat by the hearth and reminisced for a while, my inquiries innocent enough as I screwed up the courage to open a door that felt as forbidden as the fruit offered Adam by Eve. In spite of my foreboding, I eventually took a bite.

"I'm curious," I broached, "about Grandpa Harold. It seems like we never talked about him much."

My dad stared at the fire with stony concealment, as stoic as the time that he had slammed the car door on his thumb without so much as a wince. "What makes you ask about him?" he questioned.

"To tell the truth, Dad," I answered, "I get a real creepy feeling every time that I think of him."

He weighed what to say, as if determining whether something was my business to know. Apparently, it was. "It's true," he said. "Harold was not a good man." He stared at the fire some more. "Few people know this, but Harold molested your mother all the way through high school. Her two sisters too." He paused again, as if the brutality still stung nearly four decades later. "In fact, he came up to me the morning of our wedding and whispered real mean, 'I'll let Barb tell you why she won't be bleeding tonight.'"

My body recognized the truth as my dad was saying it, as if it had known it all along—my grandfather was a predator. I wanted to retch with revulsion. I wanted to weep with relief. But dread trumped both as my body knew more. I stared at the fire as impassive as my dad as I dared to press a little closer. "Did he ever visit us?" I asked.

"Sure," my dad said. "Several times. They came when we lived in South San Francisco; you must have been three or four. Your mom's little sister was still living with them. Then they came a couple of times when we lived in Foster City—once when your mom's half sister graduated from high school. She was pregnant at the time, which didn't make sense, she never had a boyfriend. And one time they stayed for weeks. Harold forced an inmate's wife to have sex with him when he was a prison guard in Nipomo and they had to leave town—the guy's gang was going to kill him. So they lived in the camper on the back of their truck in front of our house trying to decide where to go next. They stayed so long they got warnings for vagrancy. Your mom was beside herself with how long they were staying. They ate us out of food. They made her do their laundry. I even had to run an electrical wire from the house to the camper. They lived off us for weeks. We thought they'd never leave. Finally, they moved to Oregon and bought that trailer in the woods."

"Where were we when he was around?" I asked, already knowing the answer. "Us kids, I mean?"

"Where would you be? At home with your mom. I was away at work all day. The rest of you were at the house putting up with Harold."

LATER THAT DAY, I drove with Justin to my mom's condo. The closer we got, the more fear I felt, like the terror of descending a cellar's stairs where a sadist lay in wait in the dark. To be sure, my dad's revelations gave credence that my feelings and fantasies had substance to them. But I still lacked any solid evidence that my grandfather, or even one of his prey, had actually victimized me. I arrived at my mom's nauseous with foreboding. What horrors awaited hidden in the dark? It was Saturday afternoon before the face in the cellar revealed itself and struck.

I had put Justin down for a nap in the spare bedroom upstairs and walked down to find my mom alone in the living room. Like with my dad, I had mentioned to her that I wanted to talk about my years growing up. Unlike him, my mom, though agreeable, was on her guard. I started the conversation casually enough. To be honest, I felt mixed—I was horrified at the abuse that she had endured as a child and could appreciate her right to keep it to herself. And yet, I ached to know the source of my shame, and I feared that she concealed how hers may have bled into mine. So I made gentle inquiries about our life together with the caution of a cop teasing out a few details from a witness who saw more than they were divulging. I asked about our home in South San Francisco, the timing of our move to Foster City, the birth of my three younger siblings, about her mom, her sisters, and how she met my dad. As is her way, once she got going, she stared off dreamily and meandered through the shallows of our past remembering anecdotes, connecting them to others, circling back to forgotten details, then jumping ahead to others in a spaghetti noodle stream-of-consciousness monologue through the years of my childhood. She shared easily and amply, the current of her memory drifting without effort, needing only an occasional nudge to keep it flowing along.

Until I brought up her stepfather.

"You know, Mom," I finally risked. "I don't really know much about Grandpa Harold."

As if cut short by the snap of a guillotine's blade, the ease of her reminiscence halted. Her lips pursed as she still stared off. "There's not much to say, really," she offered with measured vigilance. "I don't see him much anymore."

"How about when we were growing up? Did we see him much then?"

"No." She shook her head. "Not really. They stayed in Lakewood for a while, then moved to Nipomo when he got that job in the prison. Then a couple of years later, they moved up to Oregon—into that trailer in the woods. We didn't visit them much."

"How about when they visited us?"

"No . . ." She shook her head again. "They didn't visit us either."

I thought that maybe she needed some prompting. "What about in South San Francisco? And in Foster City? Didn't he visit us then?"

"No," she said matter-of-factly, without any need to double-check her memory. "We never saw them. I haven't seen Harold since I married your father."

It didn't make sense. I wanted to be clear that I was hearing her correctly. "You're saying that Grandpa Harold and Grandma Cushing never visited us when we lived in South San Francisco, or when we lived in Foster City?"

"No," she said. "They never visited. They never came to our house, any house."

I paused, trying to take it in. I couldn't. "Are you sure?" I asked.

She turned to me. It was not clear what I saw in her eyes. Was it dogged denial, a fogged-out forgetfulness, the unquestioned certainty of her own truth, or the desperate plea that her lie be believed? I could not tell. All I know is what she said. "It never happened. He never set foot in our house."

I had nothing to come back with. Which was just as well. My mom was weary. "I'm going to rest for a while," she said. And she walked up the stairs to her bedroom.

I sat for a few minutes reeling. I could not put it all together. The puzzle pieces of my past that were just slipping into place had exploded into splinters of disorienting uncertainty. *He came to our house,* I insisted to myself. *I know he came to our house. My dad remembers it in detail. How can she pretend that he was never there? Is she lying? Is she mistaken? Am I misremembering what my dad really said?* I did not know what to believe. I had no clue how to tell fact from fiction. It was crazy-making. Beyond crazy-making. I was in the cellar's darkness, no sadist in sight, with neither sanity nor sound judgment to discern a way out.

My infuriation only spiraling as I struggled to make sense of it, I went upstairs to check on Justin. The spare room was quiet, the door still ajar. I nudged it open. Justin was gone. Panic snapped me alert. There was no doubt—I would have seen him if he had come down the stairs. I scanned the room—he wasn't there. That left only one place.

The shower in my mother's bedroom was on. The doorknob was locked. I pounded so hard the door buckled. "*Mom! Is Justin in there?*"

"Of course," she answered, as if it were routine.

God no. "*Open the door!*" I shouted. She did. She was in her bathrobe, the top draped open to her belly button. My three-year-old son was sitting on her bed. "What are you doing?" I demanded of her.

"What?" she said. "I was just going to take a nap. I shower with all of my boys, and then we take a little nap."

I did not scream. I did not strike the door. I did not strike my mother. But I was insane with rage. I whisked Justin off the bed, threw our belongings into our bags, and hauled us both out to my truck. I buckled him in, tossed the bags in the back, then hustled into the driver's seat. I had backed out into the street when I saw her. Still in her bathrobe, she was standing on the curbside. I pulled up, glaring out my windshield. She stepped close to my side window.

"What are you doing?" she asked. "I thought you were staying until tomorrow."

"Something came up," I seethed, barely able to contain myself. "Something came up at home. I have to get back. Right now."

"Okay," she said. "Okay." She smiled softly—perhaps with resignation, perhaps with wistfulness, perhaps with the coyness of two conspirators sharing a secret that bound them for life. Then she took her middle finger and slid it down my chest like a lover's farewell caress. "Don't ever forget," she said, "how much I have always loved you."

I hit the gas and fled.

I DROVE THE four hundred miles back home in nearly one sitting—stopping only for gas and fast food for Justin. I held it together through the night until Sunday at noon when I delivered Justin back to his mom's. For better or worse, throughout my freefall into madness, I fiercely maintained the pretense of stability whenever Justin was with me; in my fights with Cathy, he had seen enough of his dad out of control. But the moment the door closed harboring him at his mom's, I became unhinged. I howled and wailed in my truck, drove back to the mountains, and stormed through the woods for hours, pounding trees and screaming obscenities until darkness forced me back to my cabin. I paced and fumed into the night, trying to journal my feelings to calm myself down, but only attacking the paper with slashes and scribbles, so I paced and fumed some more.

Then I took it out on my cabin. Wielding my baseball bat like an angry God of vengeance, I pummeled my sofa, my bed, my lamps, my books, the glasses on my drainboard, the plates on my table, the sappy ceramic Pietà—Mary cradling the dead body of Jesus—smirking from the mantel on my fireplace. I swung at it all—beating back my mom's finger on my chest, beating back the thought of her taking a nap with Justin, beating back the sight of my mom and my grandfather beckoning me into their bed—pounding it all away, piercing the alpine silence with my screams and the sound of glass shattering against the walls.

Someone knocked at the door. I glanced at the clock. It was two in the morning. I opened it. It was my neighbor—a grad-student reference librarian at my workplace who lived down the hill from me. I was so loud I had wakened him up through the woods a hundred yards away.

"Are you okay?" he asked, worry creasing his face.

My chest was heaving. My cabin was thrashed. He had heard the screams and the smashing of glass so loud they still echoed from the litter all around me. What could I say? "I'm fine," I replied in defiance of the obvious. "I was just cleaning up. I'll keep it down."

He studied me, both of us knowing the truth. "Okay," he yielded, "I was just checking." He stood another moment, too concerned to leave me alone, too out of his element to know what to do.

"Really, I'm fine," I reaffirmed, prodding him along.

He stared at me, buying time for the right words to come. There weren't any. So he just bobbed his head. And, all else futile, he left.

The next morning, I woke up drained of all life. I was so depleted that breathing was a labor, so despairing that staying alive felt cruel. I left a message for my dean, telling her that I was not feeling well and would not be able to teach that day. She called back immediately. I did not pick up. As her voice carried through the answering machine, my fears were confirmed. She knew. I could tell by the masked concern lacing her voice. My grad-student neighbor had already reported to her my dead-of-night rampage.

"Of course," she consoled through the answering machine, "you shouldn't teach when you're not feeling well. But I would really like to see you this afternoon. Please call me to confirm that you'll be here at three." The subtext was loud and clear—*You really shouldn't be isolating yourself*, she was subtly admonishing. *Not at a time like this.*

I could not bear to face her in my state, so I ignored her request. I spent the morning staring into my cold fireplace, the debris of the night's outburst strewn all around like mutilated remains on a battlefield. For me, however, the battle was over. I had lost all fight. Too weary to rage, too numb to cry, too bereft to take comfort in the carve of cutting myself, I simply craved to be dead.

My dean called three more times, each one more urgent in its plea that I call back to confirm my appearance. Each call a knife twist of humiliation, I answered the next one just to make her stop. She told me how much she wanted to see me. I told her that I wasn't feeling very well. She said that it was really important to her. I told her that I was a mess—too sick to clean myself up. She said that she didn't care, she just wanted me to come, no matter what I happened to look like. We both knew what was going on. I wasn't really sick. And after weeks of worry, and now the report of my acting out, she wanted to gauge my mental state for herself. She wasn't going away. So I gave in. I told her that I'd be there at three. Just to be safe, she suggested two forty-five.

I was true to my word. I did not shave, shower, or change my clothes. I arrived at my workplace at a quarter to three wearing a long-sleeve thermal T-shirt, blue jeans ripped at the knees, a knit stocking cap pulled over my ears, and hiking boots with the shoestrings untied.

The campus was unusually crowded. I lifted the collar and shrunk into my wool-lined jean jacket to skulk in unnoticed. The dean was standing on the patio out in front of her office, huddled with three men—two in suits, one decked out in a vicar's ecclesiastical garb. When she spied me, she rushed over bright with cheer, her academic gown draped over her arm.

"I'm so glad you made it," she said, oblivious to my appearance. "You're just in time. Go get your robe."

"My robe?" I wondered, momentarily bewildered. Then it hit me. It was November 30—the day of her official inauguration as dean. Some five hundred people were expected at the installation ceremony—bishops, university presidents, former professors, distinguished alumni, the mayor and city council—the entire coronation commencing with a faculty procession in full academic regalia. "Of course," I said, recovering. "It's in my office."

I was as trapped as an insect pinned into place inside a glassed exhibit. Now that it was known that I was there, I had no choice but to take my place in the academic procession. I slunk into my office, removed my stocking cap from my scuzzy hair, and covered what I could with my neon-blue robe with its scarlet trim and hood. But it was no use. The boldness of my academic attire only accentuated the deadbeat that it sought to conceal. Haggard and grungy, I looked like I had crashed the pageant by mistake, wandering in off the street and copping some scholar's gown after a weekend bender in some timberland brothel.

The concern on the faces of my faculty colleagues as I joined them in the robing room only mortified me all the more. Mercifully, they did not say anything. They simply made space for me to slip into the line as we made our way to the ceremony. The audience rose as we marched down the center aisle, serenaded by "Pomp and Circumstance," and approached our seats up front. To my horror, I discovered that the faculty were bestowed unusual seats of honor—not in the front row as was our custom, but up on the dais itself, forming a single row of brightly colored professors, backdrop to the podium, on display for the whole crowd to admire. With no way to escape, I followed suit, stepped up onto the platform, and stood in place facing the sea of onlookers—students, academics, and invited dignitaries—all seeming to avert their eyes from the obvious standout who either did not have the shame enough to cover up his pitiful foulness or was dissing the whole affair in disheveled defiance.

Toward the back, off to the side, I recognized my grad-student neighbor. He did not look at me either, his gaze buried within his program. I did not blame him. My disgrace in front of all my peers was complete and irrevocable. That's when I decided it. Locked in the pillory of professional humiliation, no longer able to conceal my filth from myself or from others, I made up my mind to end the charade of my life for good.

I sat through the speeches, stood through the hymns, and mouthed my way through the prayers, the solidifying of my resolve my only lifeline in suffering through the public debasement. When the program ended, I joined the procession back out and made for the door, bypassing the receiving line forming in the foyer. I was nearly out when the dean called my name. I turned.

She asked me if I was leaving. I told her that I was. She reminded me that a formal dinner and evening discussion followed the inauguration. I told her that I could not stay. She could see that my mind was made up. Perhaps she saw more. She asked me if I would be okay. I assured her that I would be. She was not convinced. But she did not push. She said that she would check on me in the morning. I told her that was fine. Then I turned toward the door and left. Without looking back, I discarded my robe, drove to the drugstore, and stood for an hour staring at sleeping pills.

AFTER THE PHARMACIST thwarted my purchase of Tylenol PM, I shuffled out of the drugstore and plopped into my truck. The long, slow leak of my spirit depleted the last residue of vitality within me. And a weight of weariness descended upon me that was almost immobilizing. Turning the key in the ignition felt overwhelming. Hunting for another drugstore inconceivable. All I wanted to do was to get myself home and pass out in my bed until I could regroup in the morning. Even this proved to take more than I was able to suck up.

I willed some spark of volition and found myself driving in the direction of my cabin, but my muddled mind strained to track my truck's movement. I made the turn onto Mount Baldy Road before I realized that I had neglected to turn on my headlights. They did not help much. Even with their illumination, the road faded in and out of focus. I could barely follow the flow of the curves in time to turn into them. I continued to wind my way up the mountain, but energy was hemorrhaging from my body. I fought to keep my eyes open, my hands from losing their grip on the wheel, my lungs to remember to take a breath, each puff of air now a forced labor.

Just get home, I goaded myself like a murmured mantra. *Just get home*. Still, my spirit bled from me, as if every cell within me was draining into a paralyzed stupor. I pushed through the dopey fatigue. Pushed to keep my foot on the gas. Pushed to keep the truck on the road. Pushed to keep my body upright. Until I could push no more. My hands slipped off the steering wheel. My foot fell off the pedal. My torso slumped over onto the seat at my side. And my truck veered off the road. The last thing I saw as I collapsed was the yawning darkness of the cliff in front of me. I did not care. I was ready to be swallowed into oblivion.

Fortunately, I had been plodding uphill. I did not veer far. With the truck still in gear and my foot off the clutch, it sputtered, then stalled a few yards before the edge. There I lay, immobile and on the edge of consciousness. I was still several miles from the cabin, then a twenty-step climb up to its perch. I did not have it in me. I hardly had the juice to keep a beat in my heart. So I just lay there, dimly hoping that someone would come—a cop, a neighbor, a hiker lost in the dark—anyone to help me get to my cabin and carry me into bed. It was a winter evening on an isolated mountain road. Nobody came. And somewhere between wondering if I would freeze to death in the night and absorbing how close I had come to really driving off a cliff, I realized: I needed to get some help.

With none coming to find me there, I knew that I needed to get back into town. As the night's cold seeped into my cab, I blew the dying embers of my spirit into some semblance of flame. I harnessed what strength I could, grabbed the steering wheel, and pulled myself upright. Each act required resolute concentration, like a rock climber scaling a precipice one fingerhold at a time. *Push in the clutch*, I exhorted myself. *Turn the key. Shift into reverse. Back up the truck.* The truck jerked onto the road. *Turn the wheel. Shift into first. Let out the clutch. And steer.*

Though sensing my truck's motion, I struggled to keep up. The engine over-revved in a grinding roar. *Shift into second*, I willed myself. *Now into third.* It was like I was stuck in a dreamlike slow motion while the world around me moved at full speed. *Seventy miles an hour*, I registered from the speedometer. *Going too fast. Put foot on brake. Shift down.* I took a few breaths from the effort. *Tires on gravel.* I could hear from the sounds out my door. *Turn truck right. Bushes scraping door. Turn back left. Ten miles an hour. Going too slow. Give more gas. Going too fast. Slow back down. Keep truck between lines. Just stay . . . between . . . the lines.*

In a sleepwalker's daze, I slowed and sped, swerved and veered down the mountain road, through the stop sign and the two familiar turns, until I pulled up back at the school where I worked. My truck promptly stalled at the curbside. I let go and fell limply against my door like a barely conscious castaway washed up on a shore. It had taken all that I had to get there. The flame of my spirit was out. My muscles had no life even to quiver. Unable to flick my headlights or press the horn for help, I stared out the window, beaten and blank, waiting for someone to find me.

The dean's post-dinner discussion was still in full swing. A maintenance worker in a golf cart was maneuvering for the cleanup. He noticed the headlights and drove over. He recognized me at once.

"Frank, are you okay?" My vacant stare said it all. "I'll be right back," he assured.

A few minutes later, the school president and a pastoral counseling colleague arrived, both dressed to the nines. I must have looked drugged-out and on the edge of an overdose.

"We need to get you to a hospital," my president exclaimed. I did not argue. He retrieved his car. "Can you get yourself in?" he asked. I couldn't. The two of them navigated me from one car to the other, then raced me to the ER.

In the hospital, I lay on the gurney and stared at the ceiling longing to be free of it all. The doctors asked questions. I mumbled replies. Vitals were taken, then taken again. Blood was tested, then tested again. Perhaps to their surprise, they found no drugs or alcohol or any other chemical substance inside me. Neither did they find much potassium or phosphorous. They told me that these are the electricity in your body. Without them, the spark to move, to think, to breathe, to move blood through your heart, would lose its charge—the physio-logical impulse to keep you alive would dissipate altogether. After months of neglecting to feed myself, my levels were so low I could have died within hours. My body starved for the electrolytes that would bring me back to life, the ER staff needled me with an IV and kept me overnight for observation.

I AWOKE THE next morning strangely revived. I could think again and was able to mobilize. However, though I had more energy, I was no less depressed. I was ready once more for the drive. Not to my cabin. Up north. I wanted out of the hospital so I could find that beach in the redwoods and put an end to the pain once and for all. A nurse came in to check on me. I told her that I felt much better. When I asked her about leaving, she said that it was not up to her. A psychiatrist would be coming in to evaluate me shortly.

Midmorning, the psychiatrist arrived. She was warm but wary with concern.

"How're you feeling?" she asked.

"Fine," I said, "much better. I just needed some rest, I think. Do you know when I can go home?"

"Well, that depends," she said. "I have a few questions first." I knew what was coming. "Can you tell me what happened last night?"

"I just got tired," I said. "Depleted, really. They said something about a deficiency of potassium and phosphorous."

"Yes, that would do it," she said. "Yours were dangerously low. You could have died." I nodded that I understood the gravity of the situation. "Have you been depressed?"

Here it came. "No, not really." I played it straight.

She considered me. "Have you ever thought about killing yourself?"

"No," I said with a deadpan calm.

"Have you ever made a plan to kill yourself?"

"No."

"Have you ever tried to hurt yourself?"

"No."

"What can you tell me about those cuts on your arm?"

I was ready. "I live in a cabin," I said. "I was taking out some shrubs. The thorns must've cut me up a bit."

She looked at me, unconvinced, and angling for a last foothold in. "So, if we let you out of here, you won't hurt yourself?"

"No. I won't." I played the deception straight to the end.

She knew that it was over. She wasn't beat. I was beating myself. "Okay," she gave in. "I just have some paperwork to complete. We'll have you out in an hour or so." Closing her chart, closing her book on me, she turned and left.

I lay there alone, letting in what I had just done. I had lied to lose my life. I rehearsed exactly what I would do the moment that I got out. I would stop in to see my boy, gather some things at the cabin, then drive to the redwoods, face the ocean, and swallow a bottle of pills in my car. I was really going to do it. I was really going to take my own life. Like sand giving way underneath my feet, I could feel the slide into an abyss from which I knew that I would not climb back out. The certainty of my death, but hours away, encompassed me. *My God*, I realized with the freefall dread of a future already determined. *If I get out, I'm going to do this. I really am. My God, is this really what I want?*

I cannot say that any renewed will to live suddenly resuscitated itself. I can only say that, if I had left the hospital, I knew for sure that I would have put myself to death. And I was not yet ready to live with that.

The nurse came in with something for me to sign. I asked if the psychiatrist was still available. The nurse left. The psychiatrist came back. I tried to look at her but couldn't. I wasn't sure that I could say the words.

"I lied," I finally confessed. "If I leave here, I will kill myself. I want nothing more than to be dead. I need some help."

She nodded, sobered that her suspicions were true. Then she said with neither the promise of recovery nor the platitude that the road would be easy, "We have a place for you."

A few hours later, on the far side of town, pushed in a wheelchair, I was admitted. A seventy-two-hour involuntary hold was placed on me. With the schizophrenics, the suicide survivors, the catatonically depressed, and the dually diagnosed with both addiction and psychosis—the people that I would come to see as my tribe—I was sequestered in the tombs of a psychiatric hospital like a modern-day demoniac.

I did not know it then, but it was the first step toward my healing.

In fact, it is where I encountered God again.

Locked up and left alone in the padded room of an insane asylum.

Claremont, CA—Age 57

Good Friday 2016

———◆———

OVER TWENTY YEARS had passed since my internment in an asylum when my little sister reached out for me from the tomb of her own psychological distress. It was the morning of Good Friday, and I had yet to leave the house, when the phone rang. I assumed that it was one of my students confirming my attendance at a class project that they were installing that afternoon. The class was entitled Compassion-Based Personal and Social Transformation—fruit of my decades-long journey to discover psycho-spiritual resources that genuinely heal trauma and restore relational connection. As one of their assignments, I had asked the students to create ministerial resources that would raise awareness around some social wound that plagues our world. A few of them worked together to recast a Stations of the Cross into a memorial for victims of child abuse.

It was as provocative as it was creative.

As with tradition, their fourteen stations laid out the condemned Christ sentenced to death, shouldering his cross, stumbling three times on the path, being stripped, nailed, then hung and bled before being hidden in a tomb. But the students reconstructed each site to commemorate a specific child whose innocence was lost to violence. The face of Jesus at each scene was superimposed with a childhood picture of a real-life survivor violated when they were young. Each survivor's story was chronicled on an elegant backdrop penned to resemble pages from scripture. Children's drawings framed the narratives—scribbled sketches in crayon depicting the bestial brutality that was described in the stories. Smashed toys and mutilated dolls were arranged around unlit candles making each stage of the Via Dolorosa a roadside altar of grief and affliction. At the final station, the body of Jesus—now dead—was wrapped in strips of torn-up baby blankets, then laid in a tomb whose interior walls were covered with photographs of victimized children from around the world, the pictures arranged to form a collage of haunted faces and vacant eyes too many to number. As the body of the crucified Messiah decomposed in the dark, the untold stories of nameless multitudes wasted away with him.

My students intended to scandalize the spectators—to sear into their minds images that would transform their passivity into outraged compassion. And they were eager for me to feel the full impact firsthand. I assured them that I would come to their Good Friday unveiling.

Unfortunately, they were not the ones who were calling that morning.

"FRANK. IT'S KYLE." My little sister and her husband had moved to the northwest corner of California a few years earlier. Linda and I kept in touch by phone; Kyle never called. He wasn't calling now for small talk. "I have something to tell you," he continued without a pause. "Linda's in a mental hospital."

If he had been calling to tell me that the sky had tumbled down and that the earth was caving in next, it would have made more sense. How could Linda be in a mental hospital? I had just talked to her a few weeks earlier. She had been her usual buoyant self. She had called to tell me that her oldest daughter was pregnant. She was going to be a grandmother. At forty-nine. She was tickled and talkative—the upbeat Linda I had known all my life. Linda's sanity was solid ground.

"A mental hospital?" I asked, that ground beginning to buckle. "What is she doing there?"

Kyle told me. And the ground gave way altogether.

The trouble had started about a month before. Nightmares began invading her sleep—savage beasts in the dark smashing her windows to attack her in her bedroom. She would wake up screaming, certain of intruders, trembling with panic until dawn. Then the nightmares invaded while she was awake. She was convinced that people were trying to kill her—at first breaking in through doors that she had locked and bolted, then poisoning her with toxic vapors. She removed from the house anything with a scent—cologne, deodorant, ant spray, laundry detergent. She refused to eat anything that she had not prepared for herself; then she refused to eat anything at all. Still, the terror overcame her. She lay in her bed, curled up in a ball, quivering and vigilant for hours. The shaking impaired her walking, then became so severe she fell to the floor in convulsions.

The first time she collapsed, Kyle took her to the emergency room. Her blood tests coming back normal, the doctors stabilized her with a sedative and sent her home. The second time, they admitted her and administered more tests—blood panels, urine analyses, CAT scans, an MRI. They all came up with nothing—no evidence of drug use, no signs of cancer, no tumors in her brain, no growths in her organs. Psychiatrists came in, and in the ensuing weeks, meds were prescribed and tried—tranquilizers, antidepressants, antipsychotics— rounds of pharmaceutical roulette placing bets on which drug would yield a result. For brief intervals, a spark of lucidity flickered in her. She pulled herself together enough to get to the couch and watch a video. Then the spark would go out and the horror repossessed her. On the third trip to the ER, she kept trying to leap from the moving car as Kyle fought to restrain her while he drove. With no other options, the doctors admitted her into a psychiatric facility. She had been there for two days.

"We haven't told anybody," Kyle confessed, diffident and defeated. "I don't know why. It's just been so bizarre. I mean, this came out of nowhere. And no one can tell us for sure what's wrong with her."

I could hear the dejection in his voice. He had been a seaman in the navy and was now an electrician working the poles in the remote reaches of Northern California. Mental health crises were waters far from anywhere he had ever sailed. And he was navigating with neither a compass nor coordinates. I could understand. It was so disorienting I had yet to get my own bearings. I grasped for something to steer by. "What are the doctors saying?"

"You know doctors. They don't know what they're doing. They just give her more pills and hope for the best."

"What are they giving her?"

"I don't know. Nothing I've ever heard of. We've got pill bottles all over the house." His frustration was palpable, as was his despondency.

"How is she now?"

"Frickin' crazy. She just lies in her bed staring at the wall. Won't talk to me. Won't talk to anybody."

"Jesus," I said, somewhere between prayer and profanity.

"There is one thing," he offered. "She's asking for you. She says you're the only one she will talk to. What do you think? Would you be able to come up?"

It was a fourteen-hour drive from Southern California to the rural coast of Eureka. It was Good Friday. I had commitments to my students. I was expected at my school's Tenebrae service—the liturgy of darkness—later that evening. We had company coming for Easter brunch.

Nonetheless, I answered in a heartbeat.

"Of course. I'll be there by morning."

IN AS LONG as it took to pack a bag and secure the house, my wife, Alane, and I were on the road up north. The ominous synchronicity of the drive was not lost on me. The itinerary that we were traveling was precisely the one that I had mapped out for my suicide twenty years earlier—up the 101, across the Golden

Gate, through redwood country, to a beach off the coast of Eureka where I would swallow a bottleful of Tylenol PM. Only now, the journey's end held my sister, not me, sequestered in a psychiatric facility.

Driving up that route—through the town in which we had grown up, across the Golden Gate Bridge from which so many have leapt, through the tangled ancient forest to my sister on the far side—was like journeying back into the vortex of my own psychological breakdown. It all came back. I had been where she was now. I knew what it was like to be assailed by beasts. I knew the dread of violation disguised as love. I knew the walls of the asylum from the inside, the cage of madness from behind the bars. And as the image of my sister, locked away like I was, pierced my gut like shards of shattered glass, tremors of recognition surfaced something more—I also knew at least some of the faces on the beasts that were assaulting her.

As we wound our way through the redwood groves, Eva Cassidy serenaded us through the car stereo, the mournful foreboding of her own premature death lacing the standards she so hauntingly sang. Her music nursed my gloomy musings, scoring the tears that stung each time that I imagined my sister an inmate in a madhouse. I knew that I had been to hell. But please. No. Not Linda as well.

As I drove, however, my melancholic ruminations about my tormented sister kept colliding with my sense of the person I had known since the day she was born. The Linda that I knew loved life. She carried a self-conscious coyness like a hand that covers a smile, but the grin underneath was indefatigably bright-spirited. Her favorite flower was a daisy. She giggled at wisecrack greeting cards and sent one on every birthday. She loved to drink red wine and flavored martinis—pomegranate, pineapple, peach-raspberry, chocolate. She changed her hairstyle almost daily, mimicking fashions she found in borrowed copies of *Glamour*. She hated her voice but cranked up the Dixie Chicks and belted out "Landslide" at the top of her lungs in her car. If Linda had a spirit animal, it would be a butterfly; she had them everywhere—glued to her rearview mirror, stenciled on the walls of her kitchen, hanging from a porch mobile. One was tattooed on the back of her shoulder. And like a timid but intrepid monarch, she fluttered through raising three kids, volunteering in classrooms, chaperoning at youth camps, coordinating snacks at Vacation Bible School, then winding down with a romantic comedy, a game of Yahtzee, or shopping for cute accessories at the local Target. She was Meg Ryan as a working-class homemaker. Holly Golightly on a blue-collar budget. Or Princess Di, perhaps, hidden as a humble commoner.

To be sure, she coped with various afflictions: back pains occasionally immobilized her for days; obscure food allergies would come and go, not just gluten and lactose, but citrus, red meat, and spices like coriander and cinnamon. And she weathered her share of more severe adversity. I knew that more than most. Throughout the years—during the seasons in which our families camped together regularly and those where distance reduced us to phone calls every several months—one constant remained. I was her big brother, a port of refuge when the seas of her life became stormy. I was the one whom she called—when she ran away from home in high school; when she got pregnant at nineteen with Kyle, her navy boyfriend; throughout their marriage when escalating tensions led to short-term separations; when a need for a biopsy portended a sinister diagnosis. She would generally downplay the squall that had darkened her horizon, insisting that it really wasn't that bad, certain that things would work out. And she always bounced back when the weather broke. But while the waves were choppy, it was my role to be a safe haven, the stable ground to hold her anchor firm for a while until she came back home to herself.

It had always been that way.

THE SUMMER BEFORE our father moved out—I was thirteen; my brothers, Jim and Rich, eleven and seven; and Linda, the youngest and the only girl, barely turned five—our family spent a day in panic.

We thought we had lost Linda for good.

We lived in the town where, the previous fall, eight-year-old Susan Nason had been abducted and murdered. The unsolved horror still haunted our community. The story had gone national, tapping into the primal terrors of parents and caregivers everywhere. After school, Susan had left her house to walk a couple of blocks to a friend's. She never made it. Without a single clue or promising lead, divers dragged the local lagoons, the coast guard trolled the bordering bay, and neighborhood patrols escorted children to and from school out of fear that an assailant was out on the loose. She was missing for two months. Then her body, beaten and violated, was found tossed over a roadside cliff in the hills a few miles away. Her story went national again some twenty years later when another one of Susan's friends—a friend that my mother once babysat for—recovered repressed memories enough to convict her own father of molesting them both and murdering Susan. But that summer when Linda was five, the unknown killer was still at large.

One Saturday morning that summer, Linda walked down our cul-de-sac to play with a friend. She was told to be home by lunch. When she was late, my mom sent me to retrieve her. Nobody was home. And as far as the neighbors were concerned, the family had been away all day. Immediately, we were all on alert. We called every friend that Linda had. We searched the parks, playgrounds, convenience stores, and shopping plazas. We knocked on every door on our street. By midafternoon, the police were brought in. Fearing a second abduction, they expanded the search throughout the city.

Around dinnertime, I was patrolling our street on my bike when I spotted her. Her friend's family was driving back home; Linda was in the back seat. The parents had decided to take their kids on a day trip to the Santa Cruz boardwalk. They had invited Linda that morning and told her to go and ask her parents for permission. Linda had walked halfway home, then turned around and went back to her friend's place. Fearing her parents would refuse her the fun, she lied. She reported that her parents had approved, then she had slumped down below the back window to assure that she would not be seen when the car pulled out of the neighborhood.

I hurried her home and ran into the house shouting, "I found her!" My parents shrieked their relief, then demanded that she explain her whereabouts. Their relief was short-lived; it quickly morphed into fury. My mom stood Linda in the corner and beat her backside with a wooden spoon. My dad followed suit, using his hand to smack her into her bedroom where she was banished for the night. My parents then took it out on each other for a while before my mom retired to the TV in her bedroom and my dad drank beer while working wood in the garage.

Later that evening, I was on the couch, alone in the family room, reading a library book—a Willie Mays biography or a Hardy Boys mystery. Linda snuck out from her seclusion and crept into the family room. Loving to dress herself up as if she were her own doll, she was decked out in attire worthy of Sunday Mass—a frilly dress, shiny shoes, white stockings, her hair clumped in barrettes. In her fist, she clutched a Snow White Pez dispenser—no doubt a souvenir from her day on the boardwalk. She sat on the couch, a timid length away, opening and closing the empty dispenser.

After a while, she offered, "I have a new friend."

"Yeah," I said, my head in my book.

"She likes to read too."

"Does she?"

"Yeah." She paused. "Her favorite is *The Cat in the Hat*."

Even at thirteen, I knew when a hint revealed the heart. And I also knew that she already had mine. "Why don't you go get it?" I said.

She retrieved the book and snuggled close to my side. As I read to her, Snow White followed every word as if she were a searchlight leading a ship to shore. That's what I did. When my little sister was lost, I found her. I led her home. And if it was not altogether safe, I provided a place of refuge—solace enough to find a way forward.

Like I said, I was her big brother.

ALANE AND I needed a roadside catnap around midnight—more restive than restful—but we made it to Kyle's shortly after dawn. My dad was already there.

Kyle had called him right after me and, though elderly and recently diagnosed with Parkinson's, he had loaded the truck within the hour and, with Dona, my stepmother, driven up from Sacramento. They were as shell-shocked and sleepless with worry as I was. Still groping to make sense of it all, we pressed Kyle for details seeking an illumination he was at a loss to provide. Then we freshened ourselves up and proceeded to the facility with the foreboding of being summoned to a morgue.

Driving into the psychiatric complex only intensified my dread. Founded over a century earlier, it had deteriorated with no evidence of care since its construction. The chain-link fence, rimmed with razor wire, was ripped and splayed at the seams. The parking lot was pocked with potholes so large we had to maneuver our cars around them. The patch of lawn had long since degenerated into dirt clumped with weeds and crabgrass. Bars covered opaque windows with panes cracked or replaced with plywood. Crumbled remains of brick bordered the building's decaying façade. It lacked only Dante's signpost to Hades to seal the despair of the banished and forgotten: "Abandon all hope ye who enter here."

A few minutes early, we found the front door locked. With no signs to guide us, no visiting hours posted to orient us, no evidence of life at all either inside or out, we were unsure what to do. We walked around to the back door; it too was locked. So we wandered back to the front and waited in the foggy chill.

Eventually, an orderly came from within and allowed us to enter, locking the door behind us. Only two people at a time were allowed to see patients, so the others waited on benches in the vestibule while Alane and I followed the orderly as he unlocked another door and led us into the building's interior. The entire place seemed deserted—no sound nor sight of a single person, whether staff or sufferer or fellow visitor. The three of us not saying a word, we walked down a long corridor, up a flight of stairs, through another locked door, down another corridor, across a deserted rec room, then through a final locked door into the secured unit for the most psychiatrically disturbed.

This place, too, seemed deserted. It was just as well. The ward reeked of despair. The antiseptic white walls were dingy and mildewed. A fluorescent light cast sterile shadows on antiquated wheelchairs lining the walls. Rows of rooms on either side barricaded against breach with padlocked crossbeam bolts. A faint odor of urine was laced with chlorine cleanser. The caged-stare glare of a clock's face was screened by a grate. And a dead-calm silence hung like a shroud, with the unseen patients—we knew them to be there somewhere—neither whimpering, nor shuffling, nor distracting themselves with the steady drone of solitaire or daytime TV. The whole place hearkened back to an era in which hysteria was treated with straitjackets and lobotomies. I remembered what I knew. Having been shackled in one myself, the locked unit of a psychiatric ward is one of the most godforsaken places on Earth. If you were not depressed to the edge of madness before you came to such a place, you would be within an hour of being holed up within it.

The orderly ushered us down a hallway, then into a small break room where the patients, a few at a time, were allowed supervised snacks of Costco crackers and instant coffee. The room empty, we had our pick of several round Formica tables. We sat in plastic chairs suited for a high school cafeteria, then waited as the orderly went for Linda.

IT SEEMED LIKE hours had passed before a nurse ushered Linda through the door, guiding her by the arm as if stabilizing an infirm elder. It seemed like a lifetime had passed since the person being led in had been the Linda that I once knew. If I had harbored any hope that the whole thing was a hoax, it evaporated the moment I laid eyes on her. She was emaciated, her drab prison-garb jumpsuit draping her bony body. Her face was death-mask pale, her eyes cavernous and vacant. Her lips were withered and cracked as if blistered in the Arctic cold. And her mouth gaped open as she labored to suck up the power that she needed to propel herself. When she saw me, her eyes did not register recognition. She merely stopped and opened her arms just a fraction. I went to her and embraced her, afraid to press too firmly against a body so brittle. She offered a feeble squeeze in return, an anemic nod toward affection, then released her arms as if the strain had become too much.

I helped her to a seat and pulled a chair close. She searched me, her hollow eyes still not conceding that the apparition before her really was her brother. I could relate. The specter before me really was my sister, but not in any way that I could recognize. I wanted to tap on the window of the vacant ruin of her being and call out, "Linda, are you in there?" She was. But barely, like a wispy phantom, fading slowly, deep in the shadows within. And that phantom was crouched in terror.

She waited for the nurse to leave, then she leaned in and whispered almost inaudibly, "Frank, you have to get me out of here."

I had no idea if she needed to stay or to leave. I could only see that a malevolent force of some kind was assailing my sister's spirit. And so far, it was winning.

"I'm here, Linda," I replied. "Tell me, what's been going on?"

She glanced around to scope out the privacy. Then she resumed her whisper.

"I can't say much. They're recording everything. But they're all trying to kill me—Kyle, the nurses, the doctors, everybody. I need you to get me out of here."

To be honest, I could not imagine how such a place could be the least bit restorative. Even so, I knew that the people there were not conspiring to kill her.

"How do you know?" I asked to tease out the extent of her delusion.

"I can't tell you everything right now," she confided, still whispering. "I will when you get me out of here. But they're poisoning everything—the food, the water. They don't know that I know, but I can smell it. So I don't eat or drink a thing they give me. But they're trying to force me anyway. If I stay here, I'll die."

I have to admit I was torn. Some malignant pathogen had erupted in my sister and was eating her up from within like a virus. She needed help. But I tended to agree—the rather crude psych ward of Humboldt County was probably not the help that she needed. The staff were not actively trying to kill her, but if she stayed, she would die from the emotional distress alone, if not from dehydration long before that.

"Would it be okay if I talk to the doctor?" I asked.

"Yes," she answered clandestinely. "But only you. Nobody else."

THE CLINICAL DIRECTOR—the sole psychiatrist assigned to the ward—was helpful, even if also somewhat mystified.

"I'll be honest," he said when Alane and I asked for his diagnostic assessment. "We're not exactly sure what's wrong with her. I've talked to the psychiatrist she's been seeing—he suspects some form of schizophrenic psychosis, perhaps paranoid, or maybe schizo-affective disorder. He's got her on a lot of meds."

Something about his forthright demeanor inspired a measure of trust in me.

"What do you think it is?" I asked.

"I don't know," he answered. "She's on some hard-core antipsychotics. It's difficult to separate the impact of those meds from acute psychological disturbance. I've reviewed her records—she's clearly had some type of episode. There is certainly some biochemical component, but it does not seem like standard schizophrenia. And it doesn't appear to be substance-induced."

"What else could it be?" I asked.

"For me, the suddenness of its onset, her age, the severity of her tremors, the assaults she hallucinates—it has all the earmarks of PTSD. It's affecting her physiologically to be sure. But my guess is that some form of childhood trauma is breaking through her defenses and wreaking havoc on her body."

The nausea in my own body belied the truth in his words.

"What do you suggest we do?" I asked.

"I don't think she belongs here. It's obviously only increasing her agitation. She's not eating any food, nor drinking any water. She'll end up on an IV and a feeding tube if she's forced to stay. If there's someone who can watch over her, I'd say take her home and help her feel safe again."

"Sure, we can do that," I said. "But then what?"

Alane and I both noticed it—a trace of compassion tinted his clinical demeanor.

"Therapy," he suggested. "She needs good therapy. With professionals who know the world of trauma."

IT TOOK A few hours, but we put a plan in place. Dona, my stepmother, would stay in Eureka for the foreseeable future providing in-home care for Linda and some relief for Kyle. Alane, a professor at Cal Poly on the physiological dimensions of emotional well-being, would research both the chemical aspects of trauma-induced mental illness and the side effects of the various meds Linda was prescribed. Kyle, reluctant to attribute Linda's condition to trauma, was still willing to scope out the alternatives for mental health care within the region, coordinate diagnostic consultations, and monitor Linda's meds while we found her the right kind of help. And I would call Kyle for daily briefings, tracking our accumulation of questions, vetting the therapeutic options, and keeping Kyle's spirits up as he negotiated both the bureaucratic intricacies and the confounding uncertainties of the kind of care Linda most needed. Mobilized by our strategy, we were ready to free Linda from her institutional captivity.

We immediately ran into a hitch. Linda would not sign the release documents.

I sat with her back in the break room, the nurse across from us equal parts professional forbearing and weariness at Linda's relentless recalcitrance. My sister was adamant.

"They're trying to put me away," she whispered in my ear, though the nurse could hear every word. "I'm not signing it."

"Linda," I assured, "these are the forms that will let you go home. They won't release you until you sign them."

She was unconvinced. "It's in there somewhere—something they'll use against me."

The nurse suggested an option. "We could release you under your husband's custody."

"No!" Linda fired back to the nurse. "Never." She turned to me. "You've got to help me."

"Here," I said, like talking a toddler into a needed vaccination. "Let's go through this together." Though her fogged-up mind could not hold all the details, she followed my finger as I read and explained every line on the form. "Really, Linda," I reassured, once we were through. "It only says that you agree to them releasing you."

She was still not ready. She needed to think. The nurse left us alone. Linda weighed her options—staying in this prison or signing an uncertain document.

She had only my word to rely on. She took her time, but my word won out. She signed the form and we got her out of there.

JUST LEAVING THE building eased her distress a degree or two. She needed help into the car, but she buckled herself in and took sips from the water bottle we bought at a gas station. An Orange Freeze slush from Burger King sounded good to her, so we stopped on the way home long enough to purchase one. She spooned a few bites, then was done, gripping the cup in her hand for the rest of the ride home. Once there, she lay on the couch and dozed, too weary to converse. We got a few sips of soup into her for dinner, then, exhausted, she retired to her bedroom for the night. The rest of us spent the evening finding and listing all her meds; creating a log to schedule and record their consumption; compiling a list of doctors, therapists, and clinics to consult; and surfacing all the questions that we wanted to pose to the professionals. Then, like the disciples holding vigil outside of Jesus's tomb, we spent the rest of Holy Saturday in wait, not knowing what the morrow would bring.

NONE OF US went to church on Easter Sunday. Linda slept in. Kyle took a motorcycle ride. My dad and stepmom went to the store to round up something for a last-minute holiday meal. Alane and I went for a run. Easter being something of an afterthought, we also opted out of colored egg hunts and hiding baskets of candy. I had but one agenda for the day on which we celebrate life rising up out of death—I wanted a private talk with Linda to hear for myself the story of her disintegration.

Once she was up and fed some toast and jam, I took the initiative. I asked her if she wanted to go for a drive. So while the others cooked a ham and scalloped potatoes, Linda and I drove up the redwood coast highway in search of a site hallowed enough to hold the intimacies of the conversation to come.

It was a lovely spring day—still chilly, with billowy white clouds peppering the sky's pastel blue. Whether it was the recuperative power of some food in her system or simply the relief of being liberated from the state institution, a spark of Linda's spirit was resuscitated. She was still subdued, and heavy with fatigue, but the desperate vigilance had softened into a sober introspection. She sat in the passenger seat, wrapped in the comforter that she had brought with her, and stared out of her window. We meandered north, past Agate Beach, until the road veered into the interior of the massive state forest. Preferring a view of the ocean to the shadows of the woods, we turned back, then pulled off the highway at Patrick's Point. We followed a dilapidated lane, its disrepair promising solitude, past the state park and parallel to the ocean. Hidden in the hillside, still a couple of miles before the hamlet of Trinidad, we came upon a grassy bluff with a gravel turnout to pull into. I parked the truck and we took in the view.

The vista was panoramic. We could see the rocky coast to the south extend for miles before us, while to the west, the Pacific reached out as far as the horizon. I shifted in my seat to better face Linda. She was framed by the passenger window, the sea behind her a tranquil backdrop.

That's where we talked—like any other time that she had opened her heart to her brother. Only this time, she did not downplay the storm that had marred the horizon. Nor did she bounce right back after confiding about it. I asked her what had been happening in the weeks since I had last talked to her. She pulled her comforter tight as if bracing for the words that she would be voicing. Then she shared, the darkness of the storm mocking the springtime vista that held it.

She told me about her nightmares—sometimes bullish beasts, sometimes ravenous dogs, breaking into her bedroom to violate and devour her. She described how hard it was to rid herself of those images, that even when she was awake she could not keep from seeing their faces. She elaborated on her growing aversion to smells—how it started with a mild nausea at a whiff of Kyle's cologne, degenerated into a repulsion at the smell of his deodorant, then spiraled into fits of panic at the slightest odor at all. She related how her aversion to smells became an aversion to touch as well. The slightest contact with her skin—Kyle's hand on her shoulder, a hug from her daughter, a brush against her body in a crowded grocery aisle—induced shivers of revulsion so severe she wanted to rip her flesh and scream. She conveyed the terror that would drive her to hide herself in her closet, certain that the monsters that she had imagined were real, and were stalking the house to get her. She detailed all the ways that Kyle was trying to kill her—sneaking into the house scents that would poison her, sprinkling insecticide into her food, plying her with pills that were inducing insanity—how she knew it sounded crazy, but it was Kyle who had orchestrated her commitment. It was his friends masquerading as doctors at the ER, his coworkers driving the ambulance that ferried her from there to the asylum.

She sounded surprisingly coherent as she recounted the horrors of her experience, narrating it all with the detachment of a reporter writing copy for a newspaper. As she spoke, I simply listened, occasionally asking for some elaboration, and assuring her throughout that it all sounded awful. It did. It sounded like a living hell—both the very real torture of her psychological terror and the obvious fabrications that distorted her perceptions like a funhouse mirror mutating reality. It also sounded eerily familiar.

It took several hours to exhaust all the contours of the maddening netherworld within which she was imprisoned. When we were through—me with my queries for particulars, her with her elucidations—I offered her words of consolation. As she gazed out the window, lost in the Pacific, I told her how sorry I was at what she was going through, and that others had been there too. I told her that I knew how hard it could be, and that it really was possible to recover.

I told her that she was not alone—that I, for one, would be with her to help her get through it. Then I stopped telling her anything. I could see. My words were not seeping very far into the vacant stare of her suffering. So I simply held the silence with her as the ocean held her gaze.

Apparently, with the present sufficiently plumbed, Linda was now dredging through the past. As if the sea at which she was staring cradled all time and was disclosing fragments for her to behold, Linda began musing through a series of memories, adrift in a reverie of random remembrances.

She asked if I recalled a camping trip to Memorial Park when we were young—how she and I hiked all the way to the village store, quite a trek for a seven-year-old, while our mom entertained the date that she had brought. Or the time that a family day trip was aborted because of a fight between our mom and our stepdad, so I commandeered the car, drove us four kids to the coast for the day, and, having no money for food on the way home, pretended that we were orphans and snagged us free meals at a roadside burger joint.

Or the one that really returned light into her eyes, the time that she had visited me for a week when I was a grad student at Presbyterian Seminary. We'd spent each day in New York City seeing all the sites on the dream list that she had started as a child, including watching a Broadway show after appetizers at the Plaza, shopping at the largest shoe store in the world, playing "Chopsticks" with our feet on the giant keyboard at the FAO Schwarz toy emporium, and searching out the locations of all her favorite Big Apple movies where we posed and took pictures as if we were the celebrities.

She peered into those memories, surfaced by the sea, and sipped from their nectar, thirsty for the hope that life could one day feel that good again. But after a while, the memories slipped back into the sea, as did the hope. The length of her silence grew longer. The soundings into the depths grew darker. When her absorbed retrospection continued, it came without restorative promise.

"Do you remember how we made forts in the park and hid in them whenever Mom left us alone with Grandpa Harold?" she pondered as much to herself as to me. "Did you ever notice how much Stepdad looked like him?" To be honest, I hadn't—until then. "Did you ever wonder why Mom never left her bedroom? All the things she did not want to know about. All the things she did not care about even when she *did* know?"

She was not asking me to disclose any details that I knew of the secrets to which she was alluding. It was more like she was standing at the gateway to the sanctum within her where those secrets were locked away, and she could sense the savages lurking on the other side of the door. She was not ready to face them quite yet, but she knew that they were there. And she wanted to know if I knew as well. I did.

"Yes, Linda," I said. "There are some ugly things in our family."

She nodded, still within earshot of the horrors howling within her. "Yeah, we have some more things to talk about. Maybe when I feel better."

"Any time, Linda. It's important to talk about it."

We sat in the silence, poised alongside the secrets that we had never discussed. This was the closest we had ever come to acknowledging out loud the abuse that we had both endured. For her, it was close enough.

Except for this.

Another question came to her. She turned to face me. This time, she wanted to see my answer directly.

"Tell me something," she said. "You were like this once. You were as messed up as I am. You were even in a mental hospital for a while, I remember. What did you do? What did you do to get better?"

In that moment, I struggled with how to respond. I could see the ache in her eyes for some lifeline that I could throw her within the tempest in which she was drowning. But I had no crisp summary of my years-long search for how to live and love again once damaged by violation, no pithy recovery checklist that distilled all that I had discovered about healing from the abuse that I had known. What handful of words could possibly encapsulate it? *I stopped pushing it away and faced the truth of my past? I learned how to trust what my body was telling me? I found compassion for my pain instead of shame and revulsion?* Every line that I could think of was a pale platitude before the depth of trauma's torment. And it was certainly not the time for a lengthy discourse culled from my class lecture notes, nor even for an abbreviated form of my own resurrection narrative. No, I had no neatly rolled-up rope to toss to her. So I threw her what I could.

"I got good help," I told my sister—the hint of advice only thinly veiled.

She dropped her gaze as she let the words uncoil within her to see how far they would reach. "Good help," she said, mulling it over. "Do you think there's any out there for someone like me?"

"I do, Linda. And we're going to do everything we can to find it."

She turned back to gaze out the window. I feared I could see her slipping away once more, on a drift that would take her far beyond the length of any rope. When she spoke, I do not know if she addressed me or the sea.

"I hope so," she said, without conviction. "I hope it's out there somewhere."

That was the last day I ever saw Linda alive.

THE REST OF Easter was rather subdued—we ate the ham and had store-bought pie for dessert. With Linda napping on the couch, we watched a Sandra Bullock video she had in her collection. Once it was over, we said our goodbyes to her, and she went to bed. The rest of us reviewed the plans we had made to get Linda help in the days ahead. Then, after a few hours of sleep, Alane and I left before dawn for the long drive back home.

FOR THE NEXT two months, our search for quality care for Linda was far more frustrating than fruitful. The medical doctors in Eureka were stumped in ascertaining the chemical, behavioral, and psychological causes of Linda's condition. The region was bereft of mental health facilities that could provide comprehensive diagnostics and up-to-date treatment. The clinics we did find would only consider her if she was dually diagnosed with a substance abuse problem. The psychiatrists—several in a row as Kyle became increasingly infuriated with each one in turn—only adjusted and readjusted her meds in an attempt to subdue her deliriousness and constrain her tremors. And the few therapists we found who were trained to treat complex trauma were rendered helpless when Kyle couldn't get Linda to her appointments.

After weeks of one setback after another, we were elated when a promising path finally opened up. We found a research hospital at the University of California at San Francisco that was willing to admit her. It specialized in diagnosing patients with compounded psychological and physiological trauma symptomology, and it offered integrative treatment where medical doctors, psychiatrists, therapists, family counselors, and even nutritionists and exercise physiologists worked together as a team. Kyle's insurance approved it. Linda agreed to go. The path posed only one obstacle—its first opening was not until August 15, some two-and-a-half months away. We reserved a space and dug in for the wait. Relief was a ways off, but hope had arrived.

Through the fits and starts of finding her effective mental health resources, Linda continued to struggle. At first, she became increasingly withdrawn—isolating herself in her room, refusing contact with Kyle, and rebuffing the care that my stepmom offered her. She resisted taking her meds, fighting over each dose, threatening to go cold turkey regardless of the risks to her system. Her trembling continued unabated, subsiding a bit periodically, but then escalating so badly Kyle took videos to convey their severity to the doctors. She declined to talk with anyone on the phone—her friends, family, her children. My only communication with her was channeled through my daily briefings with Kyle, whose irritability, both at the obstinacy of Linda's distress and the interminable length of time before relief was in sight, simmered precariously at the breaking point. While the research hospital brought hope, Linda's unrelenting affliction was a continual reminder that hope is a far cry from recovery.

Then, inexplicably, she rebounded. For a couple of days in June, she seemed like her old self. She came out of her room and did a load of laundry. She made a pan of chicken enchiladas. She visited with her daughter, Lauren. They watched a video together that evening. The next morning, she even went to the beach with Kyle. She suggested their favorite—where they once loved to picnic. They sat and watched the waves. They walked along the water. They held hands. For a while, they were young and in love again.

A few hours later, Kyle called.

"YOU'RE NOT GOING to believe what your sister's done now." His exasperation was unrestrainable. "It was a good day . . . *a good day!* We were on our way home from the beach. She wants to pick up some ice cream at Walgreens. So we go in, and I get a call. I'm talking on the phone when I look across the store and you know what she's doing? She's buying a bottle of sleeping pills. I mean, my God. I run over and pull her out of the store. She doesn't say a word the rest of the way home. But as soon as we pull up to the house, she jumps out, runs into the garage, and locks herself in her car. I'm banging on it for her to open up and she just sits there. So I run into the house to get the other keys and she drives off. She just frickin' drives away. I jump into my car and go after her, but I don't know which way she went. I mean, she could've gone anywhere. I don't know. Goddamn it. She just frickin' drove away. Can you believe it?"

And so it began.

I helped him calm down a bit and then mobilize with a plan. It had been about an hour—it was starting to get dark. We made a list of all the places that she might drive to—the store, the beach, a friend's house—and a list of people to call. He set off, both to search the spots she frequented and to telephone her friends. A couple of hours later, he called back. Nothing. She wasn't anywhere he checked, and no one had heard from her. We considered the local clinics, thinking perhaps she had checked herself in somewhere—they wouldn't divulge that information to us, but they would to the police. He called them. Again, nothing. She hadn't shown up at any of the clinics, nor at the regional hospital.

It occurred to me that Kyle could access his credit card records online to see if any charges had been made since she left; perhaps she was at a motel nearby. He got on his computer. Two charges were pending, both recorded within the last hour—one from the Sav-On Pharmacy around the corner, the other at a Chevron for a full tank of gas. The pharmacy charge was ominous, but if she had filled up her tank, then she was planning on driving for a while—perhaps to my dad's, perhaps to be with her pregnant daughter in Bend, perhaps down to see me in Southern California. It was a flicker of hope. A few hours later, Kyle rechecked his credit card. The gas charge had brought false promise—it had taken until then to process, but it was Kyle's charge from a few days earlier. Our hope took a blow. Linda was still local.

With nothing else to do, we held vigil.

We held vigil through the night and into the morning, though we should have thought to light candles. We held vigil all the next day, waiting in vain for the phone call that she had turned up someplace safe. We held vigil into the evening, as her absence grew oppressive.

We held vigil until the police car pulled up in front of Kyle's.

FROM EYEWITNESS ACCOUNTS, credit card receipts, and forensic analyses, we were able to reconstruct Linda's final hours. When she left the house, she did drive to the Sav-On Pharmacy a couple of blocks away. She purchased a five-hundred-count bottle of Tylenol PM and a liter of Arrowhead water. She returned to her car and drove toward the road, less than a mile away, that turned west and led to the ocean. She turned one block too soon and found herself in a deserted cul-de-sac. She circled at the end and stopped the car facing the foothills, her back to the sea visible in her rearview mirror. In front of a wooden fence screening an older gentleman's home, she started swallowing the pills. It was early evening. A couple, strolling, saw her in the car. She looked disoriented, so they walked over to check on her. She said that she was trying to get to the ocean and was lost. They told her that she had turned down the wrong street and they pointed to the road that she wanted just one block away. She thanked them, and they resumed their stroll.

The next morning, the couple walked by once more. They spied the car still parked across the cul-de-sac. It appeared to be unoccupied. They thought it unusual but continued on their way. Later that evening, the same couple walked by a third time. The car still there, they decided to investigate. Linda was slumped down below the window line. According to the coroner, she had been vegetative since dawn, dead since noon. By his count, she swallowed 166 Tylenol PM capsules.

"How many would it take to kill yourself?" I asked him when I got up there the next day.

"Twenty would have done it," he told me.

Linda had taken no chances.

AS PROMPTLY AS I had that previous Good Friday a mere two months earlier, I made another tear-stained drive up the 101 and through the coastal redwood forest. Kyle needed help with the funeral arrangements. Through the ensuing few days, the two of us tended to the myriad of details when someone you have loved has died. We secured a death certificate; picked out a casket; arranged the cremation; selected a burial plot; wrote an obituary; notified friends and family; decided upon the right clothes for the body; coordinated flowers, music, and viewing particulars at the mortuary; and designed both a vigil and a memorial service. With help from loved ones trickling in through the week, we gave thoughtful attention to every dimension of celebrating and commemorating Linda's life.

The services themselves were packed to capacity. The viewing of her body was held at the funeral parlor; the memorial was at the Baptist church Kyle and Linda occasionally attended. Every member of the immediate family was at both—a combination of four blended families interlaced together—as were dozens of friends, fellow volunteers, and distant relatives unseen in decades. My memories for the two gatherings are more impressionistic, forming not so much a single narrative as a collage of poignant and incongruous moments that epitomize both the pathos and the senselessness of the tragedy we were facing.

Alane unpacking pictures of Linda out of the sealed box from my mom's storage bin, pulling out clumps of childhood Polaroids to display at the vigil, only to find, tucked at the bottom, a single Tylenol PM.

The moans of my mom's sobbing, wailing over the casket, an inconsolable chorus of heartache, regret, and shame from regions within her only she will ever know.

The granite face of my carpenter dad, staring at his daughter's body while blinking back tears in eyes that no one has ever seen cry.

Matt, Linda's son, flown in from Okinawa, striding down the church aisle to the closed casket up front, spit-polished in his Marine dress blues and standing at attention with a salute to the mom to whom he never had a chance to say goodbye.

The always boisterous brothers—duded up in pressed Levi's and dress shirts—loading the casket with white cloth gloves, then standing helplessly as the hearse drove Linda's body away.

The montage of pictures during the service of a Linda who loved life, projected onto the overhead screen that veiled the church's cross, while the Dixie Chicks sang "Landslide" to a piercingly silent assembly.

The Baptist pastor surmising that Linda's soul is most likely secure since, even though suicide is an unpardonable sin, she did once commit her life to Christ.

Me, offering the family eulogy, witnessing to Linda's anguish in a sanctuary full of people who had no idea that she had been struggling in the first place, reminding us all of the Linda that we loved, and assuring each person that the God I knew beams at Linda's beauty like we do and holds her with nothing but pride and compassion.

And the wake that followed—wine glasses and beer cans clinking with abandon throughout Kyle's crowded house. Then Lauren, Linda's homebound middle daughter, announcing that she too was pregnant, the father unknown to this day. Through two solemn memorial services, our family remembered and mourned our beloved Linda, then let loose and partied into the night at her place.

WITH THE MEMORIALS over, the toasting complete, and Linda's ashes securely interred, friends and family returned to their homes to settle into routines forever marred by Linda's absence. I, however, was not yet ready to make the long trek back home. My grief needed a final observance. Something in me felt compelled to follow Linda along the path of her final hours on Earth. I needed to make a solitary pilgrimage along her Stations of the Cross, and companion her, even if delinquently, on the way that she had walked to her death.

I sat in the car in which she had killed herself, taking in the texture of the seat, the tan of the interior, the faded butterfly decals, in the compact cubicle that held her last breath. I roamed the beach where she had spent the morning walking the waves with Kyle, and as she once loved to do, I gathered rocks worn smooth by the pounding of the surf. I drove the route that she followed after that peaceful interlude—from the beach to the Walgreens where she was thwarted in her first attempt to purchase pills; from there to the garage from which she fled in the car that would become her coffin; on to the Sav-On Pharmacy where she prevailed in her second attempt to purchase pills; then out toward the sea, turning one street too soon, and into the cul-de-sac where she parked, sat, and consumed the pills that would kill her. I lingered at this final station, meditating on Linda slouched in her car, alone in the dark, feeling abandoned by God and loved ones alike as she swallowed as many pills as her stomach could hold. Then later, with Alane, I dug out a patch of dirt at the fence next to where she had sat and fashioned a roadside memorial—a bouquet of daisies, a butterfly pin, a piece of chocolate, a splash of red wine, and "Linda Lu" laid out in stones collected from her favorite beach. Not resurrection so much, but at least death named and remembered.

These scenes on my sister's Via Dolorosa are the beads on the rosary of my grief. Each one has become a sorrowful mystery that I contemplate while mourning her loss. In prayerful recollection even now, I return to these sites and meditate. I imagine Linda swallowing handfuls of pills in her car, and I ponder the horrors she kept secret that drove her to choose death's relief over life's unlivable dreadfulness. I picture her, in the cul-de-sac of her Calvary, waiting alone for death to envelop her, and I wonder what she was thinking about, what her final fading feelings were, as her spirit expired in the casket of her car. I see her there, bled of hope, and I speculate on the presence of God in the midst of godforsakenness, where a credible sense of the sacred really does reside within the tombs of those for whom suicide is salvation. And I reflect upon where Linda's spirit escaped to, if it hovered for a while on that abandoned street, haunted by the brutality that still remains hidden; or if it floated to someplace peaceful, perhaps fluttering like a butterfly on the breezes of forested beaches, free of the pain that once crippled her wings. Unlikely icons to mediate the divine, these are the beads with which I pray to metabolize my sorrow.

These, and one more.

As I finger this chaplet, already well worn, one other scene has slipped onto the string that I carry. I find myself back at the bluff where Linda and I talked that Easter afternoon. She has turned to face me, the ocean at her back, her eyes yearning for a North Star to guide by, a map to navigate the seas back to sanity.

"You were like this once," she said. And I was. "What did you do?" she asked. "What did you do to get better?"

I did not have wise words to offer her then—no strategic advice to point her the way, no magic pills to prescribe that ease the pain. Such is the tragic truth about trauma; its recovery defies uncomplicated answers. And pills, either medicinal or suicidal, may alleviate the pain for a while, but the wound continues to wail unhealed.

All the same, her question still haunts me. It hangs in the air, across time and beyond death, unsilenced and unatoned. The bitter synchronicity is not lost on me. Linda and I were both mired in madness. And our madness played out in parallel storylines. We grew up in the same family. We were raised by the same mother. We were raped by the same man. We were both left on our own to fend for survival in the face of violation. And, with macabre similitude, we each, independently, plotted with precision the very same path to escape this world should the torment become too much. Here, however, is where our stories grievously diverged. One of us never followed the suicidal plan; the other one did with prescient exactness. One of us discovered a path of healing and restoration; the other one found life's brutality unbearable to the point of self-immolation.

SO HERE I am, Linda. I am ready, now, to answer your question. I will tell you the story of how I got better, and how I stumbled upon a source of compassion, sacred and sustaining, that not only restored me to sanity, it resuscitated my capacities for care and connection. But as I tell my story, I will tell yours as well. For both are true. And both bear light on the journey of the abused, and how God is known—or not—within it.

For some, Good Friday really is the last word; suffering finds no relief, and the story ends in death. For others, Easter's daylight truly liberates from the tomb of debilitating pain, and the story of death gives rise to life.

I will tell of the two together.

I will bear witness to the one; I will hold you through the other.

I will be apologist and pietà both.

For God does birth life out of death. But God is also dead, crucified in the car, hidden in the darkness that, for far too many, never yields to dawn this side of the grave.

Part II

Presbyterian Seminary, NJ—Age 27

Spring 1986

———◆———

EVEN AFTER ALL these years, the memory warms me like a smile from a co-conspirator after pulling off a con. For a few days there, Linda and I stole some happiness from the gods while they were off elsewhere plaguing somebody else.

LINDA WAS EIGHTEEN years old, fresh out of high school, when she snagged a part-time job as a stock girl at a Longs drugstore. The decidedly low person on the totem pole, her sole responsibilities were to keep the shelves supplied with goods and the stockroom floor swept and tidy. She was not authorized to ring up sales, bag merchandise, or parley with the customers—let alone answer the telephone when someone was calling. So when the stockroom phone rang just as Linda was passing by, she was disregarding company regulations when, on a spontaneous lark, she picked it up and said hello.

"What's your name?" asked the man on the other end of the line.

"Linda," she replied.

"Well, Linda, what is your favorite radio station?"

Linda remembered. It was all around town. A local radio station was giving away a thousand dollars to any person, randomly dialed, who answered with the station's call sign. Linda never listened to that particular station—seldom listened to the radio at all—but she had seen the promotion on all the billboards. So without thinking twice, she declared, "WYUU."

And just like that, she won a thousand dollars.

She knew immediately what she wanted to do with the money, for she had dreamed of it for years: visit her big brother at graduate school and, with him as her escort, take a once-in-a-lifetime sightseeing tour through New York City. I was a grad student studying spiritual formation, married just under a year, when Linda came to stay for a week. While Cathy took some time to herself, Linda and I took day trips to Manhattan by train to Penn Station or across the Hudson on the Staten Island Ferry. For those seven days, we had the city, in all its splendor, to ourselves.

Linda's itinerary was as meticulous as it was ambitious—her dreams collected and collated since childhood. And we followed it to the letter with the devotion of two disciples on a pilgrimage. We marveled at Times Square, the Statue of Liberty, Rockefeller Center, the Twin Towers. We whistled and cheered at both a Broadway musical, *42nd Street*, and the Rockettes' dance routine at Radio City Music Hall. We shopped at all the world-class department stores—Saks Fifth Avenue, Barneys, Bloomingdales, Macy's—she knew them all. We gawked at the opulence of the Ritz Carlton, the Plaza, the Four Seasons, the Waldorf Astoria. We rode a cab, a subway, a horse-drawn carriage, and a rickshaw pulled by a bicycle. We even paid a visit to the world's largest shoe store—five stories tall—where she must have tried on every sandal in her size.

But the most memorable moments came as we fulfilled the quintessential Linda desires on her well-culled must-do list. We role-played scenes from her favorite films. Linda had fallen in love with New York City through the movies, and she wanted to experience in person the cinematic enchantment that had moved her on the screen. So, though she had never fashioned herself as either an actress or a filmmaker, she directed us through location sites, insisting that we reenact them as if we were in character.

She made us go to the Empire State Building at night and stay until we were the last ones there, just like Cary Grant did when he waited in vain for Deborah Kerr in *An Affair to Remember*. We demonstrated with protesters in the square outside of the Plaza where Barbra Streisand bid farewell to Robert Redford in *The Way We Were*. She talked a street performer into hamming it up in Central Park, pushing him down in the middle of his act like Dustin Hoffman did to a mime walking the tightrope of a curb in *Tootsie*.

And we had to browse for high-end jewelry at Tiffany's.

Breakfast at Tiffany's was Linda's all-time favorite movie, and Holly Golightly—the free-spirited social butterfly escaping an abusive hillbilly past—was her lifelong luminary. From the time that she was an adolescent to the day that she died, Linda hung in her bedroom the iconic poster of Audrey Hepburn from the film—the socialite decked out in evening wear and wide-rimmed sunglasses, adorned in diamond brilliance, clasping a croissant and takeout coffee while staring through Tiffany's storefront window. With countless viewings to prepare her, Linda needed no rehearsal. When we stood outside the very same window at which she peered every night in her bedroom, she channeled Ms. Hepburn, inspired in me some George Peppard, and sauntered into the jewelry store like Holly on a shopping spree.

We pretended to be siblings shopping for our mother—heiress to the Colgate estate—who was soon to be celebrating her fiftieth birthday. Though our disguise belied it—jeans, sneakers, tourist maps poking out of our pockets—money was no object. Whether the tailor-suited salesclerk fell for the ruse, or was simply well used to two rubes sniffing around Tiffany's as if we were nobility, he waited on us with the courtesy of an aristocrat's valet. Like he would for royalty, he displayed for us rings encrusted with emeralds, bracelets of solid gold, watches studded with sapphires and rubies. Linda, playing her part, wrinkled her nose and bemoaned that, while certainly beautiful, they lacked the certain panache for which we were looking. The jeweler, playing his part, said he did have something rather exquisite tucked away for only the most refined of tastes. With ceremonial care, he opened a safe and slipped out a black velvet case with a platinum silver latch. He laid it before us as if preparing to unveil a sacred relic. From behind, he lifted the top so that we could see it straight on. Inside, nestled on a pillow of ivory-colored silk, a brooch necklace of diamonds and pearls—dozens of both—glistened with elegant extravagance.

"Would the lady like to try it on?"

The lady was tempted. Gazing upon it, her eyes mirrored the glimmering gemstones. She was no longer playacting. She was transfixed, perhaps beholding herself wearing it at some glamorous event—a ball, a banquet, a gala for the Academy Awards—sampling, for a moment, a life of radiant possibility.

But she declined to touch it. Being this close was enough; any closer may have burned.

"That won't be necessary," Linda said. "I think it's perfect. I assure you, we will be back when we are ready to purchase it." I have no doubt that, in her mind's eye, she did go back many times over throughout the ensuing years.

For a solid week, we two drifters were off to see the world, coursing along a "Moon River" current through the streets of the city where hayseed impersonators take a stab at their dreams. We laughed, we played, we followed every adventure that promised a rainbow's end. And Linda lit up. She shone like a princess on holiday. She shone like an international movie star glittering in tasteful elegance before the window of the world's most famous jewelry store.

She shone so much that she remembered it thirty years later.

We were in my truck that Easter afternoon, parked on a bluff overlooking the ocean. In excruciating detail, she had shared with me the torture that her life had become. Then she stared into the sea, lost in the pain, longing for a relief that was well over the horizon.

And it came to her. "Remember that trip we took to New York City?" she mused. "Remember when we went to Tiffany's?" If not the sparkle, at least its shadow returned to her eyes. "We had such fun," she said. That we did.

She gazed into the memory as if trying to conjure, one more time, the diamond dazzle vitality that it promised. "I just want to feel like that again," she said, the dazzle already fading into the sea. "I just want to be happy and alive."

If there is a heaven, I hope Holly—and Linda—now have their jewels.

LINDA'S WEEKLONG VISIT was soul-restoring for me as well. She did not know it—and I did not let on—but I was floundering as a doctoral student. Not academically. Spiritually. The quest that had driven me to seminary in the first place had proven to be as infuriating as it was ill-fated.

I ached to know God. But God was nowhere to be found.

TWO CAMPUS VISITS set the course for both my spiritual search and my eventual vocational direction. One ignited my longing to know the sacred; the other promised a route toward satisfying it.

The journey had yet to deliver.

The day before I started high school, my dad moved out of our home. The weekend before that, he had had a conversion experience. My mom had told him that she wanted a divorce—that she was planning on marrying the California highway patrolman with whom she was having an affair. Reeling from the revelation, he went to a Sunday evening revival service. That night he accepted Christ and forswore—for good—drinking, smoking, watching porn, and sleeping around himself. He was baptized into a conservative church, the Church of God (Anderson, Indiana), that understood itself as a holiness movement as opposed to a sectarian denomination. Convinced that his salvation and sobriety depended upon it, he scrupulously devoted himself to studying his Bible day and night. He attended prayer services throughout the week and twice on Sunday, took classes on orthodox doctrine for new believers, and served on congregational committees and then as a board member. He volunteered his carpentry skills to retrofit the church's facilities and would steal away for days at a time to conferences on Christian discipleship and camp meetings at the mountain retreat center.

When he came back to the house to pack up his things the Labor Day before school started, he did not want any help. He was in such a rush it was as if every second in that house caused him physical pain. I followed him from room to room, lamely throwing a baseball in and out of my mitt, as he dumped dresser drawers of underwear into cardboard boxes, hustled armfuls of hanging clothes from his closet to his truck cab, stuffed paper bags with file folders and blueprints from his den, and shoved crates full of hand tools from the garage into his truck bed.

As he pulled away from the house—his secondhand sailboat trailing his truck as if setting off on an adventure without me—I stood on the driveway and watched him go, wishing that I could go with him. It was not only that his leaving us left me, the oldest child, to contend with our mom on my own. He was my idol—the hero whose Cool Hand Luke nonchalance was my icon of masculinity, and the godlike personage whose favor I craved to win over every chance that I could get. It was his pride that I sought when I got straight As on my report card, when I outran his boss's son at the carpenter's union annual picnic, or when I raced home on my bike after pitching a one-hitter in Little League. It happened infrequently, but that faint smile with an approving nod of his head felt like a blessing from on high. Staring at his back as he drove away from his marriage, his home, the Catholic church of his childhood, I was chilled with a near-religious dread—maybe my dad was turning his back on me too.

So when he charted a new life for himself and found a church family to replace the family he had left, I ran after him as best as I could. I got as involved in his church as he was. Nothing purely pious stirred me; I became devout out of an attempt to gain my dad's attention—that and to stomp down the shame that burned as the taboos of puberty began to throb.

Throughout my high school years, I pored over the scriptures at early-morning Bible studies, filled out reams of discipleship workbooks, sang praise songs with gusto at glory gatherings, and prayed fervently at biweekly worship services. I became so involved in teen ministry that my youth pastor, Dave Miller, earmarked me for religious leadership. When it came time to decide upon college, Dave suggested the school that he had attended—Anderson College, the religious movement's hub of higher learning at the Church of God headquarters in Indiana. To help me discern, he offered to pay for a campus visit. My dad, having already ordained me to become the first to go to college from our blue-collar family, gave his imprimatur. So, the June of my senior year in high school, I found myself on an airplane to the Midwest, scoping out the college that would dictate the course of my life's spiritual quest.

I ARRIVED AT Anderson with some seven thousand fellow pilgrims. It was the week of the church body's annual convention—equal parts camp-style revival, international family reunion, and ecclesiastical business meeting. I quickly discovered that it was also the week that a theological controversy—contentious enough to split the church—was coming to a head. People throughout the campus grounds, venting in huddled packs, were worked up about it. The Reverend Doctor James Earl Massey, a former senior pastor at a prestigious big city church and at that time a professor at Anderson College, had been nominated to become the Christian Brotherhood Hour speaker—the movement's sanctioned spokesperson who preached weekly on their radio station that was broadcast throughout the world.

A fiercely devoted contingent—led by the outspoken Reverend Lillie McCutcheon—was determined to block it. Apparently, Dr. Massey refused to condemn the practice of speaking in tongues—believing it to be a legitimate form of spiritual expression for those who possessed the gift. Rev. McCutcheon thought otherwise—that not only was the practice unbiblical, it was all that separated the church from the heresies of Pentecostalism. She insisted that the official voice of the Church of God movement preach nothing but scripturally sound doctrine, and commit himself to preserving the purity of their holiness identity.

Skeptics throughout the convention suspected that racial dynamics were at play. Dr. Massey was Black—the first African American to ever be nominated for the flagship position of Christian Brotherhood Hour speaker. His supporters were equally outspoken, indignantly defending their colleague's impeccable faith, his erudite biblical scholarship, and his unimpeachable doctrinal orthodoxy. By the day of the vote for his official ratification, positions were drawn and tempers were hot. The confrontation promised to be messy.

Though a neophyte in the world of ecclesiastical politics, I found myself swept up in the crowds swarming to the high-steepled Park Place Church, the site of the proceedings. As if cast as an extra in the courtroom scene from *To Kill a Mockingbird*, I ended up in the back of the packed balcony, the rest of the church so crowded that people were jammed in the pews, lined along the walls, and huddled outside each wide-opened window. From my crammed perch, I gazed across the teeming commotion in search of the person who incited such theological hysteria. He was not hard to pick out.

On the dais up front, immaculately dressed in a three-piece suit, facing the buzzing throng, James Earl Massey sat with contemplative calm. Something about him inspired in me an immediate awe. He bore the presence of a medieval cathedral in candlelight—at once majestic and serene, venerable and gentle. I did not know it then, but Howard Thurman had been his spiritual mentor, Martin Luther King Jr. his friend and colleague. He imbued them both, mystic and prophet, a steel rod of strength and a soft-hearted expanse of love. As he would throughout the years to come, the very sight of him reduced me to a whispered reverence. For the first time in my life, I felt in the presence of a true man of God.

Throughout the several hours of testimony, he sat in silent attentiveness, extending the same courteous countenance to critic and advocate alike as one after another paraded to the standing mic up front and vigorously extolled their views. His critics maligned his theology, questioned his ecclesial loyalty, and attacked his biblical exegesis. His advocates impugned his opponents, defended his theology, and vouched irately for his faithfulness to the church. The climax came from Rev. Lillie McCutcheon herself.

Summoning up her considerable oratorical skills—a veritable Clarence Darrow on the offense—she commanded the room with rhetorical relish and stentorian fervor. She summarized the long list of objections, dismissed the counterpoints with dispatch, then remonstrated that the very authority of the scriptures was at stake, as well as the holiness of the movement that they followed, as she built toward a moment-of-decision crescendo like the revivalist preacher that she was. She crested with a demand pointed directly at Dr. Massey. Knowing full well that he would never disavow his convictions, she looked him in the eye and distilled her discourse into a single public ultimatum.

"Dr. Massey," she avowed with a culminating flourish, "I will be the first one to ratify your nomination if you promise before us all that you will never preach in support of speaking in tongues. Give us your word right now, and I assure you—all opposition will be withdrawn."

The crowd hushed as Rev. McCutcheon stood her ground and waited. The gauntlet thrown, Dr. Massey was called out. It was time for him to speak, and to defend both his biblical scholarship and his faithfulness to the movement. With the dignity of a statesman poised to ease the fears of a nation, he stepped to the pulpit and turned toward Rev. McCutcheon.

"My dear sister Lillie," he said, holding her stare. "I promise you one thing and one thing only—I will preach none other than the living Word of God that leads to love and everlasting life."

With that, he sat down. Four hours of debate; one sentence of response. But that one sentence came with such spiritual authority, he not only was overwhelmingly ratified, he unwittingly recruited a new student.

The radiance of his character shimmered all the way to the back row of the balcony where I sat with a certainty that matched Dr. Massey's. My longing echoed from depths within me of which, until then, I was unaware. Though unplumbed, it rose up with an urgent directive to myself: *I want to know what that man knows.*

And I matriculated to Anderson College.

I WASTED NO time in finding a way to study under him. The fall of my freshman year, I enrolled in his class entitled Introduction to the Old Testament. His teaching did not disappoint. His academic intelligence was as brilliant as his spiritual presence. His lectures were peppered with quotations from writers both ancient and contemporary. He quoted great swaths of scripture verbatim. He was fluent in the original languages of the Bible, translating and elucidating texts of Hebrew and Greek right before us. And he surveyed the history of the ancient Israelites with such clarity and detail it felt as if we were wandering with God alongside them.

My spiritual crush on him burned with a young adult's idealism. Or perhaps it was what Jung would call a golden shadow projection—an external embodiment of qualities within me, both academic and soulful, yearning to be cultivated. Either way, I was determined to impress my new professor with my worthiness of being his student. I gave everything that I had to that class. I scoured all our textbooks, including the suggested supplementary readings. I scribbled down notes from his lectures as if I wanted to transcribe them verbatim. I researched obscure journal articles at the theological library for my exegetical papers. And I collated a semester's worth of material in a binder filled with outlines and diagrams, a butcher-paper timeline coordinating text compilations with historical events, and a pile of hundreds of notecards with significant names and dates to memorize. By the time of our final exam, I was armed with enough knowledge to debate a PhD candidate. I wanted not only to impress Dr. Massey, but to secure his patriarchal blessing.

Our final was a one-on-one oral exam—a thirty-minute tête-à-tête during which he could quiz us on anything that we had studied throughout the course. He scheduled the exams at his home, mine for a late afternoon in mid-December. As I approached his house that wintry day, the afternoon was drifting into twilight. I knocked on his door fighting my nervousness by riffling through the Rolodex of facts and figures I had at my recall's fingertips.

Dr. Massey welcomed me like a minister receiving a parishioner dropping by for a pastoral visit. He held the door with a warm smile and invited me into his living room. The parlor was immaculate, decorated with a museum-like simplicity—a sofa and two stuffed chairs, a coffee table with a centerpiece of freshly cut flowers, a few artifacts from around the world in a display cabinet, and a grand piano in the corner. I sat on the couch as he settled into a chair. He opened a Bible and began the exam.

"Psalm 46:10," he read, inquisitively. "Be still and know that I am God." He paused. "Tell me, Mr. Rogers, what does this verse mean to you?"

I leapt right in with my intellectual acumen. "Well, I see this as an eschatological hymn most likely written after the deliverance of . . ."

"No, no," he interrupted. "I'm wondering, what does this verse mean to *you*?"

"Well, the Hebrew word for 'know' is *yada*, which is a uniquely intimate form of knowing . . ."

"No," he interrupted again with the patience of a schoolmarm tutoring a child who is just not getting it. "I want to know what it means to *you*, personally."

I looked at him quizzically. "To *me*, you mean, personally?"

"Yes. I know you're working your way through college; your family is in California. Where are you finding stillness in your life right now?"

And for the next thirty minutes, we had a pleasant chat about the busyness of college life, the elusiveness of stillness, and the whispers of God to be heard when the whirlwind settles and one's soul opens. It felt more like a session with a spiritual director than a final exam with a biblical scholar. Then he brought the chat to an end by saying, "Thank you, Mr. Rogers, for coming by. This was a lovely conversation."

I sat there incredulous. "You mean we're done?" I asked. He nodded. Then I became a tad irritated. "But, Dr. Massey, you hardly asked me a thing. I mean, I studied everything we did. I can ace this test. Go ahead, ask me something. I *know* this stuff."

He considered me with a patient tenderness. Then he said, "I'd like to give you a gift." He stood up and walked to the piano stationed in the corner. I learned later that he had trained to be a concert pianist, until a call to the ministry reoriented him. He sat on the bench, placed his hands on the keys, and closed his eyes as if listening for the source of music itself deep within his soul. Then he played. He played a music unlike anything that I had ever heard before—a classical concerto that murmured through the room like a brook rippling through a springtime meadow. For a moment, my soul almost settled into a stillness so quiet a whisper from God could be heard.

When he finished playing, the melody lingering in our midst, Dr. Massey held the moment, then faced me. "I have been playing this piece for over forty years," he said, "and I still do not know it the way that I yearn to. When you know sacred texts like I'm trying to know this concerto, trust me, you will pass any exam in life that is important."

I DID YEARN to know sacred texts in the way that Dr. Massey described. So the next two semesters I took two more of his classes—Introduction to the New Testament and Biblical Exegesis for Preaching. Then he taught a class that expanded my horizons even further. It was not about knowing texts; it was about knowing God.

The intensive weeklong seminar during January term was entitled Spiritual Disciplines for Ministry. In it, he expounded upon his book, *The Hidden Disciplines*, where he described the spiritual practices that cultivate a vital relationship with the living presence of God. Foundational to them all—worship, fasting, works of service—was prayer and meditation. God meets us, he taught, in our inmost center, in the hearth of the house of our soul. Contemplative prayer can settle us into that sacred residence within. Christian forms of meditation include *lectio divina*, quieting one's mind with a sacred word during prolonged sits of silence, and, like Ignatius of Loyola, pondering the presence of God within the mundanities of our everyday lives. As we give ourselves to these practices, we can sense this divine presence. Like the psalmist that invites us to "be still and know God," we can know this sacred presence intimately and know ourselves as beloved in the care of a heavenly Father. In that week, Dr. Massey rocked my world with the possibility that God can be found within the hearth of my own soul, and that, having never left, God is already there waiting for me to come back home to myself.

That was my last class with Dr. Massey. His added responsibilities as the Christian Brotherhood Hour speaker forced him to reduce his course load, and I had other classes to complete for my religious studies major and my minors in psychology and sociology. I did, however, intensify my push to embody the piety Dr. Massey so exemplified. I yearned to know this God in the house of my inmost center, so I strove to construct a residence in which God would want to dwell. I started a routine of contemplative practice, beginning each morning with *lectio* and silent meditation, and ending each evening with an Ignatian awareness examen. I also committed myself to the other Christian disciplines. I studied sacred texts and theological writings not just for class but for my personal edification. I attended daily chapel and weekly worship on Sunday. I got involved in ministry, designing Bible studies and weekend retreats as a youth pastor for teens at a local congregation. I even engaged in Christian service, tutoring kids as a volunteer with Big Brothers of America. And yet, as hard as I tried to be pleasing to him, I could not get God to come visit me in a way that felt intimate and real.

If anything, I felt that, for all my religious activity, my impure inner world was actually driving God further away.

No matter how steadfast I was with my regimen of spiritual discipline, I could not restrain the affliction of unholy emotions. I knew that it made me dirty and undesirable, but I seethed with petty irritations at my roommates. I burned with libidinal attraction to coeds, wallowed in a despondent sense of aloneness when I could not sleep at night, and boiled with anger at God for refusing to grace me with his caring presence. No matter how much I gutted my way through a pious routine of spiritual study, prayer, and good works, I could not cleanse my soul of the vile feelings that defiled it, while being painfully aware that this vileness was what was making my soul unfit for God's habitation. Then my pietistic resolve cracked altogether, and I acted on the more debauched passions that were prowling around within me.

I knew that the fleshpots of sexuality were off-limits. Not only did the Christian traditions that bound me see all carnal behavior as sinfully perverse, but a chasm of dread in the pit of my stomach warned that hidden horrors lay in wait whenever flesh gets too close to flesh. I was a young adult and I had been on only one date in my life—and that was when my high school English teacher set me up for the Christmas formal after I told her that I was not going. I took the young lady to the dance, moved with her to the music with enough space between us to satisfy a Mother Superior, then took her home and fled, not daring in the days that followed so much as an acknowledgment that we had been out together at all. No, the iron doors within me that kept Eros at bay were made of a well-congealed compound of my own shadowed psychological trepidations and the puritanical religious strictures that reinforced them. Still, midway through college, I crept through and trespassed anyway. I succumbed to my lust for a girlfriend and then to the erotic play that enticed me.

Leigh was a Southern belle from West Virginia, a music student at Anderson College with aspirations of becoming a folk singer. She also had a lighthearted sensuality that so aroused me I muscled down my inhibitions and asked her out. After two dates, our affair was aflame—just two kids, really, discovering together the amorous delights of young puppy love. Those first forays into physical touch, the tingle of skin against skin, the melting bliss of naked bodies interlaced with each other, were simultaneously intoxicating and castigating. My desire for her body was ravenous; my shame at my lack of self-control—leaping into sex before marriage—was befouling. I longed to be good, holy, unblemished—the kind of young man of whom God would be proud, to whom God would want to come home. And yet, my premarital sexual activity stained me with a sinfulness that felt unforgiveable. I tried to strap myself inside a psycho-sexual straitjacket by imposing platonic boundaries on our affections, sometimes for weeks at a time. But then my urges would writhe free for a libidinal frolic that only compelled me to cinch the straps tighter for another sentence of penitential abstinence.

Eventually, the strain became too much. After nearly two years of lascivious fickleness, Leigh and I broke up. She found a guy less tortured and sexually complicated. I sought relief from my constant state of abasement. I revived my rigorous spiritual discipline, imploring God to look on me with mercy, to visit me with the assurance of his loving forgiveness. But it was too late. His back turned to my depravity, God, I imagined, had long since pulled away. I was waiting in the house of my soul alone, soiled and growing weary of waiting for him. I could not meditate; I could not pray; I could not care enough to crack a book. I plunged into a depression, sleepless and suicidal, lying in bed each night wishing that I was dead. I should have gone into counseling.

Instead, I went to see Dr. Massey.

THE SPRING SEMESTER of my senior year in college, I was celibate once more, spiritually in crisis, and clueless about life after graduation in June. I had heard that Dr. Massey was leaving—starting that summer as the dean of the chapel at Tuskegee University. Desperate for guidance on how to climb out of the abyss of my life, I made a final appointment with him. The reason that I gave was not entirely dishonest. I told him that I wanted some last words of advice on how to improve my prayer life.

We met in his campus office this time, though the warmth of his welcome was just as gracious as when I had met him in his home. He invited me to sit in one of the chairs, the table next to his holding a well-worn Bible and a childless picture of him and his wife. When he asked me how he could help me, I maintained an academic façade. Not about to lay bare all the prodigal details of my backsliding, I simply shared, as if it were an intellectual curiosity, that my meditation practice was not as satisfying as it had been right after his class.

He responded with a similar pedagogical detachment. He told me that this was nothing unusual—that an initiate's natural enthusiasm is like a flare that burns bright for a while, but, at some point, flames out precipitating a season of spiritual dryness. That dryness is the crucible for the truly transformative work—the day in and day out discipline of sustaining one's practice, striking together the arid stones of one's prayer until the spark of an enduring flame from within is ignited. I asked him what one should do if the issue was not so much dryness, but being afflicted by destructive emotions. He suggested that one should pray the emotions, to bring them before God, that in the purifying fire of divine presence, the dross of even our basest instincts can be refined into a precious metal. Given the depth of my baseness, this seemed most improbable.

"Aren't there some instincts," I asked, "so base that they cannot be refined?"

"What might those be?" he queried.

"For starters," I said, inadvertently becoming even more self-revealing, "acedia—a fever of despair that God is so deliberately absent that the desire to pray at all is completely extinguished."

"What might that despair feel like," he asked, "if you were to sit with it?"

"If I sit with it?" I pondered. "I long for God to look at me with mercy. I long so bad it hurts."

His look was filled with care—like a physician who knows that the prescription is painful, but also knows, firsthand, that it really does heal. "That ache," he suggested, "is the backside of God, God's presence in the form of absence. It is how God clears away the false deities in our souls, and prepares a place within us to dwell."

"So what do you do," I yearned to know, "if the ache is overwhelming?"

His prescription was as sincere as it was severe. "Stay with the ache," he said. "Let the longing do its work. Let it strip you bare to the bone."

As dismal as this spiritual purgatory portended, I had deeper concerns. "Dr. Massey," I said, "maybe there's another reason why it's so hard to pray. Maybe there are some souls that are just too dirty for God to want to dwell in."

He looked at me with concern, wondering, I suppose, where this was coming from. "No," he said, as one who knows. "Nothing is too dirty for God to touch. God can be found in even the most depraved iniquity. God holds it all, the good and the bad."

As good as it sounded, it did not ring true. "But what about God's holiness, Dr. Massey?" I asked. "How can a holy God let himself be tainted with depravity?"

He searched me with eyes that bore depths of knowing culled from a lifetime of intimacy with the divine. Perhaps he saw in my eyes the depths of the lifetime of dread from which my question came. For a moment, the two depths met. Then, for the only time in my memory, he used my first name.

"Frank," he said, "God's first, last, and only impulse for you—and for everyone else—is always compassion. If you know this, you know everything."

Those are the last words that I remember from my final meeting with Dr. Massey. They have echoed into my soul's center and across the intervening years. He named the ache that drove me. *That* is the God that I yearned to know. *That* is the presence that I craved to encounter within the hearth of the house of my soul.

But goddamn it—where do you find that God?

THE SECOND CAMPUS visit that dictated the trajectory of my spiritual journey likewise excited my soul's longing to know God in a real way. It promised that God could not only be found, but that God can be experienced in moments of such transformative power that our lives are forever reconstituted around the center of a benevolent presence that never goes away. As if illuminating the location of the Ark of the Covenant, that second visit rekindled my quest for the elusive reward of glimpsing the very face of God.

It also launched my vocation. Both, for good and for bad.

THE SUMMER BETWEEN my junior and senior years of college, I fulfilled my field requirement for my religious studies major by serving as a student intern at my dad's church in South San Francisco. Among other ministerial duties, I helped with the youth group, made hospital visitations, taught Sunday school classes, and preached occasional sermons. Early one foggy Saturday morning, I arrived at the church eager to put some finishing touches on the next day's homily. A young boy, maybe twelve years old, was waiting alone in the vacant parking lot. Wearing ripped blue jeans, an army trench coat, and a bandanna around his long frizzy hair, he paced nervously as if uncertain that he was welcome on such holy ground. As I pulled up, he rushed toward me and asked if I was the priest. I told him that though I was not a priest, I was the summer associate pastor. That being close enough, he asked if I would come to his house and talk with his mother. The night before, his older brother had shot himself. His mother was distraught, and without a soul to talk to.

A few minutes later, I pulled up with the boy in front of his house. The paint was peeling from the sides. Oil stains splotched the driveway. Automobile parts were strewn across the dirt front yard. In the darkened living room, his mother sat, whimpering uncontrollably as she stared down the hall into the bedroom where her sixteen-year-old son had taken his dad's handgun and decided that life was just too hard to continue. I stayed with her for several hours. Having no words of comfort to offer, I simply sat with her on her couch—she crying, me shaking my head, the unimaginable grief overwhelming us both. When it was time for me to leave, the boy, Tony, asked if he could ride with me back to the church. We sat in my car in the parking lot, the late morning still gray, as Tony laid bare some of his pain.

It quickly became clear how much he adored his big brother. He tried to dress like Danny, tried to walk like Danny, liked to hang out with Danny and his friends. He revealed how Danny was his sole refuge at home. His dad was an alcoholic who would come home at random times both tanked and violent; his mom was so depressed she could not leave her own bed to prepare meals for her sons. But Danny watched out for him and would let him tag along when he stole a few hours away from the house. As Tony shared, something of the impact of Danny's death on this boy came over me. I had no words of comfort for him either.

Once Tony talked himself out, we sat in silence in my car. Then, after a while, he shared something else.

"I want to ask you something," he said. "Something happened a few months back I've been wondering about. Dad came home, really ripped, ready to beat up anybody who was there. Danny and I ran out of the house and tore on down the street. We got ourselves a couple of Cokes at the liquor store and hung out at the park. It was nighttime, and the two of us just sat against the handball court, waiting until we thought it was okay to go back. We didn't talk much. We just looked up at the stars. All of a sudden, this shooting star just flies across the sky. And the two of us, we started wishing on this star." And Tony described a litany of wishes—two boys, back and forth, with Danny, the older, leading, and Tony, the younger, responding in kind.

"I wish I could play baseball like Willie Mays."

"I wish I could pitch like Juan Marichal."

"I wish I had a brand new car."

"I wish I had a ten-speed bike."

"I wish Regina had the hots for me."

"I wish Suzie would leave me alone."

"I wish Dad would stop hitting everybody."

"I wish Dad didn't drink so much."

"I wish that Mom were happy."

"I wish that she would cook us dinner."

"I wish that Mom didn't need me so much."

"I wish that she would talk to me."

"I wish that Dad were dead."

"I wish that Mom would clean his clock."

"I wish, I wish that I was a long, long way away from here," Danny mused absently.

As Tony described it, he did not offer a wish in reply to that one. It was as if Danny really was a long, long way away.

But then Danny came back. "You know what I wish?" he said. "I wish that I could fly. And if I could fly, I wish that I could fly right up into heaven. And I would fly right over to where God is sitting and I would sit myself down right in front of him. And do you know what I wish? I wish that I could look into his face, and he would look back at me, and he would smile." Then he took his empty soda bottle, shattered it against a concrete wall, and spewed, "But the bastard would probably turn his back."

And Tony turned to me, on that gray Saturday morning, and he asked me, "What I want to know is, was Danny right? I mean, I know you can't, but if you could. If you could fly and see God's face, would God smile at us? Or would God just turn his back?"

WHEN I GRADUATED from college, I had as little vocational clarity as when I had begun. I had earned a rather unmarketable degree in religious studies and, though the senior pastor at the church where I interned urged me to join his staff, I had no desire to become an ordained minister. In part, I knew that the daily grind of pastoral visitations, sermon preparations, and congregational management was not for me. The deeper truth is, I did not have an answer to Tony's question. I could sense the desperation with which he asked it. And I suspected that a similar yearning was hidden within every query that prompts a person to call on a pastor—if we could find ourselves before the presence of whatever is ultimate in our world, would that sacred reality be welcoming and benevolent, or simply cold and capricious? I knew the textbook response from a pastoral care class, the one that I recited for Tony.

"Of course God would smile at you," I assured him. "He would welcome you with open arms."

But I did not know that to be true for myself. I was closer to Danny than to the textbook—certain of divine disavowal. And like it was for him, it was a life or death question for me. It is hard to hang on at all when you know that your own repugnance brings disgust to the all-seeing face of God. I simply had yet to pull the trigger. Certainly, I had no business serving as a pastor.

Vocationally bereft, I flirted with becoming an attorney. A local lawyer in Anderson, a friend of one of my professors, had hired me during my senior year for a few hours a week of clerking. It went so well that he took me on full time. Then he offered to pay for my law school if I partnered with him upon passing my boards and securing my license. With nothing else to sail toward, I took the LSAT and was admitted to the Indiana University School of Law. And I almost went. The night before classes started, however, I thumbed through the catalog perusing the courses that I would soon be taking—Torts, Civil Procedures, Contract Law. Uninspired by what awaited me, I opened a random school of theology catalog and surveyed its array of course offerings—The Varieties of Mystical Experience, Spiritual Disciplines across Traditions, God and the Problem of Evil in the World.

I knew immediately. My spiritual quest, far from satisfied, was not yet ready to concede defeat. So I declined my law school admittance, took a gap year clerking in Anderson, and went on the hunt for a theology school at which I could resume my studies. Having no idea how I would parlay it into an eventual job with a living wage—pastoral ministry still not an option—of all things, I decided to get a degree in divinity.

ONLY BECAUSE I recognized their Ivy League locations, not from any awareness of their theological distinctiveness, that November I arranged a series of campus visits through Princeton, Yale, and Harvard. I figured that I would swing by a few other schools of theology while I was in the neighborhood.

I could have concluded the tour after the first stop.

Presbyterian Theological Seminary's stone buildings and hallowed grounds conjured in me images of robed academics—descendants of medieval scholastics—poring over ancient texts in monastic cells to elucidate the mysteries of God's eternal being. With its massive library, enormous classrooms, and scores of book-laden intellectuals immersed in the world of the mind, the campus seemed to bulge with knowledge. A handful of prospective students gathered for the visit day. The admissions office scheduled the morning with an orientation, a walking tour, faculty interviews, and lunch with assorted students and staff. Then we had the option of visiting the historic township or sitting in on an actual class. I decided on the class—and thereby unwittingly stumbled upon the man who would become my academic mentor and, eventually, my *Doktorvater*.

Somewhat unpromisingly, the class was entitled The Educational Ministry of the Church. Envisioning comparisons of Christian education curriculum and tips for crafting Sunday school lesson plans, I was somewhat skeptical as I joined perhaps a hundred students scurrying into the antiquated lecture hall as if a dignitary was soon appearing. My first impression of the professor shuffling in close behind us did not raise my expectations. Overweight and easily winded, he had driven the short block from his campus home to the classroom. Climbing the building's few porch steps left him panting as he hobbled to the podium that was mounted on a dais and proceeded to pull out handfuls of lecture notes seemingly at random from his battered briefcase. With his disheveled thinning hair, stubble of whiskers, wrinkled tweed jacket, loosened tie splayed over his spotted button-down shirt, and the tousled disarray of pages in his fists, he looked like a paunchy Oxford don who had been napping in his office after a pint at the pub when it dawned on him that he was late for his afternoon lecture.

When he spoke, however, every trace of the befuddled professor persona evaporated. Forty years later, I still remember the exposition that he delivered that day. Dr. James E. Loder, a PhD from Harvard in religion and mental health and a Danforth Fellow recipient at the Menninger Foundation in theology and psychiatric theory, kept us spellbound for three hours with a tour de force discourse that integrated psychoanalytic studies, mystical theology, existential philosophy, contemplative spirituality, biblical exegesis, and theories of religious formation. Yet it was not his scholarly virtuosity that was so memorable. It was the incisive clarity of his spiritual analysis. I felt as if he had lifted the veil of my daily existence and dissected my soul.

He began by inviting us to consider the phenomenon of gazing into the face of a smiling infant. He wanted us to recall the numinous splendor of such moments—a baby taking in our features, then beaming at us with such unadulterated delight that we cannot help but smile in return. It can be enrapturing—even transformative—a moment of pure and complete loving connection. Sitting there, I had an impression of what he was talking about. My own family struggled with straightforward affection, but I had seen babies, with a simple smile, light up strangers in supermarkets. Since then, I have experienced the theophany for myself. The first time that my own son smiled at me was downright magical. Dr. Loder was right; the spell it cast turned stone into gold.

CATHY AND I were eating dinner in our apartment, facing each other across our paltry dining room table for two. Justin, perhaps a couple of months old, was nestled in his Baby Bouncer propped on the floor angled toward Cathy. His infant eyes not yet registering concrete objects, he nodded about in dopey abstraction taking in the murky collage of colors in his blurry world. Cathy and I were not conversing. I was lost in thought, ruminating on the final edits of my dissertation for Dr. Loder—a five-hundred-page tome on "Karl Barth's Faith Epistemology of the Spirit as a Critical and Constructive Framework for Christian Formation"—fancy words for how to know God for real according to a theological giant known more for his towering intellect than for his personal spiritual experience. It was fitting. All that I knew about God at that point was in my head. The house of my soul was still vacant—the hearth stone-cold.

Cathy had long since given up trying to connect. My withdrawal from her was impenetrable. It was not just the pressure of a dissertation deadline. I had shut her out, in almost every way, since we had been married four years earlier. She was well acquainted with the wall of my unavailability. It was better that than the fury on the other side.

Dabbing her mouth with a napkin, she glanced down at Justin. Still wiggling in random distractedness, he bobbed his head toward her. For a moment, he fixed on her, staring with puzzled inquisitiveness as if this blur in his world held a special fascination for him. Slowly, the blur came into focus. For the first time, he saw a face. He stared at it, captivated, as if wondering how it got there. Then he recognized it. The face was his mother. And he did the most incredible thing. He smiled.

Cathy instantly gasped, "Did you see that? He smiled at me!" Breaking into a grin herself, she knelt down beside him, brought her face close to Justin's and, fluttering her head from side to side, swooned, "Yes, you did. You sure did. You smiled at your mommy."

For several moments, they beamed at each other, rays of pure love and delight shining back and forth between them. Justin gurgled and shimmied in joyful abandon; Cathy cooed and gushed in playful reply. Both of them were so radiant in the giving and receiving of infinite affection they were like two mirrors reverberating sunlight between them, the dazzle so bright it spilled out in every direction. It even spilled out onto me.

Cathy turned to face me, her countenance glowing like one beholding the burning bush. "Frank," she said, "you have to see this." She grabbed my hand and pulled me down, scooching over a bit as I knelt at her side. Like a cloud passing over the sun, Justin's smile dimmed as his gaze shifted from Cathy to me. He took in the features of this strange new face as if ascertaining if it were friendly. Then he recognized who it was—his dad—and once again, he beamed, his whole face radiant with delight. It was like peering into a looking glass of gladness. I could not help but smile back. Justin gazed at me with such boundless pleasure I bubbled over in waves of loving bliss. He giggled and babbled and bounced in buoyant rapture; I tickled and snickered and kootchie-kootchie-kooed in childlike abandon; the two of us aglow in a sunburst of happiness. Cathy leaned in close to me, creating a visual feast for Justin. He bounced between us, grinning at one—arms flailing, feet kicking—then wiggling back to the other, the three of us giggling ourselves into a mystical moment of effervescent unity.

It truly was transformative. For a few minutes, I was restored to what a human being looks like when we are alive and flourishing with affection. Loved and loving, I came back home to my self, my true self—seen and celebrated, seeing and celebrating. The splendor of such glory burns with a hearth-like warmth. For a moment, it was able to soften a heart as hard as mine.

Even God may have cracked a smile.

For a moment.

IN HIS LECTURE, elaborating on material from his recently published book, *The Transforming Moment*, Dr. Loder expounded upon this universal phenomenon. A baby at birth, he illuminated, is unable to differentiate distinct realities within its perceptual world. Embedded within a soupy sea of light and shade, they navigate their environment through the physiological functions of sucking and grasping. As psychoanalytic researchers have documented, and attachment theorists have corroborated, the primal object that the infant first distinguishes, sometime in the first month or two, is the human face. When the infant does perceive a face—any face in those early months—the infant smiles. Wired for relationship, the baby is making a primordial bid for secure connection. With almost reflexive regularity, the person who receives the smile will smile right back.

What ensues is nothing short of mystical—two people gazing at each other with unequivocal love and delight, each person seen in their particularity and beheld with abundant, effortless care. In that moment, Dr. Loder suggested, personhood is imprinted. This is what it means to be human—to be in a relationship that simultaneously confirms individual identity and secures relational attachment, a relationship that both recognizes you without rejection and loves you without absorption.

For the infant, these spiritually restorative encounters, experienced with a self-authenticating immediacy, are primal moments of cosmic-ordering wholeness where all is right with the world. From this point on, the infant's entire development will pivot around the drive to secure and sustain such enlivening connections with the primary figures within its environment. These moments are also the prototype for all religious experience. Encountering God—like the infant beholding the smiling face that reveals itself—is the numinous experience of finding oneself in the presence of a cosmically ordering, self-confirming, loving transcendent other. For Dr. Loder, infants are mystics innately.

At some point, the infant becomes aware, albeit preconsciously, that the loving face is not everlasting. Even under the best of circumstances, the face is not always there when the infant needs or desires it, nor is it always smiling when it is there. As this realization solidifies, the infant exhibits anxiety—an instinctive angst that perhaps the face will not come back at all, or that the face will bestow disapproval instead of loving delight and connection. This anxiety forebodes an existential dread—the soul-chilling possibility of absolute aloneness, the unlivable void of a life without love, the unbearable despair of living in a world where you are unseen, unheard, unknown, un-smiled upon.

To alleviate this metaphysical anxiety, the infant develops adaptive strategies to secure for itself the love and attention that it craves and needs. In crude efforts to make the face come back and smile, the baby endeavors to wail, to pout, to rage, to withdraw, to placate, to perform—whatever is needed to retrieve and sustain the attachment on which it existentially depends.

This sets off a lifetime of ill-fated pursuits to secure enough love and sense of self-worth to hold at bay the dread of rejection and abandonment. The faces on the figures whose loving approval is sought will shift throughout the years—from caregivers to friends, teachers, lovers, employers, the general public, and perhaps eventually, even one's own children. And the adaptive strategies will take various forms—finding true love that will never leave you, earning the esteem of mentors or peers, accumulating wealth to secure one's value, even submitting to the rigors of religious devotion to make one worthy of everlasting love.

And yet, each pursuit is but the desperate and ineffectual attempt to escape the abyss of unlivable aloneness. The terrifying truth ever haunts—no one's care can be so enduring, no accomplishment can be so resplendent as to assure that, in the end, we will not find ourselves in a world alone and unloved. The essential yearning that plagues every soul remains unsatisfied. Deep in the shadowy recesses within, each of us longs for a self-confirming, loving face that will never go away.

This longing is archetypal. It is the God-shaped hole in every human being. The desire to see the glory of God's face permeates Western mystical traditions. The Hebrew psalmist seeks God's face, pleads for God's face to shine upon us, and implores God not to hide God's face in the midst of our distress. The Quran frequently refers to the face of God that can be glimpsed by the faithful anywhere in creation and extols how bright our faces will be when we see God's face fully on the Day of Resurrection. And Christian writers describe our unveiled faces reflecting the glory of God like bright mirrors and proclaim that the living Christ is the face of God whose loving gaze sustains the entire cosmos.

For Dr. Loder, the good news is that the face of God yearns to be seen. God wants to be known—not intellectually, not dogmatically, but directly and convictionally. Knowing God is a transformative event in which we encounter a transcendent loving other who sees, hears, and delights in our own unique particularity. It is an intimate type of knowing—immediate and self-authenticating in precisely the same way that an infant just knows that it is seen and celebrated by the face that smiles upon it. Knowing God in this way is life-altering. It heals developmental wounds, eases existential anxiety, regulates us psychologically, and regenerates us spiritually. It not only meets the deepest longings of our soul, it reconstitutes the center around which our lives are lived. No longer driven by anxiety to secure love and worth in transient pursuits, we give ourselves abundantly to becoming instruments of the loving presence that has so graciously bestowed itself upon us. Seeing God's face, we now bear God's face for others.

Then, breaking all protocols of academic detachment, he shared with us how he knew this. It was not from books, not from others' eyewitness accounts, not even from sacred writings. He had encountered this presence himself. As the class hushed in reverent anticipation, Dr. Loder shared the story of his father's death from brain cancer. He had been a first-year graduate student when his dad was diagnosed and already in the advanced stages of the disease. His father, a former elementary school principal, had always believed in his son, even when his son did not believe in himself. Through long seasons of doubt and depression, it was his dad's unwavering support that sustained Dr. Loder as a young man. Now, a cornerstone in the foundation of his mental health was days away from dying. He rushed home immediately, the despair overwhelming him as the reality sunk in. Once there, he fled to his childhood bedroom in a desperate attempt to collect himself. In rage and grief, he pounded his bed and pillows, screaming at God to step in and do something.

As he recounted it, a physical sensation of warmth inexplicably rose up within him, a liquid heat easing through his body from his toes to his head. As it passed through him, it washed away every drop of despair from his being and replaced it with an undeniable sense of divine presence. In that moment, he knew that he was not alone. No matter what was to come, God would be with him through it all.

He looked out upon us, from his raised lectern, with the majesty of Moses on Mount Sinai. Many in the room were holding tissues to their eyes. He gazed at us all, eyes sweeping the room. Then, with the authority of one with the power to bestow it, he gave us his benediction. Quoting the Pentateuch, he blessed us each one, "'May God make His face shine upon you and be gracious to you; may God turn His face toward you, and give you peace.'"

Once more, I was ready to matriculate on the spot. Dr. Loder not only diagnosed my spiritual condition with poignant precision; he promised that I could glimpse the very face of God. And that God would smile kindly even upon me.

It turned out too good to be true.

I SPENT EIGHT years at the Presbyterian Theological Seminary—three devoted to a master of divinity, five to a PhD, all in dogged pursuit of the God whose face is well concealed within the throne room of a distant stronghold inaccessible to the undeserving. I did not find him. But I became well acquainted with the desolate landscape outside the castle walls.

Aching for a convictional experience like the one that Dr. Loder described, I set about studying them with the single-minded intensity of a Round Table knight combing through ancient scrolls for clues to the location of the Holy Grail. Taking all his classes, then petitioning him for two independent studies, I pored over the primary psychological sources that informed his work—Freud, Ferenczi, Spitz, Suttie, Jung, Erikson, and Kegan. I used my courses in systematic theology to understand the doctrine of the knowledge of God in classical figures like Augustine, Luther, Calvin, and Barth. I took classes in the history of Christian spirituality, delving into the deep waters of mystical writings by Cassian, Climacus, Eckhart, à Kempis, Saint John of the Cross, and the author of *The Cloud of Unknowing*. I supplemented my studies with personal reading of contemporary contemplatives like Nouwen, Merton, Main, Keating, Bloom, and Basil Pennington. And I took full advantage of the free audit policy, sitting in on classes throughout the university on Dante, Dostoevsky, Camus, Kant, and the primary inspiration for Dr. Loder—both spiritually and philosophically—Søren Kierkegaard.

In fact, for those first three years, I fashioned myself after the melancholic Dane. I holed up alone in my dorm room taking reams of notes from my readings. I brooded through long solitary walks, pondering both my metaphysical loneliness and my inability to manipulate an epiphany with the divine. And I filled binder after binder with pages of journals dissecting my moods, venting my frustrations, and taking desperate stabs at disentangling the Gordian knot of my spiritual despair—indeed, my tailor-made *Sickness unto Death*.

To be sure, it was an addictive defense. Many, as my own family has known, are gripped by the insatiable urge for drugs, alcohol, sex, or gambling to muffle the feelings that overwhelm when facing the true depths of one's pain. The monkey on my back—equally efficient at first—was deciphering esoteric theological texts, constructing grand theories of the human predicament, and intellectualizing the puzzle of my spiritual plight. It was a habit that compelled me to write a two-hundred-page master's thesis articulating, in meticulous detail, the existential double bind of either denying the abyss of our aloneness through self-defeating ego projects, or facing the abyss head-on and being immobilized by the despair of eternal nothingness.

At the time, I was unaware that the real double bind was that the abyss was not composed of eternal nothingness. Hidden in those shadows was a mirror that exposes the secret shames of the one poised on the edge. I was not about to peer into those pernicious depths, so I doubled down on my ego projects and found another stash for my habit. I accepted Dr. Loder's invitation to continue my studies with him as a doctoral student.

And just to be sure that I kept the abyss of aloneness at bay, I also got married.

My secret shame was about to erupt.

CAMP GOOD NEWS was a Christian summer camp nestled alongside a small lake in the woods of Cape Cod. Founded by a navy chaplain with the United States Marine Corps, its primary purpose was to win boys and girls to Christ. The children—ages six to sixteen, many on scholarship from disadvantaged communities—came for one or both of two four-week sessions. They stayed with a college-aged counselor in cabins of six—the girls' camp at one end of the lake, the boys' camp at the other. From morning until night, they were herded through a wholesome array of invigorating activities—hiking, archery, volleyball, softball, lessons in swimming, sailing, and wilderness survival skills—all constellated around morning chapel, afternoon Bible study, and evening devotions where staff took turns offering their personal testimonies of how they came to Christ. Buttressing its piety, the camp maintained a strict moral code. It forbade drinking, smoking, swearing, dancing, card playing, and physical touch of any kind between boys and girls and men and women—a six-inch separation rule was in effect at all times, with any offender subject to the penalty of wearing a bright-red life preserver for a day as a public badge of shame.

THE SUMMER BEFORE I started at Presbyterian Seminary my roommate in Anderson suggested that I join him and a handful of other recruits from our Christian college as a staff person at the camp. The junior boys' program needed a waterfront director to lifeguard and teach swimming lessons, and I was certified in both. Two months in Cape Cod sounded Edenic—both tranquil and sexually chaste. I took him up on the offer.

The camp turned out to be neither.

Despite the prohibitions, a large portion of the young adult staff paired off for summer romances—my roommate included. It was largely at his prodding—insisting that the junior girls' waterfront director was not only perfect for me but was "impressed" with my faith and character—that I broke the six-inch rule. I passed her a note during chapel asking her if we could meet during the afternoon downtime. She agreed.

Cathy, having studied piano at Interlochen and the Westminster Conservatory, was a music teacher at a private Christian academy in Des Moines. As prim as her English ancestry insinuated, and as prudent as her Midwestern roots, she met me with her button-down shirt and khaki shorts crisply pressed, her short blond hair wrapped in a scarf. She stayed only long enough to share with me that, indeed, she would be interested in going on a date—perhaps coffee on our day off—but she had three conditions. One: since she was living at home, under the authority of her father, I needed to write him a letter and ask his permission. Two: I needed to attest my assent to the fundamental principles of her faith—a list of ten doctrines including things like the inerrancy of the Bible, the total depravity of humanity, and the saving atonement of Christ's sacrificial death. And three: I needed to honor the vow that she had made when she was in college and her boyfriend was tragically killed by a drunken driver— that she would never kiss a man until the day of her wedding when she and her partner were formally pronounced as husband and wife.

I pledged myself to all three. All three harbored deceptions. I did not believe that a father had authority over his twenty-five-year-old daughter, but I wrote a letter to him anyway. I took issue with almost all the principles in her statement of faith, but reinterpreted them for myself with enough theological gymnastics that I told her that I could affirm them in spirit. And though I had every intention of honoring her sexual boundaries, I did not submit to such prudish parameters merely to maintain my moral purity. I agreed out of relief. I am sorry to say that, deep down, I mostly pursued a romance with Cathy because she was safe. Untroubled by erotic arousal, the secrets that shamed me could sleep peacefully in platonic suppression. Unfortunately for us both, though sleeping, their dreams were far from peaceful.

It took a couple of weeks, but I heard back from Cathy's father. He was a bit bewildered at my request, but he approved with graciousness. Thus Cathy and I began our decidedly virtuous, though somewhat hampered, summer romance. With but a single day off each week—the only time that the staff had to do laundry, catch up on chores, and run into town for supplies—and with the rest of the days dedicated to shepherding several hundred kids from early-morning prayer to late-night songfests around the campfire, our developing dalliance was less torrid and more Jimmy Stewart with Donna Reed. The few hours a week we did have for a private meal or a stroll off-site were woefully insufficient with our desires to become as well acquainted as we could. And we were simply unable to find cracks in the Christ-intoxicated schedule for even a few moments during the day to wish each other well as we marched along. So we resorted to writing letters and leaving them for each other. That summer, our romance was primarily epistolary. It was also clandestine—our correspondence was carried out completely in secret.

Midway between the boys' camp and the girls' camp, Cathy and I found a rendezvous point where we could hide notes for each other throughout the day. A single cabin faced the waterfront just outside the field of vision from the grounds' main paths. The lone occupant—Richard Smith—was seldom around. As an assistant to the director, his responsibilities engaged children from all over the camp. And even when he was inside, he kept to himself in such reclusive quiet we had no idea that he was there. As far as we could tell, the place was always deserted.

A few feet in front of the porch steps, in the shade of a cluster of pine trees, a park bench was perched facing the lake. Between it and the trees, we buried a flat stationery box, covered it with dirt and pine needles, and marked it with a stone that had two cracks along the top forming a cross. Cathy and I considered it an omen. It was the perfect spot to slip over from the path, uncover the box, deposit a letter and pocket the one there, then slink back into the daily routine without ever being noticed. Those letters, buried in the shadows, foretold it all. Combinations of expressions of affection, tidbits of camp gossip, biblical forays into theology and morality, and get-to-know-you queries into everything from our favorite foods and music to our visions of love and family life, they laid the foundation on which we would later build the home of our marriage.

During the second half of the summer, those hidden notes became all the more important. Between the two month-long sessions, my responsibilities shifted. Several kids were acting out in the junior boys' camp. As I had a strong rapport with them, the junior boys' director asked if I would become a cabin counselor. Six of the more troubled boys were assigned to me, and for the rest of the summer, I was their chaperone day and night. If not for our private correspondence, Cathy and I would have hardly connected at all.

And as we came to find out, it was not all that private. On the day that we were leaving—the kids all gone home, the camp stowed for the winter—Cathy and I took a last stroll to our secret hiding place to retrieve the stationery box as a souvenir for our summer romance. As we lifted the box, now damp with decomposition, from the ground, we both gave a start. Having slid silently from inside the cabin that we had thought was already vacated, Richard Smith was standing on the porch staring at us. Though he had caught us in the act, he did not look surprised.

"Did you know about this?" I asked, feeling rather exposed.

"Of course," he said, smiling furtively. "I've known the whole time. You two have been so cute, leaving each other your notes all summer."

Glad that we did not know what we did not know, we thanked him for his discretion and dismissed the creepiness. As it turned out, the stationery box was spoiled beyond salvaging. We tossed it away and left the camp. I would not return for over three decades.

IT WAS FOUR years before I even thought about Camp Good News again. A fellow counselor from that summer was driving by Presbyterian Seminary and asked if I wanted to share dinner. After catching up and reminiscing, he asked if I had heard about Stewart Brooks—the grandson of the founder, son of one of the codirectors—a rather withdrawn boating instructor the summer that we had been there. My friend relayed the news. The previous winter, Stewart drove his car to a beach parking lot just outside the camp. He doused himself, and the car's interior, with gasoline, then lit a match.

In stunned disbelief, I asked my friend why he had done it. My friend did not know—but rumors of sexual abuse were whispered among some of the staff. Stewart grew up in the camp—he would have been vulnerable to some of those suspected. My friend surmised that Stewart had been abused. And that— either taking his secret to the grave with him, or having divulged his secret, perhaps to his own family, and being disbelieved—he torched himself in rage-filled defiance and burning despair. My friend had no evidence for this, only suspicion and conjecture. But he would not have put it past the place.

Stewart's self-immolation seared me. It was not just the reality of his sui-cide; it was the violent and vengeful way in which he had done it. I could rec-ognize a similar fire smoldering within me. My friend's conjectures felt haunt-ingly plausible. Secret sexual abuse permeating our surroundings, yet hidden in the shadows just beyond our awareness—something in me knew that this could totally happen. But at the time, it was only conjecture.

Until *60 Minutes* got involved.

Thirty years later, in February 2011, Massachusetts Senator Scott Brown appeared on the news program in conjunction with the imminent release of his autobiography, *Against All Odds*. In his interview with Lesley Stahl, and as elab-orated in his brutally honest memoir, Senator Brown, for the first time in his life, revealed that he had been sexually abused in the 1970s by a counselor at a Christian summer camp in Cape Cod. Though he did not mention the camp by name, it quickly surfaced that Camp Good News was the site of his moles-tation. His very public self-disclosure inspired scores of others to come forth with further allegations of sexual abuse at the camp spanning from the 1970s through the 2000s. The accounts were so credible, and the disregard by the administrators so egregious and chronic, the camp lost its accreditation. After a police investigation, charges were filed against one of the accused—a handy-man, Chuck Devita, who had been a fixture at the camp for decades, even ris-ing to become the director of the physical operations and an honored board member. He was never brought to trial. The day after the charges were announced, Devita drove his pickup to the camp's backwoods and killed him-self with a shotgun.

Living across the country, I was oblivious to the scandal for another few years. The spring after Linda's suicide, Alane and I were in Boston attending a conference. With some unexpected free time, we decided to rent a car and take a day trip to the Cape. Wanting to share a piece of my past with my wife, I suggested that we drop by Camp Good News. When I Googled the directions,

I stumbled upon links alluding to sexual-abuse allegations at the camp. With a dread that knew what I did not know, I clicked on the links.

It was all there—years of counselors caught with child pornography but merely being prayed over by the directors, then promoted. Multiple staff people from all sectors of the camp accused of fondling, fellating, and raping children in their charge. Predatory pedophiles singling out the most timid and disenfranchised to prey upon for a summer. And a culture of silence, denial, and dismissiveness that sustained it all. Newspaper accounts in *The Boston Globe*, *The Patriot Ledger*, and *The Cape Cod Times* recounted a police inquest, a civil lawsuit, and statements from both victims and corroborating witnesses whose reports to the staff were repeatedly rebuffed. Devita's suicide was depicted, as was the tragedy of Stewart Brooks. A janitor was named; an apology letter to Senator Brown was quoted.

Then I noticed that the DA had actually secured a recent conviction. After a two-year investigation, involving over a dozen allegations against him, the former counselor pled guilty with no contest to two counts of indecent assault and battery on a child under fourteen and one count on a child over fourteen. The man, also convicted of molesting children in another state, had only been at Camp Good News for one year—the summer of 1981.

The man's name was Richard Smith.

In the depositions, one counselor testified that Richard Smith treated Camp Good News as a "buffet for young boys." During the day, he would pull a child out of an activity and take him to Smith's secluded cabin. During the evening, he would enter one of the several dozen boys' cabins and select a child for the night. The counselor complained to the directors, but nothing was done, beyond shuffling some of the cabin assignments. Richard Smith continued, day after day, night after night, escorting children to his waterfront cabin, walking them up the porch steps, and confining them in the concealment of his quarters to violate them at his will. The counselor testified that watching one of those boys leaving his cabin, the boy looking back at him with eyes that cried for someone to intervene, was like watching the boy walk to his own execution. It certainly was to the death of his childhood.

THE CAMP GATES were open when Alane and I drove onto the grounds more than thirty-five years since I had last been there. Seeing neither a person nor a car, the camp seemed abandoned as we drove into the heart of the compound still nestled alongside the lake. In the chill of the early spring afternoon, I returned to that waterfront cabin—scene of both romance and assault alike. I stood beside the park bench, my back to the lake, and stared into the shadows of that vacant shack. Though the grounds were dead-calm silent, I could imagine the cacophony that should have filled the faithless and defiled landscape.

The trees, aflame, should have crackled in an inferno of rage. The waters should have frothed and pounded in waves of fury. The stones—both cross-faced and bare—should have cried out with shrieks for vindication. And the winds should have howled with the wails of countless child spirits unavenged in their violation.

And the young Cathy and I, with our notes of affection and our chastity-belt courtship, should have stood there still, recognizing the harbinger and weeping with foreboding. Our romance was incubated within earshot of young boys being stripped and assaulted. From the cocoon of our secret rendezvous, we could have heard their whimpering through the walls—if they were crying; if we were listening; if the love that we were cultivating could have acknowledged and held the abuse that was beside us the entire time.

The tragic truth of our doomed marriage is that our love could not. Even while the foundation we were laying for a happy home life was fresh, the fault lines for its collapse were already in place.

Like at Camp Good News, abuse was hidden in the shadows of our marriage.

All the more destructive for being forced to suffer in secret.

OUR SUMMER COURTSHIP only lasted a few more months. After our time at Camp Good News, Cathy went back to teaching music in Des Moines; I started my studies at Presbyterian Seminary. We carried on for a while with weekly long-distance phone calls and a couple of brief visits, but the dimming flame of our righteous ardor grew harder to keep lit. I grew weary of contorting myself theologically to conform to Cathy's fundamentals. Cathy feared that her very faith was at stake—the precepts and practices that kept her secure. Our conversations degenerated into debates about my orthodoxy that blazed with all the romance of an academic inquisition. By Thanksgiving, I broke up with her, able then to concentrate all my energies, spiritual and romantic, into my single-minded intellectual quest—if not to know God, at least to know what it means to know God.

And that would have been it. Except that the following summer, Cathy wrote me a letter. She assured me that she was not nursing any amorous desires, but she had decided to enroll in a two-year master's in Christian education program at the same school where I was. That fall, she was becoming a student at Presbyterian Seminary.

For those next two years, Cathy and I studied on the same campus, slept in the same dormitory, ate at the same cafeteria, and even took several classes together. She was not true to her word—she nursed a relentless amorous desire. Sure of her love for me and convinced that we were destined to marry, she fended off the advances from numerous other suitors even as I fended off hers toward me. Every couple of weeks, she would try again. Coming up to my dorm room or asking me to take a walk, she would request my assistance in processing her theological evolution. The rigid walls of her fundamentalist jailhouse were breaking open. She was discovering new vistas of faith that were both freeing and enlivening.

While this was all entirely true, our colloquies, however, inevitably would devolve into pleas, often with tears, for me to reconsider the rationale for our breakup. To be sure, I sent her mixed messages. On the one hand, my heart remained hard and my resolve firm. I had no desire to get back together as a couple. On the other hand, I would sit with her, for hours on end, affirming her theological liberation and consoling her in her relational grief. Through countless parleys, often late into the night, Cathy clung to her hopes, while I continuously repelled them. As graduation came near for us both, Cathy finally came to realize that I meant it. While I made commitments to stay at the seminary for doctoral work with Dr. Loder, she accepted an offer to return to her old teaching position. Though not to live with her parents, Cathy was moving back to Des Moines. In the face of my consistent callousness, she had given up trying.

Almost.

The night before her return to the Midwest, she invited me to her dorm room for a final farewell. She made hors d'oeuvres and had chilled a bottle of wine. She did not pledge her love for me; she did not plead for mine. With neither tears nor reproach, she simply wanted to wish me a good life. In the spirit of friendship, we embraced our goodbye. She looked at me with a smile, and she meant it. Then, casting aside her high school vow, she sprinted toward first base and kissed me with an open mouth. We continued to run all of the bases, touching each one in turn, in a night of passion I would never have imagined.

The next morning, she left.

During the ensuing few weeks, my tortured loneliness felt existential. I filled my journals with self-doubt and self-castigation. I ached for companionship but turned cold when it was offered me. I yearned to see God's face but spurned the cute one eager to delight in me. I longed to be an instrument of love in the world but could not find it in me to care for the winsome young woman right next to me. I even admonished myself that, at twenty-five years of age, I was so old I was most likely staring at my last chance at a stable and enduring relationship. Kierkegaard may have been right—if faith in God was like swimming over an abyss of uncertainty seventy thousand fathoms deep, perhaps faith in love was cleaving to the raft of committing oneself to another to survive the infinite seas of aloneness.

To this day, I am not totally sure why I did it. I may have been taking the leap of faith, or I may have been running away from my loneliness. I may have been seeking a safe refuge to escape the terrors of the deep, or I may have sensed that seeking such refuge was the best way to surface those terrors to tame them.

Or perhaps it was as simple as, once let loose, my horniness was ready to make some hay. Whichever the reason—or all of them at once—by the beginning of July, I called Cathy up, pledged to be her boyfriend, and asked her to move back near me. She was there by month's end—giving up her music teaching job in Des Moines and securing another in the town next to my school. Act of faith or failure of character, it inaugurated the chapter in my life for which I carry the most regret.

MY FIRST SEMESTER in the doctoral program, I took a seminar on Christian Formation and Moral Philosophy. In addition to studying Kantian deontological philosophy and Aristotelian character ethics, we considered Iris Murdoch's understanding of morality as right vision. Ethical behavior, she argued, is not derived by deciding upon right action through the application of moral principles or from the habit of cultivated virtues; it comes from just and loving *seeing*. When we take the time to truly *see* another in the unique beauty of their particularity, we are moved by their experience, and right action flows as an organic response. Regardless of the school of thought, I failed my first ethical test as a serious romantic partner.

Unfettered by either a high school vow or a six-inch rule, as soon as Cathy moved back, we bit freely into the fruit of sexuality's garden. We tasted enough that, within three months, she was pregnant. You could chart the lunar calendar by the regularity of her cycle—after two days of being late, she was certain. The pregnancy test, a few days later, confirmed it. We had barely entered the Eden of our relationship and we were already being kicked out.

For me, this precipitated a moral crisis. At that time, both in my family of origin and in the Christian circles where I was studying, getting pregnant out of wedlock was a scandal. I was driven to shine as a beacon of piety and responsibility, not only before God but in the eyes of my mentors and colleagues as well. With herculean tenacity, I strained to keep my shames in the shadows. Now I was on the verge of public disgrace. I could only imagine the looks of disappointment on the faces of my teachers, not to mention my God, and the shaming disapproval in the frown from my father. Such degradation felt unlivable. I had to prevent it at any cost—even at the cost of losing what was left of my moral decency.

It would never have occurred to Cathy to consider getting an abortion. Sure, becoming pregnant so soon was rushing the timeline that she had imagined for herself. And being unmarried may be cause for some passing embarrassment. But we would make it work. We would be in it together. And, in the end, we would have a child to celebrate. If I had taken the time to see her in the truth of her particularity, I would have noticed a young woman, apprehensive but in love, aching to hear from her partner that we would get through this, that I would be with her no matter what, that having a child together would be a joy, and that we should get married right away and launch our future of raising a family together. That is the right action that would have flowed from right seeing. But I did not see her. Nor did I act rightly. Instead, I broke her down.

For days, I berated her about our predicament—hiding out in Cathy's car after she got home from school so we would not be overheard in my dorm room. Like a prosecutor wearing down a witness to coerce a confession, I exposed her uncertainties, countered her arguments, and bemoaned the consequences of having a baby so soon in an all-out attempt, not just to get her to agree to an abortion, but to manipulate her into saying out loud that she was the one making the choice. After endless hours of my passive-aggressive polemics, she halfheartedly conceded—sensing, I suspect, that if she had the baby, I would abandon her emotionally, if not literally. The only choice she really had was a choice between me and the child.

If she was going to do it, she wanted to get it over with immediately. We found a clinic in a blighted section of Newark and—Cathy taking a sick day from work—we made an early-morning appointment. We drove over in silence. As we crossed the overpass into the city limits, I had the dire but certain sensation that I was staining myself irrevocably. Not only was I terminating a life out of cowardice, I was also denying a woman's right to choose for herself. And I was betraying both her and myself so completely I would never be able to wash myself clean of the soiling.

I drove on anyway.

We pulled up to the storefront dispensary. We sat in the grimy waiting room. Cathy went in for the procedure. I drove her back to my dorm room. She napped. And I went to my afternoon class—my seminar on morality. While Cathy cramped and grieved alone, I resumed my role of pious respectability.

No one could see the soiling but me.

I PROPOSED TO Cathy a month later. I would like to say that I drew the water from a well of love within me—at once compassionate and wholehearted—fed by the springs of tender care from our weathering such a painful time together. The truth is, the well water, already reeking with shame, was now polluted by the guilt of my weakness of character. I asked Cathy to marry me to expiate the sin of my failure to do so when it mattered—that, and to intensify my resolve in sculpting the persona of a wholesome man of faith and family. Maybe in acting the part I could become the part, I thought.

Even then, however, I knew better. As I stood at the altar on the day of our wedding—the church filled with family and friends, my dad stolidly pleased in the front row—I watched Cathy as she walked toward me down the aisle. She was dressed in white and was as beautiful as I had ever seen her. And yet, my only thought was, *This is a mistake.* Years later, I confessed this to Cathy. She told me that she knew. Then she confessed to me—she had been thinking the same thing.

OUR MARRIAGE WAS not able to expiate my guilt. The sin of my emotional abandonment only grew more egregious. Something in me simply shut down. When we were home together, I did not feel like talking about my day, nor did I want to hear about hers. I resented intrusions when I withdrew into my studies. I prickled with annoyance when she needed help with a chore. And I lost interest in sex altogether. As awful as it is, the very sight of Cathy, in a moment of amorous hope, coming out of the bathroom in a baby-doll nightie turned me so cold and irritable she quickly turned back and retreated for good into the unseductive protection of her flannel pajamas.

To be sure, I detested myself for being so hard-hearted, and I tried to castigate myself into caring for her. Every once in a while, I would have a fleeting moment of seeing Cathy in her unique beauty—draping a napkin over her knees in her car as she daintily nibbled the treat of her White Castle hamburger, playing Keith Jarrett standards on the piano when she was feeling forlorn, or sitting on our balcony, sipping her cinnamon-laced coffee, as she found solace in her grandmother's copy of Anne Morrow Lindbergh's *Gift from the Sea*—and I would fan the resolve to love her as she deserved. But the moment that I stepped toward her to demonstrate care, I ran into a gale force of internal resistance as strong as a hundred-mile-an-hour headwind. By the time my caring sight turned into concrete action, my heart was stone-cold again.

Eventually, the impenetrability of my withdrawal prompted Cathy to voice her frustration, which only incensed me with fury and indignation. Within a few months, we were fighting so loudly, and so deep into the night, we were asked to leave our first home together—the servant's quarters that we rented from a seminary board member, the true heiress to the Colgate estate, who lived in a manor down the pike from the seminary. Cathy and I simply transferred our hostilities to the seminary's married-student apartments. When Linda came to visit toward the end of that first year, Cathy declined the day trips to New York City not because she needed a little downtime; she needed a break from me. The weeklong respite with my little sister was only temporary, however. A short while after Linda returned home, my rage at Cathy escalated exponentially.

We started fighting about my mom.

CATHY AND MY mom never hit it off. My mom thought Cathy prudish and uptight. Cathy thought my mom invasive and shameless. To be sure, Cathy was reserved in expressing any endearments to my mom. Then again, the first time that they met, my mom was half-dressed.

The winter break after we were engaged, Cathy and I flew to the Bay Area to meet both sets of my parents and her two brothers in San Francisco. Borrowing a car from my dad, we drove to my mom's for a few days' visit. We arrived midmorning and were greeted in the entryway by Linda—then seventeen—and Michelle, my ten-year-old sister from my mom and my stepdad with whom I shared a love for backgammon, reading, and all things left-handed. My mom was still in her bedroom upstairs; my stepdad was in his downstairs den where he slept next to my two sisters' bedrooms. My mom waited to make an entrance, but not long enough to finish dressing herself. When she sashayed down the stairs, with her hands outstretched like a diva descending upon her fans, her tight blue jeans were splayed open to reveal her underwear and her unbuttoned blouse exposed her breasts.

"Who's here to see his mother?" she cackled, making a beeline toward me. "Plant me a big wet one." She kissed me on the lips, then wrapped me in a bear hug, squeezing and wiggling with affection. She did have enough decorum to snap a couple of shirt buttons before pivoting to wrap her arms around Cathy.

Cathy beat her to the punch and escaped my mom's embrace by reaching out a hand and saying, "You must be Barbara." When my mom moved onto the kitchen, Cathy hung back and whispered at me, "What was that all about?"

"What?" I responded. I was genuinely perplexed. "That's just my mom being my mom. Don't start reading into things." I wrote it off as Cathy being territorial.

Cathy also had issues with my stepdad. He would sit on the end of the couch in our family room, his feet propped up on the table, with an arm around either Linda or Michelle pressed against him so tightly they looked like they were being held hostage. A man of few words, he had a silent system when he needed something—one snap of his fingers beckoned Linda to report; two snaps called for Michelle; a flick of his fingers meant he wanted his cigarettes; a twist of his wrist meant a cup of Nescafé coffee.

My mom, irritated by my stepdad's smoking downstairs, spent her evenings in her bedroom. Just like she had throughout my childhood, she asked me to come up to say goodnight each evening before I went to sleep. She would be perched on her bed, clad in her negligee, reading a novel and fingering her popcorn. I would sit on the side of the bed as she rambled on about her day until she was ready to release me with a hug and a kiss. Before I left, she held my face in both her hands and reminded me, "I love you, Frank. You're my number one."

After three nights there, Cathy was determined to spend as little time with my family as possible.

IN THE MID-1980s, childhood sexual abuse was just beginning to appear on our culture's radar screen. Ellen Bass and Laura Davis's landmark book for women survivors, *The Courage to Heal*, did not come out until 1988—the same year as Mike Lew's book for male survivors, *Victims No Longer*. Judith Herman's groundbreaking work on PTSD in general, *Trauma and Recovery*, was not published until 1992. Before then, most people considered the topic of childhood sexual abuse taboo and incidents of it extremely rare. Even in as enlightened a community as a leading theological school, the issue was hardly ever mentioned, and then only in whispers.

For my circle of friends, Sharon Nelson changed all that.

Sharon was a bright, vivacious young woman studying to be a minister at Presbyterian Theological Seminary. Once a month, Cathy and I would join her and her husband, Tommy, and two other seminary couples for an evening of contemplative prayer, theological discussion, and fellowship over food and drinks. Within ten years, all four couples would be divorced. Sharon and Tommy were the first.

Seemingly out of nowhere, Sharon was assaulted, first by nightmares, then by fragments of repressed memories of sexual abuse throughout her childhood by her father—a rather prominent minister in Minnesota. The psychological rupture was so destabilizing, Tommy would come home to find Sharon clawing at her skin to the point of drawing blood, or curled up in a scalding shower, or cowering under a pile of clothes in her closet unresponsive for hours at a time. They hid it from us and from everyone, until it got to the point that Sharon had to be institutionalized in a psychiatric facility a couple of hours away. She never came back to Presbyterian Seminary. From that point on, we only heard about her from the edges—that she confronted her father about the years of childhood molestation; that her family subsequently disowned her; that her husband, hanging in for as long as he could, met somebody else and divorced her; and that it took years of therapy, in and out of hospitals, before she could finally function and fashion a life as an advocate for women survivors.

The bombshell of Sharon's abuse and disintegration sent shockwaves into Cathy's and my marriage, detonating well-buried explosives within me whose trip wires were just waiting to blow. Cathy began to suspect that I had been sexually abused as well—something that Sharon herself surmised based only on the intuitive sense that she and I were similarly wired. For Cathy, it explained so much—my disdain at being touched, my aversion to sex, the intensity of my withdrawal from her as a woman, the fitful nights of sleep that I refused to discuss—and my mom's sexualized behavior was so over-the-top that it must have seeped into her child-rearing. For me, Cathy's suspicions were enraging. The very suggestion of it set me off in an atomic blast of fury and indignation.

"How *dare* you imagine something so sordid in my family," I would seethe at her whenever it came up. "How *dare* you see me so damaged and defiled. How *dare* you blame all of our fighting on me. How *dare* you scapegoat my mom for all of our marital problems."

The more she considered her conjectures, the more intensely I went after her, getting livid beyond reason, beyond civility, beyond my capacity to contain it. I would find a newspaper clipping on the counter of a "Dear Abby" column on abuse, or I would come upon an article on her nightstand with tips on being married to a survivor, or I would simply see it in her eyes when I recoiled at her touch—and I would yell at her, berate her, and batter her verbally to obliterate the lurid obscenities from her mind: "*Keep those filthy ideas out of this house, do you hear me? You fucking bitch. How dare you. Keep it away from me, or by God, you fucking bitch.*"

To be sure, my pummeling of her shamed me excrementally. I would wake up each day determined to resist another night of attacking her. I would steal away to my study for morning prayer and beg God to forgive my despicability and to still the storms of rage within me. I would leave the apartment in khaki and tweed, a masquerade for both our neighbors and myself to fortify my resolve to be a paragon of academic and domestic stability. I would drive back in the evening determined to contain my fury, when it inevitably ruptured within me once more. But no amount of spiritual practice, façade of civility, or emotional resolve could hold back the tsunami of abusive bile with which I accosted Cathy.

It got to the point where anything could set it off. If Cathy sought comfort from her best friend, I screamed at her for talking about me behind my back. If she suggested that I talk to somebody myself, I yelled at her that who I talked with was nobody's business but my own. If she tried to appease me by cooking my favorite meals, I would spit at her insincerity since I already knew what she really thought about me. If she winced as I approached her while screaming my vitriol, I would harass her for the demeaning innuendo that I would ever actually hit her.

She pleaded that we get help. I refused.

She begged that we talk to our friends for support. I forbade her.

She cried for me to just calm down a little bit so we could talk about things quietly, and I erupted that I had a right to my rage, that *she* was the one who brought all of this on.

To our neighbors on all sides, it must have sounded like I really was beating her up. I wasn't. Not physically. But I beat up her spirit so severely she would hide out in our bedroom—terrified to speak—determined not to provoke me even inadvertently.

If God was watching, what he saw turned his stomach.

In the end, it did take an all-seeing face to wake me from the nightmare that I was inflicting onto my wife. If it was divine, understandably, it was not benevolent.

A doctoral student, teaching an adjunct course for the seminary, moved in next door. An emerging womanist theologian studying Hebrew Bible, she was working on a book, soon to be published, using feminist biblical criticism to explore the experience of Black women in the Bible. Our two apartments were separated by a wall so paper-thin you could hear the clatter of dishes on the other side. The piercing screams of my tirades would have ripped right through that paper like a knife blade. She only lasted two weeks before moving to the far side of the apartment complex. I did not think much of it—until I saw her, a few weeks later, at a campus reception.

Perhaps forty or fifty faculty and students were milling around with glasses of wine and small plates of appetizers. Costumed once more in my Ivy League respectability, I was taking in the room when we happened to look at each other. It took her a moment to place me. Then she did. The look on her face gave it away instantly. Hardly a smile of delight, it was also not a look of scornful disgust. She looked at me with terror. She was afraid of me. She could see right through the part of the scholar that I played with such sociopathic calm. She knew the violence of which I was capable. And it frightened her. Who would I attack next? How far would it go? How badly would I hurt, if not her, then one of her sisters?

I hated the man that I saw in the mirror of her expression—the terrorizing horror that I had become, absurdly trying to hide his shame behind the fig leaf of tweed. I had so lost my way, God would not have recognized me if I could ever have found him. I no longer recognized myself. I needed to get away for a while to get my mind straight. It is testimony to how bad things were that Cathy did not object.

A PHONE CALL from Linda provided the cover. A few months after her trip to see me, she met a navy seaman on shore leave for a couple of days. They hit it off so well he called her on his next leave a few weeks later. Linda was phoning to tell me that she was now pregnant. Sucking up the courage that I had failed to call upon, she was going to tell Dad, then she and Kyle were getting married. I told her I wouldn't miss the wedding.

I bought a yellow Datsun pickup—the one that, a few years later, I would almost drive off a cliff—and I decided to make a road trip out of it. I would drive cross-country to attend Linda's wedding, then head up north to a friend's cabin in the remote regions of the Idaho Panhandle. On the pretense that I needed some time for renewal before I prepared for my doctoral exams, I asked my friend if I could borrow the place for a personal retreat. He graciously gave me the keys. After Linda's wedding, I had a quiet cottage in the woods for eight weeks of solitude and soul-searching.

Witnessing Linda's bravery was both a source of shame and encouragement. Just barely showing, she wore white and stood tall throughout her formal church wedding. My dad, proud in his tuxedo, escorted her down the aisle with the cool debonair of Paul Newman playing it straight in *The Sting*. Not only did he applaud her for doing the right thing, he dressed up and stood at her side as she did it.

The smile on his face was no con.

LINDA'S STRENGTH STAYED with me through my weeks of retreat in northern Idaho. My entire time there was devoted to getting right with God and resetting the course of my life. I prayed, I journaled, I meditated, I read devotionally, I beseeched God to forgive my sins, and I walked the woods for hours at a time with a relentless introspection determined to break through the impasse of my psycho-spiritual torment. Linda helped me to see how much of my turmoil was connected to my father. I related to him like I related to God. I ached for his approval; I was petrified of his rejection. I was all too aware of the depths of my unworthiness, so to secure his love, to glimpse even a faint smile of pride and approval, I dedicated myself to becoming worthy in every conceivable way—morally, religiously, sexually, relationally, even endeavoring to purify my passions interiorly. Of course, I failed spectacularly at becoming worthy—in every conceivable way—which only intensified my shame and redoubled my efforts. The truth is that I yearned to feel seen and loved, but I hid from everybody how despicable I had become. The me that I did let people see was a sham. How can you find a face that smiles when you hide your real face behind a mask?

The true leap of faith that would break the cycle became clear to me. I needed to stop hiding. I needed to come clean about how low I had sunk. I needed to bring my blemished face before the faces of others and begin to live with honesty and integrity.

And I needed to start with my dad.

I rerouted my itinerary back to Presbyterian Seminary so I could stop overnight at my father's. I found him in the garage, unloading his tools from his truck after work, and asked for a few minutes to talk. To secure some privacy, we stepped into the side yard where his sailboat was trailered and dry-docked. As if he had become my priest, I told him that I had a confession. A few years earlier, I had got a woman pregnant, I told him. I was afraid he would be disappointed in me, so I made matters worse by talking her into getting an abortion. It had weighed on me ever since. To make peace with myself, I wanted him to know the truth.

He took it in stride, his face not frowning but stoic, and he offered what comfort he could. He told me that, to be honest, it was nothing compared to some of the things that he had done in his past. That was why he took it to God—only God could wash away our sins. And he suggested that I bring mine to him as well. I told him that I already was, that I was talking to God quite a lot these days. He told me that I was on the right track. Then, with nothing else to say, he nodded his head and, with a faint smile to suggest that it would all be okay, he hustled off to take a shower before dinner. That was it. No mystical epiphany of divine affirmation; no thunderbolt awareness of God's, or my father's, proud and everlasting love. Just the mild relief of coming clean with a piece of who I really was.

And this.

As I was leaving the next morning, my dad handed me a care package for the drive—a paper lunch bag with a couple of cans of Diet Coke and a package of Hershey bars. When I pulled over a while later to view the contents, I found the message that he had left as well. On a page ripped from his pocket spiral notepad, he had scribbled with his dyslexic scrawl, "Frank, Mark 1:11. Dad."

With all my years of study, you would think I would have known the passage. I didn't. I retrieved a Bible and read the words: "And a voice came from heaven, 'You are my son, my beloved, with whom I am well-pleased.'"

Maybe a glimpse of God's face after all.

BETWEEN LINDA'S WEDDING, eight weeks of solitude, and the revelation of my dad's affection, some of the hardness of my heart softened during that cross-country trip. By no means was I healed. Nor was I under any illusion that the minefield of my reactivity around Cathy was now swept clean. I could still so feel the bone-bruise sensitivities just under the surface primed to be triggered and explode that, once back to graduate school, I rented a room just outside of town. Taking another step in public vulnerability, I acknowledged to my friends and colleagues that I was struggling in my marriage. Cathy and I were officially separated.

I was, however, ready to take a first sweep at deactivating the bomb-laden field of our marriage. With the aim of mending our relationship, I started counseling. Cathy and I started marriage therapy, and Cathy started sessions for herself with Dr. Loder—with my blessing to share what she wanted about the challenges that we were facing. I cannot say that we rid the field of the mines that were there—they remained buried and fused with their network of coils deeply rooted in regions we did not explore. Rather, Cathy and I built something more like a boardwalk through the field of our relationship that avoided triggering the landmines, or at least gave us a safe place to leap back to if we got too close to one still exposed. We developed ground rules for our conversations, designed a system of pauses and time-outs to de-escalate any activation, practiced skills of emotional self-regulation, and created a covenant of ways to treat each other with care and civility. If not a thorough excavation of the hidden explosives, we at least succeeded, for a spell, in evading them with well-intentioned diplomacy.

We were separated for a year. I studied for my doctoral exams; Cathy taught music at the elementary school. We went to our respective therapists, and, for the first time, we actually courted. We settled into a comforting routine—I went to daily Mass first thing each morning, then drove to our apartment in time to kiss Cathy goodbye as she left for school. I would study all day in the apartment. Cathy would come home in the late afternoon. We would have dinner together. Then I would drive back to the room I was renting for a few more hours with the books before bed. Weekends, I stayed over with Cathy.

That year was healing enough that, once I passed my spring exams, I moved back in. The seminary asked me to teach a fall class, Spirituality and Christian Formation, and I began the research for my dissertation. That following academic year was the best year of our lives together.

It was so good, we planned to repeat it. The seminary asked me to teach another class while I finished my dissertation, and Cathy signed on for another year of teaching music at her elementary school. We would have followed through with our plans, too, if it were not for the weekend in April when two days changed everything. On Friday afternoon, the dean of the Claremont School of Theology phoned our apartment—he had talked with my advisors and wanted to know if I would come to California to interview for a full-time, tenure-track faculty position. On Saturday, we found out that we were pregnant. Within a few weeks, our new plans were set—a family of three to be, we were moving to California.

It had taken a while, but God was finally smiling upon us.

AS A FINAL farewell to this chapter of our lives, Cathy and I, with a few of our friends, planned a two-week stay in June at a cabin on an island off the coast of Maine. The place was so remote, it took an hour-long ferry ride to get there from the mainland, then a thirty-minute drive across ill-paved roads. All of us had vacationed there together each June of Cathy's and my marriage. This was our last trip with our circle of friends before Cathy and I were moving out west.

The second night that we were there, Cathy woke me up at three in the morning horror-stricken. Her body was releasing clots of bloody tissue. Something was very wrong with the pregnancy. We called the island doctor on the party line and secured emergency transportation on the early-morning ferry; then, once on the mainland, we sped for an hour to the nearest hospital. The doctor in the ER did a sonogram. It was the first time that we had seen the fetus. Maybe ten weeks old, its heart was beating with a hummingbird rapidity. A shadow encircled one of its sides. The doctor shared the heartbreaking news— that shadow was where the placenta was separating from the uterine wall. We were in the early stages of a miscarriage. It may be hours, it may be days, but no fetus could survive such uterine interruption.

Crushed that our child was on the verge of death, we called our doctor back home. He cautioned against us making the ten-hour drive home—the miscarriage could be induced by the drive itself and then we would be stuck on the road. He suggested that we return to our friends where we had support, have emergency transportation from the island prepared, then wait for the miscarriage to follow its course.

It took the rest of the day to make all the arrangements, then drive back to the terminal for the late-afternoon ferry. By the time we were on the boat ride back, we were exhausted, grief-stricken, and terrified at what lay in the days ahead. Sitting in our car, first in line at the front of the ship, Cathy leaned her head against the passenger window for a few moments of quiet. Needing some air, I got out and stepped to the bow. The weather matched my mood—the sea was enshrouded in a canopy of misty gray, visibility only a couple of hundred feet. Staring into the soupy nothingness, it all spewed out of me.

Silently, I dumped my prayer before God. *Why are you doing this?* I implored. *It is so unfair. We've had such hard times—things are finally looking hopeful—and you throw this at us. Goddamn it, why? It's just not right.*

I tossed all of it at him—my anger, my grief, my fear—out before the distant divinity enthroned God knows where. His face was not only invisible; it was unresponsive as well. I was broken and alone, unmasked and unseen.

Then something happened. Of all things, a scripture verse came into my mind, and with it, a sense of warmth eased through me, both inside and out, massaging away every knot of my turmoil. The verse was from Psalm 139: "I created your inmost being; I knit you together in your mother's womb."

I turned to look at Cathy, her anguished face pressed against the glass. And the assurance came over me that the microscopic being in her womb, clinging for its life, was not alone—God was with him, knitting him stitch by stitch. And I just knew—with an intimate immediacy, the knowing of *yada*—that everything was going to be okay. The outcome was unclear—I had no reason to doubt that our miscarriage was imminent. But whatever was to happen, I knew that we were not alone—a sacred presence would see us through.

Then it became mysteriously cosmic. I looked back at the boundless gray, and my knowing expanded. We were *all* in a womb; this vast creation—every cell of it—was held within the womb of God. We were all fighting for our lives, yet none of us were alone. God was with us, each one, knitting us stitch by stitch. And we were *all* going to be okay.

The mystical sensation lingered as we approached the dock. I returned to the car, stroked the back of Cathy's head, and waited for the crew to work the lines so we could leave the ferry. The ground was wet, and the crew was slipping as they struggled to unlock the chains. A man in a pickup truck beside us—lumber piled in his bed—honked with impatience. I looked at him with tender understanding. *Don't you know?* I wanted to say to him. *It's going to be all right—you're in the womb of God.*

I had sense enough to keep that to myself, but the feeling lingered as we drove back to our friends, embraced each other with our tears, and waited for the miscarriage to come to termination. The miscarriage did not come that night, nor the next, nor anytime during our remaining two weeks. With fear and trepidation, we drove back home, then met with our gynecologist. He performed another sonogram. The tiny hummingbird heartbeat was still visible, as was the ominous shadow beside it.

The doctor studied it. Then he said, "Do you know what that shadow is? It's an empty sac. You had twins. One of them miscarried—but the other one is hanging on."

Cathy's mobility was limited throughout the rest of her pregnancy—but on Christmas Day, Justin was born.

THAT MISTY AFTERNOON epiphany that I had on the ferry was not a spectacular encounter—numinously transcendent—with the God who occasionally deigns himself to make an appearance before a loyal and watchful subject. It was more as if, for a moment, the veil of this world became sufficiently translucent that I could perceive the silhouette of a sacred reality that is always already there, whether we know it to be or not.

To my surprise, that reality was more maternal than paternal. It was not an all-powerful Father-God—whose scornful face I feared—with the ability to change the fate of his serfs should it ever happen to please him. It was rather an all-embracing oceanic presence that enfolds every particle of the universe with a womb-like warmth of love that sustains and companions us through whatever our fate happens to be.

The truth is that some babies live, some babies die; some conditions are treatable, some conditions are terminal; some wounds heal, some bleed on in secret. And yet, a cosmic sacred reality holds it all—the good and the bad, the hope and the despair, the joy and the sorrow—grieving the pain, aching for new life, and celebrating the flourishing whenever it comes. With eyes moist when we suffer life's heartache and glistening when we shine like a jewel, it companions every being, every molecule, every moment of existence, with compassionate, restorative care.

It was only a glimpse, but that silhouette was the face that I had been seeking. That was the divine presence that I yearned to know. And here, I had been in the hearth of its house all along. The divine presence is as close as a mother to the newborn that she embraces.

Whatever was to come—times of stability or turbulence, delight or desolation—that compassionate reality would be there when Cathy and I made our way to California.

Which was a good thing. There would be a lot more to companion. The fault lines were still in place; the explosives were ready to blow.

As I was about to find out, with the birth of my son a few months away—the fear of a father's frown is nothing compared to the terror of a mother's touch.

Part III

Foster City, CA—Age 10

Spring 1969

IF SHE HAD been raised under different circumstances, my mom could have been an actress rivaling any cinematic siren of her era. The come-hither coquetry of Raquel Welch, the schoolgirl sensuality of Marilyn Monroe, the sweetheart lasciviousness of Ann-Margret, the magnetic carnality of Gina Lollobrigida—my mom would have smoldered with the hottest among them. She did not turn her charms off and on for art's sake—her needs for sexual attention had far more sinister roots. But she had a Hollywood allure when she teased and toyed with you, then turned on the stiff-shoulder scorn of Mrs. Robinson done with her Dustin Hoffman fling.

A housewife and homemaker—with four kids to tend to—was too dull a role for the star-power sex appeal that sizzled within her. She had a public to please, and the wiles with which to please it. When my mom went out, she stepped onstage and stirred up her audience with a flirtatious effervescence. Whether shopping at the grocery store, visiting the doctor's office, volunteering at the elementary school, or coordinating a blood drive at the local fire station, my mom focused more on getting a rise out of the men present than getting the business at hand completed.

She turned errands into amorous subjugations.

Retail managers, school principals, bank vice presidents, fathers of friends—it did not matter. She smooched cheeks and squeezed love handles, admired physiques and showed off her own, fussed over disheveled shirts and smirked at lipstick stains with a footloose and fancy-free esprit that, if harnessed, could have landed her a role on Broadway. Literally. Though she had never acted a day in her life, she played the role so well she was cast on the spot to portray it in a local repertory production.

Hillbarn Theatre—a playhouse under the auspices of the College of San Mateo with the reputation of staging some of the finest drama in the Bay Area— had recently relocated to a site a few blocks from our house. It came to my mom's attention when a police car pulled up one day with my younger brother Richard in the back seat. Four years old at the time, he had wandered from our front yard and was found playing with construction materials behind the newly opened place of business. When my mom breezed over to get acquainted with our new neighbors, Sam Rolph—cofounder and casting director—recruited her within minutes to play a part in an upcoming production for which my mom would be perfect.

The Paisley Convertible was a 1960s farce satirizing the partner-swapping sexual liberation of the free-love milieu of the time—the convertible in question being a sofa that transformed into a spur-of-the-moment bed. The bed becomes most well used when the former lovers of a recently married couple crash the newlyweds' apartment. The husband's previous paramour—the comic-relief instigator for the frolicking bed-hopping to follow—is a free-spirited, scantily clad, libidinally insatiable sex kitten who jumps in and out of the unfolded convertible with multiple partners, sometimes at once, throughout the course of the play.

Needless to say, my mom stole the show. Everyone who saw it was enamored. The audience singled her out for standing ovations at the end of each performance. My dad was so titillated he never missed a show. I was only ten when he took me to the final night of the run, but I followed along well enough to know what everybody found so arousing. Even the reviewer for the *San Francisco Chronicle* was enthralled. He had seen the original production when it opened at Henry Miller's Theatre in New York; as far as he was concerned, the actress who played the part on Broadway did not belong on the same stage as my mother—she seemed downright prudish compared to the unfettered sexual abandon of the newly discovered Barbara Rogers.

In a better world, my mom would only have performed professionally.

MY GRANDMOTHER AGNES was a single-mom divorcée in the 1940s, working as a nurse to support four children, when a bus driver—Harold Cushing—took an interest in her. To her astonished relief, Harold was undeterred by either her divorced status or the fact that she had four young children—three of them girls. My mom was third-born of the four—six years younger than her older sister, Elaine; four years younger than her older brother, Bud; and two years older than the baby of the family, Maryanne. If some part of her believed that men only valued her for sex, she learned it young. She was six years old when Harold moved into their house.

Agnes worked nights at the Catholic hospital, leaving Harold alone to attend to the children. It began with Elaine. When he called for her to bring him cigarettes in his bedroom, she would be gone too long, then come back distressed. When he called for my mom, she learned why. The two of them endured it differently. Elaine fought back, which provoked Harold's brutality; my mom placated him so he would not hurt her. Depending on his mood, he called one or the other.

When he called for the baby, Maryanne, my mom and Elaine took turns offering themselves instead. They were determined—though they were held captive to Harold's desires, they would do anything necessary to keep that beast away from their little sister. Their she-wolf protectiveness was also needed for the other girl soon born into the family. Agnes and Harold had a child of their own. Fruit of his loins or not, Harold did not discriminate.

My mom was twelve when Elaine met a man, married, and moved out. For the next six years, my mom was on her own. She brought Harold the cigarettes no matter whose name was called. She was eighteen—a senior in high school—when she met my dad. He was a cousin to her best friend, with a year left in the army after a stint in Korea. He asked her out; she said yes and gave him her address.

When he came to the house, my mom answered the door all dolled up for an evening at the drive-in. Harold was sitting in the living room, stretched out in his recliner. He did not get up to greet my dad. Instead, he requested a kiss from my mom before she left. She walked over and pecked him on the cheek. Staring at my dad, he told my mom that he wanted a real kiss. My mom sat herself astride his lap, smooched him on the lips, then wrapped her arms around his neck. Harold never stopped glaring at my dad, as if making sure that both of them knew just whose property this little plaything really was.

The glare was so menacing my dad almost missed the look in my mom's eyes. Still clinging to Harold's neck, straddled across his lap, she glanced back at my dad. Her eyes were easy to read. *Please*, they pleaded, *get me out of this house.*

Six months later, my dad did. They married and moved to the army base in Barstow. Eleven months later, I was born.

My mom was nineteen.

WHEN I WAS in the fifth grade, I ended up in the emergency room with my mom and my elementary school teacher. It happened while playing softball during afternoon recess. I was sitting on the bench behind home plate talking to my friend while waiting for my turn at bat. At the crack of the ball being hit, I instinctively turned to catch the play. The hitter had lost his grip on the bat as he swung for the fences. I turned right into it. It struck me on the forehead with such force, I was knocked backward onto the ground behind me.

Dazed to the edge of blacking out and frantic with panic and shock, I jumped up and scrambled about aimlessly, shrieking, "Don't touch me! Don't touch me! Don't touch me!" The stricken school kids gave me my space as I tried to will my way back into some measure of mental clarity. After a few minutes, one child dared to approach me to make sure that I was okay. As soon as he saw my face, he blanched. I had a lump at the center of my forehead the size of a golf ball.

We were followed by a herd of concerned schoolchildren as the boy hustled me back to the classrooms. My mom happened to be volunteering that day and was in the arts and crafts room with Mr. Borel, my fifth-grade teacher. As soon as he saw me, Mr. Borel insisted on driving my mom and me to the hospital. We sat three abreast in the front seat of his car, my mom scooching over to sit in the middle. At the hospital, the two of them accompanied me into the examination room as if they were both my parents. It was a good thing that Mr. Borel was there. My mom was so upset she needed him to query the doctor about my condition and treatment needs, then usher her back to the lobby for comfort. The nurse tended to my contusion, then walked me out and released me to their care.

On the way home, Mr. Borel bought me a giant popsicle shaped like a missile, then we stopped at his house so I would have some place to eat it. I sat on his couch, licking at my ice cream, and watched cartoons on *Captain Satellite* while he and my mom discussed "school business" in his bedroom. The popsicle was too big for me to finish. It melted into a puddle on the plate that Mr. Borel had left for me.

I also was not up to finishing my dinner that night. My mom had made my favorite—hard-shell tacos with ground beef. But after a couple of bites, I felt like going to bed. Usually, I slept on my side, curled up and pressed against the wall, my back to the door, with my blankets wrapped over my head like a protective cocoon with only a slit open through which to breathe. That night, I had to lie on my back, my face exposed, because my forehead was too tender to be touched. Since I could not go to her room to kiss her goodnight, my mom came to me. She slunk up alongside the top bunk of my bed.

In my ear, she whispered, "I love you, Frank. You're my number one. You're my number one. You will always be my number one." Slipping her hand through my covers and underneath my pajamas, she stroked my bare skin while I drifted asleep. I was so concussed; I did not grow rigid.

Needless to say, Mr. Borel gave me straight As at the end of the school year.

MY MOM WAS hardly alone in her free-love promiscuity. During the course of their marriage, she slept with my father's boss, our dentist, the convenience-store manager, our next-door neighbor—three different ones along the way—my Little League coach, my fifth-grade teacher, and, in partner-swapping escapades, her sister's husband. My dad kept pace. As he later disclosed to me, in addition to his various neighborhood dalliances, he slept with my mom's sister, her sister's coworker, and the sister and the coworker together when they stayed at our house for vacations. He even drove his car off an embankment while being pleasured by my mom's best friend.

For my part, I was ignorant of it all—not of the special relationship that my mom had with me, but of the extramarital lovemaking in which they both so freely indulged. I took it at face value that one or the other was out late with their friends, that the banker had business in the bedroom, that the snapshot on the counter of my aunt's breasts was really a picture of her bent knees, that my dad had fallen asleep at the wheel when he lacerated the left side of his face through the windshield. I lived snugly in the illusion that my parents loved only each other, and if sex was a thing, they kept it to themselves.

I was so oblivious that, the summer before my dad moved out, I vandalized a neighbor's door over it. It served him right. Phil Sullivan—the boy who lived across the street—was badmouthing my mother by making up rumors that a California highway patrolman was sleeping with her every night, his cop car parked in front of our house during the wee hours of the morning. I was playing catch as he was heckling me about it. Claiming that it was an errant throw, I hurled a baseball at his front door so hard it got lodged in the splintered wood. My dad repaired it the weekend he came home after supposedly working out of town. I was as stunned as he was when my mom disclosed that it was true and that she wanted a divorce to marry the cop. After repairing the neighbor's front door, my dad moved out.

The affair with the highway patrolman only lasted a few more weeks. Once my mother was available, he reconsidered and chose his wife over her. Devastated, my mom begged for my dad to come back. By then, however, my dad was too involved—both with Christ and with the woman who would become my stepmom. Scorned twice within weeks and suddenly finding herself single and alone with four kids, my mom took a job as a bank teller and sought comfort in a series of liaisons ranging from one-night stands to lovers who lasted for as long as a few weeks.

Since I was the oldest, my mom looked to me to make sure that my siblings were fed and put to bed—or kept out of the way when she brought a guy home while we were still up. Some nights, she did not make it home at all, and I woke up the kids in the morning and made sure that they got off to school. Once, I thought that she had left us for good. The police called the house, waking me up at one in the morning. Her car had been found abandoned in a Safeway parking lot some forty miles away. I told the officer that, no, she was not at the house, and I had no idea where she was. She showed up a couple of days later—she had hooked up with a bank client and took a spontaneous trip to Tahoe.

For a year and a half, so many men came in and out of the house—or chaperoned us on weekend camping trips—that when my mom informed me that she had gotten married over the New Year's weekend of my sophomore year in high school, I simply responded, "Yeah? To which one?"

It turned out to be none of them. She had met Frank Ovalle at a New Year's Eve party. They drove to Reno and tied the knot the next day. He, too, was undeterred by my mom's divorced status and by the fact that she had four kids—he had three of his own. He moved in that week and became our stepdad.

My mom quit work. I took advantage of the reprieve from having to take care of my siblings and stayed away from the house as much as I could. A year later, my sister Michelle was born. Within a year after that, I had gone off to college in Anderson.

It took Linda, over thirty years later, to help me make the connection. Our stepdad bore an uncanny resemblance to our step-grandfather Harold.

Linda was six years old when Frank Ovalle moved into our house.

Upland, CA—Age 35

December 10, 1993

ALTHOUGH I HAD consented to being sent to the asylum on the night that I nearly drove off a cliff, the moment that I entered it, I wanted out. Once you are in, however—voluntarily or not—you are at their mercy. You leave when they deem you sane enough for the outside world.

I was in for three weeks, out for one, then in for two more. Even then, I was hardly sane. It had taken that long for me to want to be sane, lost as I was, consumed by rage and despair.

SAN ANTONIO HOSPITAL's mental health facility was a psychiatric wing adjoined to the back of the main medical building. Like Dante's *Inferno*, it enclosed its patients in concentric circles—each chamber deeper into the interior sequestering the increasingly disturbed with ever more intensive surveillance and confinement. Entered into through the single external doorway, the outer circle entailed a large lobby with meeting rooms on either side for outpatients attending day programs and support groups to sustain a recovery that had already taken hold. The entrance doors were unlocked from the inside—anyone within could leave whenever they wanted.

At the far end of that lobby, alongside a nurse's station, double doors were located that locked from both sides. Hidden behind them were inpatients too debilitated to function day-to-day on their own but not so unbalanced as to be an immediate danger either to themselves or to others. More sanitarium than asylum—with couches, ferns, and stuffed chairs in a central commons, private bedrooms along the sides—this unit sheltered the clinically depressed, the anxiety-ridden, the chronically fatigued, and the addicts still stabilizing after a fitful detox. Supervision was minimal. They were not free to leave on their own, but they did not constitute much of an escape risk.

The back wall of that unit bordered a ward for the deeply disturbed. The doors that bound them were not only locked from both sides, they were dead-bolted by a metal beam clamped into place that could only be opened with a security code. Here were detained the suicidal, the delusional, the obsessive self-cutters, the psychotic, the potentially violent, and the severely addicted in the throes of a feverish withdrawal—people who could not constrain their tortured impulses, nor regulate them for very long. These tormented individuals were under constant observation—both from the viewing window of the perpetually staffed nurse's station and from the surveillance cameras mounted to spy into every corner of the bedrooms, the eating area, the smoking patio, the TV lounge, and the consultation room used for both private counseling and group therapy. The escape for which these souls yearned was as much internal as it was external.

On the far side of that ward, at the darkened end of the last corridor, a padded room was reserved for the most deranged—those in the midst of a psychotic episode so severe and unrestrainable it defied any intervention by either staff or security. The size of a prison cell used for solitary confinement, the floor and four walls were covered with cushions so thick they could absorb someone's fists, feet, shoulders, or forehead being slammed into them with frenzied fierceness. The door was not only locked from both sides—dead-bolted and padlocked—the viewing window within it was barred on the inside and latched from the outside.

A throwback to the days when isolation was used as both treatment and deterrent, it was seldom deemed necessary anymore. During the entirety of my stay—some five weeks in total—I only saw two people so insanely crazed that they needed to be caged within such a godforsaken enclosure: Marcos, a young man off his meds for schizophrenia who was so convinced that he saw ninjas invading the building that he went on a ballistic rampage, flailing at walls, tables, chairs, and fellow inmates until the orderlies—four of them—could wrestle him down and drag him, writhing, into the padded cubicle.

Marcos. And me.

THE LABOR DAY weekend before I started high school, my family went on an overnight camping trip to Memorial Park—a favorite site of ours in the red-wood forest about an hour from our house in Foster City. I thought nothing of it when my dad slept with us boys in the tent while my mom spent the night with Linda in our Volkswagen camper. I also missed it when my mom asked the people in the campsite next to us to watch over the little ones—Linda and Richard—while she and my dad took Jim and me to some place secluded so we could talk. We sat alongside a dried-up creek bed a short hike from our campsite—Jim and me on the ground in front, my mom behind me on a fallen tree trunk, and my dad beside her, behind my brother. We all four gazed at the cracked dirt. I still saw nothing coming.

Then I saw nothing at all.

As they told us that they were getting a divorce and that my dad would be moving out as soon as we got back, I lost all sense of time and place. My mom and my brother were crying, and my dad fumed and fidgeted, but I stared out into an indiscernible void—not seeing, not feeling, not thinking a thing. It was as if the ground of everything stable in my life had given way and I had collapsed into an abyss so dark that neither I nor the world existed at all anymore. I looked so blankly into the nothingness that it scared my mom. She scooted down and, wrapping me from behind with her legs and arms, she pleaded with me to say something, to express my feelings, to cry if I needed, anything, that it was just not healthy to hold it all in. Still, I stared, encased in stoic senselessness.

It was the shrieking that brought me back. As if distraught after stumbling upon the remains of his bride in a shallow grave in the woods, my dad scurried off into the forest to collect himself in private. He did not flee far enough. Hidden in the shadows behind us, he pummeled an impervious tree trunk with shafts of timber. The smacking echoed into the creek bed and carried all the way to my stone-walled vacancy. And then, when he screamed—in waves of fury and futility—his cries shrieked with such raw desperation they ripped through the trees and broke down the walls of my numbness altogether. The pain engulfed me like a plunge through ice into a glacial ocean. Swallowed in anguish, I wept—howling and heaving as I clutched my belly and rocked with sobbing spasms. My mom, still enfolding me from behind, bawled as well, squeezing me into herself as if trying to meld her pain with mine. We wailed as one, my brother Jim leaning against us, while my dad wailed alone.

And yet, even as I was drowning in my desolation, I felt the concrete hardening into place. A resolve was solidifying within me—a vow with the fierceness to fight back the floodwaters and dike them behind a granite stronghold.

Never, I told myself, as I willed the sobbing away. *Never will I feel pain like this again.*

Wrestling down the last of my whimpering gasps, I pulled myself together, wriggled free from my mom, and, with the wall of my impenetrability firmly in place once more, I locked away the first thirteen years of my life and walked alone back to the camp.

Twenty years later, I still had yet to shed another tear. Not until I was admitted into an asylum.

FOR MY FIRST few days in the mental hospital, I was too beat to rebel against being there. Whether my electrolyte levels had yet to replenish themselves, or the pit into which I had descended was so cavernous it rendered futile any attempt to climb out, I had neither the energy nor the resolve to do anything but lie in my bed and stare at the wall. I was not particularly suicidal, nor was I immobilized by shame. To be sure, I had ample cause for humiliation. I was separated from my wife. My public debasement had been on display at my workplace. I had to be delivered from my truck by my boss after nearly driving off a cliff. And, after plotting a way to kill myself with sleeping pills, I had been committed to a mental institution. And yet, the truth was, I did not care anymore. It was not rock bottom; to truly hit bottom you have to regret your condition. I simply no longer gave a damn.

For the most part, I was left to myself. The sanitarium unit of the hospital only offered refuge to a few of us convalescents dispersed throughout the commons and within our bedrooms in solitary introspection. And the days were relatively unstructured. Besides the decidedly somber mealtimes, we had a life-skills workshop each morning, group therapy in the afternoon, a few minutes with the psychiatrist when he monitored our meds during daily rounds, and an evening craft time to keep us occupied where we dripped drops of paint into plastic stencils of fir trees and candy canes to make Christmas ornaments. Other than that, we sat and brooded, paced the commons, or napped in our bedrooms, left alone to deal—or not—with whatever maladies so afflicted us.

After a few days curled up in my bed and coursing through the insipid schedule, the senseless tedium became too much and I was ready to leave and be done with the place. I was tired of sitting around and moping. I was not about to crack open the crypt of my psyche with total strangers in group therapy. The workshops on life-skills were absurdly inane—like taking the time to count to ten would dissipate the hellfire of a rage that is homicidal. And if I had to drip one more drop of paint into a piece of plastic, I was going to decorate the walls with Christmas projectiles.

I wanted out. And I let the staff know, calmly and rationally, that I was back in my right mind and ready to go home. That was when I found out that it was not up to me. I had been placed on a seventy-two-hour involuntary hold. After the mandatory three-day commitment, it was up to the staff to determine when I was stable enough to be released. They could keep me there indefinitely. And so far, I had shown no signs of taking seriously how ill I was, nor had I made any effort toward getting better. They had no intention of releasing me anytime soon.

The panic snapped me out of my stupor. I got—like a gut punch—the double bind of my predicament. They had already marked me as mad—so mad that I needed to be committed. To be set free, I had to own the severity of my madness, and yet it was that very severity that made my committal a psychiatric necessity. I had conceded to some institutional downtime and had awakened in a Kafka novel. I was damned if I admitted that I was deranged, and damned if I denied it; damned if I hid the derangement, and damned if I displayed it. Well, fuck that. I was sick of holding it all back anyway. To hell with the consequences—if they needed to see me facing my shit, I would face it in all its excremental foulness. Like a cornered bobcat, I would go down fighting.

They wanted me to spend time with my feelings, so I spent hours pounding the tetherball in the patio, punching its ever curling face first one way, then the other, until my fists were swollen and cracked. They suggested that I draw pictures of my inner experience, so I filled pages with erect penises dripping with blood, wide-open vaginas with tongues licking out from within, and cyclones of black scribble crushed into the paper then attacked with slashing slaps of crimson red. They insisted that I describe my symptoms to the psychiatrist, so I told him that I felt like I was possessed by demons—rage, despair, sordid fantasizing, and a lethal self-loathing—all taking their turns to dominate me. And they encouraged me, in group therapy, to share the struggles that had brought me to the hospital, so I laid it all out for them: how I caught my mother about to mouth my son's penis; how I stopped her from sharing a shower with him, then sleeping with him naked; the nightmares and daydreams invading me like flashbacks—of me mouthing penises too big for my toddler hands, of me being raped from behind, of me cupped naked with my mom while she pleasured herself behind me, of me curled up in my bed with my mom's hand sliding under the covers to stroke me.

It was hardly a genuine attempt to work through my issues. It was an act of defiance. If they wanted crazy, I would give them crazy. And I dared them to throw up their hands and admit that some people in this world really are inexplicably damaged beyond repair.

With the array of afflictions endured within the subculture of psychiatric inmates, my obscene disclosures in group sessions were met with varied reactions. A few of my fellow sufferers were so submerged within their own private hells, my sharing barely raised an eyebrow. Marcos was more representative. Joining us for groups when he felt safe from the ninjas, he not only raised his eyebrows with disgust, he offered his unfiltered commentary: "That's some pretty sick shit."

A couple of them could relate—like Jean. She was admitted when she sliced both her arms and her legs with razor blades after coming off a high and discovering that she had left her two daughters in the car all night when she traded her dealer sex for cocaine. She kept the secrets of her own abuse to herself, but she revealed enough when she retorted to Marcos, "It may be sick, but that shit happens."

If I was trying to impress the staff with my acknowledgment of how seriously disturbed I was, I would have to get crazier still. For the most part, they were unfazed. The small-group leader—more facilitator than therapist—would nod sympathetically, then call on somebody else to share. The psychiatrist only furrowed his brow and confirmed that I was speaking metaphorically—that I could not actually see the demons right there in the consultation room—before readjusting my meds. And the nurses merely kept me supplied with scrap paper and hunted down fresh crayons when I wore the others down to the nub. If I wanted to leave, I would have to do more than vent the filth that stewed in my depths. I would need to hit a rock bottom that was deeper than I knew was there.

THE ART THERAPIST came once a week. Although it was a slight improvement over filling Christmas stencils with paint drops—at least we were invited to express ourselves—I still scoffed at how uncensored creativity could tame demons as destructive as mine. The first week of my stay, she had us make collages. In the center of the paper, I pasted a picture of a naked young boy from a *National Geographic*, then engulfed him in an inferno of rage—filling the page with every image of fire that I could find in her tubs of ripped-up magazines. The second week of my stay, she had us work with clay.

We were each given a brick of it as we entered the art annex. It was an appropriate descriptor. The clay was not only the size and shape of a brick; it was equally as hard. When I received mine, I sneered—how in God's name were we supposed to express anything with this unyielding piece of stone? I took it to the far end of the workbench in the back corner of the room and stood glaring at it.

The art therapist instructed us to soften the clay by massaging it—pressing the heels of our palms firmly into it and kneading it with our fingers. As we worked it, she suggested that we not think, that we not set out to make anything specific. Rather, we were to let the clay speak to us—to let it be and become whatever it wanted to embody. I tried rubbing the rock-hard brick, stroking it with my palms and fingers, but it was impervious to my manipulations—the surface skin barely smudging, the stiffness unrelentingly hard.

Frustrated to the point of giving up on it, I slammed it onto the wooden workbench. The corner dented with a thud. I picked it up and slammed it again—another thud, another dent. I did it again—another thud, another dent. This was far more effective than caressing it with my hands. I did it again—another thud, another dent. I found different edges still crisp and creased and pounded each one in turn onto the bench—another thud, another dent; another thud, another dent. The brick began to round but was still too hard to work, so I reached back further and hurled it at the bench like a baseball. A big thud, a big dent. Another big thud, another big dent. It was steadily becoming more malleable, the thuds splatting into deeper dents, but the clay wanted to keep on pounding. So I capitulated. Take that. And that. And that. Another thud, another dent; another thud, another dent.

And as I stared at the tabletop and watched the clay thud and dent, thud and dent, time and again on the surface, I stopped seeing the clay at all. I saw an image of me—maybe three years old—lying naked on my mom's bed. My mom was curled up alongside me, in her bra and panties, dreamily watching her hand as she stroked my bare chest, then caressed my privates. Another thud, another dent; another thud, another dent. She leaned over and kissed my forehead, my cheek, my chest—another thud, another dent; another thud, another dent—and was making her way down toward my penis—another thud, another dent; another thud, another dent—when she started to mouth me and I lost it.

The demon of rage rose up from the molten lava fields of my core and I screamed with a soul-piercing fury, "*Stop doing that to me! You fucking bitch! Stop doing that!*" The clay turned into cannonballs, my arm into a field gun, as I propelled blast after blast at her head, at her back, at her bra and her panties, at the fucking bitch bent over that stiffened boy. I could not throw them hard enough. I could not throw them fast enough. Specks of clay flew about the table. I was losing my grip on the dwindling mass, but she was still there. I shook off somebody touching my shoulder and kept pummeling my mom with all that I had left. She would not stop; she would not fade; she would not explode into a billion bloody pieces. She kept mouthing that boy and I kept pelting her with cannonballs of clay, thudding and denting, faster and harder. The clay slipped free from my hand, so I pounded her with my fist, beating her into oblivion, screaming at her to stop, spraying her with my spittle, until I was pulled to the floor from behind and pinned by two men, one on each of my shoulders.

The bitch was still with that boy so I fought to get back up, but somebody else arm-locked my legs. I thrashed as if my boy's life was at stake, kicking a leg free before another man cinched my ankles with the force of a vise grip. Beside myself with wrath, I shrieked and battled as the four of them muscled me out of the art room, through the secured locked unit, and into the padded room where they released me onto the floor, then scurried back to slam and lock the door.

I rose up insane with rage. I screamed so loudly they could hear me throughout the ward—my profanity-laden fury echoing down the corridors at that bitch who had mouthed that boy and at everyone that tried to keep me from her. "Fuck you! *Fuck you! Fuck every goddamned one of you! Ahhh!*" That demon of rage in the underworld of my soul had fused itself to my being and was ready to spew its ancient wrath onto the world. And, for once, I was willing to let it have its uncensored say. I was done diminishing it, done fighting it, done apologizing for it, done tempering its intensity. It had every right to its madness, and if it wanted to unleash the full force of its venom, so be it.

Come on, some distant voice in me goaded, *give me everything you've got; then give me some more.* And I did. Those padded walls took the beating of their lives. I pounded them as if my mother had followed me and had found a way to embed herself within them. I punched her; I head-butted her; I kicked her; I took running starts and threw myself at her. The rage within me yelled and howled, ridding her from one wall, then another, while the dim voice within me grew stronger—unafraid and unashamed—inviting the full brunt of that rage's torrent. It wanted to beat that bitch bloody, and I said, "Go for it." It wanted to scream obscenities and howl, and I said, "Louder." It wanted to rip this violating world apart, and I said, "Get every last thread of it." I did not resist its fuming and flailing, nor dilute it even an iota. I went with it in a ranting admission of its right to its wrath, while it took full advantage of the permission to expel its ire in all its entirety.

And as it spewed its unhinged malice, it became something of a yoked coupling. It was as if the rage was disengaging itself from my being and becoming its own entity—one with which I was thoroughly attached in a contest of endurance. It felt akin to Jacob wrestling with the angel—except that the angel was a demon inhabiting me from within, and it was not so much a battle as a ride on a bucking bronco. It was a maddened dance of defiance not being defied, but not merely venting either. Two of us were there: the demon using my body to disgorge its lifetime of fury, and some fledgling "me"—the willing vessel—being with it, encouraging it, even validating it, as I accepted its wrath and flailed along with it. It was as if the rage was testing me—to see how much I could take, how much I *would* take. And I took it all. The two of us going toe to toe writhing, screaming, cursing, bludgeoning until, finally, the rage spent itself out and gave up.

Heaving, I fell onto the floor. Like a wild animal that has been ridden out, the rage within me subsided. It was still there—this was not an exorcism—but it had receded and relaxed. We were disjoined from one another, no longer fused nor yoked. I was aware of this energy of rage within me, but I was no longer the rage itself. I had an image of it as a wolf-fiend of rabid ferocity now tamed and facing me from the mouth of the underworld cave from which it came. Seeing it there, I had an intuitive sense that it did not come to do harm—to capriciously wreak havoc on me or my world. It came as an ally, not as an enemy. It fought for some truth that was of life or death importance to it. And now that I had acknowledged it fully, it no longer needed to possess me, with all of its feral fury, to get my attention. It had it—I wanted to know the real reason for its wrath. And it needed me to know, and to take it in completely.

"It really happened," that demon of rage was saying to me with an eye-to-eye directness. "All of it—it really happened. And that boy is still suffering all of it alone."

With that, the wolf-fiend of rage dissipated, and a different image emerged. Not of the boy on my mom's bed, but of a skulled face, like the head from Munch's *The Scream*, with haunted eyes and a wide-opened mouth howling without sound. It was the anguished soul of that boy on the bed and a composite of the soul in all of the boys buried within me that had been touched, stroked, mouthed, penetrated—all of them aching for someone to see their pain, to hear their silent scream, to put an end to the abuse from which they could not escape, and to hold them with a compassion as pure as it is protective.

Recognizing that skull's suffering, recognizing that its suffering really was my own, that it really was me being mouthed on that bed—I gave voice to the scream that it longed to howl. In waves of guttural wails, the horror of what that boy had been through came over me and gushed forth as if it was happening all over again. I could feel it in my body—the violating touch seared into my skin, the burning down my chest and belly, the moist stinging in my prepubescent genitals. A lifetime of sorrow, a lifetime of sorrow being silenced, erupted in spirit-chilling shrieks of agony. Doubled over and rocking with pain, I wept with the anguish that could cut through my decades-old heart of stone.

And yet, once more, as that boy's soul wailed through me, some "I" in me was wailing along with it. That same solid ground core of me that accompanied the rage through its savage frenzy was now companioning this boy as he sobbed in his suffering. And somehow, the boy knew. His pain, every intimate detail of it, was being seen, heard, known, understood. He was no longer alone in his torment. He was with *me*. He was held. *I* was holding him. An "I" that I had not known before—with a steel spine of resilience and a vast reservoir of abundant compassion. I loved that boy within me. I would do anything to protect him. And the boy, now safe in my loving embrace, felt it. His sobs turned into whimpers, then stilled altogether. He took in my presence. He absorbed my tenderness. And like a distressed infant now secure in a parent's arms, he drifted off to sleep in the cradle of my care.

I, however, was wide awake. Lying on my back on that padded floor, every molecule of tension and turmoil within me drained from my body. I gave myself to the gravitational pull of a profound peace that pervaded my being. I became absolutely still and intensely present. It was like a new "me" had emerged, one acutely alert to my inner world. I was aware of the tamed energy of rage on the edge of my consciousness, and of the wounded boy slumbering before me. But the "I" that was aware of them was qualitatively different. It was unshakably grounded, infinitely calm, and infused with a love that held them both with affection.

I felt like the mirrored surface of a pond, utterly without a ripple in its stillness—a pond that could hold in its reflection, without judgment or distortion, anything that came to it. I had a vague sense of other beings peering from the shadows of my underworld—my other demons of despair, self-loathing, and sordid fantasizing; the other boys trapped in abusive nightmares throughout my childhood—all of them longing to be seen, honored, and held as well. In the still waters of that loving reflection, every one of them was welcome; every one of them could come and be met with grounded presence and unqualified care. This "I," capable of such absolute calm and abounding compassion, was an "I" that I had not known before. It was the "I" that I yearned to be, the "I" that I longed to never stop being, the "I" of both restored sanity and spiritual expansiveness. I lay there, as still as could be, savoring what it was like, finally, to be the me that I had found so elusive.

Then it intensified exponentially. As I rested in that peacefulness, the sense of presence began to swell. I felt the unmistakable certainty that I was not only holding, I was also held. The still pond of my caring openness was nestled in a cosmic ocean of compassionate presence. I was but a tiny molecule of a boundless sea that holds, without judgment or distortion, *all* things in the reflection of its unequivocal love. As I lay motionless on that padded floor, the waters of that cosmic presence seeped through all the crevices of our universe and flowed into every particle of my being. The veil that separates this world from the numinous did not merely lift its corner for a peek at the sacred reality behind it; it had dissolved altogether. I was fused with the energetic force field of love that holds and enlivens all things—its currents were coursing throughout my body. These were the waters into which all the world's pain flows for healing, the glassy depths where all the world's rage is received and restored. This was the sea of celestial compassion, and I was totally immersed within it. The stillness was so complete, the care so expansive, the hum of its vitality so energetic, I did not want to breathe. I did not want to move a muscle. I did not want to trouble the waters of that oneness with even the tremble of a heartbeat. I lay as motionless as possible, my every cell charged with sacred presence.

Some voice within me—some spiritual ethnographer part of me—sensed, even then, that this was the sphere that mystics like Teresa of Ávila and Julian of Norwich describe. As if stumbling upon a mythical lost land, that part of me was amazed that it really does exist, and it yearned to find the cartographers who had been there and could map the pathways back to it. But even that voice, lost in awe, quickly quieted. I simply soaked in the energizing stillness, alive in a way that I had never been before. It was a painful labor, but something new had been birthed within me. Or if it had been there all along, it was new to my experience. And for the first time, I felt aligned with the God of infinite love.

My life had a new "before and after."

ALTHOUGH I WAS unaware of it, I was being watched. The staff had called Helen, my therapist, when my fit with the clay grew out of control. She arrived shortly after I was sequestered and witnessed the entire journey—from enraged torment to mystical communion—through the door's barred window. She let the episode run its course and waited until I was lying peacefully before she entered the room. I was still steeped in the sea of cosmic oneness when she knelt by my side.

Not wanting to disturb the energetic tranquility, I whispered as inaudibly as I could, "Helen, this is amazing. The peace, the compassion. I just want to stay here. It's indescribable." I sounded like I had discovered a world the likes of which we had never seen before.

"Shhh," Helen comforted as a matriarch who knew this world quite well. "Just rest. Stay there as long as you like."

When we processed it in the days to come, Helen shared that I resembled an infant as I writhed on the floor of that padded room—one enduring an abuse for which there were no words, and then slowly calming as if being newly birthed into a world that received it with love. That was why, on an instinct, she sought out a hospital blanket and brought it with her into the room. As she quieted me and lulled me back into my soak in the maternal waters of sacred care, she used the blanket to swaddle me. With deft efficiency, she slipped the blanket under my side, covered my entire body, and tucked in all the edges until I was snugly wrapped in downy warmth with only my head showing.

It may well have been the first time that I had been swaddled in my life. If so, it was appropriate. I was a newborn in the world of cosmic love.

IT WAS LATE into the evening by the time that I emerged from the padded room and walked into the lobby of the secured locked ward, some eight hours after the art-therapy session had commenced. I was reluctant to leave the padded room even then. The stillness was so soothing, the oneness so restoring, I lay there timelessly, saturated in sacred presence, until the spiritual sensation subsided a bit and I wriggled free from the safety of my swaddling ready to reenter the world.

As I stepped into the lobby, the half-dozen psychiatric patients sitting there turned and stared. The looks on their faces were self-evident. They had seen me dragged away like a madman possessed. They had heard the banshee-like wails. And now I was standing there with all the appearance of a man suddenly sane.

Marcos's skeptical eyes summed it up for the lot of them, seeming to say, "We may all be crazy in here; but that guy's nuts."

Apparently, the staff concurred. After such a severe episode, they thought it prudent that I spend a few days in the secured locked ward. I did not mind. It was where I belonged—among the tombs at the edge of town with my people, the crazed and the outcast. My tortured companions left me alone. Whether wary of the fury of which I was capable, or because they were consumed with furies of their own, they kept their distance from me and never inquired about the brawl in the padded room that they could not have helped but overhear.

One thing was clear, however. I had been possessed by demons. Now I was clothed and in my right mind. Mercy had come upon me. A new world of love and resilience had revealed itself to me.

I now knew.

If healing and restoration were possible, the path led from there.

I WISH THAT I could say that I did not stray from that path—that from that day forward my sanity was secure and I walked steadily toward my well-being. The truth is, my toehold on sanity was so unstable it could not keep me out of the hospital for even a week.

I did not lose my footing straight away. During the days immediately following my padded room theophany, a sober tranquility lingered. I spent hours in the locked-ward lounge journaling about the experience and absorbing its revelations. I drew, in meticulous detail, the images that I had envisioned within my interior landscape—a collection of underworld caverns with demons peering attentively from within; a wolf-fiend of rage at the mouth of one, tamed and befriended; and skulled faces lurking in the depths, each awaiting their turn to be tended with care.

I even cooperated with the treatment plan—participating in groups, paying attention in the workshops, and dutifully taking my meds when prescribed. I became such a compliant patient that the staff determined me fit for release a couple of days before Christmas. I deemed that I was ready as well.

I barely made it past Boxing Day.

RETURNING TO MY cabin brought me back to the depths of the pit into which my life had descended. The place was still in shambles from the thrashing that I had given it the night before my breakdown. Toppled lamps, flung sofa cushions, splayed books, and broken pieces of ceramic crockery were strewn about in such violent disarray that the place seemed to have been ransacked by thugs with a vendetta. My baseball bat hurled at the coat tree sharpened my recollection that I was the one who had wrought the blood feud damage. That and the razor blades left on the table after doing their work scarring my skin. With

Justin coming over for Christmas Eve, I cleaned up the mess and hid all evidence of my self-destructive instability.

The gut punch to follow reminded me that the mess of my life was on public display. I got a phone call from my boss—the president of the school where I was a professor. After sharing his pleasure that I was well enough to be discharged—and his pledge to support me in whatever way that he could—he informed me that he and the dean had decided, and the board of trustees had approved, that I was to be placed on medical leave for a semester. The fragility of my mental health and the liability to the school made it necessary to relieve me temporarily of my institutional responsibilities. He assured me that this was not a punishment, nor a retraction of the school's commitment to my future as a faculty member. It was meant to provide me the space that I needed to focus on my recovery full time. I told him that I understood, and that I was grateful. I lied. I could not have felt more reproved and defrocked if I had been a priest suspended for sexual misconduct.

Even so, the fatal blow to my resolve to claw my way out of the abyss of my life, I did to myself. I thought that I was stepping out on the emboldening path of a determined self-reliance. Instead, I lost my way altogether.

FIRST THING IN the morning, on Christmas Eve, I picked Justin up from his mom's at the house where the three of us had lived. Having had no time to shop, I took him to a Toys "R" Us to let him pick out some presents for himself. To be sure, I did so clandestinely. I told him that Santa had asked for our advice on the perfect gifts for boys turning four on Christmas Day. Justin was on it. It turned out that their favorite games to play involved dinosaurs and baseball—just like Justin. Under the pretense that we would send to Santa precisely the right items for him to deliver to four-year-olds around the world, we bought enough toys to satisfy both Christmas and a birthday. Then, after stopping for candies to stuff into stockings and supplies for homemade pizza, we made our way up to the cabin.

We crafted a rather crude Christmas tree out of pine branches and balls of tin foil, then played several rounds of hide-and-go-seek—both inside and outside the bungalow. During one of them, we were surprised to discover that Santa had come early, leaving gifts beneath the makeshift tree while Justin was buried, and impossible to find, under the tarp draped over the firewood. We spent the afternoon reveling in the stash—creating forts out of building blocks for the plastic dinosaurs to demolish, piecing together a giant floor puzzle of a *Tyrannosaurus rex*, and running the bases around the living room after hitting Nerf ball homeruns with a Bam Bam-sized baseball bat. For dinner, we shaped our pizza like a Christmas tree—sausage crumbles the ornaments, a sculpted cheddar cheese biscuit the star—and blended homemade chocolate mint milkshakes with extra Hershey's syrup. Then we curled up in front of the fire to peruse the holiday books that Santa had also left. With Justin on my lap in the armchair, snuggling his powder-blue blankie with the hole in the corner for his thumb, I read to him each one—*'Twas the Night Before Christmas, How the Grinch Stole Christmas, Polar Express*, Tomie dePaola's *The Legend of the Poinsettia*. By the turn of the last page, the fire was low, and it was time to take Justin back to his mom's.

I had him go potty, then bundled him up in his jacket and cap for the drive. Having to freshen up myself, I returned to the bathroom, then washed up at the sink. Justin followed as far as the doorway, his hand clutching a container of his favorite orange Tic Tacs as if they were his staples to survive the ride back. As I toweled my hands, he noticed the row of pill bottles lined along the back of the counter.

"Daddy," he said, "why do you have so much medicine? Are you still sick?"

Not given any details about my absence since Thanksgiving, he knew only that I had been in the hospital because I was not feeling well.

"Oh, no, honey," I said. "I'm fine, really. I'm all better. Those are just to keep me from getting sick again in the future."

"I can do that," he said. His face turned as serious as a doctor squeezing drops from a final vial of serum. Coaxing a single Tic Tac into his hand, several others slipped through as well. He set the container onto the floor and returned the extras one by one. Then, looking back at me, he held out the remaining piece of candy. "Here, Daddy," he offered. "This is magic medicine. You'll never get sick again."

I received it and placed it into my mouth. "Thank you, Justin," I said. "That's all the medicine I need."

"See?" he said. "You're all better."

WHEN WE ARRIVED at Cathy's, he leapt into his mother's arms as she opened up the door. Through the entryway, I could see the tree lit up in lights, the living room table laid out with Christmas cookies and sparkling cider, and the fireplace donning but two stockings—one for "Mommy" and one for "Justin."

Still holding his mother's neck, he turned toward me and asked, "Can you stay home tonight, Daddy?" His question pierced me like the sight of an orphaned toddler staring out the window for parents who would never come.

"No," I said. "I can't. But I'll call you tomorrow. It's your birthday—four years old." Still only three, his searching eyes knew when it was no use to try and ask again. "How about you give Daddy a big hug goodbye?" I said, snuffing out the last flicker of his hope. He let go of his mom and came into my arms, squeezing me as tightly as he could. "We had fun today, huh?" I said, hanging onto the day's festivities even as they were fading away.

"Yeah, Daddy," he returned, not ready to let go. "When will you be back?"

"Soon," I assured him. "Your mom and I will talk about it. No more than a couple of days." Neither one of us had any way of knowing that it would be much more than a couple of days, that the next time he would see me would be to visit me when I was locked back up in the asylum.

"Okay," he said. He squeezed me tightly once more. "Goodbye, Daddy." Then he scurried into the holiday scene waiting inside to receive him.

I looked at Cathy as she held the door between us on her porch. Her eyes said equally, *Why are you doing this to our family?* and *Are you sure you won't reconsider?* That sugarplum vision danced to its death, I told her goodnight and turned. She locked the door behind me. From within the house that I had once called home, I could hear Justin's squeals as he discovered Cathy's parents, hidden in the kitchen, having flown in for the holidays from Des Moines. The sounds of his glee stabbed like a blade. Their celebration no longer had a place for me. So I left it behind and stepped into the night, walking into the wintry chill of a divorced parent spending Christmas alone.

I had considered hanging out about town and attending midnight Mass in a few hours, but the service commemorating light within darkness no longer seemed consoling. The luster of my soul swallowed by the shade of Justin's absence, I drove back up the mountain by myself and without the comfort of faith. As I reentered the cabin, the residue of our earlier cheer only mocked my aloneness. The dinosaurs buried under building blocks, the pizza picked clean of its sausage ornaments, the books splayed on the table beside the cold and darkened fireplace—it all merely deepened the hollowness of being away from my boy for both Christmas and his birthday. The silence of being alone out-screaming any echoes of our merriment together, I tidied up, not to be neat, but to dull the pain of a gutted holiday.

My despondency persisted until bedtime. Pulled only by the gravity of routine, I stepped into the bathroom to prepare for the night. The line of pill bottles stopped me cold. Like a taunting mirror, ruthless in the precision of its reflection, the pills seemed to throw into my face the mental case that I had become, and the mess that it had made of my life. Perhaps that is why I did it. Perhaps the sheer quantity of the medication that I required to be functional— enough to get the attention of a four-year-old—intimated a depth of malady too shaming for me to bear. Or maybe I wanted to cast my lot with the recuperative powers of a single Tic Tac of care over the fistful of pharmaceuticals I ingested each day. Or maybe I was simply sick and tired of the bloated and dopey side effects with which my prescriptions plagued me.

Whatever the truth, what I told myself was, *I am done being mentally ill. I am taking control of my life. I will walk the long road to health and well-being. But I will do it on my own terms.*

With that, I emptied the bottles into the toilet and flushed the meds to where they belonged.

I AWOKE THE next morning in a mood foul and forlorn—the ghost of Christmas future had not come in the night to terrify me into the holiday spirit. I was staring at a Christmas Day listless and alone. No gaggle of children to smile at as, giggling with rapture, they ripped open their presents. No beloved to squeeze and peck on the cheek as we exchanged tokens of our care. No holiday feast to attend with family and friends sharing our cheer with toasts around a table garnished with garlands, crackers, and candles. While the rest of the world held poses worthy of Hallmark cards, I lay in bed by myself, mired in the misery that my own stab at domestic bliss—as misguided from the beginning as it was—had self-destructed so excruciatingly it turned Christmas into a torment to endure. So much for celebrating the sacred being birthed within our world. I just wanted to find a way to fill the day without imploding.

Without a clue as to how, I got out of bed and freshened up. I brought my coffee out to the porch and sat a while. Though I had brought them too, my journal and coloring pencils laid impotently at my side—I just did not have it in me to write or draw what I was feeling. Instead, I stared across the alpine valley immobilized by the weight of my loneliness. It took the phone's ringing to spur me into motion. My dad's voice on the answering machine wished me a Merry Christmas and asked me to phone him back when I could. I did not get up to answer. I got up to leave. I was not ready for his call—nor for the other holiday calls that I was already dreading I would have to make at some point during the day. I was buying time when I left the cabin and drove down into town.

THE NEIGHBORHOOD'S DESERTED streets only depressed me all the more. The town's entire population was preoccupied with holiday celebrations inside their homes. I stopped at the grocery store to pick up something to microwave for dinner, then drove by a Blockbuster for a video to take me through the evening. It did not open for another hour, so I drove to a park to kill some more time. It too was deserted, or nearly so. I walked the paths through the grassy fields and came upon a baseball diamond. A young boy and his father were on the infield breaking in what was clearly the boy's Christmas gift baseball mitt. The boy was calling out, "Throw it right here, Dad."

He had his finger in the center of his glove as if the dad had perfect aim. The dad didn't. The ball sailed past the boy and bounced up against the backstop. Undeterred, the boy scrambled to retrieve it, crying out as he heaved the ball back to within a few feet of his dad, "That's okay. I'll catch the next one. It's a great glove."

The whole scene made me want to scream. I was better off back up the mountain where my holiday desolation was not rubbed in my face. I scurried to my truck and headed back. On the way, I breezed by the Blockbuster. No sentimental Christmas specials for me. I found a movie to match my mood, then ditched the populace and made my way back to my hideaway.

Once back home, I busied myself with cleaning. Knowing they would bring more pain than comfort, I put off for as long as I could the holiday phone calls before me. I pulled a hairball from the shower drain. I scrubbed scum off the bathroom sink. I took Clorox cleanser to the tub and Comet to the porcelain. Such were the depths of my dread—on Christmas Day, I chose cleaning a toilet over calling up my loved ones.

Perhaps I should have kept on scouring.

I CALLED JUSTIN first. It was mercifully brief. I wished him a happy birthday, listened to the haul of presents that he had taken in, then told him that I loved him as he rushed back to resume playing dinosaurs with his granddad. He was in so much of a hurry, he neglected to return the phone to its receiver. Cathy and her mom chattered in the background while cooking in the kitchen. I hung up before they discovered the phone dangling by its cord.

I then called my dad. I knew that all of my paternal siblings would be gathered at his place as well. When Dona, my stepmom, answered the phone and returned my greeting with, "And Merry Christmas to you, Frank," I overheard my dad jump up from his chair exclaiming, "I want to talk to him."

Knowing that I had been in the hospital, he asked me how I was. I lied and told him that I was feeling much better. Ever awkward about expressing his emotions, he moved on to tell me that he was making homemade pasties for Christmas dinner—the family favorite meat and potato turnover that took him three days to prepare. I told him that I wished that I was there, that my mouth was watering already. He told me that he was saving one for me in the freezer—the biggest and juiciest that he had ever made. It turns out that he could express his emotions rather well after all.

The phone was delivered down the row of my siblings—each one expressing their season's greetings with an exaggerated cheer. Not one of them made mention that I was fresh out of an asylum. From their eagerness to pass the phone down the line, I could sense their awkwardness in how now to treat me and the tremor of worry that my breakdown had stirred—if the supposedly stable member of the family had ended up in a mental institution, what did it portend for the rest of them?

Only Linda alluded to my troubling demise, and even she had to work up to it. She grabbed the phone with her distinctive butterfly brightness and said, "Hey . . . When're you comin' up?"

"I don't know," I answered. "When're you comin' down?" It was not a veiled reference to our emotional states—it was our customary telephone banter, bouncing the ball into each other's court about whose turn it was to make the drive for a visit.

"Actually," she let on, "I was thinking of taking the kids to Disneyland. What do you think? We could come down for a few days after New Year's."

"I think it's a great idea," I said, continuing the pretense that everything was fine, and that the secrets we steered clear of only needed a hit from the happiest place on Earth. "Justin's four and he still hasn't been. Let's do it."

We discussed the details, then she caught me up on her children before one of them needed her and it was time to say goodbye.

"It's all set then," she confirmed. "I'll see you in a couple of weeks."

"Great," I said. "I'm looking forward to it."

She paused. Perhaps she heard the quiver in my voice—the one that knew that things were far from fine, that our secrets resided in the bowels of the earth with demons that obliterated all joy.

"Get better, Frank," she said. "I need my big brother."

It would be some time before her big brother was back. Our trip to Disneyland would be postponed. It was just as well. She, too, would discover, soon enough, the demons of despair unappeased by amusement park happiness.

MY MOM'S CHRISTMAS blessings were hidden within her offensive. She answered my greeting with a full-scale invasion, blasting away any remnants of the solid ground supporting my path to recovery.

"Oh, so my eldest son has decided to call his mother on Christmas Day. Where have you been? I haven't heard from you since Thanksgiving. I have to learn from everyone else that you've had some kind of a breakdown—that you're in some mental hospital. I only know that you're not still there because Richard thought to call me. You have no idea what you're putting me through with all of your problems and all of your questions. I've never been so beside myself. I'm sure you're telling your doctors all kinds of things about me. It's always the mother's fault, isn't it? I never hurt you, Frank. I could never do any of those things that I know you're thinking that I did. What kind of a mother do you think that I am? You were always my number one. Always. I never did anything to you but love you like no mother has ever loved her son. And this is what I get from you? You can't even call me to tell me where you are? I'm afraid every time that you call me anyway—who knows what new 'revelations' you'll start accusing me of next. Why are you doing this to me? I raised you better than this . . ."

And on it went. As only she can, she talked nonstop for some thirty minutes in a meandering monologue jagged with accusation, defense, declarations of love, and pleas for pity. At the time, I could not hear the desperation hidden behind her onslaught, nor the terror hidden behind that. I heard only a rant of self-preservation determined to put me in my place before she took me down in her place. And it worked. Every word was a knife wound to my spirit, slashing away my will to respond, my will to defend myself, my will to hold onto any truth of my own. Dutiful son that I was, I took it all in without retort. Then I made an excuse and got off the phone.

All at once, a deluge of despair engulfed me—a morass of shame and lacerating self-doubt. She was right. I was making it all up. Nothing bad ever happened to me. She would never have let it. What kind of a depraved person would think his own mother capable of the vile things that I imagined of her? I wanted to rip into my skin for ever feeling otherwise, to punish it with cutting. Then the savage wolf-fiend came back. An inferno of rage erupted within me and went on the attack.

Fuck her! What kind of a mother is **she***? She did not even care that her own son was on the verge of killing himself! It did not even occur to her to ask him how he was doing! She was more put out that she had to suffer watching her child in pain. What kind of a mother would rather defend herself and pounce than ask how she might help her obviously distressed child?* **Something** *has to be disturbing him. How is he to get to the bottom of it all if all that she does is insist on her denials? Doesn't she know? She's driving her "number one" insane. Or maybe she does, and that's the whole point—better him than her, better to grieve his self-slaughter than face the shadows within herself. What kind of a fucking mother, indeed?*

Needing to beat the bloody hell out of something beyond my cabin's confines, I grabbed my bat and made for the woods. I came upon a deadened evergreen the size of a large Christmas tree. Smote by either lightening, drought, or wood beetles, its bark and needles were bone-dry brown as it stood atop a small rise. Like a deranged woodcutter without his axe, I beat away the brittle branches until the trunk was a stripped pole spearing the sky with splintered knobs spiking its entire length. I then attacked the trunk itself. Though its base was no more than eight inches in diameter, I could not budge it with my bat. It stood erect like some primitive weapon barbed to harpoon a harpy on the prowl. Out for prey myself, I hammered that spurred shaft of a pine trunk as if each swing were an impaling blow to the crazy-making woman who bore me. I gored her until my arms grew leaden, and the day's light dwindled into dusk. That spiked spear still stood firm. I, however, was spent. Having wrought all the damage of which I was capable, I made my way back to the cabin, the final vestiges of fight leaking out behind me like a beaten warrior returning to a conquered homeland.

Once inside, the deluge of despair flooded back in. I had nothing left with which to combat it. It was Christmas. I was alone. And the darkness of my desolation was shaded by lewd fantasies that I could not confirm and volcanic furies that I could not explain. The day had been the nightmare that I had foreseen. I just wanted to suck it up through the rest of it and put it all behind me.

So, while the rest of the world feasted on home-cooked delicacies, I microwaved a cup of noodles and closed the holiday out with my Christmas movie— *Sophie's Choice*. As Stingo recounted Sophie's doomed journey through the underworld of her past—and, with Nathan, her subsequent descent into despair—I descended along with her. Not yet penetrating the truths of my past, but equally uncertain if morning would come, and come excellent and fair.

THAT NIGHT, I had a dream.

I am in my bed in my childhood home at Foster City. I have the sense that my mom is on her way into my bedroom. I look out the window and see smoke from an approaching fire. I leave through the front door, and the fire has suddenly become engulfing—devouring our house with my mom still in it. In terror, I flee toward the city, San Francisco. The fire is huge—bigger than words—and is chasing me from behind. Somehow, my mom is not dead—she is a charred carcass in a wheelchair pursuing me in the fire's wake. The flames are advancing on me, my mother behind them. I race past my first home in South San Francisco. A young boy appears at my side. I grab him and we haul toward the city, to the tip of the peninsula where the bay water will protect us. We get there and the fire, abruptly, stops. We turn to see that everything behind us is now a scorched wasteland. No one has survived. Not even my mother.

I walk back toward my childhood home. It is now in ruins. Somehow, I have lost the young boy. I am panic-stricken, as if I had lost my own child. With my foot, I scrape away some ash from the sooty floor and a stairway appears—descending infinitely into the darkness. I know that the boy is at the bottom of the stairway. I walk down the steps—twenty, thirty flights of stairs. A dread comes over me that I am not supposed to be there. I keep going. I reach a door. It is locked. Suddenly, a savage wolf appears from the other side, snapping fiercely at me.

"You should not be here," it shrieks. "If you come down here alone, what you find will kill you."

I am beside myself with fear. I flee back up the staircase. The wolf chases me, baring its teeth and growling to ravage me. I get to the top, hurtle through a door, and slam it behind me. The door is thin and flimsy. The wolf rips through it with its claws.

I am frozen with terror and wake up.

THE NIGHTMARE LEFT me rattled and on edge—a surge of buzzing irritability coursing through my body as if I had taken speed and chased it with a double shot of espresso. It was morning and, once again, I was facing a day without plans or direction. I had hoped to see Justin for a couple of hours, but Cathy informed me that she was taking him on a day trip with her parents to marvel at the holiday displays at Universal Studios. That left me with stewing about the cabin, alternately fuming about my son's sightseeing without me and my mother's filleting of me while feigning to love. I felt as tortured as ever. And now, I not only had my mom forbidding me from delving into our family secrets, I had figures from my nightmares warning me away at the risk of painful death.

My agitation could not be distracted by household chores, the running of errands, or escaping into a novel. I paced and seethed, scribbled in my journal, and slapped paper with crayons until my distress reached a frenzied pitch. Needing to release the pressure with something more physical, I hiked back through the woods for another rendezvous with that limbless tree. This time with an axe. The barbed spike of a trunk still stood like the skeleton of a scaled totem. It did not stand much longer. I spent the afternoon chopping it down, hacking it into hunks of firewood, and lugging armloads to the cabin's woodpile.

The manual and mutilative labor did not help. By nightfall, the agitation had intensified into a fevered affliction. Literally. I felt like my skin was burning with a soiled repugnance that seeped cellularly into my pores. It was all that I could do to ward off cutting myself until it was time to turn in.

Bed, however, brought no comfort. As if they were set free from their netherworld captivity, fantasies forced their way into my mind. I tossed about in a restless delirium, with each fantasy playing out in agonizing detail as if compelling me to try it on to ascertain how well it fit—my mother caressing me in my bedroom, my grandfather raping me in his camper, my mom and my grandfather both as one watched the other strip and suck me. Instinctively, my body would recoil with shudders of revulsion trying to expunge the lurid images out of my being. But they kept coming back, their presence asserting their veracity and demanding their assent. And I would know. This really happened. I could feel it. My body remembered it as if the abuse were seared into my tissues. Then my mother's denials left me screaming in tormented self-doubt. *What is wrong with me? What am I imagining? What kind of filth have I become?*

I writhed in my covers, twisting between sordid fantasies and self-laceration until I worked myself up into a crazed hysteria. Sleep an impossibility, I had to get out of that bed, that cabin, that anguish, that life. Though well past midnight, I got in my truck and drove down the mountain. I had no destination—just a need to find some way to let off some of the steam of my fury. Once in the neighborhoods, I prowled the streets, randomly turning on different roads. At some point, a homing device of habit must have clicked into place. I was not planning on it, but I found myself driving on the boulevard passing by my workplace. As soon as I saw it, I knew that I had found it—the object on which to unleash my rage.

It was hideous. Perched front and center in the entrance courtyard at the mouth of the seminary, an enormous, freestanding pulpit had been erected. Some thirty feet tall and fire-engine red from top to bottom, it was wrapped in siding, wide at the base and narrowing as it rose to a railed podium thrusting itself onto the world to proclaim the good news and subdue the masses for Christ. A phallic monstrosity if ever I saw one, its public installation on our campus must have been a magnanimous gesture to appease some donor who fancied himself an artist of ecclesiastical sculpture.

For me, it was an in-your-face declaration of ejaculatory subjugation. And I was done being subdued and violated. I stopped my truck, grabbed my bat, and beat the bestial satisfaction out of that cocksure pillar of proclamatory conquest. My bat punctured the particle-board siding with only a couple of thwacks, so I worked my way around the base, pounding gouging rips and gaping holes from the ground to as high as I could reach. If a car had driven by, it would have seen a grown man, in the middle of the night, taking on a bright-red wooden leviathan like a child going up against a beast larger than life. If the police had driven by, I would have been cuffed as a vandal and taken away in a squad car. The indignity of arrest would have been a new low in my humiliation. I was so distraught that I did not care. I battered the massive pulpit until it was thrashed and splintered. Then I whirled my bat onto the administration building's roof and made my getaway back into the night.

I AWOKE THE next morning as dejected as I was depleted. As if the blood-sugar level of my spirit had crashed during my sleep, I lay in bed with no energy to move and no will to live. My suicidal fantasy returned to taunt me—*Why not drive up north, find that redwood beach, and swallow a bottle of sleeping pills? I could end this all for good. Nothing is stopping me. I could leave today.*

Not yet ready to commit, but needing an outlet for the internal anguish, I stopped resisting the other pull and turned to the razor blade. In the window's light, I lost myself in cutting. It hurt so bad it felt good. I needed to feel the pain viscerally; I needed my skin to consolidate and absorb the torment. So I sliced slits up and down my arms, not deep enough to nick an artery, but enough to watch streaks of scarlet flow into and fill the white flesh of my scratches.

I had scored my second arm when the president of my school called. He asked me to come see him in his office—just to confirm in person that I was doing okay. I could tell from his tone that I had no choice. I told him that I would, then decided that I would keep on going—a fourteen-hour drive to Eureka. I packed a small bag to sleep on the road and gathered a couple of toiletries. The last item I took came as an impulse. I saw it on the table and thought it a good idea. Just so I would always have it with me, I tucked the razor blade into the sole of my shoe, then I drove down to see my boss.

THOUGH BOB PRESENTED with his former congressperson can-do optimism, his eyes betrayed the depth of his worry. Seeing the despair seeping through my indifference to my disheveled appearance, he was not buying for a moment that my mental health was no longer a matter of grave concern. He sized me up as if able to surmise, from just one look at me, that my hospital release was a critical mistake. It may have been. But I was not ready to concede it. Then again, with my choice between the gallows and a prison, I lacked the resolve for a vigorous defense. I responded to his queries less like a defendant protesting his innocence and more like a death row inmate with nothing left to appeal.

He asked me how I was doing, and he meant it. If it was an opening gambit to secure an admission to my mental instability, it came from genuine care. I said that I was fine. Then, not to appear too deflective, I added that the holidays were tough but that I was doing a lot better. He took in my scant offering and considered how to proceed. He went with empathic understanding— again, his sincerity self-evident. He shared that he knew all too well how the first days out of the hospital could be harder than expected, and he went on to confide in me that his wife had been institutionalized after the birth of their first child. After several weeks of treatment, she seemed better and came home. Within a couple of days, she was more depressed than ever. Tending to the mundanities of living day-to-day proved to be too much for her. After an attempt to no longer try, she had to be rehospitalized. Thank God there was someone to find her. It would be months before she was functional enough not to be left alone.

I got the admonition hidden thinly within his disclosure and told him that I was sorry to hear about his wife, but that I really was readjusting just fine. He expressed his concern about how isolated I was up in my mountain cabin and offered me an apartment on campus to see me through the next few months. I told him that that was kind but really not necessary—the solitude was good for me. He nodded as if he was not satisfied but was willing to drop it for now. Then he redirected, under the guise of changing the subject.

"Say," he said, as if a mild curiosity had simply come to him. "You don't know anything about that pulpit, do you?"

Though I knew that the vandalism could never be traced back to me—and that I, a respected professor, was a most unlikely suspect in the first place—the question did not surprise me. Somehow, I felt like he already knew, and that denying it would only tighten his case. So I fessed up.

"Yeah," I said, with a resigned nonchalance. "It was me."

He sighed as if he had hoped that what he knew to be true was not. "As soon as I saw it," he said, "I had a feeling it was you. When did you do it?"

"Last night," I answered, not caring what it insinuated about my mental health. "I don't know, sometime after midnight."

His fears confirmed, he shook his head. "You're lucky nobody saw you. I'd have a professor locked up in jail." He was not trying to pile on guilt; he was simply underscoring the depth of my distress.

"Yeah, you're right, Bob," I admitted. "It's been harder than I thought. I'm sorry. I'll pay for it."

"I'm not worried about the sculpture," he said. "The artist has already said that he can fix it. I'm worried about you."

"Really, Bob," I continued, "it was just a hard night. I'm doing better now. I'm thinking of driving up north for a few days—get a change of scenery."

He saw right through it. "Why don't you stay down here? I think it'll be better for you."

"No, that's okay," I said. "I can really use some time away."

"I'm not so sure it's a good idea," he said.

"Yeah, why not?" I countered, as if all that I needed was a good vacation.

He stared at me with pained seriousness. Then he called my bluff. "Frank, what's that?"

He motioned toward my wrists. From underneath my shirtsleeves, blood was trickling toward both of my palms. I had no reply. The wounds spoke for themselves.

"I think you should go back to the hospital," he suggested with paternal tenderness. "There's no shame in it. It's an illness. These things take time. What do you say? I'll take you right now."

What could I say? I had trashed a donor's artwork. I was bleeding in my boss's office. And out in my truck, I was packed to die.

"Yeah, Bob, maybe you're right."

I WAS NOT admitted as a convalescent merely in need of some seclusion in the sanitarium. Having so severely self-injured, I was sequestered in the locked unit where I could be observed around the clock. As soon as I was caged, I regretted my submission to the pointless indignity of another stay at the hospital. This was more than humiliating. This was humiliation with commitment papers. In a place that promised no hope for renewal. No longer the compliant patient, I stared at the floor in wordless defiance as the doctor scolded me for going off my meds. I refused to say a word during groups and gave none of my attention to the drivel doled out in the workshops. I snuck out my razor blade and cut myself in the isolation of the bathroom stall. And I stood before the plexiglass window that faced the outside world, positioning my body to obstruct the camera as my hands used my razor to scratch futilely at the pane.

Then I planned my escape.

I noticed that the lunch cart was wheeled into the locked ward at the same time that the convalescents on the far side of the sanitarium were let out into the main lobby for day programs. I picked a day when Lupe—a nurse nearing retirement who had looked after me during my first institutional tour—was on rotation. As she shuffled the cart through the door, I left my appointed perch against the back wall and walked toward her, pretending to offer her assistance. I laid hold of the cart and swiveled it to gently pin her in place, then pivoted and slid out the door.

With professional calm and matronly concern, Nurse Lupe simply offered, "Frank, you don't want to do this."

I did. And I kept going. I whisked across the commons and toward the far door. An orderly was holding it open for the last straggle of convalescents. I vouched that I, too, was in the day program and, not giving him a chance to verify it, I slipped through the door. Day patients were milling about in the lobby. I paid them no heed as I beelined through them, made for the entrance, and strode through the parting glass doors into my freedom. I was astounded at how easy it all was.

Having no idea what the protocol was for an inmate going AWOL, I got off the main road and hustled through some neighborhood streets in case a security guard was sent out to chase me. I never truly believed that my escape plot would work, so I did not have a plan for once I got out. My truck was still at my workplace, but my keys had been confiscated. I had a spare back at my cabin, but that was over twenty miles away. I needed someplace clandestine to sit and think it through, then came upon the perfect spot. A small Roman Catholic church offered sanctuary on a quiet residential corner. Its parking lot deserted, it promised not only concealment, but privacy with anything sacred there that deigned to offer me direction. I scurried up to the front door. It was locked. That felt perfect too. God was not home. Or if so, I was barred from any audience with the preoccupied Almighty.

Left to myself, I hoofed it toward the highway with the vague notion of hitchhiking up to my cabin. As I approached the main intersection, I noticed a police car stopped at a light prepared to turn toward me. I could not imagine that the police would be on the lookout for me, but just in case, I ducked into a strip mall and made for the Circle K at the far end of the parking lot. I was halfway there when a second squad car emerged from a side street and pulled into the lot in front of me. I turned around to retrace my steps as the first squad car was pulling into the parking lot behind me. Coming at me from both sides, they had me cornered. For a split second, I flashed on running toward the highway. Before I could bolt, however, words boomed from a squad car's intercom, "*Stay where you are. And with your hands up. Now!*"

As terrified as I was shamefaced, I froze, then held my hands high. Onlookers ogled from the sidewalks, heads stared from the cars driving by on the highway, as I was approached by an officer with his hand on his gun, cuffed, then secured in the back seat of his police car. I had not been gone for more than fifteen minutes.

The officer was polite but firm. He reported my custody into his radio, then informed me that he had to return me to the hospital. Once there, he gripped my bicep with the force of a stranglehold and escorted me in. As he marched me, still cuffed, back through the lobby and into the locked ward—both patients and hospital staff gawking—I did not don a Cool Hand Luke grin of defiant aloofness. I was shamed into sheepish capitulation. I saw for myself what I was. I was a convict escaped from an asylum, apprehended in a police manhunt, and paraded back into captivity in conquered ignobility.

How much lower could I fall?

IT WOULD TAKE another theophany before I truly got my mind right—one decidedly more corporeal but no less restorative. Before it came, though, the steam propelling my acting-out was already beginning to dissipate. Like the wounds that reveal that the bullets are real in the gun with which one is playing, the reach of my behavior's harmfulness started to hit its mark with me. The psychiatrist was shooting with live ammo too. He got my attention when, while adjusting my meds, he pressed upon me that the one I was most hurting was myself. I could resist the staff's care as much as I wanted, but I was only making the case for a judge-ordered involuntary commitment of indefinite length to the state-run mental institution.

The shot from my fellow inmate Jean hit flesh. She figured out that I had smuggled in a razor blade—it takes a cutter to know a cutter—and begged me to let her borrow it. I knew that when she cut, she went for the vein. Imagining my blade responsible for her self-immolation sobered me a bit further—enough to realize that my influence was only hastening her descent into destruction, and to tell her that I had already tossed it away.

Nurse Lupe hit an organ. Sitting me down while making her rounds, she went straight for the heart.

"I hear you have a son," she said.

"Yeah," I replied.

"What's his name?"

"Justin—he just turned four."

She paused before taking aim. "Have you thought about what it would be like for him to grow up without a father—whose father thought so little of him that he took his own life?"

That bullet was already lodged deep within, causing more pain than Nurse Lupe could ever know.

"Yes, I've thought about it," I told her point-blank. "The thought pierces me to the bone every second of my life."

I DO NOT know if Nurse Lupe, in a flash of therapeutic creativity, suggested the idea to my therapist. Perhaps Helen came up with it all by herself. Or maybe it should all be taken simply at face value. Whatever the earthly source, it was divinely inspired.

During one of our therapy sessions in the hospital consultation room, Helen mentioned that Justin had been asking for me. She wondered what I thought of him coming for a short while during visiting hours one evening. It might help him to feel more secure if he saw firsthand that I was alive, at least, if not well. To be honest, at the time, I was more concerned that the sight of him would only intensify my shame. The apprehensive look on his face when he saw his dad in a facility would burn with the coals of mortification. I only agreed because parental responsibility brought a searing burn of its own.

A family friend agreed to bring Justin to the hospital one evening right after dinner. The locked ward no place for a child, we would meet in the commons of the sanitarium between the ward and the main lobby. I waited inside the locked unit and watched for him from behind the barred door—peering through the meshed window as my worry drowned me with dread.

As soon as I saw him, his look of dislocated confusion ignited the flame that was all set to scald. Let in by an orderly on the far side of the commons, Justin paused, holding the hand of our friend, and looked about the vacated sanitarium bewildered about where I was. Nurse Lupe opened the locked-ward door and I stepped out into the commons. The second that he saw me, all bewilderment evaporated. His face lit up like a child's at the sight of his POW dad disembarking from the plane that had just brought him back home. Unable to restrain himself, he dashed the full length of the commons squealing with euphoric delight, "Daddy, Daddy, Daddy!" Orange Tic Tacs shook in his fist as he raced toward me and leapt into my arms, squeezing my neck with euphoric joy and affection.

That was the moment that I came back home to myself, the moment that my resolve to find healing solidified and took root. My heart broke for that boy and overflowed with love's determination. Through everything—the pain of me separating from his mother, the mystery of my prolonged and cryptic absences, my plunge into despair and madness that landed me in the abyss of an asylum—in the midst of it all, his love endured, his beauty still beamed, the radiance of his countenance could shine on without shadow. I wrapped my arms around that adorable boy, soaking up the rays of sunlight as his care brought to bloom the loving father within me. The conviction rose up inside me like the greening power that fuels a flower's flourishing—*Never will I do a thing that might dampen that boy's spirit; I will do all that I can to be the dad that he deserves.*

"Daddy," he asked, when he released his embrace, Tic Tacs still gripped in his fist, "can we play the medicine game?"

"Of course," I said, checking the crack in my voice. Then I added, "If we can also play the 'Run, Run, Run into Daddy's Arms' game."

And so we did. He placed Tic Tacs into my mouth, a single pill at a time, to make me feel better. And I would walk the length of the room, turn, and match his beaming grin with my own as he raced and squealed with abandon, "Daddy, Daddy, Daddy," into his daddy's arms. He had no way of knowing. For me, it was more than a game. It was a restorative spiritual practice. One that we would play for years to come—in living rooms, parks, lobbies, and hallways the longer the better—until he grew so big his leap would knock me down. Even then, our giggling embrace, each squeezing the other for dear life, was solid and sacred ground.

JUSTIN'S VISIT WOKE me up to why my well-being was worth fighting for. Not only did I want to protect and promote the thriving of this beautiful young boy, I glimpsed again the person that I wanted to be and become—a man who could receive the delight of another and who could mirror it back with grounding enough to catch the leap of their love. When I returned to the locked ward, my stride was determined. I would walk the path toward healing and recovery. And I already knew the first step. That very night, I gave Nurse Lupe my good faith deposit, my pledge to secure psychological sobriety. I turned over the razor blade that I had smuggled into the hospital.

Its days of cutting were over.

FOR THE NEXT week and a half, I not only cooperated with my treatment, I set up a support system to see me through a season of healing. The sexual-abuse counselor and writer Mike Lew, offering guidance for those first turbulent months of recovery, recommends that survivors nail up a shingle in the storefront of their lives saying, "Temporarily Closed for Repairs." I closed up shop and set out my sign.

I agreed to move down from my mountain cabin isolation into a single-bedroom apartment in student housing on campus. I applied for disability to offset my salary loss through my semester-long leave of absence. I scheduled semiweekly therapy sessions with Helen and outlined contact procedures should I ever get suicidal. With my psychiatrist, I settled on a tolerable regimen of meds and set up weekly consultations to monitor them. I signed up for an outpatient support group that met as part of the hospital's day programs. I wrote a letter to my mother, explaining to her that I needed a period of prolonged separation, that any contact with her whatsoever could undermine my tenuous emotional stability, and that she should wait for me to initiate any future reconnection.

And coming with the power of a revelation, I stumbled upon a contemplative practice that held uncommon recuperative promise in guiding me through the journey ahead.

IN MY FINAL days at the hospital, I resumed my practice of morning meditation. Helen had mentioned that Carl Jung would take imaginative journeys into his inner world, engaging the psychic symbols that emerged with the intention of harnessing their power and integrating them—a process he called active imagination, or wakeful dreaming. He trusted that the images produced by our unconscious—whether we are awake or dreaming in our sleep—came with some life-promoting purpose, and that they could be queried, befriended, and assimilated in constructive ways. Active imagination involves noting such images in our mind, what is often called the mind's eye, and with a grounded curiosity, inviting them to reveal their psychic gifts.

This resonated with my experience in the mental hospital when throwing clay erupted into a fit of fury. In my extended rage and despair, the images emerged of a rabid wolf-fiend and a Munch-like skull. When I noticed them, the possessive grip of those emotions relaxed as if they had been screaming to get my attention and, once they had it, they did not need to shout anymore. From the ensuing grounded space, I could engage the images in a way that felt profoundly restorative. It even evolved into a mystical encounter with the sacred.

Ignatius of Loyola likewise prayed through his imagination, meeting God within the images that emerged through contemplation. And when a prayer experience was particularly consoling, he engaged in the practice of recollection—remembering and savoring once more the grace of that meditation. Buoyed by both Jung and Ignatius, I ventured to embark on a meditative journey of my own, returning to the captivating images that came to me in the padded room.

My first contemplative adventure into the underworld within me took place in the privacy of my hospital bedroom. Lying on my bed, I breathed into a grounded calm and recalled the energetic connection that I had experienced in the padded room with a cosmic sacred compassion. Wrapped in a remembrance of that safe and healing presence, I pictured the underground caverns that I had envisioned during that mystical experience. Each one was guarded at the mouth by a passionate energy with the power to possess like a demon. And each one harbored, deeper in the depths, wounded children aching to be seen and held. As foretold in my dream, and as had happened with the skull-faced boy that I had held on the padded-room floor, I had the distinct sense that the path toward healing entailed descending into the underground caverns and tending with care whatever I found there.

As I took a step toward one of the caves, the menacing wolf from my Christmas Day nightmare leapt from the mouth of the cave. Growling and baring its teeth to attack me, it repeated its former threat, "Don't you dare come down here alone—what you find here will kill you." A tremor of fear rumbled in my belly, but I held my ground. Breathing in the sacred energy that surrounded me, I told the wolf that it was okay—that I was not alone—that I was partnered with a sacred presence that could hold and handle all things. The wolf took that in, still poised to pounce if it was not true. I continued to stand my ground and told the wolf that I believed the wolf to be a treasured ally guarding against danger, not an enemy out to hurt me. I invited the wolf to escort me as we descended into the depths together.

To my astonishment, still a neophyte in this inner world exploration, the wolf instantly transformed. Like the demon of rage with which I had wrestled, its hostility evaporated as it morphed into a benevolent companion, coming to my side like a long-cherished four-legged friend. Affection washed over me, as did wonder at the power of grounded and courteous presence in transforming the seemingly malevolent into psychic strength. I came to name that wolf Gubbio, after the one that Saint Francis tamed in the legend. I even found a medal of Francis and the wolf that I wear to this day like a talisman. In the years to come, Gubbio and I would take many journeys into the underworld of my soul together.

During that initial foray, we did not go far. Just inside the mouth of the first cave, the Munch-like skull reappeared—its silently howling mouth and haunted, vacant eyes, all wide open. The compassion that I felt before washed over me once more. The skull transmuted into the face of the three-year-old boy lying naked on my mother's bed. His eyes bore into me with wordless certainty.

"It really happened," they implored me to hear.

I replied with equal wordless certainty, "I know."

He came into my arms and I held him. With each heartbeat of care that I breathed into him, the pulse of his spirit resuscitated. Our hearts were beating as one, sustained by the heartbeat of cosmic compassion. As I soaked in that restorative oneness, the words came to me as if whispered in my ear by the presence in whose lap I rested.

"This is the path," that compassionate source assured. "Be Pietà to yourself. Like Mary cradling the body of her son, hold all of it—the demons, the nightmares, the lurid fantasies, the wounded ones within you. It all cries out for healing. It all can be held. And it all can be restored. This is the way. Be Pietà to yourself."

The words were as secure as the arms in which I was held.

A FEW DAYS after the first of the year, I left the safe harbor of the hospital with the sober optimism of a voyager launching on an odyssey in a stocked and seaworthy vessel. To be sure, this was not the maiden voyage of my quest for psychological and spiritual well-being. I had spent years studying its various paths. I had splashed around in contemplative practices from a variety of traditions. I had sought counsel from an array of therapists and mental health professionals. I had turned introspection into a life's work, filling reams of journals exploring the depths of my madness.

And yet, this leg of the journey felt different. My resolve was rooted in cautious confidence, not last-ditch desperation. I had supports in place that felt sound and sturdy for when the seas inevitably became stormy. And I had set foot on the shore of sacred oneness already, so I knew that the region that I sought was not a mere myth.

But most of all, I had, if not a map, a compass. Though the twists and turns of the itinerary were yet to unfold, and gale-force winds were sure to knock me off my course across the waters, I had a fixed coordinate by which to orient and course-correct along the way. The needle of the compass pointed to the Polaris star of true North. I wrote the coordinates of that star on an index card and framed it with a photo of the original.

When my way was lost, I needed only to fix my eyes on the icon over my desk: Mary holding the broken body of Jesus. And underneath, "Be Pietà to yourself."

Part IV

Whitethorn, CA—Age 36

July 17–25, 1995

——— • ———

A YEAR AND a half after my hospital stay, still lost at sea on my therapeutic odyssey, I retreated to the redwoods for some psycho-spiritual reorientation. To be sure, other factors contributed to the storms that had swept me off course in my recovery. Cathy and I were still tangling about custody schedules and property settlements. Justin was struggling to adjust to two households, his anxiety disturbing his ability to sleep. And a publishing deadline to secure my academic tenure had me blocked to the point of jeopardizing my career trajectory. All of that played a part in it. But the prevailing winds of my interior turmoil came from my obsession to determine the truth of my past. With the absence of actual memories of abuse, the insidious doubt tormented me that all my suspicions were entirely made up. My journey toward recovery could not stay the course when I could not concede a trauma from which to recover. It was as exasperating as breaking a rudder while tacking through a tempest to safety.

The problem was that I could feel it all in my bones. Everything about me bore the marks of violation. I read books compulsively on sexual abuse and wept with recognition at the profiles of survivors. I spent my leisure time absorbed in Holocaust depictions—films, memoirs, the music from *Schindler's List*—my soul resonating with the tsunami of suffering it somehow knew innately. I ruminated over scenarios from my past, visualizing scenes of molestation while my body confirmed each sordid sensation as if it were seared into my skin. With a detective's determination, I pored over the evidence—patterns from the generations, the congruence of my symptoms, false testimony from the one suspected, the indiscretions of her past that were incontrovertible—certain that the clues disclosed unequivocal episodes of lurid sexual assault.

And then the notion that it was all nothing but unsubstantiated speculation would suck the winds from the sails of my certainty. The scenes I played out were imaginative fictions, it insisted. My body's recognitions came with no reliable details. And the evidence over which I brooded so excessively was all purely circumstantial—with neither eyewitness recollections nor confessional admissions to corroborate so much as a shred of it. My drive to uncover the abuse of my past gave way to a dead calm of dejection and self-castigation for consuming myself with such despicable conjectures. Far from the certitude that I had felt when I had held the skulled boy within me in a protective and paternal care, I now felt stalled and adrift in a sea of infuriating uncertainty.

I went to a monastery to regain my bearings. I wanted to recall what I had known to be true in that hospital epiphany—perhaps, even, to sense again the womb-like waters of sacred connection that I had experienced while I was knowing it. I did not expect to meet, in person, the feminine presence of the divine. Her appearance in bodily form was a surprise. So too was the restorative power of her simple care for the bereft and broken down.

OUR LADY OF the Redwoods is about as far from my home as I can drive without leaving California. Hidden in the aptly named "Lost Coast," in the northwest corner of the state, it is a twelve-hour car ride from Claremont—the last leg of which twists along a craggy country road from the interior 101 Highway through the shadowed forest highlands toward the sea. As the crow flies, it is a mere fifty miles from Eureka, the coastal town further north that had been the destination of my previous suicidal fantasies. Eighteen months earlier, I would have stayed on the 101 in search of a beach just past the borough where I could escape into an eternal oblivion. This time, I turned off the highway, into the barren remoteness, and made for the monastery as far from town as life is from death. Which is to say, sitting side by side.

The Trappistine community of Cistercian nuns had come to my attention years earlier when I was studying Thomas Merton. The famous monk had stayed at the monastery on his way to an interfaith conference in Bangkok in 1968. He found the primeval landscape indescribably beautiful. The cathedral quiet of the dense old-growth groves, the ancient thirty-story redwoods towering into the sky, and the sea mist stillness encircling the silence had so moved his soul that he had hoped to move into a hermitage nearby upon his return from Thailand. At the age of only fifty-three, Merton died at the conference from a freak accident. Though his dream to soak in that old-growth sacredness was denied during his lifetime, the sacred presence that permeated the place was still there for others, perhaps laced with a mystic trace of Merton's still living spirit. I longed, if not for a soak, at least for a brush with that sacred presence that seeps through such silence. I did not have to wait long.

I passed through the monastery's entrance gate into a wide grassy field edged by lofty pine trees and majestic redwoods. A single gravel road led to a cluster of attached buildings at one end of the field. Though a few cars were parked at some cabins off to the side, the grounds were otherwise deserted. I drove toward the buildings with some trepidation. The trip had taken longer than I had expected. It was after the dinner hour, the summer's dusk was descending, and the arrival time for registration had long since passed. I hoped that I would still have a bed for the night—the closest motel was back at the main highway over an hour's drive away.

I pulled up in front of a sign indicating the hospitality center. The office toward which it pointed looked vacant, as did the complex of monastic living quarters behind it. With nowhere else to go, I walked toward the office door with the cautious quiet of one intruding into a convent after hours. Inside the screen, a note was taped to the door. With the precise printing of a practiced calligrapher, it read, "Frank, We're at vespers. Come to the chapel." Though the instructions were eerily personalized, I hesitated, reluctant to disturb a group of nuns already deep in prayer. Yet something about the note's directness pressed me to obey. Still wary, I crept toward the door marked "Chapel." I paused before it, listening in vain for any movement within. I hoped to God that my interruption would not be a bother. Then, with the chagrin of one showing up late for Sunday morning service, I entered the sanctuary through the side door.

I saw her at once. She was directly in my line of sight, sitting on a bench along the far wall, and of the dozen or so nuns and fellow retreatants facing each other on parallel benches across the worship space, she was the only one whose head was not bowed in prayer. She was looking straight at me. Somewhere in her sixties, with her upright posture, crisply ironed nun's habit, and Germanic face creased from age and long hours of toil, she epitomized for me the stern Catholic sister whose life of discipline, self-sacrifice, and back-breaking labor did not suffer profligates lightly. Except that she was smiling faintly, with a glimmer of mischief in her eyes, like I need not worry, we were in it together, co-conspirators in my prayer-time tardiness.

She nodded toward the empty space on the bench a few steps in front of me. A book of the hours was splayed open to the page for that evening's vespers. Atop it was a napkin and a freshly baked oatmeal raisin cookie. I glanced back at her. She lengthened her smile. And, triumphant in her hospitable sneakiness, she winked. Then she closed her eyes and continued with her prayer.

After vespers, she hastened over to greet me—like a grandmother rushing to welcome a grandchild coming home from college.

"You vill be Frank, no?" she said in a guttural accent still thickly clothed in its Flemish countryside roots. "It is very gut tat you are here. Ve are so glat you have come to be wit us. I am Sister Veronique. Come, you must be tired after traveling so far."

She retrieved a room key from her pocket and escorted me to my cabin not far from the complex. She left me to unpack, then returned a short while later with a tray bearing a hot bowl of soup and a half round of bread.

"You vill be hungry, no? I hope you like lentil," she said, her English enunciated as if clear diction could make smooth the hard edges of her Dutch. "The vegetables, they are from our garden. The bread, I am sorry, it may be a bit coarse for you. But tomorrow, we have baguettes." She laid the tray on the desktop, centered the bowl, and straightened the cloth napkin that wrapped the silverware. "Very gut," she said, turning back to me, "I vill let you rest now. Morning prayer is at six. Gott's peace during the night." Then she looked about to confirm that all was just right, clasped her hands together with nothing left for them to do, and slipped back into the shadows of the monastery's silence.

MORNING PRAYER CONSISTED of two twenty-five-minute sits of silence with a ten-minute walking meditation in between. Though I had made sure to arrive early, Sister Veronique was already perched on her bench. Her eyes had been closed, but she opened them when I walked in. Once more, she nodded toward the seat prepared for me. The prayer book was open with a note on the page that read, "Orientation at 8:30. I will meet you in the chapel." I nodded my confirmation. She smiled that she was pleased. Then she closed her eyes and settled back into her meditation. I followed her lead and plunged into my first soul-sounding of the week. The quiet was soothing, but the sacred encounter was yet to come.

After prayer and a bite of breakfast, I returned to the sanctuary well ahead of my appointment with Sister Veronique. Expecting nothing more than a briefing on mealtimes and property boundaries, I wanted some time to myself to survey the prayer space. Something about it was contemplatively compelling and elicited in me an instinctive stillness. Though a box-shaped construction of gray concrete—the floors polished granite, the two-story walls cinder block—the cavernous spaciousness felt neither hard nor cold. A Zen-like simplicity pervaded. A single row of benches lined three walls, Zafu cushions on meditation mats were laid out before them, and a few simple images decorated the otherwise barren cinder block.

The chancel, in the corner off to the side from the door, was spare as well: an unadorned cement block for an altar on a slight slab of concrete for a dais, one white paschal candle holding vigil alongside, a plain wooden tabernacle housing the host against the wall, a modest freestanding pewter crucifix on a pole, and a single vase of purple irises providing the only touch of color.

The most distinctive feature of the unassuming decor came from outdoors. Behind the altar, where a cross would normally hang, a twenty-foot-high wall of window showcased a mammoth redwood just outside the building. Only the base of the trunk was visible, a broad pillar of bark rising up that dwarfed the chapel it shadowed. If a symbol for a site of death, that tree was very much alive, its unseen crown of branches reaching high into the heavens out of sight.

I pondered the subtle aesthetics of the space trying to pinpoint what I found most enticing about it. When it dawned on me, I did not know how I missed putting my finger on it. Once recognized, it was inescapable—its invisibility only intensifying its all-pervasiveness. It was the silence. Merton was right. I could not imagine a quieter place on the planet. Into this void of stillness, sound itself ceased to be, the silence so absolute it had its own palpable presence.

"It is okay to come in further." Sister Veronique had slipped in through a back entrance and found me standing just inside the door.

"I was just taking it all in," I said from the refuge of the chapel's edge. "I can't get over how quiet it is."

"Yes," she said like a connoisseur savoring a rare vintage. "The silence of the redwoods is unlike any silence that I know."

Still taken, I ruminated aloud, "Thomas Merton once wrote that God's speech is silence; only in silence can you hear it. If that's the case, what better place is there to hear a word from God?"

She let the words dissolve into the silence that held us. Then she asked, using Merton's monastic name, "So you read Father Louis?"

"I do," I said. "Especially when I was in grad school. I considered writing my dissertation on him."

"He was here, you know—him and his beret. And his camera." She warmed to the memory, her affection for him obvious. "He loved it here."

"I did know that he was here," I said. "That's how I first heard of the monastery."

"Then you may want to see this." She walked us to a tapestry hung on a side wall—an Asian Jesus in Hindu garb shouldering a mystical cross. "This is from him. He sent it to us from Calcutta, on his way to Bangkok, just days before he died. We heard of his accident and it crushed us—just a few weeks earlier, he had been here. Months later, this comes in the mail. It felt like he was sending us a gift from the other side of the grave." She gazed pensively at the hanging, perhaps dropping another pebble into the well of her grief now over twenty years deep. When the pebble settled, she turned. "Come, let us sit."

She led us to a bench alongside the chancel and next to the window facing the poled crucifix inside and the trunk of redwood outside. She asked about what I had studied in grad school and was delighted to find out that I was a professor of spirituality. Sharing my enthusiasm for the subject, she was eager to hear what I taught, what I read, what I would recommend for her to read as if I would have suggestions for the seasoned contemplative that she was. And I, in turn, asked about her—where she was from and how she found living in this monastery out in the wilderness.

She shared that, growing up in the Belgium countryside, she knew that she wanted to be a nun the moment that, as a young adult, she saw the Cistercian monastery on the outskirts of Antwerp. In 1962, after her novitiate, she was one of the first four nuns who sojourned from the motherhouse in Belgium to found this sister community in the redwood wilds of Northern California. The first years were grueling: freezing winters in drafty canvas shelters, forests so dense that one seldom saw the sun, a wild terrain that defied traditional gardening. The noonday demon of depression was a perpetual specter in the shadows. And yet, she suggested that it had all deepened her faith. Stripped of all that was familiar—and of all that was comfortable—thousands of miles away from her homeland, she was forced to find her refuge in God or fall prey to that which devours. Like the early desert mothers—the Ammas of the second century who likewise forsook the world to pray and to fast in desolate conditions—her steadfast desire to love God and the world had clearly kindled a divine fire within her that now stayed aflame through times of comfort and affliction alike. To my wonderment, I found myself sitting next to a modern-day Amma as if she had been carried through the centuries.

Then the Amma turned back to me.

"So, tell me, Frank," she asked, with the curiosity of a soul friend companioning another along their spiritual journey. "In the silence, what do you seek to hear from Gott?"

The question caught me off guard. I was not expecting a spiritual-direction query about the intentions that I was bringing into my retreat. Uncertain how honest I wanted to be, or how honest she really wanted me to be, I offered something cryptic.

"The truth," I said, neither concealing my desire nor disclosing it, yet doing both at the same time.

She held my veiled longing with a tender regard, sensing the hidden depths that were revealed in my words. Then she followed up, genuinely wanting to know.

"The truth about what?" she asked, her eyes peering into my own.

By then, her kindness had already inspired an intuitive trust in me. Her Amma's compassion now promised a knowing care. Something in me ached for that care, ached to be known and met with an Amma's understanding. I had no need to share details, and she had no need to hear them, but into the expanse of her openness, I came clean about the anguish that besieged me.

"The truth about the pain," I said, "and how the pain is healed."

She let my words drift down into her own hidden depths, into seabed crevices that sheltered ample pain of her own. In those sun-starved waters, she knew the same longing—perhaps she had brought it with her from her homeland as well. And she, too, had listened for God in the silence. In the ensuing years, however, with her soul exposed to the redwood quiet, she had heard something along the way—something that she now wanted to share with me. An enigmatic smile lightened her face.

She leaned in close and whispered with intrigue, "Do you vant silence? I will show you silence."

AFTER DISAPPEARING INTO her living quarters to bundle up for the morning chill, Sister Veronique met me outside wearing a denim jacket over her work habit, a woolen scarf wrapped around her neck, and hiking boots laced tightly on her feet. With a gait that belied her years, she strode us across the grassy grounds toward the forest on the far side of the clearing. As we traversed the field, she recollected how, a number of years earlier, the monastery had had to fight for the quiet. The constant thumping of police helicopter blades sliced the skies like a war zone. The nuns joined forces with the local farmers to petition the government to cease and desist with the incessant surveillance. The courts ruled in their favor—to the relief of farmer and monastic alike. The farmers wanted to prevent the confiscation of their marijuana crops; the nuns wanted their silence back.

Across the field, we passed through a wooden gate and entered the darkened forest. After a short walk along a footpath, Sister Veronique stopped and turned toward me.

"Are you ready?" she asked, poised to escort me into some mystical land. I was. "Come," she beckoned. "This is my true place to pray. This is my true cathedral." She led us between two trees and into a hollowed pocket encircled by redwoods so ancient they may have been saplings at the time of Christ. The handful of trees were so huge, the ring so tightly packed, it hushed all sound; while the canopy of limbs and needles above was so thick, and rose so high into the sky, it shrouded all light. We had slipped into a vaulted grove of such fecund quiet it could have been an Edenic cocoon.

Sister Veronique solemnly stepped to the widest redwood in the circle and placed her hand on the bark as if paying homage to an elder high priestess before treading upon her sacred ground. Once her reverence was received, she turned back to me, grabbed my arm, and beheld the wooded tabernacle. After calibrating herself to the quiet, she softly spoke.

"Father Louis also said that out of the dark heart of the forest comes the secret that can only be heard in silence." She closed her eyes. "Listen, you can almost hear her heartbeat."

She did not elaborate on whose heartbeat she was hearing—that of the maiden tree, Mother Earth, the divine feminine, her own. She simply soaked in the silence, perhaps all of them beating as one. Then, with her eyes still closed, she leaned over and whispered as if confiding in me a secret that she held close to the bone.

"And believe me," she shared, "that heartbeat knows all about the pain."

MY WEEK OF retreat followed a rhythm of early-morning meditation with the nuns; a few hours of journaling and rumination after breakfast; midday prayers, lunch, and afternoon walks through the wooded hills; Eucharist before dinner; then an evening of reading and reflection before vespers and bed. Sister Veronique receded somewhat, leaving me to follow the lead of my soul's descent into the silence. Yet her presence hovered all around the edges as a continuous backdrop of hospitality and kindness.

She noticed that I journaled by the chapel window in the midmorning solitude, so she placed a cushioned chair next to the planked bench so my sit would be more comfortable. At communal prayer times throughout the day, a breviary on my chair was always opened to that hour's daily office—no longer bearing notes, but occasionally offering a trail map, a wildflower, an icon of the Black Madonna. Freshly baked cookies would be wrapped on a plate and set outside my cabin's door to greet me upon my return from an afternoon hike. And in case I happened to be interested, I found, tucked into my door, a hand-drawn map to the secluded coastline a few miles away where Thomas Merton had dreamed of hiding his hermitage.

Like a self-appointed acolyte to the rites of my retreat, her care-filled attentiveness was so devout it could have invoked the sacred reality that I was seeking. Maybe that is why she came. One thing is certain—some wisp of spirit from Sister Veronique found its way into my prayer that week.

AFTER MY MEDITATIVE forays in the hospital—where I had harnessed the wolf-demon of my rage into a resilience to face my pain, and where I could hold and grieve the Munch-like skull of my anguish externalized into the form of a child—I continued my experiments with using my imagination to personify and engage my emotional states. Emboldened by my subsequent studies of spiritual writers in the tradition of Carl Jung—Robert Johnson, Morton Kelsey, Ann Ulanov, among others—I would summon up images in my contemplative practice to signify the passions and impulses that blustered within me. And I found that this freed me, at least temporarily, from their possessive clutch on my being.

A consistent process began to emerge for me. When an emotion or impulse overwhelmed me, I would cultivate a grounded awareness of the energy being present within my inner world—something akin to mindfulness. Then, trusting that the emotion or the impulse or the hounding inner voice came with some life-promoting purpose, I invited it to personify itself as some image—a symbolic object, for example, or an animal, or a human figure. Once the image solidified, I could query it; I could hear its deeper cry; I could tend to its hidden need; I could even invite the sacred to come and comfort it.

For example, when I could picture my harriedness with all the demands at my workplace as a street musician flailingly trying to play five instruments all at once, or my guilt at Justin's divorce anxieties as a spear pressed to my gut from a garrison charged to protect the boy from a callous disregard, I was able to separate from the all-consuming charge of the emotion. I no longer *was* my harriedness or my guilt, engulfed by their overwhelming energies. Rather, I was able to settle again into my solid center where I could hold those images in my grounded awareness. Then, with resilience and curiosity, I could interact with them, tend to their concerns, and allow them to evolve in a mysterious yet restorative process. The street musician could pause for a moment, then play his music one instrument at a time; the garrison could be reassured that Justin was well loved, and withdraw the blade knowing that my love for him would hold steady through whatever we had to endure.

Jung compared it to alchemy, transforming base materials into gold—the reeking manure of one's unfettered passions becoming the radiant ore of inner strength and capacity. I engaged this process through meditation, though it could be practiced just as effectively through drawing, creative writing, playing with puppets or objects like sand tray figures, creating characters for the stage, dialoguing with an empty chair, talking it out with a confidant, or whatever reflective process is most accessible to one. For me, sitting in my craftsman armchair in the early-morning quiet, a candle lit by my side, coaxed open my imagination and eased me into the process soon to take on a life of its own.

While the practice proved invaluable in regulating me through my day-to-day functioning, I had yet to employ it to plumb the stormier waters that swirled around my recovery from abuse. Now, with the spaciousness of a week-long retreat, and with my responsibilities at home on pause, it was time to take another dive into the more turbulent regions of my soul—perhaps, at least, stilling that storm for a spell, if not surfacing again that boy hidden within its squalls. As it turned out, he was there. And he had a few places that he wanted me to see.

During my first contemplative sit with the nuns, my internal agitation about my inability to remember any episodes of sexual abuse whipped me about in its tempestuous whirlwinds. Several shifting gales of emotion hurled and howled within me. A fierce resolve to force my memory into surrendering some form of self-confirming flashback vied with a nauseous dread that dared not face the truth to be revealed from my past. My body's searing insistence that my flesh had been violated did battle with my castigating self-doubt that I was fabricating filthiness from my own deceptive depravity. And my fidgety frustration that the monastic quiet could not quell my inner discord aroused the reproach that my time on retreat was only serving to avoid my work back home.

With so many conflicting emotions, all tangled together in a brawling mass, I was not able to single one out for long, let alone personify them with psychic images. I was tossed about in the tumbling tumult without a toehold to anchor me. I was about to concede to an hour of contemplative exasperation when the obvious image, hovering there offshore all along, presented itself and materialized before my mind's eye. Taken all together as a gestalt, I felt as if I were caught in the throes of a typhoon out in the middle of the ocean, the various emotional pulls conspiring together to suck me into an escalating cyclone of dizzying distress.

Incongruously, the mere appearance of the image—giving expression to my emotional state with such resonant precision—was itself enough to dissipate its tenacious grip on me. It was as if the image now contained all the energy with which the cacophony was possessing me, and I was now free to acknowledge and observe it all. I was still in the middle of a typhoon, but I was standing securely in the eye of the storm. I could sense the various emotional energies hidden in the whirling spray, but I was no longer captive to their gusts. The patch of sea in which I was centered was rippleless in its calm, a faint reminiscence of the oceanic oneness that I had felt in the hospital.

The reprieve from the turmoil was such a relief, and the serenity so restoring, that I felt no need to journey any further. My soul was now soaking in the monastic silence permeating my prayer. For the rest of that early-morning meditation, I simply rested in the grounded stillness and, with each breath, absorbed the regenerative balm.

ON THE SECOND day of early-morning meditation, back with the nuns in the cathedrally quiet chapel, I returned to the same image.

I could still sense the swirl of discordant emotional charges coalescing into a hurricane of distress, and I settled once more into the center of the storm, into the eye of grounded awareness. Though I could envision the foggy whirlwind before me—sleet pelting the pounding waves in windswept angles—the eye was a space of untroubled resilience. With an inner strength swelling from someplace within me, I could face the typhoon and observe its features with a confident sense of inquisitiveness. As with the rage-demon before—befriended into the wolf-escort, Gubbio—I had the intuitive sense that the storminess served some life-promoting purpose, and that the various emotions shrouded within it came as allies promising some form of companionship on my journey toward healing. With poised expectancy, standing imaginatively in the still, dry eye of the storm, I parleyed with the downpour before me.

I queried the storm about the reason for its ferocity, and waited for a disclosure. I invited the various emotions generating the storm to emerge from the spray and let themselves be known, then waited some more. I asked the storm for guidance, to reveal for me the route to take to find the truth that I sought. I needed to wait no longer.

That is when she came.

Emerging from the gusty mists, walking across the water as Jesus was reputed to have done on the stormy Sea of Galilee, a young woman approached me. I am not sure how I knew it, perhaps the numinous quality that permeated her, but she was different from the personifications of my various psychological states. She was a being from another realm—a divine figure, clad in a white gown, her dark features unmistakably Jewish. Not knowing if she was a spirit guide, an angelic emanation, or merely an hallucinatory trick of my mind, I could see in her eyes that she had known suffering in its most barbaric form—some blend of Rachel weeping for children dashed on the rocks; the young mother Mary fleeing with her baby as innocents all around her were slaughtered; and Etty Hillesum tending the sick, sharing her food, and comforting the grief-stricken in the Holocaust concentration camp that would kill her. Over time, I came to call the figure Shekinah (shuh-KEE-nuh), the feminine presence of God within the Jewish tradition whose power is compassion, and whose glory sits undulled with the lost, the soiled, and the desolate ones still weeping in our world.

I asked her who she was, and she said that she was a manifestation of the divine, not God in God's fullness but an embodied particle like a hologram of the holy. I asked her where she came from, and she said that she dwelt at the sacred source from which all waters flow into our souls. I asked her what she did there, and she said that she tended to the wounded there, that she mixed her tears with theirs. I asked her why she was there with me now, and she said that she had come to take me to the source of my soul's waters.

She explained to me that the waters that were surrounding us were actually tears, my *tears—all those within me that have not been shed, an ocean's worth of buried pain longing to wail in lustral lamentation. They swell into an all-engulfing tempest, and whip me about in its gusty violence, but the storm's intent is merely to get my attention, then direct me toward the source of my suffering. Her words were both validating and galvanizing. The suffering that I carried within me felt like it*

*could fill the Pacific, and I ached to know the wounded wellsprings whose unap-
peased weeping still fed it. I asked her what that would look like.*

"Follow me," she said.

*As if belted with deep-sea diving weights, we dropped below the water's surface
and descended, for some time, through miles of pitch-black depths until we arrived
on the ocean floor. I sensed a vast topography of underwater canyons concealing
enough caves and secret passageways to promise endless possibilities of places to hide
thousands of fathoms from the light of day. In one such passageway, in the cliffside
before us, a young boy, battered by life, cowered in the shadows.*

"Who is he?" I asked Shekinah.

*"An outcast," she answered. "A thrown-away street urchin, fending for himself
in this underworld darkness."*

*Something about him awakened a paternal care within me. I took a step
toward him. He jerked back, recoiling into the darkness out of sight.*

"Why is he ducking away from me?" I asked Shekinah.

*"He is afraid of you," she replied. "He thinks that you are ashamed of him—
that you banished him down here, then turned your back on him forever."*

*A pang of guilt confirmed the truth in her words. But tenderness now replaced
the shame. "You're right," I called to the boy in the darkness directly. "I did banish
you here. But it was only to keep you safe—in the only way that I knew back then.
I am not ashamed of you—not in the least."*

*His silence might have signaled that he had disappeared into the tunnels that
interlocked the caves in intricate stealth. He hadn't. From within the darkness, he
spoke.*

"I've been waiting for you," he said. "And you never come."

*The sting of his words deepened my care. "I really am sorry that it has taken so
long," I said. "I am here now. And I am here to stay." He absorbed my words, longing for them to be true, terrified that they may not be. I reached out further. "I
would like to know whatever you have seen," I offered.*

*"I've seen it all," he said. Then he added with a hint of puckish pride, "I know
every inch of these depths. That's what I do—I explore all the secret places."*

"Would you be willing to show me?" I asked.

*"Yes," he said, somewhat tentatively. "But not yet. I have to be sure that you're
not ashamed of me."*

*An abandoned boy longing for me at the bottom of an ocean of tears? I was as
far from ashamed as compassion is from callousness. "How can I help you be sure?"
I asked him.*

*With the timidity of one beaten for ever baring his face, he eased an eye from
the shadows to see me more clearly. It glistened with cautious hope.*

*"It's okay," I reassured him. "I really am here now. And I really will give you
whatever you need."*

He poked the rest of his head out from the darkness and weighed my every word. Then, when his desperate desire out-scaled his tired trepidation, he darted. Like Justin had in the hospital—and countless times since then—he ran, ran, ran into my arms where I wrapped him up in the warmth of my embrace. Shekinah looked on, the sacred energy of her caring presence surrounding us and fusing with the love coursing through me as I embraced the boy. The divine flow of love felt so restorative, I immersed myself in the warmth of its rush.

When I emerged from that morning's sit, I was the only one left in the chapel.

MY SKEPTIC KICKED in later that morning. After journaling it all in meticulous detail, I subjected the encounter to critical scrutiny. In the light of rationality, it seemed so bizarre. How could I be sure that this was not just an imaginatively inventive defense mechanism—an elaborate spiritual bypass to shield me from a painful reality? And was it even healthy to surrender myself to such an entrancing process—was I opening the door to an invasion of unconscious forces so dangerous that I risked a psychotic break from reality?

I needed to get my bearings a bit with a walk in the redwoods or sitting beside the sea's surf before giving myself to another meditative journey. I got in my truck and followed Sister Veronique's meticulous map to the site of Merton's dream hermitage. I parked at the end of a dirt road and hiked the half mile to the location. Sitting among the trees where he would have built a small cabin, I gazed upon the ocean pounding the rocky coastline and pondered my doubts.

Scrutinizing them, there in that grounding landscape, I could not help but sense that my second-guessing cross-examination did not ring true. I had had agency throughout the meditation. At every point in the midst of it, I had been capable both of bringing it to an end and impacting its direction. Furthermore, the prayer had opened my heart to pain, rather than harden it in avoidant defense. And the imaginative journey restored my psychic functioning; it did not undermine it. I emerged from the meditation more grounded, more aware, more emotionally and spiritually expansive. In the brighter light of the truth of my experience, the contemplative encounter felt extravagantly consoling. With the solidity of the rocks withstanding the relentless crash of the waves, I decided to continue the journeys—but limit them to one a day. I returned to the monastery, ate and slept, and in the early-morning silence returned to the chapel to join the nuns for another meditative sit.

SHEKINAH APPEARED AS soon as I invoked her, and we descended through the depths to the same ocean floor. The boy was there waiting.

He said that he wanted to take me somewhere—to the source of the waters within my soul's sea. He explained that the ocean within me was fed by rivers and tributaries that coursed through canyons from hidden headwaters. The inverse of dry land, where rivers flow downward from the mountains to the sea, these waters flowed upward from the deepest regions of the psyche. He led us down a ravine forged by a stream that we followed like discoverers in search of the wellspring of the Ganges. At points, we climbed down cliffsides into chasms, descending ever deeper into the darkness, alongside cascading waters that flowed upward.

"Notice," the boy pointed out. "They're not 'waterfalls.' They're 'water-rises.' They flow up from the very bottom."

Eventually, we reached the bottom. We dropped down to a still pond nestled in a grotto of absolute quiet. We sat beside the pool, against walls made of a tough but moist tissue, and rested in the hushed calm. I asked the boy how, with the headwaters so still, they could flow upward to feed the sea above us.

"Watch," he said, and pointed to a section of wall behind the pond. As if the wall were a living organ, its soft membrane contracted—receding and opening up into a deeper chamber—then pulsated back closed as it released a wash of fluid into the pond and up through the "water-rise."

"Come on," he said, "I want to show you. This is where I feel most at home. I come here and sit for hours."

With a seasoned ease, he approached the wall, with Shekinah and me at his side, and waited expectantly. When the membrane contracted once again, we slipped inside the deeper chamber—this one also, though much more expansive, with a pool of water and walls of moist tissue.

Somehow I knew at once that, with the womb-like warmth that pervaded and the palpable presence of tenderness and care, we were in the sacred center of the universe. Without using words, the boy communicated that this is where all suffering is received and grieved. We were inside the heart of God, the One who holds all the world's pain and weeps with everlasting sorrow. Her tears seep through the lining of these walls like a compassionate condensation that drips into the pond, fills it up, then pulsates out into the person's soul to mingle with their own tears already there.

As he shared all of this, I peered into the shadows that stretched into the heart's interior. Children, in pain, their numbers too many to count, were rocking in the crevices. Some of them, I recognized: Justin, sleepless from the stab of his parents' separation; Cathy, a disremembered young girl dreaming of a love both true and enduring; my dad, a boy abandoned by a father that not even God could replace; my mom, only six years old, caved in on herself after a visit to her stepdad's bedroom.

As is her way, Shekinah slipped over and tended to the children. I stayed with the boy and watched. The sight of the children's suffering—both those that I could see, and the abused, battered, and bullied that I could not—moved me so much that my eyes teared up in my prayer. Perhaps they mingled with the tears, even then, filling up the pool within God's heart.

I leaned into my heart as it softened, even toward those against whom I most often harden myself, until it dawned on me. One boy was missing from the children that I gazed upon. I was not among them. When I turned to the boy with my realization, I discovered that he had moved. He was lying in a crevice of his own, hunched over and holding himself. When I knelt down beside him, he looked up at me. Then he put into words that which had neither been named nor fully comprehended.

"I am you," he said. "And this is where we belong. Everything that you feel, it is true. The terror that recoils every time that you are touched, the sensory sensations that your privates have been violated, the nauseous certainty that you were a plaything for your mom—it is all true. It is the truth of your experience."

As he said it, I knew that he was right. It was a relief to admit it. "Yes, I was molested. I do know depths of pain that yield an ocean's worth of tears. It really is all true."

But the relief of validation gave way to pathos for the boy. He was looking at me with pleading eyes. Then he added, "And I am the one who carries it all."

My heart, already softened, broke open for that boy. I lay down beside him and held him in my arms. Shekinah came over, her sad eyes confirming the truth that had been spoken. "I will be with you," she told me, "as you grieve and heal. But it all starts here. In knowing that it is true. And in knowing that all of it is held in the heart of compassion."

I pulled the boy closer. His chest pressed against mine. Our hearts were beating as one. As one with each other, and as one with the sacred heart in whose beat we were nestled. And as steady as the love that sustains the universe, the wall of membrane contracted once more, then pulsated out into me.

THOUGH THESE JOURNEYS seemed suspect from the outside—something you would think was psychedelically induced, something Carlos Castaneda on LSD might dream up—being on them felt extraordinary. The depth of at-oneness with sacred presence, the soulful expanse of poignant compassion, the energizing vitality surging within me, the truthful power of the fictive images—all were so compelling that I continued the adventures throughout the week at the monastery.

On one such adventure, we returned to the sacred heartbeat and, with the boy in my arms, Shekinah swaddled us in the baby blanket from which we had been so abruptly weaned as toddlers when our parents tossed it into the fireplace right before our eyes. On another, Shekinah took us to some sacred pools, ringed with wimpling waterfalls, where all the world's children, now healed and whole, splashed and played with abandon. And on yet another, the boy took us to where he slept at night—a burrow hidden in the darkest tunnel of the darkest cave in the darkest canyon to be found, where he snuggled a rubberized toy Gumby that I had long since forgotten from our childhood.

On the last day of my retreat, during early-morning meditation with the nuns, the contemplative dives took a turn. Shekinah, once more, came when beseeched and took me down to the ocean floor. The boy was there but nervous. This journey would be different. I assured him that I would be with him through anything that he wanted to show me, that I would hold him with protective care in whatever way that he needed. By then, the boy trusted me. With him leading, we set off.

We negotiated a labyrinthine web of canyons and rocky descents, the cliff-sides camouflaging hundreds of cave openings, each one a passage into another boy's pain, each one with that boy, hidden in the shadows, peering out with hope to witness for themselves what was about to happen. After navigating the convoluted network of ravines, we stopped before a cave opening as nondescript as all the others. The boy gazed into the mouth at a darkness as deep as an abandoned mineshaft. He seemed to be gathering his courage.

"You don't have to do this," I offered.

Gathering enough, he said, "I do."

He walked us into the passageway, and we drifted down through the interminable darkness until we ended up in the living room of my childhood home in South San Francisco. The house was vacant. With the fireplace cold, a dusky chill pervaded the place. The boy had become me at three or four years old. He was naked but for his briefs and was huddled on the floor in the corner shivering.

"Something happened here," he said. "Something I want you to know."

From outside, the music of an ice cream truck could be heard in the distance, slowly getting louder as it neared. In terror, the boy started and glared at the window. "Please," he implored. "No. Don't let the ice cream truck come. Please, not yet. Don't let it come."

I do not know how, but I made the music stop and the ice cream truck disappear. I found a blanket and, sitting down next to him, I wrapped him warmly. He leaned into my embrace.

"I can take you away from here," I told him.

"No," he said. "I want you to see. Just not yet." I pulled him close. "There's more of us, you know," he added.

"I do," I answered.

"We all want you to see," he said.

"I will," I assured him.

"In time, though," he added.

"I understand," I said. And I meant it.

Safe enough for now, his chest against mine, he drifted into sleep. Shekinah, standing by, wrapped the whole room in a warm, golden light—a protective bubble of healing presence holding us in sacred care. The boy rested in my resolve to be with it all however it needed to unfold. As I held him, I noticed that the bubble's walls were perspiring with tears. Compassionate waters were seeping through and bathing the boy and me in their warmth. When we were soaked thoroughly, the bubble pulsated. The tear-steeped waters flowed out and into the back rooms of that house, and into the camper parked out on the street, and into the bedrooms to come in Foster City, and on into every cave and crevice hidden in the cliffs of my soul.

I knew.

I would be following those waters soon enough.

THAT EVENING, IT was my turn to pass a note to Sister Veronique. Leaving early the next morning, I asked for a few minutes after vespers to bid her farewell. Once we prayed the day's final office, we sat on the planked bench near the chapel's wall of window. It being dark, the pillared altarpiece of redwood trunk was swallowed in the night's shadows, the glass's view now limited to the single flame of candlelight reflected on its surface.

"So, you will be leaving in the morning," she confirmed.

"Yes," I replied. "I'll be heading out early—before morning meditation. It's a long drive and I need to get back in one day."

"You have much to get back to, I guess?" she asked.

"I do," I admitted, not yet ready to face all the work that was waiting for me. "Plus, my son is way past ready for me to be home. A week is a long time."

"Ah," she understood, "it will be gut to be with him again."

"It will indeed," I said, wondering if she harbored any regret at never having had children of her own to return home to.

"So, tell me," she inquired, "how was your retreat?"

"It was amazing," I said. "I could never have imagined all that has surfaced this week. I will be praying with it for some time."

"And in the silence, did you hear your word from Gott?"

I smiled at what we now shared. "Something better," I said. "I heard her heartbeat."

She showed no doubt that the divine that she knew would come through. "And the truth about the pain?" she asked.

"You're right," I answered, as one who now knew. "The heartbeat knows all about the pain. That is the path to healing."

"Gut," she said, as if her job were finished here. "I will be praying for you." And I knew that she would.

She looked ready to retire, but I had one more thing that I wanted to tell her. "Before I go, Sister Veronique," I said. "I want to thank you—for everything: your guidance, your presence, but most of all, for your kindness. All week, your caring gestures have touched me deeply."

She nodded with understanding. "Well," she said. "One thing I know. Kindness does not take the pain away, but it can keep the spirit alive while going through it." She paused as her words echoed down to places that needed a reminder. Then she added, "It may be the only thing that does."

The Shekinah presence, tending the wounded ones within me, was keeping my spirit alive even as we spoke. "I am very grateful," I said. "More, maybe, than you know."

"Very gut," she said, knowing the more, no maybe about it.

With it time to turn in, I thanked her once more and told her that I hoped to see her again. She assured me that this was not a goodbye, that our paths would cross again—on this side or on the other. Then, as was her way, she bid me God's peace during the night and made to leave.

"Oh," I said, suddenly remembering. "One more thing. I'd love to spend a few minutes in prayer before I leave in the morning. Will the chapel be open that early, say, around five?"

She answered as if bestowing a final blessing upon my leaving. "Your prayers are always welcome here. Anytime. Day or night."

That would have been benediction enough.

I COULD NOT have foreseen the kindness about to come. But with its ability to keep one's spirit alive, I should not have been surprised by the resuscitative power with which it would impact me.

With a long day ahead, I awakened earlier than I had expected. I washed up, tidied the cabin, packed the truck, and arrived at the chapel at a quarter to five. Sister Veronique had already been there to light the candle beside the chair on which I prayed. The halo of flame a portal into tranquil presence, I dipped into a brief meditation—more to soothe my feet in the contemplative waters than to take another full dive. When I opened my eyes, I savored my final few moments in the chapel's palpable quiet. The words that were about to seep into the silence did not come from God—at least not directly. They came from Sister Veronique. Slipping up behind me, with more than a trace of mischievous pleasure in her voice, she whispered into my ear, "Breakfast is served."

A bit bewildered, I followed her—not to the dining hall, but past it, through the metallic double doors, and into the monastery's kitchen. On the counter, as prepared for me as the Passover meal awaiting the astonished disciples, a spread was laid out worthy of hosting our own storied seder—several varieties of bread for toast, with as many canisters of homemade granola; opened jars of jam already planted with serving spoons; fruit ripe from the garden, both lush in a colander and sliced on a plate; an array of lunchmeats and samples of cheese fanned in rows on trays; juice squeezed fresh into a glass; organic coffee brewed in the pot; a bowl of boiled eggs; a pitcher of milk; a dish of nuts. And for dessert, I saw baked goods pillaged from the pantry—an assorted selection of scones, muffins, and slices of coffee cake enticingly bundled and wrapped in cloth in a handmade wicker basket. With all that to feed us, we could have feasted for hours, sharing stories of our liberation from the captivities of cruelty.

Sister Veronique leaned against the drainboard and sipped her coffee, as pleased as a great-aunt from the old country who insists on stuffing every guest that comes by. To her delight, I ate what I could. She refused to let me rinse out my dishes, pressing me to get on the road and take advantage of my early start. To be sure that I was provisioned for the long drive back, she brought out a bagged lunch, the size of a small backpack, that she had already assembled and set aside in the fridge. Eager to divulge its contents, she unfurled the grocery sack and pointed out what she had packed—a couple of sandwiches on artisanal bread amply piled with sliced turkey; lettuce and tomato in a separate plastic bag; fruit keeping crisp in another; cut vegetable sticks in yet another—finger-lengths of carrots, celery, and cucumber—with a bleu cheese dip poured into a cup sealed with wax paper and rubber bands; a can of smoked almonds; boiled eggs in tin foil; salt and pepper in plastic thimbles; paper napkins folded and stacked; a sprig of rosemary to keep it all fresh; and a bottle of Belgian beer with the stern directive, "Only for when you make it back home."

She started to fold the bag closed, then stopped.

"Oh," she exclaimed, "we must not forget." She whisked across the kitchen, clearly enjoying her run as a homemaker, to a tray of cookies straight out of the oven. Deftly wielding her spatula, she slipped eight or ten into a paper bag, then hustled back.

"They have been cooling," she explained as she added them to the lunch sack. Then she eyed me with glee at the decadence of the treat and reveled, "Chocolate chip!"

By now, I was overwhelmed. "This is all so incredibly kind," I stammered. "Thank you."

"Ah," she said, "every young man deserves to go out into the world well fed—food for the body, and food for the soul."

Wanting to salute the abundance of her care, I offered the most truthful words that I could think of, unwittingly unveiling the fanciful longings of the orphaned one within me. "Sister Veronique," I said, "you would have been a great mom."

She received my words, whether from him or from me, and replied with a smirk, "Who says that I'm not?" Both he and I heard her.

Time for me to go, I embraced her goodbye, picked up the lunch, and made for the door. Before I slipped through, she stopped me. "And don't forget," she offered as her final words of consecration. "What you found at the monastery, it is not here. It is in you." Then confirming precisely where in me it was to be found, she placed her hand on her chest. The heartbeat of sacred care—be it hers, God's, or my own—is found within. It stays with us wherever we go. And with that, having given all that she had, she patted her chest twice like a heart's single beat, then turned to attend to the tasks at hand—putting away the food, cleaning up the dishes, and freshening herself up before slipping back into the rhythm of that day's morning prayer.

I got in my truck and drove into the darkness. I made it about a mile down the road. The reason for my meltdown was sitting in the seat beside me. Like a sacrament, it symbolized the whole in the everydayness of its elements. A simple sack lunch did me in.

I have no recollection of my own mother ever making for me a single bag lunch. Not because I have repressed the memory, but because my mom simply did not have it in her. The maternal gene—the one that gets expressed in putting together a meal, baking treats, and sending your child into the world well fed—had been, if not obliterated, then beaten to the point of inaccessibility during her years of suffering sexual assault. She left her children to mother themselves.

When we stood beside her bed each morning, before we left for school, she scrutinized the lunch bags that we had made to take with us. A single slice of paper-thin lunchmeat was all that was allowed in our white-bread sandwich. An apple and one store-bought cookie could accompany it. The cookies, of course, were the true contraband. But if we ever tried to sneak out with extras, pilfered in our pockets or knapsacks, she would know. She kept count of all the sweets stashed away in the cupboard. And if a single cookie ever went missing, she would stand us in the kitchen corner, once we got home, and take a wooden spoon to our backsides until the culprit fessed up. The tragic truth is that she was too unfed herself to be able to feed her children, either in body or in soul.

The grocery bag beside me—filled with its effervescent affection—stood in such striking contrast to the love-starved lunches of my childhood, it pierced me to the point of tears. I sobbed so hard that I had to pull over, barely out of the driveway from the haven of silence that I had just left. The schoolboy inside me, hiding out in one of those underwater caverns, was now shedding his share of the ocean of tears with both grief and with gratitude. He wept at the ache of never having been mothered, of missing out on a mom whose care was as generous as that of Sister Veronique. And he cried at how resuscitating a single act of kindness can be, even when it comes decades later. For the first time in his life, that young schoolboy had been lavished with love from the feminine divine. For that, he wept. And I wept with him.

It really was so basic, and yet so recuperative: a note in a breviary, a bowl of soup for a weary traveler, a cushioned chair for prayer, a lit candle in the darkness, a breakfast buffet, a bag lunch, and freshly baked chocolate chip cookies. With simple acts of everyday care—both mundane and extravagant—Sister Veronique incarnated the loving presence that restores a depleted heartbeat. For me, she pulsated as one with the sacred. She was an icon that cracked me open to the restorative truth. Even in pain, Shekinah kindness keeps the spirit alive.

The cookies were gone by the time that I reached the highway.

UNFORTUNATELY, SHEKINAH WOULD not have long to wait before her kindness would be requested once again. Just north of Petaluma, not yet halfway through the drive, my Datsun pickup overheated. I pulled onto the shoulder, let it cool, then limped into a grimy auto shop barely on the rural edge of town. It took the mechanic there but five minutes to pronounce my truck's demise. With all of the symptoms of a blown head gasket—on a vehicle already gasping at 320,000 miles—the repair was not worth the expense. Now stranded over four hundred miles from home, I used the shop's landline to reach out to someone on whom I knew I could count. I called up my little sister.

"Hey, Linda Lu," I greeted with a casual chumminess. "It's your favorite brother calling."

"Yeah," she played along without missing a beat. "Which one? I have three favorite brothers."

"The one who would drop everything in a second if his sister ever called him in need."

"Okay, I get it." And she did. "So what do you need? Jim? Or is it Richard?"

"Very funny," I said. "But really, what are you doing for the next few hours?"

Linda was living in Oakley at the time, on the outer boundary of the Bay Area and at the edge of the Sacramento River Delta. Using the backroads that bypassed San Pablo Bay, it was an hour-and-a-quarter drive from her house to Petaluma. I asked her if she would do me the favor of coming out and fetching me, then taking me down to the Oakland airport where I could catch a flight home that evening. Like I would be for her years later, she was on it in a heartbeat.

"I'm leaving right now," she said.

Thirty minutes later, the mechanic found me in what passed as his waiting area—the grungy chair next to the washroom with an end table covered with tousled old car magazines. Taking pity on my predicament, he had spent some more time with my truck. Replacing the coolant, administering some sealant, and jury-rigging the radiator, he told me that he could get me five hundred more miles out of it—enough for me to make it back home if I then promptly ditched it in a wrecking yard. For his time, his additives, and the use of his phone, he would only take twenty dollars—a far cry from the price tag for a last-minute flight to Ontario. I paid him, thanked him profusely, then sat in my truck on his potholed lot. With no way to contact her, now that she was well on her way, I waited for Linda to arrive for the rescue operation that was no longer necessary.

She pulled up in her Isuzu Rodeo—butterflies stenciled to the rear window—with a thermos of coffee brewed and an overnight bag in her back seat. Instead of taking me to the airport, she was planning on ferrying me the whole way home, then driving back up by herself the next day. When I told her about the mechanic's patch-up job, she suggested that she follow me in case I didn't make it. I had needlessly troubled her enough as it was. Assuring her that I would call if I needed the help, I offered instead to take her out for a meal—a quick bite at a hole-in-the-wall down the road famed for its tuna melts and chocolate shakes. We caught up while we waited for our food.

"So where are you heading home from?" she asked, once the waitress left with our order.

"I was on a retreat in the redwoods just south of Eureka," I told her.

"That's funny," she said. "Kyle and I have been talking about moving to Eureka. PG&E has a plant up there and we thought he could ask for a transfer."

"That would be quite a move," I said. "Why Eureka? Surely PG&E has plants all over the place."

"To be honest," she said, "because it's far away. I need to do what you did—get a long way away from all of the drama."

Of all people, I could understand. I could also see how the weariness was wearing on her. "Is there any new drama?" I asked. "Or just the same old stuff—not that that's not enough."

"Oh, there's new drama," she shared. "Mom caught Stepdad having an affair with an old girlfriend from Chile. She went through his bedroom and found their love letters hidden under his bed. She snuck them out and got somebody to translate them from Spanish. When she got them back, she threw them in his face. He stormed away; she threw his things out into the street. Now he's filing for a divorce and moving back to Chile."

"Wow, who knew that it would come to an end like that?" I said. "But it's not like there's any love lost between them—they've hated each other for years. They were only staying together because Michelle was still in school."

"Oh, Mom's way past hate," Linda went on. "You should hear how she tears into him, how she can't believe that she's put up with him for all of these years—his temper, how he locked himself in his bedroom all the time, how he was more married to Michelle than he was to her, how he and Michelle forced her to live alone in her own house ever since Michelle was born. Michelle says that she threatened him with a carving knife when he came back for some things. Of course, it's not like he didn't have it coming. I mean, we know—we had to live with him too."

"He was a hard man, that's for sure," I said, still oblivious to the clues, in hindsight, laid out so clearly. "What a pair. And with Michelle now in college, Mom really is alone."

"Believe me, I get an earful of that too—how nobody really cares about her, everybody just leaves her, the people that she's given everything to who just cut her out of their lives."

I could feel the barb hurled at me even delivered through a friendly intermediary. "I'm sure that I am on that list too," I acknowledged.

"We all are," she said consolingly. "But, yeah, she goes on and on about how she doesn't know why you won't talk to her, won't let her see her grandson, that she's sure you must be saying all kinds of horrible things about her. I don't know what's going on between the two of you. I'm sure you have your reasons for staying away from her; I can think of my own. But she's as upset at you as she is at Stepdad."

"It's complicated, Linda," I admitted. "I'm not out to hurt her. It just got to the point where it was too crazy-making to be around her. There are a lot of secrets in our family. A lot has happened between Mom and me, some things that nobody knows about. I just need some space to get a grip on it all."

"Do you plan on ever talking to her again?" she asked. "Not that I'd blame you if you don't."

"Sure," I answered. "Without a doubt. We have some things to set straight. But in time. When I know what I want to say. And I can say it and keep my sanity." I smiled as if half-joking at the last part. I wasn't.

Linda looked down and stirred her shake with her straw as if pondering her own soundness and considering the potion that promised to preserve it. "Well, believe me," she said to the shake. "I know all about how crazy-making it can be." She did not say that she also knew all about family secrets. Some that we shared. And some of her own. "And that's what I need too," she continued, "space away from it all. I really think that it's time that I move to some place far away." She sipped from her straw, then set her sights. "I hope Eureka will be far away enough."

It took twenty years to find out for sure. But it turned out that it wasn't. However far away we go, the secrets have a way of finding us.

BY THE TIME we walked out to our cars, the cloud of our family's craziness had receded. Linda was sunny with impish good humor. She teased me about my rust-eaten jalopy. She couldn't believe that I still had it, as it had been on its last legs a decade earlier when she rode in it during her weeklong visit to New Jersey. I informed her that the jalopy had journeyed with me, through every condition of weather, to all four corners of the country, and had yet to let me down. She raised her eyebrows as if it was about to, then wished me well on its final road trip.

Before I left, however, she had something for me to take along on the ride. She ducked into her car and retrieved a bin of her homemade cashew brittle. Knowing how much I loved it, she had brought some for us to share on the drive. Touched by her thoughtfulness, I thanked her and assured her that it would be thoroughly enjoyed. She also pulled out a gift bag, which she offered with a prankish grin.

"Here," she said. "I was going to save this for your birthday but I couldn't wait. I'm sorry I didn't have time to wrap it." I peeked inside and pulled out an eight-track tape, an antique copy of Barry Manilow's *This One's For You* album. "I know how much you love him," she added with a dig. "Now you can listen to him the whole way home."

"Barry Manilow?" I said with appropriate derision. "Right. I seem to recall that you were the one with the junior high crush on the guy."

She pretended to be offended and retorted, "I never had a crush on Barry Manilow."

"Oh yeah?" I pressed. "You were the one with the dreamy poster of him on your bedroom wall. I used to make fun of it."

"I don't remember that," she fibbed. "I just remember you singing his music all the time. You could never admit how big of a fan of his you really were."

I chortled at how preposterous that was. "I was never a fan of Barry Manilow," I made clear.

"No?" she egged on. "What about the times—when you were home from college—and Mom and Stepdad would be out somewhere, and Rich and me would play his record on the stereo that Stepdad said was off-limits. And you would come in, pretending that a turkey baster was a microphone, and sing 'Looks Like We Made It' like you were performing for us in Las Vegas, with your arms all stretched out, flashing some dorky dance moves, and then you'd say, 'Wait for it. Wait for it . . . Key change!' And you would belt out the ending at the top of your lungs, '*Looks like we made it!!!*' If that isn't a fan, then I don't know what is."

"Are you kidding?" I came back. "I was making fun of that song. Of all of his songs. They were all the same thing—some sad ballad, build it up, then a key change, and the whole orchestra kicks in for the big finale."

"No," she insisted. "Nobody pretends that good. You loved that song. You loved Barry. You just didn't want to admit it. After all, you were the one that did make it. You got out, and didn't have to deal with Mom and Stepdad anymore."

"That's not even what that song is about," I protested.

"You would know." She smiled slyly. "You're the Barry fan. Besides, maybe for us it was."

I let that pass by, still bemused that I was actually holding an eight-track tape of Barry Manilow. "Well, I promise you," I forewarned, "I will see that this gets the attention it deserves."

"If nothing else," she said, "it'll feed your addiction until your next concert. I know you go to them all—to be with your hero."

I just shook my head. "Linda," I told her directly. "There is one thing that I can assure you of. You will never find me at a Barry Manilow concert."

She smirked like she knew better.

So began the running gag that was to play out for years. Each holiday, we traded the eight-track tape in elaborately disguised Christmas gifts, even though neither of us ever owned an eight-track tape player nor seriously listened to Barry Manilow music. With the advent of cell phones, we texted each other pictures of Manilow posters or album covers that we stumbled upon while out somewhere. And voice-mail recordings bore ubiquitous allusions to the secret musical obsession of which we accused each other: "Oh, you must be out. I guess Barry's back in town." Or, "Just wanted to let you know that your birthday present is in the mail—two tickets to 'A Very Barry Christmas.'" Or, "'Mandy' just came on the radio and, of course, I thought of you."

I never foresaw that the playful banter would prove to be prescient, that my disdainful protestations would turn into crow-eating standing ovations. A few months after Linda's death, Alane saw the advertisement—"A Very Barry Christmas" was coming to the LA Forum. We brought Linda's picture, donned her favorite cabbie hats, and took our place with the other enthusiasts. It seems that his songs were able to touch me to the core after all. I cried the whole way through the concert.

That musical discovery, however, was still years away. Holding that eight-track tape for the first time, Linda was very much alive.

"Well, thanks for the birthday gift," I said, then got in the last jab. "I know how hard it was for you to part with it."

She ignored the poke and hugged me goodbye. "Call me if the jalopy breaks down along the way," she offered. "I'm already packed and ready to go."

"Thanks for that too, Lu," I said. "I really do appreciate you coming out to help."

"Of course," she said. "Anything for my favorite brother."

WITH BARRY RIDING shotgun, I made it home just fine. A few months later, Linda followed through with her designs. She and Kyle bought a house and moved to Eureka. I sent her a housewarming gift. An eight-track tape. Barry's signature song was the fourth selection: "Looks Like We Made It."

And I hoped that she had.

Claremont, CA—Age 38

Fall Semester 1996

———◆———

I AM FIVE years old. I rush into our apartment straight from the bus that dropped me off from kindergarten. I am eager to find my mom. That evening, she is taking my brother Jim and me to see "Mary Poppins" at the movie theater. To be able to stay up late on a school night, I had promised to take a nap as soon as I got home.

Jim, three years old, is already napping in his bed. I walk to my mom's bedroom. The door is ajar. I walk in. She is in her bathroom, toweling herself off after stepping out of the shower. She calls me over. Dropping the towel at her side, she says, "Give your mom some lovin'."

I embrace her. My face presses against her naked belly.

"Are you excited to see 'Mary Poppins'?" she asks. I nod. "Good. Let's get you ready for your nap."

She pulls off my shirt and unbuttons my pants. I am still wearing my pajama bottoms underneath my trousers. I was so excited that morning, for the evening outing ahead, that I had forgotten to take them off before dressing for the day.

My mom laughs, then teases, "Look at my big boy—wearing his pajamas to school. Here, let's get you out of them." She slips them off, my briefs off with them, then says, "Come, it's time for your nap." She lifts the covers from her bed and we slip underneath them. She cups me from behind. She presses herself against me. Her hand slides down to my penis. I feel myself stiffen. I wish she would stop. But she doesn't see that. She pulls me closer, moves her hips, and strokes me until . . .

The clapping brings me back to the present. I am in a partitioned hotel ballroom at an academic conference on practical theology. A paper has just been presented on "The Philosophical Foundations of Faith Development Theory."

I look around the room and want to scream, "*Who the fuck cares about the philosophical foundations of faith development theory? Don't you know that there are children being molested in their own homes? They're right in this room, for God's sake! What are the philosophical foundations of being fucked by your own mother?*"

I want to. But I don't. Instead, I politely applaud with the rest of my colleagues.

THE CHALLENGE IN going away on a retreat is returning again to the world. What seems so clear in the light of the sanctuary's tranquility becomes blurred and buried within the pressures back home. Staying centered in one's mountaintop certainty within the lowlands' daily bustle is like seeking to sustain one's inner stillness in the middle of Times Square. Or for me, like trying to stay clean while sloshing about in a sewer. Like stink rising from excrement, my day-to-day routine reeked with my soul's secret filth. It was hidden behind the mask of my public persona, but the stench was still there and the foulness revolting—for any who had the nose to smell it.

LIKE MANY SEXUAL-ABUSE survivors, I lived by the fierce imperative to present a façade to the world that was unblemished by the stain of my debasement. To be sure, it is only socially proper that, within the various contexts of our lives, we play our roles wearing some measure of a mask that is sanctioned for the scene—a papier-mâché public face that filters and screens the more shadowy impulses that simmer within all of us. For me, however, the mask was steel-plated. Less papier-mâché and more armor-metaled. And one that I cinched and scoured to keep free from any noxious disfigurement. God forbid that a colleague, or even a bystander, get a glimpse of the furies and miseries that consumed me. Goddamn to hell anyone who so much as gets a peek at the sordid fantasies that played out inside me. And God condemn me to the coldest circle of Hades before a single person surmised that I had been sexually molested, that I was soiled to my core, goods damaged beyond repair. The look that I would get—be it pity or disdain—would have been unlivable. So I concealed the truth of me behind an ironclad persona and spotlessly inhabited the part of the dutiful academic.

I taught my classes in practical theology fields and met with students to fine-tune dissertations. I attended conventions of several professional associations and symposia on the future of theological education. I participated in collaborations and grant-funded projects to promote lives of faith in succeeding generations. I chaired faculty committees and school task forces envisioning curricular reform and sustainability renovations. I led workshops at conferences and lectured at churches on spiritual formation and religious education. And throughout every second of it, I barricaded against breach the passions and preoccupations that privately laid in wait as I compliantly went about doing my work.

They did not wait quietly. At times, they would seep to the edges of my guard poised to slip through my white-knuckled restraint—a lurid fantasy from my childhood flashing me back while I was supposed to be listening to a lecture, or a senseless impulse rising within me to drop into a conversation with a coworker that I happened to be an abuse survivor. Other times, it seethed and smoldered to the brink of eruption—a rage, for example, in the midst of a curriculum debate that wanted to burst out and inquire about the relevance of requiring ancient Greek in a world where children are sodomized and raped.

At such times, Rabbi Irving Greenberg, the post-Holocaust theologian who posed the challenge to religious intellectuals everywhere, spoke my truth: When the slaughter of innocents can still play out in modern-day death camps, he implored, "No statement, theological or otherwise, should ever be made that would not be credible in the presence of burning children."

As far as I was concerned, children were burning all around us. They were certainly in flames within me. And in the presence of those furnaces, nothing in my work-life felt credible anymore. Business carried on as usual, pretending that the children were just fine, and I played along with a smile, pretending that mine were dandy as well. And yet, I would sit through committee meetings on grading rubrics, or paper presentations on post-modern hermeneutics, wanting to rip apart my academic façade and scream the truth of my experience: *There is evil in our world, goddamn it. I know it in my cells. And all I really care about is uncovering the truth of it and keeping my soul alive while facing it.*

Coming out from hiding, however, and being honest about who you really are, runs the risk of being met with repulsion and banishment. And it is hard to expect another to embrace you when you are still struggling to embrace yourself. The ability to hold with care the truth of your being must come from within. In the end, no one can give us what we cannot give ourselves.

In the safety of my home each evening, the mask would come down. I would scribble and vent in my journals or soothe myself with abuse memoirs and Holocaust portrayals—depictions by others who knew evil firsthand and dared to tell the truth about it. Then to prepare for the next workday, I would get up early and try to meditate with my emotions. More times than not, I was searching for an image that encapsulated the mounting fury that I anticipated at a meeting or a consultation on that day's agenda.

One image came often. I frequently felt like I was a cast-iron pressure cooker bolted and soldered tight, the substance within it boiling and building to the breaking point. Terrified of the impending explosion, I vigorously polished the pot as if the shine itself could prevent it from blasting. In the privacy of my own inner prayer chamber, I could step back and let it blow.

The lid flew off with the force of a volcanic eruption, the stewing substance within spewing and splattering in all directions, then gushing from the pot as a never-ending river of molten mass with enough force and fury to eventually cover the earth. The substance was not lava. It was excrement. Shit was flowing from the pressure pot within me in an unending stream of fecal defilement.

Once my repugnance relaxed, I let it flow. When it subsided to a trickle, I peeked into the pot. As if I were peering through a manhole into a sewer, I saw a young boy crouched in the darkness, sitting in a pool of waste. He had been so covered with shit, for so many years, it had soaked into the tissues of his being. He was soiled to his center. Stained beyond cleansing.

Sometimes, I just sat with the boy. Sometimes, I wiped him down and bathed him. And sometimes, Shekinah would come and hold him in a rinsing embrace. But every time, once the prayer was over, the lid would return and clamp down in place. My face mask would strap itself back on. And I would return to the stage of my workplace costumed in my professional disguise.

And nobody would know about the soiled boy still stewing in the sewer.

AS GRACE WOULD have it, the boy did have one person who saw him in his plight—the only human being at the time in whom I confided, mask and all.

When Cathy and I filed for divorce, the court appointed a local psychologist to evaluate our mental fitness before ruling on a custody arrangement. After several batteries of tests and private consultations with all three of us—Cathy, Justin, and me—he made his recommendation to the judge: joint custody with equal visitation rights. Cathy and I were so impressed with his perceptiveness into our individual psychological maladies, his insight into our convoluted relational dynamics, and his unwavering ability to offer genuine understanding to two persons as polarized as us, that we asked him if he would continue to counsel us after the divorce was settled. Helen had retired and I was without a therapeutic replacement. And both Cathy and I were determined to work out our relational conflicts at least enough that we could co-parent Justin without inflicting onto him our resentments toward each other. He agreed—not to counseling us together, but to offering us each individual therapy concurrently. The best thing that we could do for Justin, he suggested, was for us each to work through our own personal issues. We consented—and so began a therapeutic relationship that would, for Cathy and me both, last for over ten years.

Dr. Mark Reaves became much more than my psychotherapist. He became my vocational counselor as I explored career paths that promised purpose and vitality, my stalwart defender as I bore witness to the horrors of the atrocities yet to be revealed, the enthusiast in my corner celebrating talents and capacities as they were birthed within me, and the unflinching advocate for the truthfulness of my inner experience however it was expressed. A depth psychologist by training, he had companioned enough souls through the underworld of trauma that he could testify with confidence that the darkness would lead to the daylight of healing. If my path was that of Dante—finding both God and well-being by going through the hell of one's pain—then he was the Virgil who guided me.

It did not take long for him to find out how sordid the terrain would be in our journey through the inferno of my interior landscape. I caught him up on the whole sleazy affair—the chronic depressions and desires to die that sometimes consumed me, with the attacks of rage that wanted to kill; the backstories of my mom, my dad, their marriage of rampant promiscuity, and my grandpa Harold's brutality toward girls; the onset of my breakdown when my mom, right in front of me, tried to kiss my infant son's penis. I told him of my tailspin through nightmares and invasive visions that pierced my consciousness with their lurid images—my mom mouthing my own infant penis, me napping nudely in my naked mom's bed, my grandfather raping me from behind in his camper, his shaft in my mouth too big for my hands. And I finished with the trajectory of my still neophyte recovery after nearly driving my truck off a cliff—my stints in the hospital, my time in the padded room, my trying to will my way into remembering the truth of my past.

In his gentle way, sitting on his leathered office chair with me slouched on the couch across from him, Mark received all that I offered him with an imperturbable composure, a sobered understanding, and an unwavering affirmation of the validity of my experience. He had an unshakable trust that the psyche's fundamental instinct was life-promoting, and that the emotions, impulses, and physiological sensations that it generated were not only rooted in genuine experience, they sought in their own way to secure survival and well-being.

"We feel what we feel for a reason," he continuously maintained like a mantra. "The body knows what the mind forgets." He cautioned that the psyche does not always communicate literally; its images may be symbolic. But the images and passions within us are not random. They come from some place of pain that yearns to be healed. The memories proper may be slow in coming—they cannot be forced. So we hold with empathic curiosity whatever the psyche does offer, in whatever way that it offers it.

I, on the other hand, was not nearly so trusting. I insisted that I knew the difference between a memory and a fantasy, between truth and fiction, between something that really happened and something that my mind was concocting. In the absence of concrete recollections of actual assaults—at that point, I had not even remembered being molested by the priest—I took my symptoms and obsessions as evidence of how psychologically sick that I was. I also was formed in a religious tradition whose dogma about original sin, total depravity, and the intrinsically carnal nature of our bodies and their appetites suggested that I was sinful to the core. If nothing else, some people are just fundamentally flawed, I would counter. That was the truth of my experience. I was one of them.

During one such back and forth, near the beginning of our therapeutic odyssey, Mark asked me for an example of this difference between truth and fantasy that I so insisted upon. He wanted to know what my earliest memory was, one that I actually remembered as being real. If he had designs that the recollection would confirm his notion of the psyche's impulse toward wholeness, he would be disappointed. It only reinforced the pervertedness of which I was capable.

My earliest memory was a recurring nightmare that tormented me for months when I was three years old. It was as vivid as the first night that I woke up screaming for someone to come in and save me.

I am sitting, naked and alone, on the floor in the living room of my childhood home in South San Francisco. I hear, outside, music from an ice cream truck coming toward our neighborhood. I climb onto the couch to look for it from out of our front window. A green truck is parked on the street with a full-sized camper mounted on its bed. Two monkeys are holding the camper's back door open, waiting as if poised to spring a trap. Two more are in the cab, grinning at me, and revving the engine to drive me away. And two more are hiding in the bushes below the window, just out of sight from the front door, where they are ready to pounce whenever I come out.

I hear a knock on the door. I don't want to go, but some force compels me. As I open it, a swarm of monkeys attacks—from the porch, the bushes, and charging behind me from the back rooms of the house. I try to run away but I cannot move. I try to scream but I cannot speak. They grab me and drag me to the edge of the camper's back door. A bullish monster is inside waiting for me. I am ballistic with terror but my body is paralyzed, as rigid as a shaft. The monkeys hoist me above their heads. I hear grunting and snarling from the beast in the camper. Then, like a lamb being heaved into its slaughter, they thrust me into him. Before the beast can ravage me, I wake up screaming.

"That's a real memory," I attested to Mark, gearing up to prove my point. "I remember that dream vividly—the shrieking when I would wake up, my dad running into my bedroom, the pleading that became a part of my bedtime routine every evening. 'Please, Daddy, please,' I would beg him each night when I refused to go down before seeing him. 'Don't let the monkeys get me while I'm sleeping tonight.' That is all real."

"I hear that," Mark affirmed. "It sounds terrifying. Especially for such a young child."

"It was," I agreed.

"And being so chronic," he continued, "it must have symbolized some experience. What associations do you have with a green camper, or a bullish monster, or with monkeys, for that matter?"

"Yes," I said, not conceding, merely maneuvering from behind. "I've thought about it a lot. My grandfather has always reminded me of a bullish beast of a man, radiating pure evil. And he drove a green camper when he came to visit us. And I remember that he had one of those plaques above the bed in his camper, of the three monkeys—you know, see no evil, hear no evil, speak no evil. But that's as far as I get. It doesn't mean that anything bad really happened to me in the back of my grandfather's camper. It's only a nightmare, not a memory."

"Perhaps," Mark said cautiously. "Dream images are symbolic."

"Exactly," I continued, drawing my smoking gun, my body quivering with revulsion even just thinking about it. "And do you want to know how sick I am? This is what I do. I start imagining what might have happened in that camper. And once I start, I cannot stop. It's like I'm being pulled into the scene and caught in my own nightmare. I picture him at the foot of his bed, taunting me, 'Oh, you're mommy's big boy, are you? I'll show you how big you are.' And I imagine him putting his hardened penis right into my face. And it's too big—my hands can't even hold it. But I can feel it right there. I mean, I fucking want to gag. Then he turns me around, I'm already naked, and he rapes me from behind. But again, he's too big to enter me, so he comes between my legs.

"And Mark, I can feel it all down there as if it is all really happening—my anus hurts, my skin is burning, there's wetness between my legs. And all I can see are those asinine monkeys with their hands over their eyes, and over their ears, and over their mouths. And I want to explode with shame and fury. But I just stand there and I let it happen. Then he turns me around and says, 'So who's big now, momma's boy?' And I just look at him and stare, until he flicks my penis with his middle finger and says, 'This never happened. Do you hear me? You speak one word of this and I will kill you. I've done it before.' I'm telling you, Mark, I feel every second of it. In my mind, in my body, in my soul, as if I am reliving something that I can remember in detail. *But, Mark, I am making it all up! It is not a memory. It's a disgusting daydream! And I let myself experience it for no good reason. It's like I'm abusing myself through my grandfather. What kind of a sick person would imagine such filth like that, and in such vivid detail?!"*

"A traumatized person," Mark said, with a gravitas of compassion that had no doubt that my fiction was somehow truthful. I pursed my lips and glared at the wall, twitching to dissociate from the repugnance I had just retched. "I don't know what happened to you," Mark continued. "But something did. The body does not lie. It may not be a memory, but it is your experience. An experience that is screaming to be heard."

Mark was all ears. My monkey hands were still covering mine.

AND SO WE crossed the river Acheron—my grandfather Harold, not Charon, the ferryman—to survey the Hades of my past and encounter whatever sufferers and devils were hidden in the ditches along the way. My quest was to make my way into the center of the deepest shadows where whatever evil I had known was lodged. And not only to discover its true face, but to stare into its cold eyes—glazed frozen from the foulness—and not be calcified by the enormity of the chilling horror that I found there. I longed to know both the truth of my pain and the heartbeat that could pulsate with hope and resilience even in the face of it. The route that we took was far from linear. We meandered our way, back and forth, through various regions of the past and the present. We advanced through openings of insight when they presented themselves. And we paused before walls of resistance that blocked us—our wandering guided by whatever my psyche was offering us at the time.

In some sessions, we sifted through fragments of genuine memories—the time that my mother tried to kiss my son's penis, or the times that, as a child, I showered with my mom; napped nude with her in her bed; lay in my own bed as she caressed my chest; or sat in our living room, my head in her lap, her hand slipped into my shorts as she stroked the tender tissue of my bare behind. In other sessions, I played out, in pornographic detail, the fictive daydreams that sucked me into their mesmerizing pull—my mom mouthing my infant penis; my mom pleasuring herself while cupping me through our naps in her bed; me interrupting my mom with my grandpa, and she using me as a toy to appease him and to keep him away from me.

Sometimes, I sat through an entire session lost in wordless despondency. The acuteness of the pain, the intensity of the aloneness, the depth of the pit in which I was mired—all of it immobilizing me in a tomb of simply wanting to be dead. Other times, I stormed in ranting in a rage, piqued at the masquerade that I was trapped in at work, furious over a reproving voice mail from my mom, or stewing over the times that my mom dismissed me from her bed with disgust, as if I were a plaything to be disposed of after a john had been satisfied.

And often, my body took over our time together—an hour of me shivering uncontrollably at the vision of me cowering in my childhood living room, naked and chilled to the bone; or sobbing irrepressibly at the brutal reality that, as a three-year-old, I already knew evil from the inside; or flicking my fingers into the air while shuddering and twitching at the sensations of violation seeping into my privates like a stain demanding a reckoning.

Regardless of which circle of hell we found ourselves in during our weekly descent into my soul, and no matter what behaviors were on display in the ditch of that day, Mark and I could both be counted on to stay in our respective characters. Mark, the wizened companion and guide trusting the soul's unfolding in whatever way that it expressed itself, would meet it all with a nonplussed curiosity—his caring presence, neither judging nor intervening, itself testimony to the pulsating life-force that holds and heals all things.

And me—who, at some point, would step back from the horrid spectacle on exhibition that session and gaze upon it with perspective. Unlike the pilgrim poet, however, who would absorb the appropriate spiritual lesson from the scene that he had just witnessed, I would fume with exasperated desperation and insist to Mark that none of it made sense, that I was feeling things for no sane reason, that we still lacked proof that anything egregiously abusive really did happen to me by either my mom or my grandfather—the things that I could recall at that point not adding up to outright molestation.

And Mark, with Virgilian patience, would hold that as well.

ALTHOUGH THE PATH meandered, it was slowly descending. And though it often felt like we were eddied in the same cul-de-sac for months, at some point the ground would shift and an opening would appear that pointed us in a promising new direction. One such reorientation felt like something of a rumble at the time. I had no way of knowing that it was more like a subterranean earthquake rearranging the tectonic plates on which my entire life was being lived.

It dawned on me that the predominant impasse that was then keeping me stalled was the unrelenting insistence that my feelings had no basis in reality—that with the absence of actual memories of out-and-out molestation to provide proof to the contrary, the fantasies and bodily sensations and obsessive suspicions were all made up, rooted in my own perverted self-deception, not in any real pain that would explain it. If my feelings were a lie, they had to be scorned and purged. My repudiation of them sealed off any avenue to their source. Since the repudiation itself was the prevailing energy that possessed me, I decided to meditate with that—testing the limits of the hypothesis that all psychic states, even ones as self-negating as this one, were, in their own ways, allies for healing. If nothing else, personifying it could offer a brief respite from its dogged clutch within me.

AS I SIT *in my chair and turn my gaze inward, I invite the unrelenting insistence that my feelings have no basis in reality to personify itself. The image that comes to me is that of a determined sentinel standing guard at the foot of a mammoth dam. From the stench, it is clear that the dam keeps at bay an ocean's worth of excrement. I am standing at the base as well, splattered with scanty splashes of waste—soiled by the fantasized surmisings that I obsess over.*

The sentinel looks at me with disgust and voices the words that I use to excoriate myself, "You're covered in shit, but the shit has no basis in reality. You're making it all up. There is no real pain to explain it."

In the meditation, freed from its grip at least momentarily, I know better. I cannot see the particulars, but I know that the shit on me has leaked from the ocean of shit on the other side of that dam—from that hidden sea of assaultive fantasies and feelings with the untold numbers of children swallowed in its filth.

I query the sentinel. "You're saying," I pose, "that this shit on me came from nowhere—that it is just self-induced." He looks at me less like he is caught in an obvious lie, and more like he is weighing how much to disclose to me. "You and I both know," I say, with undeniable certainty, "that there's an ocean's worth of shit on the other side of that dam."

Still tentative, he concedes as much, "Yes, there is an ocean of shit over there."

"And the shit that I am wearing," I press, "is not self-induced at all. It came from the shit that really is over there."

"Of course, it did," he admits. "I'm the one that splashed you with it."

This takes me aback a bit. "Why would you do that?" I ask.

"I am the regulator," he reveals. "I want you to see all the shit that is over there. I want you, eventually, to transmute it all. I modulate how much comes out at a time, and when."

"Then why," I struggle to understand, "would you berate me that I'm making it all up—that there's no real pain to explain it? That ocean is filled with suffering that is real."

"To keep your attention where it needs to be," he divulges. "I don't want you looking at that shit right now. Or at the suffering that is hidden within it. I need to know that you can handle it first. If you can't deal with the little bit that I leak to you now, you won't be able to deal with the ocean of it that's still to come. That won't be good for you, and it won't be good for the children that are hidden in its depths."

I can sense the shift that is shaking up the ground of my perception, but it has not given way to a solid clarity quite yet. "So you're saying," I advance, "that I need to believe the fantasies that I am having even though I do not know if they are really true?"

"I'm saying," he corrects, "that you need to accept the truth of what you do already know. The truth of your actual experience right now."

"And what is that?" I ask.

"That you are doused in shit without knowing why. You don't know for sure if you were molested or raped or fondled. And if you were, you don't know by whom— your mother, your grandfather, maybe somebody else. But you do know that you feel like you were. That is the truth of your experience. You experience the world as one

who feels violated. You grew up as a child who felt like he was assaulted in a camper. Even if it did not happen exactly the way that you imagine it, that you even felt like it did is crushing enough. I need you to hold that child with pathos and compassion before I can trust you with the others in the sea of shit that I am guarding."

And with that, the opening appears, with solid ground leading me through the passageway that it offers. I understand what he is saying. I do not know the details of what, if anything, happened to me, but I do know what I feel. I am a man tormented with sensations of assault. I was a boy whose body felt like it had been raped in the back of his grandfather's camper. Whatever was historical, that I felt like it is the truth. For the first time, I hold that—the truth of my experience. I accept, with tenderness, the sensations of my soiling.

I am not the only one. I do not see her, but I feel her presence. Shekinah's compassion sweeps over me like a cleansing wash. And the shit that I am wearing is turned into golden light.

THOUGH I HAD taken a step on the path toward accepting the truth that I was feeling what I was feeling, I was far from ready to expose those feelings to the world, truthful or not. I continued to don my armored mask of the academic professional in public, even as the soiled survivor in me grew increasingly resentful of having to hide what wanted to be acknowledged and held. The survivor asked that I stop playing pretend—that I trust my experience, embrace my feelings, and live with authenticity from the inside out. The armored mask insisted on keeping up appearances—looking clean and securing external approval even at the cost of going through the motions of work that had lost its meaning. The survivor was caged, fighting to break free after a lifetime of captivity, while the mask added locks to the steel-plated doors certain that living truthfully would only be met with contempt. With one boiling to bust loose and the other doubling down to subdue, it was only a matter of time before the one forced the other's capitulation, or the other broke through in a daring bid for freedom.

That time came when I went up for tenure.

IN THE ACADEMY, tenure is the holy grail of both job security and peer approval. Colleagues from inside of one's institution, and across one's academic discipline, evaluate whether one's scholarly contributions are sufficiently plentiful, and of a high enough quality, to warrant a permanent professorial appointment. For me, it was the courtroom in which the effectiveness of my professional façade would be assessed. While a tenure approval would only reinforce that my armored mask was well polished, a tenure rejection would confirm that the stench it kept hidden had seeped through enough to repel my workmates from wanting to invest anymore in my future. I was convinced that my academic merits were not on trial; my personal worth was. And in the "publish or perish" world of higher education, it would all come down to my writing.

For the fall semester before my spring tenure review, my school granted me a research leave to bolster my application. The dean confirmed that, while my teaching evaluations, my commitment to school governance, and my contributions to the church and the wider community were all outstanding, my publishing record was mediocre. The reality of the situation was that I had not written a word in the two years since my return from my medical leave. She surmised that I could probably secure tenure on the basis of my writings before my hospitalization—several peer-reviewed articles, a couple of book chapters in edited volumes, a few essays in church publications, and a handful of book reviews—but it would be a marginal tenure. She strongly advised that I use my sabbatical to complete a textbook on religious formation that I had talked about since I had begun teaching. The armored mask in me assured her that I would. The subjugated survivor said that it would be over one of their dead bodies.

The two of them waged war with each other throughout the entirety of that semester-long leave—each of them both creative and devious in the stratagem that they employed to advance their agenda. The survivor would distract me from the textbook by absorbing me in abuse memoirs and Holocaust theologies searching for both a credible God and resources to stay spiritually vital in the face of evil and suffering. The masked academic would castigate me for wasting away my writing time. He would insist on keeping a schedule—eight hours a day at the desk—where the survivor fought back with a writer's block so severe that the day would not yield a single word. The armored professional would resort to panicked exhortation—"Just write the damn book; what is wrong with you?" The survivor would counter that the book was meaningless—despicable in its antiseptic irrelevance given all the pain in our world.

Meditative forays offered a few moments of reprieve. In one, I imagined myself sitting at my desk looking over my shoulder after each word that I wrote to see if my dean was still scowling at my production. Shekinah came and replaced my dean with Sister Veronique, who kindly encouraged me to write from the heartbeat within, from the real source of my personal truth.

In another, I pictured my writer's block as a young eaglet yearning to soar but mired in a tar pit, its wings heavy with pitch. The tar pit wanted the eaglet to dive rather than soar—the pitch inviting the bird to sink into the soulful depths where the source of truthful writing is found.

And in yet another meditative foray, I personified the conflict as a circle of colleagues surrounding me at my desk, snapping whips and entreating, "Just write the goddamned book. It's time. Why are you wasting away all of your potential?" Underneath the desk, a young boy is cowering—the same boy from the sewer, from the dam, and from the underwater caverns on the ocean floor of my soul. I ask my colleagues to leave and I sit down with the boy. Soiled in suffering, he says to me, "Please don't make me do anything that I don't want to do." I assured him that those days are over. Writing this book or not, he will not be hurt again.

The contemplative respites, however, were only temporary. After surfacing, I still found myself at my desk, pressured to produce a book, yet paralyzed by my inability to write it from the truthful depths within. The soiled survivor was dug in—if its truth could not be expressed, then nothing would be. As the weeks withered away, the masked professional was forced to give up. The textbook was not going to be written.

And that was the end of my sabbatical.

Except that, as if the universe were throwing out a consolation prize, an opportunity arose, in the final weeks of my leave, that appealed to the academic professional inside me. The opportunity also captured the attention of the soiled survivor. The latter saw a chance to express some of its truth. The academic's concerns would prove to be right. Once the survivor started speaking, it would not be satisfied until all the truth of its experience found a way into the world.

LATE IN THE fall, I received a phone call from the dean at the University of Judaism—now American Jewish University—in Los Angeles. He had heard me speak at a regional conference on religious education a few weeks earlier, where I had been asked to lecture on the spiritual lives of children and had begun my presentation with some memorable remarks. The day before the lecture, the *National Catholic Reporter* had printed a story of how the Milwaukee archbishop had written to then Cardinal Ratzinger in Rome requesting a canonical trial for a priest accused of child sexual abuse. The priest, Lawrence C. Murphy, had admitted to molesting over two hundred boys while teaching at a school for the deaf in Wisconsin. The Vatican did not respond, and Father Murphy would spend the rest of his life neither defrocked nor criminally charged. With my own priestly sexual abuse still buried but rumbling under the surface, the article so incensed me that it took an entire afternoon of power walking through the foothills to calm myself down. To appease my outrage, I opened my lecture with the quote by Rabbi Irving Greenberg. And I voiced that I hoped that my remarks would be credible in a world where children were not only abused, the flames of their suffering also burned on unatoned.

The dean was calling to invite me to attend a dramatic performance at the university and to serve on a panel afterward. The play was a one-person show, entitled *From Bubby to Bet Yam*, written and performed by a Jewish actor, Steve Greenstein. The play chronicled the actor's relationship with his haunted Belgian grandmother who had, during the Holocaust, hidden his mother—then a young girl—with a Catholic family in Antwerp, survived several years in Auschwitz, then returned to retrieve her daughter and emigrate to New York. The dean asked if I would present a short scholarly overview of the Catholic church's role in assisting Jews during that diabolical time. The budding truth-teller in me could not resist.

My remarks were brief but pointed. While I acknowledged that the lives of hundreds of thousands of Jews were saved by the heroic efforts of individual Catholics, the church itself was still in need of a moral reckoning for its complicity in the slaughter of six million Jews. The concordat in 1933 that legitimated the despotic Nazi government that had just claimed power; the silence of two popes spanning a decade while Jews were mysteriously disappearing; the anti-Semitism that seeps throughout the tradition, including papal bulls that dispossessed Jews of their property and established Jewish ghettos long before Hitler did; the continued church teachings that God has rejected the Jews and that Jews are Christ-killers guilty of deicide—all of this conspired to sustain the ideologies and policies that allowed the Holocaust to happen. As but one Catholic communicant, I wanted to apologize for the pain that my church helped bring to a people, and I hoped that the Vatican would one day do so as well.

Virtually no one in that Jewish audience had ever heard a Christian acknowledge so forthrightly complicity in their historic suffering. For many of them, my words of admission, rather modest coming from a lone layperson, offered some of the solace that comes from a moment of reparative truth-telling. One of those people was the actor himself—Steve Greenstein. Steve came up to me immediately after the discussion so grateful for my words that he asked if we could have dinner sometime to discuss the restorative possibilities of truth-telling art. I had already been moved by his poignant and compelling performance and told him that I would be honored to share a meal together. So began the collaboration that not only upended the trajectory of my vocation, it launched a new season in my recovery.

STEVE, STRUGGLING ACTOR that he was, did not own a car. He asked if I would pick him up, before our meal together a few days later, at the community center in South Central Los Angeles where he had been hired for a part-time gig. He was working with a dozen or so teenagers in an after-school program using the dramatic arts—both the creativity of playwriting and the spontaneity of improvisational acting—as a means for empowering young people to find their voice and express themselves artistically. Over the course of his program, he would invite them to create fictitious characters that, without them fully realizing it, symbolically embodied their experience, then craft and perform an original dramatic production that conveyed the emotional truth of their lives to their friends and community. The plays were, of course, works of narrative fiction.

But in telling their fictive stories, they were transforming their experience into art that told their truth.

Intrigued by the work that he was doing, I drove over early to observe his afternoon session. I sat, inconspicuously, in a folding chair at the back of the rec room and watched across the tiled floor to the school stage at the far end. Steve was up on the stage where he had scattered, on the floor, an assortment of random objects—a baseball mitt, a mirror, sunglasses, a CD case, an empty McDonald's cup, a bottle of aspirin, and the like. The teens were sitting in a semicircle around him as he began the day's class.

"I heard a story once," he discoursed, "about Jeff Goldblum—you know, the actor from *The Fly* and *Jurassic Park*. Somebody once asked him why he loved acting so much. He said, 'If I'm in a subway and someone steps on my toe and says, "Sorry," I say, "It's okay, no problem." If I'm on the stage, however, I can jump up and down in pain, scream at them to watch where they're going, step on their toes just to get even, or curl up and sob like a child.' That's what the stage is. It's one place in the world where you can be real, where you can be free to explore anything that you might happen to feel. We can't do that anywhere else—not at school, not at home, not even with our friends, usually. But here you get to express it all and discover the ecstatic rush of being emotionally alive.

"Acting is the exact opposite of what most people think it is. It is not faking to be someone that we are not. It's not putting on a mask and playing some role that hides our true feelings. That's what we do in real life. Rather, it's taking imaginary scenarios—characters and storylines that are entirely made up—and putting ourselves into them to discover what's emotionally real within us. It's not pretending to feel something that we really don't. It's being real with our feelings in the midst of something that is pretend. So, we are going to do an exercise in being emotionally honest with an imaginary character. I invite you to dig deep. Open yourselves to whatever feels real down in your gut. Don't censor it; express the deepest truth that you can imagine your character feeling."

He invited the teens to choose one of the objects on the floor and create a fictitious character of a teen in some kind of a crisis that the object somehow represents. To fill out the fictive circumstances, he gave them a series of writing prompts—questions to surface amplifying details of the character and their context. Then he had them write a brief monologue in which the character would disclose their name, where they are, what kind of trouble they are in, and within it, what their deepest fear is, and what their deepest hope is. After they had time to craft their characters, Steve invited the teens to step inside of them and, one at a time, stand up, face their thespian peers, and speak that character's imagined truth. He suggested that they do it while keeping silence in between each one. After a couple of moments of nervous shuffling, the litany of monologues commenced.

"I'm Maria. I'm studying at an all-night McDonald's. I'm in trouble because I want to go to college but I just can't understand algebra. My deepest fear is that I'll be stuck cleaning houses for the rest of my life like my mom. My deepest hope is to become an architect and build a house of my own—one so big my mom can come live and never have to work again."

"I'm Ahmad. I'm sitting backstage at a club. I'm in trouble because I'm a singer but I've lost my rhyme. My deepest fear is that my song will die inside of me. My deepest hope is that people will hear my music on the radio and treat me with respect."

"I'm Ramon. I'm at a park playing baseball by myself. I'm in trouble because my big brother is hanging out with some bad people. My deepest fear is that they'll become his best friends. My deepest hope is that they'll become my best friends too."

"I'm Alicia. I'm in my bathroom. I'm in trouble because I just want to die. My deepest fear is that nobody will care. My deepest hope is . . . I don't have one."

The monologues were so poignant—so emotionally truthful—that after the last teen had embodied their character, Steve silently gathered them in a closing circle. Making eye contact with each teen, going around one by one, he applauded, and had them applaud for each other.

"That was real," he said, obviously pleased. "You created imaginary characters and you told the truth about what they were feeling. People pay good money for that kind of emotional honesty. That's acting. Now, I want you to take those feelings and put them back into your art. Between now and next week, create an artistic piece, anything you want—a poem, a song, a drawing, a story—anything that expresses those feelings that your character is experiencing. I only ask one thing: that it be emotionally truthful."

He looked around the circle once more like a proud coach after a championship game. The teens beamed with the admiration. Then he had them shake all of the intensity off, leave it on the stage, and dismissed them back into their lives.

I was sitting on my folding chair watching the entire thing. For the life of me, I had never fantasized about being onstage as an actor. It had never even occurred to me to try out for so much as a school play. But a space where I could be fully real? Imaginary circumstances to explore my genuine experience? The invitation to honor my deepest feelings, whatever they were, and transform them into art whose fiction reverberates with my gutsiest truth? I had only experienced a handful of places where I could be truthful and where my truth was honored—in the padded room at the hospital, at the monastery in the redwoods, in my imaginative prayer excursions, in therapy—and here was a space where I could claim it publicly. As I spied upon those teens stretching their fledgling creative wings, I felt it awaken within me: if given the chance, I would say tenure be damned to be a part of that circle with them.

THAT EVENING, OVER French dip sandwiches at Philippe's, Steve expounded on his views about acting, the stage, and the artistic process itself. His theatrical mentor was Sanford Meisner—an acting teacher who impacted the craft as much as other great acting teachers like Lee Strasberg and Stella Adler. For Meisner, the essence of acting is not feigning to be something that we are not. It is about being completely real—what he called "living truthfully"—but under imaginary circumstances. We live truthfully when we are alive to our deepest, most authentic emotional experience. Too often, we flatten our emotional reality, and thus deaden our vitality, by suppressing it beneath the masks that we wear and the socially acceptable roles that we play.

The artist breaks through the numbing conformity to what's polite and conventional—takes an axe to the frozen sea within us, as Kafka would say—and accesses the primal passions that truthfully flow within their intestinal depths. The artist then harnesses that vein of raw emotion—the electrical current of vital energy that flows through us all—and makes art. No longer stifling their truest feelings, but also not merely venting them nor screaming them for them to be heard—acting is not acting out—the artist takes the raw material of their real experience, charges it with agency and purpose, and uses their particular gifts to transform it into artistic pieces that pulsate with vibrancy and authenticity.

The genius of the stage is that it offers an embodied and interpersonal space that gives artists permission to surface and externalize the vital depths buried within them—those that are processed in therapy, for example. Through stepping into fictitious characters and playing out fabricated storylines with other actors, artists discover and open themselves up to their own emotional vibrancy. By tapping into the creative vitality that flows deep within them, they become free to transform their experience into emotionally truthful art.

This is not only a path toward vibrant art; it is also a path toward a vibrant life. A living stream of creative vitality courses through us all like the subterranean current that flows fluidly under the ice of a frozen river. It is the life-force that infuses all things—that enkindles and sustains fullness and flourishing. It is the life juice that makes the rose blossom, the eagle soar, the orca dive and surface in a dance of breaching grace. It is the livingness that keeps life alive. This river of creative energy within us seeks to flow fully and freely through us, lifting us into the radiance of our own particular beauty. Like all species, human beings were made to bloom. Yet, as the poet David Whyte observes, we are the only species that forgets how. Blooming—living fully and authentically—is living artistically. It is being alive to our emotional experience—as the bard says, seeing the world feelingly—and crafting, with care and intentionality, ways of being that embody the deepest truth that pulsates in our being.

Living artistically is a spiritual path, as teacher and author Julia Cameron lays out. It is an invitation to plug into the current of vitality that crackles within us all and participate in its unceasing impulse to restore us to our splendor. When we do, we will find ourselves aligned with the universal life-force that suffuses all of existence, urging us toward life's flourishing. We will find ourselves fulfilling our God-given purpose. Drinking fully from this fountain of fecundity that flows from the very essence of the divine, we will become the beauty that we were truly created to be—we will be fully alive, and fully ourselves.

I DROVE HOME from dinner that night lit up like one who had newly glimpsed a paradisal world. It was a wondrous realm, which I had not known existed, where I could fully express precisely what I was feeling and would be judged only on how emotionally truthful I was. One that did not care a whit if the shit that I was expressing was historically rooted or literally true, only if it was intestinally honest. A realm that offered an arena where I could explore fictitious scenarios to discover my emotional truth and find artistic forms to transmute that truth into creative self-expression. A spiritual path of fictive creativity had opened up before me and I was ready to convert. To hell with the academy! I wanted to be an artist. I wanted to live artistically.

Like a devoted catechumen, I assiduously studied my new sacred text—Julia Cameron's *The Artist's Way*—and poured myself into its spiritual practices of journaling morning pages and going on weekly artist dates. I studied Steve's techniques for unlocking truthful self-expression and devoured the books on the reading list with which he so kindly supplied me. I started my search for artistic outlets where I could explore my emotional truth—narrative forms where I could live into stories that embodied my imaginative experience. And I took my first true artistic leap of faith. Having no designs on ever becoming a professional actor, yet wanting to know the liberative process from the inside, I enrolled in a one-year acting class taught by one of Sanford Meisner's last apprentices, John Ruskin.

On our very first day, John invited each student to stand on the step-high stage and share something truthful to the rest of the class. It need not be literally true; it only needed to be emotionally true. My gut immediately began to wrench. I knew the truth that wanted to be declared. It was intestinal. It reeked from my bowels. The soiled survivor inside me was wasting no time. While the others took their turn, as John called out their names from the roster that he distractedly doodled upon, I took the scat and crafted the words just right. John called my name. I walked up and took my place on the stage. I stood for a moment and stared at the audience. My glare looked like I was daring anyone to doubt the words to come. In fact, it was the heat transmuting the coat of shit that draped them. Then I told my truth.

"I fucking hate my goddamned mother. I hate her."

I held their stare. They held mine. Any doubts that they may have had about my truth were incinerated. They sat stock-still. From the corner of my eye, I could see that John was still as well—his head bent down toward the pen that had stopped mid-doodle. He glanced at me as if sizing up for real my emotional stability. Then he turned to the class and said, "Now that's truthful."

I was as stunned as John was. Who would have known that embracing fictiveness could yield the truth? Who would have thought that the stench of my defiled experience could be alchemized through artistic expression? My descent into the underworld of my trauma had found a new footpath. I did not yet know if my feelings of violation were historically rooted and literally true. But I did know that I could play the part of the violated with emotional truthfulness. I was not yet ready to expose to the world that I was a survivor of sexual abuse. But I was willing to step into the imaginary circumstance of it and express the experience with artistic authenticity.

Imaginary or not, I had embarked upon the path. I was an artist. And for the first time ever, I told the truth of my experience in public.

The soiled survivor in me was just getting started.

Claremont, CA—Age 40

May 1999

———•———

"THE TITLE OF my lecture this afternoon is, 'And God's Eyes Were Crying: The Church Responds to Child Abuse.'"

The Board of Global Ministries of The United Methodist Church had invited me to speak at their World Mission Conference spotlighting various crises around the globe. Some five hundred ministers and activists were gathering at a retreat center in Big Sur to renew their commitments to tend to the wounds of the world. I agreed on the condition that I could address the reality of child abuse. I am not sure that they knew what they were in for when they approved me speaking on the topic. In my talk, I cited the horrifying statistics: nearly three million cases of abuse and neglect reported each year in the United States alone, one in three girls sexually abused before they are eighteen, one in seven boys similarly assaulted.

I critiqued several time-honored teachings: the theology of original sin—that considers children to be inherently fallen, even proud-spirited and in need of having their wills broken; the child-rearing philosophy of "spare the rod, spoil the child" that has proof-texted the Bible to provide religious justification for children to be beaten; and the doctrine of sacrificial atonement. This final dogma, as Joanne Carlson Brown condemns, is tantamount to "divine child abuse" as it espouses a cold-hearted father, with a twisted sense of justice, so unwilling to get his hands dirty touching a soiled humanity that he sacrifices his son whose spilled blood somehow washes away all the wickedness in the world.

I told the stories, veiled in anonymity, of my seminary classmate sexually abused by her pastor father, then spurned by the church when she reported it, and of the Christian camp counselor in Cape Cod whose unatoned violation led him to set himself on fire in a car parked across from the summer camp's beachfront. I contended that some realities in our world are so piercingly assaultive that tears of wailing are the only credible response, howling with the weeping women of Jeremiah who cried for those who could not cry for themselves—that and the fire of outrage that unequivocally denounces abuse in any form and fuels prophetic action to transform the institutions that perpetuate it. Then I closed, cloaking some of my own story in a creative third-person redaction.

"A few years ago," I segued into my lecture's conclusion, "I worked as a volunteer with abused boys in a residential treatment center. I would come once a week to tell them stories and to invite them—through narrative prompts—to tell tales of their own. Something about the sharing of stories helped them feel known, even when the stories were time-worn folktales. One boy, Jason, so loved our time together that he designated himself as my assistant and shadowed me for as long as I was there.

"One day, when I arrived early, I found Jason sitting alone, staring out of the window in the corner of the community room, while the other boys played games. His gaze held the vacant stare of one absorbed in a distant scene both haunting and unabating. I wondered what stories were playing out there in the shadows of his mind's eye. I pulled up a chair beside his and stared out the window with him. If he noticed, he did not show it, his eyes remaining stony and fixed.

"After a while, I asked, 'What are you looking at?' The story unfolded as he watched it from afar. He recounted it with a reporter's detachment.

> When I was little, I used to make forts out of the couch cushions in my living room. I would hide in them and pretend that nobody could find me. One day, when I was barricaded behind the couch, I heard music from an ice cream truck outside. I knew it was bad—my mom told me to stay in the living room no matter what. But I wanted a rocket popsicle, the one like the picture on the ice cream truck door, with different colors and pointed like a missile. So I went to her bedroom and opened the door. She and this man were doing things on the bed. They didn't see me at first. But I kept standing there, hoping that the music wouldn't go away. Then my mom jumped up.
>
> "What're you doing here?" she asked. I told her that I wanted a popsicle. "Well, you can't have one right now," she said.
>
> But the man was staring at me real mean. "Oh, I think he should get a popsicle," he said. "That's what he gets for interrupting us."
>
> My mom looked at the man and started kissing him, and said, "It's okay, he'll go back to the living room."

But the man said, "No, he's going to get his popsicle. Come here," he called to me.

My mom thinks for a minute, and then she says, "Here, let me." She called me over to her. I thought they were going to give me money for a popsicle, like they said. But they didn't. My mom pulled me onto the bed, took off my clothes, and did some bad things to me while the man watched. Then the man pushed me away and they went back to what they were doing.

I lay there on the bed. I could hear the ice cream music going down the street. But I didn't feel like a popsicle anymore. I just stared at my mom's dresser. She had a picture of Jesus up above it. He was naked too, except for his privates, up on his cross. His head was bowed like he was dead, or like he just wanted to close his eyes to it all. But as I looked at him, hearing the ice cream music get further and further away, he opened his eyes and looked at me. He looked like he was real sorry, like he wished he could come over and help me, but he couldn't because he was nailed up on that cross. Like a dog I once saw who got run over and tried to crawl to its owner across the street, but just couldn't. That's how he looked at me.

And then he started to cry. His eyes filled with tears until they spilled out and dripped down his cheeks. And he kept looking at me, and crying, as the tears made puddles on my mom's dresser. And he kept looking and kept crying, the puddles getting bigger and bigger until they dripped off the dresser and onto the floor. And then the water came pouring out, gushing out of his eyes like a dam broke, filling the room higher and higher until it swirled around like a hurricane and smashed everything in the room, then crashed through the walls and flooded outside carrying me and Jesus down the street in a great big river of tears.

Except it didn't really happen. I was still on the bed and the man was all dressed. And he looks at me real creepy and says, "What a mama's boy." And he leaves the room.

My mom goes into the bathroom and leaves me on the bed. I couldn't hear the ice cream music anymore. But I could still see Jesus above my mom's dresser. Only his eyes were closed now. And he didn't cry. And I just wondered. And sometimes, I still do.

Where are those crying eyes now?

I wanted them to carry me away more than I wanted a popsicle.

"Where are those crying eyes now?" I implored the audience of church workers. "Someone summon the weeping women. As sure as violated children are a violation of God's very being, God's eyes are sobbing. The church's should be too. May all of our eyes be wet with tears. And may the flooding rivers of outraged compassion wash away all of the wickedness in our world, and carry us out to an ocean of grace where all wounds are healed, and all children are safe."

The crowd filling the auditorium gazed at me stunned. Each one was stilled into silence. The silence of staring into the face of horror. The silence of beaten impotence before it.

Until the music came. Rev. Bill Thomas, the worship leader, slipped behind the piano and fingered a few notes.

Sometimes I feel like a motherless child;
Sometimes I feel like a motherless child;
Sometimes I feel like a motherless child;
A long, long way from home.

The song took hold. The church workers took part. To the tune of an African American spiritual, they sang the tears of the violated children.

THE TWO YEARS following my creative conversion served as my novitiate into art as a means of emotional recovery and spiritual vitality. Determined to fathom the emotional truth within me, and to discover the creative forms in which I could express that truth, I threw myself into an array of artistic endeavors. I kept my day job, teaching graduate courses and attending faculty meetings, but I stole away when I could to explore a variety of narrative arts. I continued my study in the Meisner method of acting—first with John Ruskin, then with Fran Montano, and then a yearlong immersion with William Alderson, Meisner's right-hand man and associate director for over two decades in North Hollywood.

I took training intensives in Santa Monica on the theater arts as a means of personal empowerment and social transformation—plunging into Daniel Judah Sklar's brilliant approach to "Playmaking" that assists young people in creating their own scripts and producing their own plays. And I trekked to Omaha, Nebraska, for a weeklong immersion in Augusto Boal's revolutionary vision of the "Theatre of the Oppressed" where the stage becomes an arena for "spect-actors" to rehearse liberative agency within the social injustices of their community.

Recognizing my natural affinity for storytelling, I started collating the stories that I had told through the years, crafted new ones that felt emotionally truthful, and sought opportunities to flex my wings as a storyteller wherever I could. I told fables and folktales at local elementary schools. I put myself out there during open mics at regional storytelling festivals. I volunteered at a boys' home, both telling them stories and celebrating them as they told their own. And I partnered with a couple of musicians to create evening shows of stories and songs—one at a family retreat center in the remote Washington Cascades and another as a holiday celebration for friends and neighbors in Claremont. I also apprenticed as a narrative-arts educator facilitating for others what I sought for myself: I taught my son's third-grade class how to craft stories and share them at a storytelling festival for their school, showed his fifth-grade class how to write their own play and perform it at an end-of-the-year assembly, and mentored teenagers in a youth program how to do the same at a community center in Pomona.

During this season of immersive artistic exploration, I was driven by longings that felt essential to my survival. I ached to access my emotional truth, to discover and affirm the genuine feelings that emerged as I entered the imaginary circumstances that haunted and obsessed me. My emotional preparation for acting exercises entailed visualizing myself in scenes of abuse, as gut-wrenching as it was, before going onstage to improvise in character. The scripts that I wrote during playmaking intensives involved protagonists living with holocaust pasts in search of resources to keep their spirits alive while coping with their secrets. And the series of stories that I freshly crafted—some fictional, some historical—filled a collection that I called "The Cries of Burning Children," vignettes of various boys and girls whose tales of suffering are seldom told.

I also yearned to metabolize my truth—to find the narrative-art forms where I could transform the raw experience of my feelings into externalized creations charged with meaning and authenticity. Acting, playwriting, storytelling, creative writing, free-verse poetry—I was delving into them all, discerning which ones struck veins of vitality within me and quickened the gifts adequate to hold the depths of pain that surfaced. I was an artist in search of, not only my truth, but of the art form in which to express it.

And I longed to live truthfully—not only to be alive to my authentic experience and to craft that experience artfully, but to be in the world aligned with my truest depths, blooming, as it were, in the flourishing that embodied my unique beauty, and engaged in generative work that had meaning and purpose flowing from my vital core. I longed for a vocational life as animating as my closeted life as an artist.

This was where the streams of creative vitality met the polar winds that iced their waters into a hardened surface. For as enlivening as my artistic endeavors were, I was doing it all in my spare time. I kept at my job as an academic. While taking my mask off during my narrative pursuits, I was putting it back on again at work. No one in my professional life knew that I was taking acting classes and intensives on playmaking, let alone that I was using these art forms to explore my emotional truth around the imaginary circumstances of abuse and violation. As far as my colleagues were concerned, I was busily occupied as a professor. Though I increasingly detested stepping into the role, I kept on playing the part—teaching my classes on religious formation, serving on committees, attending conferences, and participating in collaborations. I faked my way through all of it seamlessly.

With one exception: I still was not producing as a scholar.

IN MY END-OF-THE-YEAR review, before the last summer research break of the millennium, my dean met with me to discuss my future. I had already been granted tenure after my last sabbatical. Even if it was borderline, my job security was not in question. The threat, however, was both to my professional reputation and to any future promotion. I had not written in four years; I had no discernible research agenda; and the long-awaited book that I had promised to produce, for all intents and purposes, remained a fantasy. She kindly volunteered to serve as my mentor, even as a writing coach. We could meet weekly throughout the summer to discuss my progress on the manuscript.

I thanked her and assured her that I worked best on my own. But I promised that, at summer's end, I would have either a full manuscript, or at least a detailed report of its development with a deadline for its completion. I kept my word. I did not come through with a manuscript, but I did come forth with a deadline. Its drop-dead date would come as some surprise.

BEFORE THE SUMMER for writing began, Justin and I had the opportunity for a brief visit to central Europe. The World Council of Churches had invited me to participate in a dialogue on theological education and the environment at their Ecumenical Institute in Bossey, Switzerland. I found that it was cheaper to purchase two tickets to Frankfurt, Germany, then rent a car and drive to Bossey, than it was for a single flight to Geneva. I made the pitch that I bring my fifth-grade son—single dad that I was—and we soon found ourselves gearing up for a road trip through the environs of Switzerland and southern Germany. We both had our must-see sites. Justin earmarked castles, medieval towns, and Lego stores with kits unavailable in the United States. I had a place in Bavaria that I wanted to experience firsthand.

After the conference in Bossey, we had four days to tour with only a vague itinerary to guide us. We drove through stunning natural beauty—Lake Constance, the Black Forest, the Bavarian Alps, and along both the Rhine and Danube rivers. We stumbled upon a spring festival at the medieval town of Rothenburg ob der Tauber and scurried through its still-intact Gothic city walls as if we were under barbarian attack. We soaked and splashed in family-friendly hot mineral springs at the spa town Baden-Baden, where royalty would come for the widely reputed medicinal value of the water. We took a guided tour through Neuschwanstein—better known as the Disney castle—and stood transfixed before Munich's Glockenspiel, the gigantic clock with life-size figurines jousting and dancing to the chiming of bells. We donned berets, shopped for Legos, and ate our fill of bratwurst and pretzels. Then on May 1, we drove northwest from Munich—a mere twenty kilometers—for a short outing to Dachau.

We arrived at the town midday. Neither of us had eaten since a small bite for breakfast, so we drove around in search of a place for lunch. Unbeknownst to us, May Day is a holiday in most of Europe—the ceremonial equivalent to Labor Day in the States. Everything was closed. Grocery stores, restaurants, corner delis; even street vendors had vanished to take advantage of the day off. The place nearly vacant, we made our way back to the main thoroughfare that connected the town to the workcamp memorial site. To our surprise, we came upon the only eatery serving food in the vicinity that day—Dachau's McDonald's.

With little choice, we stopped for Big Macs and fries, a chocolate shake for Justin, a Diet Coke for me, then drove not more than a mile to the first concentration camp that the Nazis ever constructed—the prototype for all the rest. The offensive vapidity had already struck me on that tiny distance to drive. What spiritual nourishment did we have to sustain us as we faced one of the horrors of human history? Globally commodified fast food from the fluorescently neoned Golden Arches.

To be expected, the pitifully anemic sustenance did not last long. As I walked through the iron gates—with *"ARBEIT MACHT FREI"* welcoming us—I immediately became nauseous. I felt like I was stepping into the real-life scene of a long-ago experience that I had thought was a mere nightmare. If I believed in past lives, I would have sworn that I had been there at the height of its brutality. If not, then I was at least channeling the pain of some ancestor in my bloodline, my cells suddenly sapped from the legacy of their unappeased suffering. We were in the presence of preternatural evil—and evil is not restrained by geography or generations. *Evil*, I remembered like bile in my belly, *is something with which I am familiar.* The acidic queasiness seething throughout, we walked the grounds without words. It was all as I could imagine it being, if I had lived through it myself.

The rows of barracks crowded and forlorn with the full gamut of Nazi undesirables—about a third Jews, the rest Poles, Russians, Slavs, Gypsies, communists, criminals, homosexuals, dissident clergy, disobedient Catholics, race polluters, the unemployed, the mentally disabled, and the all-encompassing enemies of the state. The bunkers hiding laboratories where medical experiments were performed—measuring how long an inmate could survive on a seawater diet, or in subfreezing temperatures, or in decompressed high-altitude chambers; and if, once unconscious, the victim could impregnate a fertile female subject. The crematorium furnaces—not as diabolically effective as the death factories in Auschwitz, but active enough to diffuse billows of ashes throughout the surrounding suburbs like snowfall dusting the landscape. The

SS quarters where off-duty officers pursued decadent pastimes to banish from their minds the atrocities to which they were party, and where they eased their stress by sleeping with the women selected for the brothel that they pimped for themselves.

And the religious memorials: the Mortal Agony of Christ Chapel with a copper crown of thorns rooftop; the Carmelite Convent of the Precious Blood with its cross-shaped compound bordering the camp; the Protestant Church of Reconciliation; the Orthodox Chapel, Resurrection of Our Lord; and the Jewish shrine with its candled menorah shining light into the darkness of near extermination. All of them were a symbolic presence bearing witness to a sacred reality that births life even out of senseless savagery, and yet their appearance posed a bitter, bold relief to the truth that none of them were there during the obscenities themselves. The causalities of Dachau died divinely abandoned.

My visceral sense of having been there myself, I knew, was not historically literal. I was not recollecting any previous internment in that workcamp, neither mine nor of one of my ancestors. But I was recognizing what it was like to be imprisoned in a sphere of unsurpassable evil—evil that is inescapable, continual, and interminable. The camp felt familiar because it mediated a confrontation with the holocaust horror that lived within me—a childhood where home felt like a deathcamp, neither God nor freedom in sight. At Dachau, I had the antithesis of a religious experience. It was a transcendent encounter without the divine, communion without the bread and the wine, a contra-sacrament: not an external sign of an internal grace, but an external sign of my internal agony. It was an encounter not with God, but with evil in its most devilish form.

Where is the food that sustains a stare into the face of absolute abomination? What meal strengthens the faith to look into the hollowed eyes of the emaciated and not cave into a despair that swallows you into its black hole as their bodies turn into ash in the furtive shadows of a deathcamp furnace? I walked out of Dachau with that question burning within me—the undesirables in me awaiting either the furnace of their abuse being discarded, or the faith that sees and resuscitates. When we arrived at our car, we found a flyer on the windshield. The Dachau McDonald's had a coupon in honor of May Day.

The fast food an obscene offense, Justin and I both vowed never to eat at the Golden Arches again.

THE DAY AFTER my seminary's commencement—the marker for an academic that the school year is over and summer has begun—turned out to be Mother's Day. I was hardly ready to dive into the textbook project that awaited me. Nor was I about to celebrate motherhood on this one day a year where, for sure, the abscesses of my maternal pain and bitterness suppurated toward the misanthropic. I wanted to be alone. Or if not, at least with one of my kind.

The Los Angeles County Museum of Art was holding an exhibition of paintings from the Van Gogh Museum in Amsterdam. The largest loan ever of the Dutch painter's artwork, the show promised to be one of the few in the world where so many of his pieces were gathered in one place. I had long been a devotee of van Gogh, moved both by his art and his life story. He was ravaged by poverty, scorned by society, rejected by the religious fanaticism of his family, and so debilitated by mental illness that he succumbed to the Dark Age terrors of a primitive insane asylum. And yet, he found it within himself to paint. Some creative spark kept pulsating within the cesspool circumstances of his life that not only sustained him, it compelled him to bring beauty into the world.

Of course, that creative spark could not carry him through the course of his natural life. At the age of thirty-seven, having sold but one painting—and that to his brother—Vincent took his own life. He shot himself with a gun used for killing crows out in the wheatfield that he had just finished painting. It took him three days to die, with the painting—his last—on the easel beside his deathbed.

The anguish of his last days reverberates throughout this obviously symbolic and cryptically self-revealing final work of art. A hauntingly troubled storm of a sky threatens a pregnant field of golden wheat. Streaking away from the thunderous threat is a flock of crows—harbingers of death—with one flying lonesomely off to the side into a swirling disc of light being swallowed by the melancholic sky.

More than his act of self-immolation, this painting is Vincent's final testament to the power of the creative spirit to resuscitate life in the midst of suffering, or its inevitable inability when the abyss is too deep. He left no other note. And his last words are lost as well, hidden in the riddle of two competing stories. They both have his brother Theo, who hurried from Paris to share his last hours, as their recipient. One story has Vincent gazing into his brother's eyes and whispering the despairingly capitulative words, "Saving me would be pointless . . . as the sadness will last forever." The other story has Vincent, flush with a final infusion of life, offering words apocalyptically hopeful with their reach for food and their promise of eucharistic consummation: "I am hungry, Theo. Please, get me some bread."

We do not know the words on his last breath. We only know the work from his last brush. Regarding the question "Is life worth living?", the painting itself is Vincent's final word. But as he took the time to touch up the crows in the hours before his death, what was he really saying? Was he saying that the wheat will always be pelted by the storms of debilitating despair? Or that the storm had passed and the stalks are still rooted in the soil that ever ripens? And the single crow, separated from the flock: Is it flying *into* the storm, its flight a resigned escape into self-abdicating destructiveness? Or is it flying *out of* the storm, its flight the soaring and determined return of one once lost now winging his way back to field and flock?

Wheatfield with Crows was Vincent's icon into either the cosmic nothingness that consumes us in the end, or the eternal pulse that ever pumps life and hope into the depleted souls of the world. And it was on display as the culminating centerpiece at the LACMA exhibition. I secured a ticket to spend Mother's Day on a pilgrimage to see from the original source what Vincent saw as he passed from this world. I have never been more viscerally slayed in the immediate presence of a painting. Icons, though, are fickle.

That painting was not the one that pierced me.

THE MUSEUM'S RETROSPECTIVE was labyrinthine—a twisting array of rooms and vestibules meandering through sketches, studies, and less significant oils spanning the artist's entire career. I glanced through the array of pieces, really only interested in seeing the one at the end, and jostled around the mass of people crowded in front of each painting until I came to the final leg of the exhibit. A series of alcoves stretched out through a hallway that culminated in a final viewing room where *Wheatfield with Crows* was perched, framed from a distance by the squared archway that opened onto it. Now that I had located it, I took my time roaming through the interceding nooks, savoring my imminent encounter with the climactic piece throbbing so near I could sense the drum of its heartbeat.

I made my way to the last alcove in the hallway and saw a gaggle of eight or ten people gathered around a painting in the corner. From over the tops of their torsos I could only glimpse a fraction of the piece. A head twisted sideways, draped in blue linen, was held in the streaks of a dimly lit sky. From the crooked head, a pair of eyes stared. The eyes, angled down, were hollow. Past crying, past caring, they were tired. A drained stare of resigned vacancy. I was more intrigued than moved. What were the cold, defeated eyes looking at?

I took a step toward them. Like a veil tearing in two and slipping away, the crowd separating me from the painting parted. I found myself face-to-face before the Virgin Mary and the broken body of Christ.

It was a Pietà.

I had no idea that van Gogh had painted a Pietà. I was well familiar with the classic one sculpted by Michelangelo—Mary, her young face bowed in depthless sorrow before her dead son's body held in her lap, revealing herself to be the Madonna, the archetype of maternal presence and compassion, the comforting model and mending comrade for all the mothers who mourn the crucified children of the world. In the rock-solid security of that sculpture, Mary holds Jesus with a mother's pity. She also holds Jesus with *divine* pity. For in that moment, Mary reveals herself to be the maternal face of God.

And here Vincent, this sad painter resting out a tempest in an insane asylum, had taken the time to paint his own Pietà. But his was different in two striking ways. First, the man held in Mary's arms was not Jesus. He had red hair, a rust-colored beard, that familiar tight-lipped scowl, and those classic triangulated cheekbones. Vincent had painted his own face on the face of Jesus. The beauty and genius struck me at once. What a poignant sight to behold. To see one's own weathered face on the face of Christ, one's own beaten body within the broken body of God, one's own dead spirit poised to descend into the abysmal tomb held by the Mother of us all, the womb-like grace that holds this whole wounded world of ours. *Yes, Vincent,* I thought, *you are right. It is your face on the face of Jesus.*

But van Gogh's Pietà was different in a second way. He was not cradled by Mary's compassionate arms. Vincent was falling out of her lap. His body was twisted and bent as if a spasm had shot through him, jerking him clean out of Mary's grasp. Or no. Worse. Mary's hands were agape, not enclosed. Her arms pushed outward; they did not draw inward. Mary was dropping him. No, she was *thrusting* him. She was actually *shoving* him into death's shadowy pit.

And then, as I looked back, I noticed that Mary's face was not grieving. It was not pained. It was not filled with sorrow. It was blank. A mask. The faint trace of a smirk at being done with this distasteful business held in check by the callous resignation from one who, quite frankly, did not care anymore, if she ever did in the first place.

And you could see it in her eyes. They weren't even looking at Vincent. They stared away in indifferent preoccupation. I mean, my God, her own son has been tortured and killed. Thugs have beaten him. Mobs have spit at him. Spears have split him open. And for the last few hours he's been hanging from a crossbeam by spikes in his hands and feet, bleeding to death in the desert sun. And his own mother could not deign to give him her attention.

But more, her eyes were cold. Unfeeling. Pitiless. Remorseless. Her eyes had no tears. They had nothing in them. They were as dry as the pathetic eyes of Pontius Pilate himself. And I swear to God: I wanted to grab the closest stick, the nearest board, the length of post from the goddamned cross if I could find it, and pound those eyes until they bled with tears. I mean, why the hell was she not crying? The bones she was holding were crushed. The flesh she disdained to touch was sliced open. The blood from the blood-let body in her lap was insufficient to even stain her virgin cloak. And now she's dumping the corpse of her own son into his grave. Doesn't she care? Doesn't she see his pain? Doesn't she feel anything? Why in the middle of this godforsaken hellhole was she not crying?

Then it hit me. The absolute horror of it. Like a sucker punch to the groin. The Virgin Mary, the Holy Mother of God, was not crying because, quite simply, she did not give a flying fuck.

It was all that I could do to turn from that searing spectacle and escape the building without wailing in pain or screaming in fury. I paused before *Wheatfield with Crows* as I scurried by, but the question that I wanted to pose to it had already been answered. Vincent van Gogh's anti-pietà was his truth. In the depths of life's pain, even God goes cold, the pulsebeat gives out, the divine bedrock gives way. Would it be my truth as well? If I were to paint a self-portrait, with my own face on the face of Christ's, would my tortured agony be held with compassion or tossed away with callous disregard? I had glimpsed, to be sure, that cosmic womb of grace, but would it be there in the cavernous depths of the pain that was yet to come?

I drove the roads aimlessly until Mother's Day turned into night; then I returned home and entered my summer of academic writing, poised at the tomb not knowing if the abyss of my still cryptic abuse had a resurrective bottom.

THE TEXTBOOK ON religious formation was simply not going to happen. I tried to force myself to my desk, but, as the yawning desolation of summer stretched out before me, I did not have the spark—either creative or vocational—to pull myself out of my bed. I awoke at dawn, lay sleepless until it was time to get Justin off to school, then came back home and crawled under my covers for the remainder of the morning. Depression swallowed me into a darkness so sunless I could only lie fetally, curled up in leaden immobility.

Dragging myself to therapy, I begged Mark for direction.

"What am I going to do?" I implored him. "I hate my life. I'm stuck in a job that sucks the spirit right out of me. And I keep living a lie. Nobody knows what I am really like. They just see the fake me. And now, if I don't get this book done, it'll all come out. They'll see me for the fraud that I am. For the life of me, I can't get myself to write it. I am totally at a loss. How do I get out of this hole?"

Ever patient, ever trusting—even before my perpetual lament—he held my impasse with infinite understanding. "The only way out that I know," he counseled, "is to be where you are."

"Where I am?" I questioned. "Where I am is so depressed that I can't get out of bed to make myself lunch. How do I 'be where I am' when I am sinking deeper into the pit?"

"What is your depression saying to you?" he asked.

"It's saying that I detest my work, and that this textbook is an insipid waste of time. So what am I supposed to do with that? Quit a good job and become an actor? What a cliché. I don't even like acting. I just like to let out my feelings in theater classes. So what, then? Make a living as a storyteller? Like that is a life plan."

"I don't know what you should do," Mark said. "All I know is that the body does not lie. What is your body telling you?"

"It's leading me headlong into a black hole," I answered.

"So what's on the other side?"

"That's just it—maybe nothing."

"Maybe everything."

That was it precisely: the Pascal's wager between living as if the abyss were really a womb, or dying in the tomb that sees no sunrise. How do you tell the difference when both are pitch-black?

BEING THE ONLY way through that I knew, I tried to honor the truth of where I really was—feeling compelled to write a book that repelled me, and stuck in a depression that disabled me. I took that truth to meditation.

The image appears of a two-ton boulder weighing me down in the bottom of a Cimmerian darkness. Struggling to resist it is futile, giving in to its paralysis defeating. Instead of being enmeshed within this pinned incapacity, I breathe into an awareness that this despairing powerlessness is present within me. A wedge of curiosity emerges, and I query the boulder.

"Why are you here?" I ask it. "What are you trying to do for me?"

"I'm keeping you from writing that book," it admits without apology.

"Why don't you want me to write it?" I follow up.

"Because," it says, "it isn't you."

"What would you have me do instead?" I ask.

"Let the boulder take you down to the bottom," it replies.

Okay, I think. If you want to know the depth of the abyss, go into the depth of the abyss. I invite the boulder to take me.

The ground beneath me gives way, and the boulder and I plummet down through the darkness. Eventually, we come to the same ocean floor that I had discovered at the monastery. Having done its work, the boulder now dissolves. The young boy that I had met at the monastery is at the opening of his cavern waiting, his lonely eyes studying me as if to ascertain if I am friend or foe.

"You promised that you would come back," he says.

His betrayed disappointment deepens the blade of my guilt. "I'm sorry," I say, and mean it. "I've been pursuing some leads—leads that will make me more available to you. I really do want to be with you. Somehow, I feel that I'm most truly me when I am down here with you."

He weighs my words for their sincerity. "I'm the one who sent that boulder," he confesses. "I'm the one that won't let you write that book."

"And why don't you want me to write it?" I ask, unsurprised by his admission.

He searches me to see if I really want to know. I do. "Because I want to write a book," he reveals.

"And what book would that be?" I ask.

"A book about the truth," he says.

I am amenable, and yet. "I don't know the real truth," I say. "I only know pieces of it."

"Don't worry," he says. "I know it. And you'll know it as you write."

"Okay," I agree. "So how do we do this?"

"You'll know," he says. "You'll know when you know."

"And what do we do for now?"

"We wait," he says.

He sits with his back against the cavern wall. I sit beside him. I have no idea what it will mean, but it feels right. Whatever book wants to be written, it needs to come from here.

THOUGH IT PLUNGED me into a limbo of vocational uncertainty, I gave up trying to force that textbook out of me. Wherever it would lead, I waited with the young boy. In the meantime, I let it lie fallow. I pulled myself out of bed to walk through the hills, to frame and hang prints by van Gogh that I bought, to journal my morning pages, and to listen listlessly to soulful music like the score from *Schindler's List*. Like a fog dissipating to reveal the landscape that was always lingering in the mist, the deep-sea longing within me sharpened even more fully into focus. It was the question that drove me into my creative pursuits, as well as to my downtime diversions.

How does one face the truth of one's pain and find the pulse that gives rise, not only to a will to live, but to the spark to live artistically? How does Itzhak Perlman stare into the savagery of the Holocaust and find the vitality to play the violin with such exquisitely exalted melancholy? How does Elie Wiesel live through Auschwitz and emerge with the tenderness of spirit and tenacity of purpose to write about it as a novel? How does Maya Angelou, sucked into the seedy underworld where children are used sexually, then disposed of like rags, rise up and write poetic memoirs?

I ached to join these surveyors of the soul, these people who plunged into the pit of their suffering and somehow, in the midnight belly of their pain's tomb, found, or were found by, a womb of grace and a heartbeat of hope that birthed them back into the world with pathos and sober gratitude. With them, I yearned to transform the filth of my suffering into something sublimely beautiful—not to suggest that evil is any less repugnant, but to attest to the truth that I too might discover, that even in the midst of perversity most vile, a creative life-force beats that can never be extinguished.

That is what I wanted to know for myself. That was the book that I longed to write. It was the one, I suspected, that the boy within me wanted to write as well. The wait, however, was on. The boy had yet to pull out his pen.

THE THURSDAY EVENING before Memorial Day unfolded like any other mid-week school night. I made Justin dinner—hard-shell tacos. I helped him with his homework. And I read to him from *The Lord of the Rings* before putting him down for bed. I tidied up, skimmed some memos for the next day's faculty meeting, then read some post-Holocaust theology before turning in myself. I offered no sacrifices of wine and barley, and I did not invoke any seers or muses—neither voiceless shades from Hades nor lovely ladies from Heaven. I went to bed without deviating from my nightly routine in any way whatsoever. The epiphany came as an unexpected bolt from the deep regions of my sound slumber.

A little after two o'clock in the morning, I was jolted awake so abruptly a seraphim could have, like it had for Isaiah, scorched my sleeping lips with a burning coal from the celestial temple's altar. It was not a dream. Nor was it a moment of creative inspiration. It happened while I was dead to the world—a flash of summoning insight that came with such convictional certainty it could have been, as for the prophet, a divine call from Yahweh.

I knew two things with absolute clarity as I snapped out of my sleep. One: I *had* to write a novel. Though I had never taken a writing class, creative or otherwise, in my life, had never fancied myself a writer of narrative fiction at any time during my years—the fierce urgency flared within me as if my life would be in peril if I smothered the fire now burning.

And two: I knew the story that I had to write. Like waking up into an alternate world that was already fully realized, the entire arc of the central plot was laid out before me. A child psychologist, using narrative therapeutically to work with abused children, is haunted by flashbacks of his own too painful to face. A young boy comes into his charge carrying secrets so traumatic that the boy has become mute. In uncovering the boy's hidden pain, the protagonist is forced to uncover his own. The healing path for each of them would depend upon the therapist's capacity to confront the brutalities of the past—both his and the boy's. The nature of their trauma, the scenes that conveyed it, the climax toward which the story built, were all etched in such vivid clarity it felt like writing it would be more like transposing than creative composition.

In addition, the characters were so fully formed, I felt like I knew them—the therapist, the boy, the boy's guardian, the creepy priest, the bullish beast of a pursuer, the mom whose sexual violation in a death camp perverted the care that she gave to her son. The existential quest that drove the protagonist was pounding in my chest. As he descends into the underworld of shadowed abuse and suffering, would he find the spiritual heartbeat to restore hope in the midst of the world's brutality, and a food to feed a life of vitality once back in the land of the living?

The prologue setting it up was clear—a Mother's Day encounter with an anti-pietà at the van Gogh exhibit in Los Angeles. The epilogue felt settled as well—the crying eyes of the crucified the last word in a tragic gospel. I even had a working title that, for me, captured it all. The novel that came like a vision in my sleep would be called *Dinner at Dachau*.

That epiphanous night, I leapt out of bed and feverishly scrawled the contours that had come to me. Through the rest of the summer, I made preparations for the narrative odyssey that would consume me for several years. I collated files for the reams of ancillary research ahead of me and collected books from the college's library that I stacked according to topic. I sketched storylines on swaths of butcher paper that I pinned to my bedroom walls and detailed a chronology for each character as their backstories began to materialize. My daily artist pages became brainstorming flurries, fleshing out scenes and scheming how to find the space in my life to follow my creative bliss.

Then, at summer's end, I made my announcement to the faculty and dean at the school year's kickoff retreat. I had already committed to teach during the next two semesters. But effective June 30, 2000, I was resigning my tenured faculty position. I would use the ensuing months to secure grant funding to direct a youth project focused on the narrative arts. While I empowered teens to tell their stories, I would be taking the time to tell one of my own. I was writing a novel.

I did not tell them that, through the imaginary circumstances of the world that I was creating, I would be surfacing and transmuting the emotional realities in my own inner landscape. For now, it was enough to step out of the role of the dutiful academic. The vocational mask was off. I was an artist. My novel would speak for itself. And those with the eyes to see would know.

That epic piece of creative fiction would be, until then, the most truthful tale that I had ever told.

Part V

Claremont, CA—Age 42

December 2001

————•————

"WHY WOULD GOD want somebody to hurt like that? She was barely seventeen years old. Can that really be God's will? Why wouldn't God want to help her? Wouldn't he want her to be healthy and happy? I know we're not supposed to question it all, but . . . what do you think?"

Linda had called after a disturbing sermon that she had heard from her pastor. A tragic death had rocked the town of Eureka. A young woman—a senior in high school—seemingly had had everything going for her. A straight-A student, the captain of the cheerleading squad, the lead in the school's production of *The Music Man*—she was the girl that all the other girls dreamed that they could be. Then she came back to school after summer vacation sullen and withdrawn. Certain that her body looked too fleshy, she barely ate and purged what little she did. Slender to begin with, in a matter of months, her bones seemed to cleave to her skin, though she tried to hide her gauntness by wearing baggy sweats and oversized coats. While running alone one evening, she went into cardiac arrest. She wasn't found for hours—too late to be saved by the paramedics called onto the scene.

The community's grief was so widespread, her memorial was held at the high school auditorium. The following Sunday, the pastor at the small Baptist church that Linda and her family had started to attend preached on the topic that was weighing down the hearts of everyone in the town. His sermon sought to reassure the congregation that, though they were experiencing a painful trial, one difficult to comprehend, this young woman's death was somehow God's will.

And his reasons for allowing this to happen were good. God's ways are mysterious, and his plans are not ours to know. He only asks that we trust him through the hardship, that we do not despair, and that we allow him to use her death for his greater glory.

Linda found it difficult to swallow. I did as well. That was the kind of theology that made me want to wield a bat at God. Or at the self-appointed surrogate purporting to speak for him.

"I think it's all so terribly sad," I answered Linda's query. "And of one thing I am sure—God had no desire for that young woman's death. It was most definitely not God's will. It's horrible what she went through. And God's heart breaks for it all—both for what she suffered when she was alive, and for the awful way that she died."

"It is awful," Linda said, as she turned it over. "So why would God let it happen? That young woman wasn't that way a year ago. Wouldn't he want to protect her from such a terrible ordeal?"

"You would think so," I sympathized. "Maybe God can't; I don't know. But I am damn sure that God doesn't plan it or want it to happen for 'his glory.' I think God wants anyone who suffers to be comforted. And when they're ill, he desires their health as much as anybody."

"I don't know how to make sense of it," she continued, still unsettled. "I just think that God should have been there. She was by herself. Nobody was there to help her when she was hurting, and nobody was there when she died."

"Maybe that's what God wants us to feel," I suggested. "Instead of trusting that he has his reasons, maybe he wants us to wonder where he was, to grieve her death, and to question how to keep such a thing from happening again to others."

Linda was lost in her thoughts, no longer preoccupied in theological speculation. Perhaps she never had been. In her mind's eye, she was with the young woman. She felt her pain as if it were her own. "I just keep seeing her lying in that street by herself," she let out. "Can you imagine how alone she must have felt?"

From this side of things, I can, Linda. I can imagine it all too well.

FOR ME, AS with many survivors of childhood abuse, the question of God's presence in the midst of suffering and evil is decidedly personal. God, as I was taught from a very young age, is an All-Powerful Being, a larger-than-life Guardian who watches over his loved ones. Where is he, then, when you are barely past being a toddler and bad things happen to you? Does he not care enough to protect you from the maltreatment? Or does he let it happen because, for some reason, you deserve it? I have been asking these questions since the first time that I remember God being there but not doing a thing about it.

The incident came back to me while I was engaged in some initial brainstorming for the backstory of the brutal bull of a man stalking a boy in my novel. As I was freewriting scenes of abuse that this man was capable of, random details rang eerily true. I began to feel nauseous. With a sickening dread rising from within me, creating a fictious scene gave way to recalling a buried memory—like wiping off the sludge from the dredged pieces of a jigsaw puzzle, slipping them into place, and discovering that the face of the puzzle is not a picture but a mirror. With the full force of a gut punch, I was there again.

The truth was not far off from my surmising riffs on the camper truck nightmares that plagued my childhood.

WHEN I WAS five years old, my dad's favorite television program was *The Red Skelton Show*. It aired on Tuesday evenings at 8:00 p.m.—too late for a kindergartner to stay up and watch on a school night, but early enough that, not yet asleep, I could hear the rumbles of my dad's laughter echoing down the hallway from the living room to the top bunk of my bedroom. When I begged him for details the next day, he would recap the sketches, guffawing at times with such boisterous abandon that he pounded the table and gasped for air before being able to get out all his words. Clem Kadiddlehopper, Freddie the Freeloader, Cauliflower McPugg, and Gertrude and Heathcliffe had clowned around the night before, but their antics were still on full display for my dad the following evening. I longed for the day when, in tandem with him, I could watch the comic horseplay for myself.

One evening—I must have already slipped off to sleep—the jiggling from my dad's muscled arm shook me awake.

"Frank," he whispered. "Do you want to watch Red Skelton tonight?"

Are you kidding? I thought. *Catching sight of Santa Claus would not be more exciting.*

"Come on," he encouraged. "But be quiet. We can't let your mom know."

He led me into the living room where he had it all worked out. The television set was on the floor where it could be seen from the end of the couch. Pretending that his back was out, he stretched out on the sofa to be able to watch the TV while lying down. He had me crawl on the floor in the tunnel behind the couch, between the base of its angled back-frame and the wall against which the top edge was pressed. Sticking my head out from the far side, I could catch sight of the screen through the legs of the end table. My dad even handed me a couch pillow upon which to rest my head.

Red Skelton was on his game, so much so that our chortling aroused the suspicions of my mom. Under the guise of hankering for some popcorn, she walked in from her perch on the bed in her room.

"There sure is a lot of commotion in here," she played along.

"Yes," my dad snickered clandestinely. "I think we have some mice in the walls. I hear them too."

"Hmm," my mom considered. "Do you think the mice would like some popcorn?"

A few minutes later, she brought out a tub's worth for my dad and placed a bowl of it on the floor just within reach of my end table hiding place.

"Don't forget," she said to my dad as she sauntered back to her bed. "The mice have school in the morning."

"No problem," my dad said. "I'm on it."

What problems could there be in such a world of slapstick conspiracy? And one where my dad had promised to be on it no matter which ones might turn up at our doorstep?

SOME DAYS LATER, my grandpa Harold came to visit, with my grandmother and their daughter, unnervingly named Harold Lee. I hustled home, one day during their visit, straight from the bus after school to find my grandfather alone in the apartment. With my mom and Jim out running errands with my grandmother and Harold Lee, my grandfather was left to watch over me until they returned. I could sense the foulness in his mood the moment that I walked in. He vacated his chair in the living room and stormed out to the patio to smoke cigarettes, snapping at me to make my own snack and then occupy myself so as to leave him alone. Only too grateful to comply, I made a sandwich with a slice of lunchmeat, turned on some cartoons, then burrowed myself behind the couch to watch TV from my new tunneled hideout.

A show or two in, my grandfather came looking for me.

"*Frank!*" he shouted through the room, vacant but for the TV turned on. "Where the fuck are you?"

"I'm behind the couch," I revealed, my voice muffled by both terror and my concealment.

"What're you doing behind the goddamned couch?" he demanded.

"I'm watching cartoons," I offered. "I like watching from here."

My covert pleasure incensed him all the more. "Get your butt out here. What kind of a pussy watches TV from behind the goddamned couch?" I dragged myself out and stood before him, too scared to look up at him. "Answer me," he seethed. "What kind of a pussy are you?" I didn't know what to say. "*Well?*" The slap was so unexpected it knocked me to the ground. My cowering enflamed him even further. "Don't look at me like that," he menaced, "or I'll take out the belt." I had no other look. He unbuckled the belt that he was wearing and, without thinking, I bolted. I had never been whipped by a belt before, but terror seized me all the same. I fled to my room and scurried under my bed, cringing into the furthest corner away from the door.

He was right behind me. "Get out from there," he threatened. "Don't make me come down and get you." I writhed against the wall so desperately I should have broken through it. He got down on all fours and peered at me with the savagery of a rabid Doberman. It took a single swipe. He grabbed me by the leg with the prison-guard grip of inescapable capture and jerked me out from under the bed. His ire became eerily calm. "Forget the belt," he said, as he forced me face-down onto the bottom bunk. "This is what you get. This is what *she* gets. This is what both of you got coming."

The body never lies. It had been telling me for years what it already knew.

LATER THAT AFTERNOON, once my mom returned home, she found me in my bed. I had crawled in and curled up once my grandfather was done with me.

"Grandpa says that you're not feeling well," she said as she placed the back of her hand on my forehead. "He says that you fell and hurt your face while you were running through the apartment."

I was incapacitated beyond the ability to respond. She petted my hair and promised to check on me in a bit. She came in later with some dinner, but I was still too nauseous for food. So she prepared me for sleep and tucked me in.

"Did you say your prayers?" she asked as she pulled my covers up under my chin. On the wall across from the foot of my bed, a picture of Jesus hung. It only showed the profile of his head looking heavenward while he was in prayer. When she had tacked it there, my mom told me that Jesus's prayers would protect me throughout the night—from monkeys, from ghosts, from anything that might want to bring harm to a child. Like an obedient Catholic schoolboy, I beseeched him every evening.

My mom lingered at my side and slid her hand underneath my blankets. Stroking my skin to comfort me, she reassured me that I was her number one and, no matter what, she would always be there for me. I fixed my eyes on Jesus. Like he had been all day, he kept looking away. His prayers must not have been heard. Or maybe they were, but God didn't care.

Some time later—maybe hours, maybe weeks—my dad came in and asked if I wanted to watch Red Skelton. I told him that I was too tired. I no longer had it in me. I could tell that he was hurt. I was too. Jesus, however, did not seem to notice. As he would through it all, in the years to come, all he did was look into the heavens—and pray his impotent prayer.

MY JOURNEY OF recovery carried on undeterred. I continued to meet with Mark weekly to explore my emotional reactivities and to process the memories that occasionally surfaced. And I sustained my daily practice of personifying and tending to my various psychic states. But my vocational life shifted dramatically. With the epiphany of a novel within me bursting to be written, I dispensed with the façade of the professional academic and came out as an artist working on a novel exploring the gritty themes of childhood sexual abuse and theodicy. I then redistributed my work responsibilities to maximize the time that I had to work on it.

The new dean at the school where I taught, after several requests for my reconsideration, finally did accept my resignation, but then he made me a rather attractive counterproposal. With the grant money that I had secured to work part-time with under-resourced teenagers in a narrative-arts project, I could stay on the faculty as an adjunct lecturer—with neither tenure nor committee assignments—and teach a course each semester on the role of narrative in spiritual formation and social engagement. The classes became lab opportunities where I took seminary students into the community centers that I was now working at, where they could observe and apprentice in the narrative techniques that I was exploring. Freed up from the institutional duties that had so depleted me and engaged in a project that gave me a genuine sense of purpose, I had both time and energy to immerse myself into researching and writing the work of fiction that not only got me out of bed each day, it proved to be a path toward both emotional truthfulness and spiritual restoration.

I set out to write a novel in which the protagonist—my narrative psychotherapist alter ego, Tony Backman, with a Jewish father who had resisted the Nazis and a Catholic mother who had lived through Dachau—is telling the story, seven years later, of his work with a boy named Carey Foster who had come under his care. The therapeutic relationship between Tony and Carey had become complicated as Tony's resolve to uncover the secrets of Carey's trauma inadvertently unearthed Tony's own secrets of childhood sexual abuse that he had yet to face. Their time together had ended so tragically that the despair-ridden Tony—whose eyes have still not watered from grief—abandoned his vocation and bottomed out as a nighttime security guard at a commercial film studio. Now, these seven years later, his hold on life has nearly slipped away. In a last-ditch effort to unburden himself from his past—or at least to make a final act of contrition before escaping from the shipwreck that his life has become— he decides to descend into the haunted shadows and tell the truth about the soul-crushing events that had befallen both him and Carey.

Tony's self-revelatory recounting is more than a tell-all confession to clear his tortured conscience. It is a make-or-break spiritual quest. In plumbing the depths of the pain that cripples him, he is seeking an encounter with some restorative reality that might meet him at the source of his shame and heartache. Allied with other underworld voyagers—most notably the poet-pilgrim Dante—Tony is journeying through the inferno of his suffering in hope of finding the divine presence that holds the world's horrors in the mirror of its compassion and births a life worth living in the midst of all the brutality.

In essence, Tony is in search of his own gospel—one akin to the sober gospel attributed to Saint Mark. Mark tells the "good news" story of how God can be seen in the Passion of Jesus, but he ends his account with a death by torture and without an observable resurrection. He takes readers to the crypt of Good Friday—where all hope is slain and sealed with a stone—and leaves them with an inexplicable empty tomb, some implausible words by a stranger, and followers who run away afraid. Without rushing triumphantly into a glorious Easter victory, he forces the reader to stare, with eyes wide open, at the horrific reality of a hero's suffering and summary execution, and to listen for ourselves, within the silence of death, for the sacred heartbeat that pulsates life and love back into the world. Mark's Gospel is tragic. It promotes neither a despairing cynicism nor a sentimental optimism. The Messiah is dead. The body has disappeared. New life is possible. But it only comes once the gut punch has landed.

Tony seeks a similar gospel truth. What is the "good news" story of how God is credibly present within the profanely defiled agonies of child sexual abuse? And for him, as for me as I was writing, the dawn had yet to come. What would Tony find as he confronts the heinous violations within himself? The question was still open. Would he find that divine spark that resuscitates a slain spirit? Or would his journey take him into the tomb that never makes it to the light of day? For the novel to be truthful, I knew that it had to tell both stories. For some people, a plunge into the abyss of one's pain comes to rest in a womb-like grace that births hope and new life. For others, facing a violation's ravaging malignance crucifies the will to live—resurrected new life is a fairy tale too farfetched to believe; succumbing to death is, itself, the last stab at hope.

What would Tony's truth be? Would his descent into the Dantean darkness of calcifying evil lead him back to the land of the living? Or would his truth-telling tale be his narrative take on a *Wheatfield with Crows*—a final self-portrait of the despair that swallowed him before ending it all with a bullet in his gut?

Would *Dinner at Dachau* be a tragic gospel, or an anti-pietà?

HOW CAN GOD *live with himself when he sees a young girl being raped by her dad and he doesn't do a thing?* This is the theological question that torments Tony throughout the course of my novel—a variation of *Where is God when a boy is raped from behind in his bedroom by his maternal step-grandfather?* or *Where is God when a high-school girl so starves herself she collapses from a heart attack while jogging?* For Tony, the traditional explanations, professed by clergy and scholars alike, are simply not credible—or if credible, then spiritually repugnant and emotionally offensive.

How is an abused child supposed to find comfort, or a balm to restore the spirit, in the suggestion that God would rather protect the free will of a pedophile than keep a toddler safe from sexual assault? Or that God allows evil in the world because he uses it to test and purify the faith of those who endure it steadfastly? Or that suffering is a result of human wickedness, the consequential punishment for the sin that stains us all, both perpetrator and victim, from birth? Or that God's ways are a mystery and not to be questioned—his absence during affliction to be tolerated with trustful patience? Or that, in Christ, suffering is redemptive, and surrendering to it willingly participates in the salvific work of atoning for the transgressor and appeasing the God whose hands cannot be soiled by human depravity?

To a survivor, such ecclesiastical platitudes seem chillingly complicit with theologies that only serve to benefit the perpetrator. Whose interests are secured by church teachings that essentially instruct those victimized by abuse to keep silent? Or to not question? Or to recognize your own complicity within it? Or to submit to the suffering patiently, and use it for your own edification; indeed, to count it all joy when you meet times of such trial because it produces perseverance? The God being espoused in such deplorable dogma not only fails to be credible, he is criminally culpable.

In my quest to encounter a God infinitely more satisfying—not just for the fictional Tony, but for the very real toddlers and kindergartners within me that had a staked interest in the outcome—I sought the oracular wisdom of post-Holocaust theologians. A God that could keep the spirit alive in the cold, hellish bowels of Auschwitz would sustain the heartbeat of a child interred in the death camps of abuse. With their help, I came to discover a sacred presence—both palatable and resuscitative—within the sordid depths of excremental assault. But before I was able to see her, the old God had to die. Tony and his band of The Bitter Truth Players would supply the nails for the task.

Tony worked in a residential facility for a dozen abused boys. His therapeutic protocols included a narrative-arts component in which he would share stories with liberative themes, then invite the boys to craft their own narrative pieces that processed their trauma symbolically. Occasionally, his wards would weave their stories together and stage a dramatic production for friends and supporters of the facility. For these public performances of theatrical originality—designed to get a rise from even the most permissive of patrons—the boys took on the provocative nom de guerre of The Bitter Truth Players.

When Carey is placed in the group home, Tony discovers that he and the boy share a macabre fascination with the Holocaust. This gives Tony the idea for a writing prompt that would not only engage the young Carey but would be sure to capture the ghoulish imaginations of the other Bitter Truth Players as well. Tony introduces the theme through a story that recounts a play written by Elie Wiesel—a two-act drama with a decidedly thought-provoking perspective on the presence of God in the midst of the world's evil and suffering.

Apparently, the fifteen-year-old Wiesel, while in Auschwitz, overheard a group of rabbis accusing God of conspiring with the Nazis. After all, God was refusing to deliver them from Hitler, and yet he had intervened to liberate the Jews when they were enslaved under Pharaoh. It followed that either God supported the Nazis, or he didn't care enough to get involved. Either way, he was an accomplice to genocide. So the rabbis did the unthinkable. They took the Master of the Universe to court. Some thirty years later, Wiesel wrote a play about it. He entitled the stage-piece *The Trial of God*.

Tony rewrites the play as a short story and shares it with the boys.

THE PLAY TAKES place in seventeenth-century Eastern Europe. It is Purim, the holiday on which Jews tell stories to celebrate how Esther saved their ancestors from a Babylonian massacre. Three strangers come to an inn at a Jewish village. The inn is deserted, except for the testy innkeeper who feeds the three strangers dinner. After they have eaten, the strangers call the innkeeper over.

"We must be honest," they tell him. "We have no money. But fear not, we will bring you bucketfuls before the night is through."

"No money?" the innkeeper shouts. "I'll have you swindlers thrown into jail."

"But we're not swindlers," they say. "We're minstrels. And tonight is Purim. Gather the entire Jewish community to listen to our stories. They'll laugh, they'll cry, and they'll eat and drink until your pockets, good sir, are bulging."

"Ha!" the innkeeper snarls. "Look around you. I am the Jewish community— the only Jew left in this village, but for my daughter who's half-dead and mad."

"But how can that be?" the minstrels exclaim. "We've seen menorahs in all of the windows."

"Let me tell you a story," the innkeeper scorns. "Two weeks ago a Jewish 'community' is celebrating a wedding. My daughter, seventeen years old, is marrying the rabbi's son. Two hundred Jews—men, women, and children—gather in this room for the wedding feast. Unfortunately, it is the night that the Christians call 'Good' Friday, the night they claim we Jews killed their God. In the middle of the feast, a mob of Christians storms in. With clubs and axes, they hack their way through the crowd until they have butchered every Jew but two. Me, they tie to a table—it takes ten to subdue me. They stand it against a wall and pry my eyes with sticks. I am forced to watch as twenty, forty, sixty men rape my daughter, then spit in her face.

Then they leave us to bury the dead and live with the nightmare. Tell me, God's minstrels, what kind of Purim stories will you tell that do not insult the dead who begged your God to deliver them?"

The minstrels are shaken. "But what are we to do? It is our sacred duty to extol God's goodness through story tonight."

"No such stories will be told here. God doesn't deserve to hear them."

"You accuse God, then?" they ask.

"That is exactly who I accuse. God abandoned his people when they cried out to him in their suffering. What does he have to say for himself?"

The minstrels are stunned. "We do not know."

"Then that is what we'll find out. You want a story for Purim? This is it. You be the judges. I'll be the prosecutor. Tonight, we put God on trial. Let him listen to that."

Just then, a priest bursts in through the door. "Hurry," he warns. "Trouble is brewing. A mob is forming to kill any Jew that still lives. You must flee to the woods until it is safe."

"We're not going anywhere," the innkeeper threatens. "We are celebrating Purim. Aren't we, minstrels?"

The minstrels are terrified and talk it over. Then they agree. "Fine, innkeeper. We will celebrate Purim as you wish."

The priest runs out to talk sense into the mob. The Jews convert the inn into a courtroom. The three judges are seated at the center. The prosecutor has a podium to the side.

"Are we ready to proceed?" one of the judges commences.

"We are," the prosecutor replies.

"Where is the defendant?" the judge inquires.

"Absent," the prosecutor sneers. "As usual."

"Then where is his defense attorney?"

"There isn't one."

"But there must be somebody with faith enough to justify the ways of God."

No one moves. "It's God's own fault," the innkeeper denounces. "He let them be killed two weeks ago."

"Well, we cannot have a trial without a defense attorney," the judge insists. "Somebody must answer the accusations made against God."

Once more, the door blows open. This time, a stranger walks in, wearing a Purim mask. "I must warn you," the stranger says. "A mob of Christians is coming this way. Their priest is unable to stop them. I suggest that you flee at once."

"We will not flee," the innkeeper insists. "We have a story to tell for Purim."

"Yes," the judge concurs. "We are putting God on trial. But unfortunately, we cannot find a defense attorney."

The stranger considers the matter. Then he removes his coat. "I would be honored to defend God's ways. What precisely are the charges?"

The prosecutor begins. "I accuse God of conspiracy with every murder, rape, and genocidal slaughter that the world has ever seen."

The defense attorney responds, "But surely you cannot consolidate every atrocity into a single lawsuit. Each act of violence is unique unto itself."

"Fine," the prosecutor comes back. "I accuse God of massacring this village, of violating my daughter, and of defiling a faithful Jewish home."

"Very well. Bring on your witnesses."

"I am the witness."

"But that will not do," the defense attorney responds. "You are the prosecutor. In your mind, God is already condemned."

"Then I bring the shrieks of all of those who were killed as testimony against God's silence."

"But you cannot testify for the dead. Maybe they rejoice to be rid of this world."

"I heard their screams as their children were hacked. Nobody rejoices at such a horror."

"Precisely my point," the defense attorney rebuts. "Death brought relief from violent suffering. Maybe they rejoice now to be with their God."

"A God who condoned their death?"

"A God who spared your life. Should you not be rejoicing now, since you were not killed as well?"

"Rejoicing!" the prosecutor spits. "That my loved ones were slaughtered, my people exterminated, my daughter defiled right in front of my eyes? How dare you suggest I rejoice in that." The innkeeper looks ready to attack. The stranger calmly looks back. Cries are heard in the distance. The Christians, lusting for blood and armed to spill it, are getting closer.

"Okay, Prosecutor," the stranger continues. "For the sake of argument, I will concede that your village witnessed a sinister night. But theologians and rabbis for centuries have concluded that God's goodness prevails even in the midst of evil. If you wait with faith, God will make things clear in the end."

"I waited for God," the innkeeper refutes, "killers came instead."

"God's reasons are mysterious; mere mortals cannot understand them."

"Evil is not—even a child flinches when stabbed."

"God uses suffering to punish the wicked; sin brings violence upon itself."

"What is the sin of a newborn baby impaled to a door with a spear?"

"Then, it's the sin of the killers that is to blame. God does not impale children."

"God does not stop it."

"God is not able."

"Then, God is not God."

"God is not willing."

"Then, God abets murder."

"God preserves freedom."

"God deserves death."

The two men glare as they pause from their sparring. Outside, the cries of the mob grow louder.

"You are a hard case, Prosecutor."

"As is your defendant, Stranger."

The stranger patiently contemplates the innkeeper. "You are right," he says. "God's ways are difficult to comprehend."

"They are more difficult to defend," the innkeeper responds.

"Perhaps. But the holy one believes in God's goodness despite God's absence."

"I despise God."

"He glorifies God in the midst of persecution."

"I find God contemptible."

"He turns to God in times of darkness."

"I turn my back on God."

"The way of life is to trust God, despite it all."

"I choose death, to protest God in the midst of it all."

"I see that," the stranger says. "Pity. For the death of a godless man never ends."

The door flies open. The priest rushes into the room. "Quick!" he pleads. "I can't hold them off. They will be here in seconds. They will kill you all."

The innkeeper looks at the judge. "I offer our deaths as my final testimony. Surely, God's silence now proves my case beyond a shadow of a doubt."

The judge turns to the stranger in terror. "But God has not abandoned us yet. Surely he will listen to you, Holy One—you who alone have defended his ways."

"But what can I do?" the stranger beseeches.

"God hears the prayers of the righteous," the judge says. "Beg him to spare us."

An axe-blade thunders against the door. Rabid cries surround the inn.

"Prayers are useless!" screams the innkeeper. "I demand a verdict before I die."

Another axe-blow pounds the door. "Please, Holy One," the judge pleads, "pray for God to deliver us."

The door splinters as the axe breaks through. An arm reaches for the lock. The prosecutor screams at the judge, "I demand a verdict, I tell you!"

The minstrel stares at the stranger. "If you won't pray for us, at least tell us who you are."

The stranger reaches for his mask. The innkeeper shouts again, "A verdict, I tell you! Now!"

"Please, Holy One, reveal yourself."

"A verdict!"

The door crashes open. Christians rush in. The stranger rips off his mask. The minstrels and the innkeeper are aghast. As the mob consumes them, they cannot stop staring.

The man before them, the only one who dared to defend God, is Satan.

IN MY NOVEL, even the coarsened adolescent abuse survivors of The Bitter Truth Players are taken aback at the twist of an ending. Tony, however, finds it brilliant. The one person with all the answers—the one explaining the offensive outrage away—is Lucifer, the Prince of Deception. The one who is truly faithful is the prosecutor—the only one gut-wrenched by the horror of evil's violation and anguished at God's abandonment within it. Significantly, the play offers no verdict. God is neither absolved nor convicted. Without a declaration of either guilt or innocence, the case remains perpetually open. God is forever confined to the defendant's chair, forced to face his accusers and listen to the stories of their savage suffering until the horror finally gets to him and he does something about it. Anyone who lets him off the hook—who holds back from interrogating him about his criminal passivity—is promulgating, not the refined faith of a holy tzaddik, a person of exemplary righteousness, but the flimsy excuses of a coldly cerebral devil.

With this cautionary tale condemning the moral and spiritual paucity of orthodoxies that exonerate God's callousness before suffering, Tony prompts the boys to surface their own dormant grievances, rooted in the wounds that they still carry. He invites them to create imaginary characters that would have a reason to put God on trial, then to sketch storylines that unfold when those characters demand a reckoning.

The Bitter Truth Players were all over it. In fact, they took Wiesel's twist and twisted it again. They not only indicted God, they sentenced Him. Their midrash, or interpretive redaction, of *The Trial of God* was the play that prompted a pivotal breakthrough in Tony's theological odyssey.

Tony's boys called it *The Night that God Got Nailed.*

THE PLAY TAKES place in an ecclesiastical courtroom. A judge's bench stands at the stage's center. Angled on one side are a prosecutor's table and three chairs, each with a boy sitting expectantly as a witness. Behind a table on the other side, a defense attorney sits. With a black suit and tie, a red dress shirt, and a deviously painted pencil mustache, he looks like a devilish cross between Snidely Whiplash and a used-car salesman from hell. And in the back corner, where the accused would answer to their opponents, God watches over. God is a giant eight-foot face—eyes open, mouth shut—painted on butcher paper and mounted on a plywood frame. The face is a cross between the majestic head in *The Wizard of Oz* and the longhaired head of Jesus pasturing sheep.

The judge bangs his gavel and calls the court into session.

"Today we hear the matter of . . ." He searches for the docket. "The People of the State of Affliction versus the Lord God Almighty." Surprised, he looks down at the prosecutor. "Is that right?"

"Yes, Your Honor," the prosecutor says. "We the people from the State of Affliction have a grievance against the Divine Governor of the Universe. We're putting God on trial."

"On what grounds?"

"Capricious neglect, criminal abandonment, and conspiracy to child abuse, racism, and murder."

"Those are severe charges, son," the judge says. "Are you ready to proceed?"

"I am, Your Honor," the prosecutor replies. Then he calls on the boy at his side. "My first witness is the millions of children born with birth defects." The boy hobbles forward, his hands hidden in his sleeves. "Please state your name for the court."

"I am Legion."

"How old are you?"

"As old as humankind."

"And what is the nature of your complaint?"

"I was born with acute skeletal deterioration. My bones are disintegrating. My hand's already decayed."

"Would you show the court?"

The witness starts to, but the judge interrupts before the hand can be disclosed. "Stop right there. There'll be no obscene displays in my courtroom."

The witness complies; the prosecutor proceeds. "What is your prognosis?"

"My bones will crumble until I die in a splintered mass. They already chip whenever I'm touched."

"Why are you here today?"

The witness motions toward the butcher-paper face. "Is that really God?"

"It is."

The witness cautiously looks over. "I'd like to know why you made me this way."

"Objection." The defense attorney leaps up from the table. "Witness can't address the defendant."

"Sustained," the judge says. "Address the court, son."

Confused, the witness glances around. "But I want to talk to God," he says.

"Absolutely not," the judge warns. "He can't be defiled by the likes of you. He's holy."

"But look at what he did to me." He pulls out his hand. His splotchy stump makes the courtroom gag. The judge pounds his gavel. "Put that away this instant!" he yells.

The witness slumps toward God, waving his deformed fist. "Why, God?" he asks. "Why did you make me a mutant?"

The judge explodes and grabs a giant foam-rubber sledgehammer and dashes around the bench. "How dare you bring such foulness before God."

Writhing, the witness squeals, "I just want to know why." His fist flails toward the face.

The judge reaches him and whales on him with the hammer. "Hide your rot, right now!" he screams as he pummels him into a splintered mass. When the witness stops moving, the judge fumes at the courtroom, "God shouldn't have to see such filth." Then he storms to his bench.

"I *object!*" the prosecutor exclaims. "You killed my witness."

"I didn't like the look of him," the judge sneers. "Now, do you wish to continue?"

The prosecutor glances at the butcher-paper God. The face stares blankly. "Yes," the prosecutor says, flustered but determined. "I call my next witness— the countless victims of child abuse." The second witness cautiously steps forward. "Would you state your name for the court," the prosecutor directs.

"Jesús de la Cruz."

"What is the nature of your complaint?" The witness lifts his shirt. Bruises and burn marks scar his chest.

The judge's gavel pounds. "Hide it, or you'll pay," he warns.

He does. The prosecutor resumes his questioning. "What happened?"

"My father said that I had the devil in me. He beat me with beer bottles and burned me with cigarettes. Then he locked me in the closet until I got my mind right."

"What did you do to bring this on?"

"He said I sassed him and looked at him bad. I didn't mean to, honest."

"What did you do in the closet?"

"I asked God to stop it."

"Objection." The defense attorney breaks in. "See that smirk on his face. He's sassing the defendant right now."

"Objection sustained," the judge barks.

"But I wasn't sassing," the witness pleads. "I just want God to stop it."

"Don't start back-talking me," the judge warns. "Or I'll teach you some respect."

"But my dad keeps hurting me," the witness appeals.

"Are you defying me?" the judge boils.

The witness turns to God and begs, "Why won't you stop this?"

"*How dare you challenge my authority!*" the judge rails.

"Please, God. Stop it."

The judge gets the hammer and rushes toward the witness. The witness stretches his arms and cries to the blank God, "Why have you forsaken me?"

"Wipe that smirk off your face!" the judge screams as he batters the witness until he's pounded the smirk clean off. "That's more like it," he scowls. "I don't tolerate disrespect." Then he storms back to the bench.

The prosecutor is aghast. "You can't keep killing my witnesses," he challenges.

"I will not tolerate back-talk. Now, get on with your next witness."

The prosecutor reluctantly complies. "I call the victims of violence committed in the name of God." The third witness, an African American teen, steps forward with a martyr's boldness. "What is your name?"

"Mohammed Elijah."

"What is the nature of your complaint?" The witness lifts his hands. Chains hang from each wrist. "Are you a slave?"

"I once was."

"But you still wear chains."

"We may be slaves no longer, but the chains of racism still bind us."

"Are you a Christian?"

"As a Black Muslim, I reject the white man's God."

"Why?"

"For three hundred years the white man used his God to oppress us. 'Slaves be submissive to your masters.' 'The Black Man bears the mark of Cain.' 'Take up your cross and submit to your suffering.' The words of Christianity are harsh for my people."

"Why are you here today?"

"I want to ask the white God why he condemns us."

"Objection," the defense attorney interrupts. "Argumentative."

"Sustained."

The witness argues anyway, directing his words to God. "In your name, Christians have persecuted my people—Arabs slaughtered in the Crusades, Africans hunted by colonizers, Negroes enslaved by white church deacons. Now your priests promise riches in the afterlife while we remain poor in this one. We're offered Heaven but we suffer on Earth. When will you stop the oppression? *When will you let my people go?*"

"That's it!" the judge screams. "I will not tolerate blasphemy." He grabs for the hammer and races around the bench to pound the witness from behind. "Take this, you cursed son of Cain," the judge spits until the witness is as slain as the others.

The prosecutor is outraged. "I demand a mistrial," he declares.

"This is the only trial you get," the judge retorts.

"Then I demand a judgment," the prosecutor insists.

"Please. You've got to be joking."

"Am I?" The prosecutor steps toward the judge. "Look at your God. He's as callous now as he's been throughout history. He neither weeps nor smiles. He doesn't cry for the slaughtered. He doesn't delight in your handiwork. He simply does not care. Not for them. Not for you."

The judge considers the prosecutor's words and turns to face his God. The prosecutor is right. God's eyes are dry. And he does not smile. The judge scans the bodies. He studies his hammer. He stares back at the face. "All the work that I do for you, and you don't even care? We'll see about that!" He wheels around and bludgeons the prosecutor to death, then spits, "Prosecution rests!"

Still burning, the judge starts toward his bench. He stops cold. A boy's head, terrified and bewildered, peeks over the top. Slowly, the boy stands. He's wearing a black suit and a red shirt, a younger version of the defense attorney. Distractedly, he wipes his mouth clean.

"Oh no." The defense attorney is repulsed. "Don't tell me . . ."

"You suckin' tease!" the judge seethes. "I told you never to come out from under there." The judge breaks for the bench. The boy races the other way. He makes for the defense attorney and leaps into his arms yelling, "Save me!" The defense attorney is too stunned to move. The judge catches up and swings at the boy's back.

"How dare you try and expose me," the judge rages as he pounds the boy to the ground. The boy's eyes plead with the defense attorney until they are beaten closed. The sight of his abused protégé makes the defense attorney snap.

"You sick degenerate. How could you?" He snatches the sledgehammer and pummels the judge with his own weapon until the judge, too, is beaten to death. Still fuming, the defense attorney turns and sneers at God. "So," he spews, "it's you and me once more. How can you just sit there? How can you let this happen? Well, this time, you're going down." Raising the hammer like an axe-murderer, he lunges after God. He slashes away as the butcher paper rips, each blow slicing another gash across God's face, each swing shredding the face to pieces until it litters the floor in a pile of scraps. Then he stops, steps back, and looks at what is left of God.

Beneath the butcher paper, an eight-foot-square mirror stares back, marred by spiderweb cracks as if cast at by stones. Graffiti scars the surface, its red letters dripping like blood leaking from a wound. "Nein Juden!" "Colored Only!" "Spare the rod, spoil the child!"

The defense attorney gazes into the mirror and shakes his head. Horrified by his reflection in God's butchered face, he slowly backpedals, trips over a body, and falls. Still stricken, he whispers, "No." Then louder, "*Noooo!* . . ." Then a piercing howl, "*NOOOOO!* . . ." as he bludgeons himself with the hammer and he, too, the last living member on stage, lies cold on the battered heap of corpses. For as long as a last breath, he's still. Then his arm swings up, arcs across, and like the final gasp from the gavel of judgment, the hammer slams to the floor.

The hammer's ring fades into silence. The pile of bodies is still. For several moments, nothing moves.

Then the curtains part. A small boy creeps out. From shoes to gloves, he is dressed in black. Moving with a weary heaviness, he positions himself behind the mutilated God, then slowly, like the sun inching into a canyon of darkness, rotates the mirror toward the audience.

The glass surface fills with faces as the spectators are gathered into its gaze. For each person in the audience, the slogans swell into cold clarity as they come more fully into view and sweep across the onlooker's own features. The spiderweb cracks sparkle in a collage of their own disfigured facial fragments. And then their face appears in unbroken purity as a clean stretch of surface slides by, each person seeing themselves, with untarnished lucidity, in the mutilated mirror of God's bloody face.

In stoic persistence, the glass keeps pivoting until its back is completely turned. The boy behind it pauses. His arms are stretched wide in their sober grip. His head is bent low. His back bears the weight of every incriminated stare that saw its own face reflected in the marred mirror of God. As if nailed to the spot, he waits.

Then he pushes. The curtains give way. Both mirror and boy recede, then disappear, into the darkness. The play is over, the final scene suspended—an impassive God now vanished, a pile of disposable bodies battered, a frozen sea of staring spectators.

For a survivor, an utterly truthful moment. An icon of violation divinely abandoned. A portal into the bottom of the abyss.

THE NIGHT THAT *God Got Nailed*, for Tony, is a truthful depiction of the Lord God Almighty's inexcusable indifference toward those who suffer at the hands of evil. As victims cry out for deliverance and beg from their knees for a savior to intervene, the Supreme Being—All-Powerful and All-Knowing—looks on in callous passivity. The institutions—whether ecclesiastical or juridical—that prop up and defend such a detached deity insidiously side with the sinister and conspire with the perpetrators that pummel the violated. Taking a hammer to the face of such heartless disregard rips away the façade of divine magnificence and lays bare the dreadful reality of those who have been beaten down: assault has claimed its victims, God is nowhere to be found, and the abyss of bespoiling violation has imprisoned the forsaken in a tomb of death and despair. Any way out is concealed in the darkness.

The abyss, however, does have a bottom. Like the glassy surface of a dead-calm sea, a mirror underneath God's paper-thin countenance takes in every scene that plays out before it. The mirror manifests all of it in its unflinching reflection. It receives the blows of the enraged that are hurled against it. It bears the bloody profanity spewed by the depraved. It absorbs the pain of any who suffer. It meets the gaze of those who stare. The polished surface reveals that God's true face is scarred; its features are splintered. And it invites all who look into it to recognize their own faces, scarred and splintered, merged with the marred mirror of divine unfaltering that holds all that the world has to offer it.

As that sacred looking glass recedes into the shadows, we who have seen ourselves within it are hung in the balance. Within this darkness of evil unblinkingly unveiled, will we hear a heartbeat of hope and compassion that replenishes our spirit and brings us back into the world alive? Or will the pulse within us fade and grow cold, hardening into incarnations of a stoic and distant deity? Like Dante standing at the axis mundi of Hades's horrors, poised before his reflection in a frozen Lucifer's iced-over eyes, Tony is at that spiritual fulcrum where descending into the pitiless depths might pivot into climbing out toward the light of day on the far side of the abyss. Here at the moonless crossroads—where the truth of depravity, and the brutal pain that it inflicts, are fully on display—where is the divine spark that can resuscitate the spirit and sustain us as we continue along the path?

Who would have known? She was there all along—a sacred presence so ordinary it is easy to miss her.

A presence with which I was, unknowingly, already well acquainted.

MELISSA RAPHAEL IS a Jewish feminist theologian whose scholarly work is focused on Holocaust studies and Jewish responses to evil and suffering. As I was researching my novel, I came across an article of hers that was so compelling it not only influenced Tony's spiritual development, it affected my prayer life. In her essay, later expounded upon in her book, *The Female Face of God in Auschwitz*, Raphael argues that the central theological question posed by the Holocaust is not "Where was God while his people suffered?" but "Who is the God being sought for within all of the suffering?"

For her, the God that skeptics decry as having abandoned God's people during the Shoah was the male God of patriarchal omnipotence and emotional aloofness—a God who could have thwarted Hitler if he had wanted to but, for enigmatic reasons known only to himself, chose not to. For Raphael, this God is not only theologically problematic, he is dangerous to the point of being diabolical. A God of absolute power—who militaristically intervenes in history when it so suits his whims, who uses any means necessary to achieve his self-justified ends, and who imposes his will as a dominating force on whomever it so pleases him to puppet—is a deity that resembles, all too terrifyingly, the totalitarian ideologies of Nazi Germany.

This masculinely conceived God is the deity assumed in every defense, given by his supporters, for God's refusal to overthrow Hitler and squash the despot's genocidal designs. That God wanted to protect human freedom, or to spur a Jewish state, or to punish Israel's wickedness, or to purify its faith through a fiery furnace, or to inspire the faithful study of the Torah—all these insufficient rationalizations presume a God that could have altered the course of human history but decided not to for some overall greater good. For Raphael, such a God never existed. Or if he did in the Jewish imagination, then certainly the Holocaust has definitively exposed his moral and spiritual deficiencies.

A more credible God was, however, present in Auschwitz and active in redemptive ways. As Raphael studies the sacred-text accounts of women survivors of Auschwitz, she recognizes that God was with God's people in their suffering, but she was with them in her feminine form. Throughout history, the Hebrew scriptures attest, whenever the Jewish people were in exile, the feminine presence of God went with them. The people built a portable tabernacle for this presence at Mount Sinai and carried it with them throughout the Egyptian wilderness.

The tabernacle was replaced by the temple in Jerusalem, but it went with the people, in spirit, when the temple was destroyed and the Jews were deported into captivity in Babylon. This dwelling, even if incorporeal, housed the God who stays with her banished people, who sees their plight and suffers what they suffer, who goes with them into the ghettos and wastelands to tend the wounded, bind the broken, grieve the slain, and inspire the down-spirited. This feminine presence of God sustains the people's spirit through her compassion.

In the Hebrew Bible, she is known as Shekinah.

With the Jewish mystical concept of *Tikkun Olam* as an interpretive lens—the teaching that humanity is invited to co-partner with God in repairing our broken world and restoring the radiance of God's dulled glory—Raphael suggests that every mitzvah, every good deed, every act of care, or encouragement, or comfort, or self-respect, in the midst of evil's degradation, is itself a tabernacle, a divine dwelling where the Shekinah is present with the people in their suffering. The real miracle of Auschwitz is that, in the midst of a quite literal excremental assault, God was not obliterated. Even in the belly of an abyss of profanity—where despair, futility, and the primal instinct merely to survive can deaden the spirit—women found ways to resist the dehumanizing fierceness of evil and to bear Shekinah's compassion.

They shared scraps of food with each other, combed lice from each other's hair, wrapped blankets around the dying, wiped tears from crying children, massaged each other's hands, lanced each other's boils, and in ritual acts of daily hygiene, they simply washed their own faces, claiming the purity of their divinely imaged radiance in a camp that sought to defile and disfigure them. This is divine power in its truest form—the capacity to extend kindness in a world of coldness, to coax beauty out of the decay of the ugly, to claim dignity in the face of degradation, and to incarnate compassion in the heart-hardening hell of unadulterated malevolence. In the tabernacles of their care, women birthed the divine into the world. It did not take the suffering away, but it kept their spirits alive while going through it. The male deity proved himself to be inept in his detachment. But the divine feminine got dirty with her people and kept their hearts beating through the putridity.

STORYTELLING HAS ALWAYS been an integral part of the Jewish tradition. For Raphael, a professor of Jewish thought, theology often, likewise, takes a narrative form. As much a work of religious imagination as of philosophical discourse and ethical counsel, theology offers structuring metaphors and symbol-laden storylines to shape perception and inspire meaning. Taking her place in the long line of Jewish myth-makers and storytellers who have come before her, she concludes her exposition with an allegory of the sacred feminine that she crafted in conversation with Jewish mysticism. In my novel-length narrative of religious imagination, Carey's religion teacher, inspired by Raphael, shares a version of Shekinah's story. For Tony, it bookends the stage-piece depicting the male God's demise.

AS LEGEND HAS it, the world was created when the Lord God, the Master of the Universe, wed his Queen, the Shekinah, in whose womb the earth was conceived. Born from such love, the world was pure and good. But the people turned wicked, and perversion covered the planet. The Master of the Universe was incensed at the depravity—the unstained glory of his holiness could not tolerate such filth—yet he refused to violate human freedom to stop it. Seething with rage but paralyzed by disgust, the Radiant God shattered into thousands of shards of light that were spewed throughout the decadent world where they faded into the foulness. The Shekinah looked upon the world and saw only suffering. Weeping with grief for the earth and her marriage, both broken, she forsook the heavens and walked the world in search of the shards of her splintered husband.

She wandered the land as a compassionate presence—soothing the wounded, nurturing hope, and inspiring the people to acts of care in resistance to evil's dehumanizing pull. In a world of obscene assault—where governments brutalize ethnic groups, overlords exterminate races, parents molest their children, and homes are rife with violence and poverty—any act of kindness and compassion, justice and beauty, is a miracle. It is a miracle that a workcamp inmate would share food with another; that an abuse victim would craft a soulful work of art; that a slave would assert their dignity within a system that tries to rob it. They are not the spectacular miracles of a Master of the Universe dividing the Red Sea. They are ordinary miracles, birthed by the Shekinah who holds everyone with compassion through whatever hell they happen to be living within.

And as people are moved to incarnate such everyday miracles of kindness, they shine with the glory of God's image. A tiny light is illuminated. And one of the shards, hidden in the shadows, is discovered in the world's muck. The Shekinah gathers each of these shards and wanders the world for more. When all the shards are gathered, so many that they have been found in every sordid crevice that evil can create, the Shekinah will remake the Master of the Universe. She will place each piece in position until his patchwork frame is reassembled. Then she will bathe those shards, and the cracks that hold them, with the tears of her compassion. The cracks will fade and disappear, the shards will come back to life, and the Master of the Universe with his Queen, the Shekinah, will wed once more, and delight together in a world of radiant goodness.

AS HE SEEKS a spiritual resource to sustain him during his odyssey through the abyss of his suffering, Tony lives between two stories. In one, an apathetic deity, impotent in his remoteness, is ripped to pieces, and we are left gazing into the marred mirror of God's face that holds, with stark clarity, the entire web of pains and complicities in which each one of us finds ourself. In the other, a sacred feminine, whose power is compassion, meets us in our suffering and, with the balm of her healing care, binds back together the broken pieces of our lives.

As Tony makes the pivot and walks toward the light that can uncover the truth of his past, he is still uncertain whether he will discover a Shekinah's care that wanders even into the cesspools of childhood sexual abuse and tends, with compassion, the soiled who are exiled there. And as I companioned him through the imaginary circumstances of my own past's truth, it remained to be seen if we would find together a mirror of grace whose face not only reflects the pain that we carried but holds it lovingly enough for new life to be resuscitated. For the wounded ones within me whose suffering was far from fictional, much more was at stake than discovering the mere ending to a novel.

Santa Rosa, South San Francisco, and Foster City, CA—Age 43

June 2002

———◆———

BREATHING INTO A *grounded calm, I descend through the depths of my soul's interior sea until I arrive, not at the ocean floor from before, but at the site of a memory that has consumed me for days. I am in the living room of my home from when I was a kindergartner. The place is creepy quiet. Like an alien abduction scene from* The Twilight Zone, *the television set is on, cartoons playing out in silence from the screen positioned on the floor. Underneath the end table, the uneaten crusts of a sandwich are strewn on a plate. But the room, along with the rest of the house, seems void of human life.*

I creep down the hallway and enter my old bedroom. My boyhood self is on the top bunk curled underneath his covers. He stares dissociatively at the far wall. The bedspread on the bunk below him is rumpled from one squirming while being pinned. An urge wells up within me to take a sledgehammer to the whole indecent scene.

"Why doesn't he come when we pray?" the boy asks, absently. "Doesn't he care enough to stop it?"

I see what he is staring at. A framed head of Jesus is petitioning a God hidden in the heavens. "It's just a picture," I tell the boy. "He can't come to stop it."

"Make it go away then," the boy requests. "It only makes it worse."

I step to the picture. As if my wrath throws flames from my eyes, the print blisters and peels away. Beneath it, a mirror peers back. I see myself as the adult that I am, my ire still burning. Over my shoulder, I see the boy staring as well. He is no longer gazing toward the vaporized Jesus. He is staring directly at me. The pain pleading from his eyes pierces me. I can see it. He now looks to me to care enough to stop it.

The fire within me turns to resolve. I do not need words for him to hear me.

"Never again," I tell him with my eyes. "I will never let it happen to you again."

EVEN THOUGH WRITING fiction is a work of the imagination, the narrative world that is created can take on a life of its own. At times, its characters, locales, and occurrences can seem as real as the solid earth on which we stand. More than once, Tony insisted on making decisions that I, as the writer, begged him to reconsider. He wouldn't listen. But then again, other times he displayed a cleverness beyond my capacity to conjure. He and his undertakings seemed so substantial that my trip to scout scene locations in Northern California felt like traveling back in time to take notes from the historical events that had already transpired there. As would happen to an attentive investigative journalist, I was about to discover events that had taken place of which, when I set out, I was entirely unaware.

THOUGH I HAD never spent any time there, beyond driving through it on the 101 highway when I visited the monastery much further north, something in me always knew that my novel was set in Santa Rosa. Sure enough, as I drove about the town, with the Yellow Pages and a Thomas Guide to lead me, fragments of Tony's life materialized like storyline puzzle pieces slipping into place. It was all instantly recognizable—the coffee shop where Tony read underworld mythology, the hospital where Carey was rushed to with both wrists severely sliced, the mall with a Baskin-Robbins where Tony took Carey on an ice cream outing. I even came across the home for boys where Tony had worked—a small-scale facility that really did exist, at the rural edge of town, tucked between the razor-wired fence behind a juvenile detention center and the spooky wilds of the Mayacamas Mountains.

I also explored the surrounding environs, and additional historical settings were disclosed—the Catholic boarding school in the foothills where Carey was a resident; the seedy cul-de-sac, in an adjacent shantytown, where Carey's mom hustled tricks for a living; the gated cemetery where Tony's mom was buried; the Petaluma park nearby where he would sit playing sad James Taylor songs on his harmonica; and the home in which Tony grew up, where his dad still lived guarding his secrets alone. Then, heading back to Santa Rosa from his boyhood town of Petaluma, I noticed a sign from the freeway. On a whim, I made a detour to Sonoma State University.

As soon as I drove onto the campus, I knew. Not only had Tony gone to college here, but something decisive happened during his years as an undergrad. I parked in a lot and walked the grounds, with only the vague hunch to guide me, until I rambled into Commencement Park. As I paused before the expansive meadow adjoining a small lake, the realization came over me as sure as if I were Tony in the flesh living it out all over again.

My God, I thought, *this is where Tony falls in love with Jen.* The sudden certainty gave way to an immediate follow-up query: *Who in the world is Jen?* In my mind, Tony had always been single, even a bit timorous around women. I knew as well as any. Men maternally molested as boys, even when still unconscious to the trauma, can see intimacy as something to be feared, sexuality something to flee and forswear. But apparently, Tony had an earlier love that I did not know about. I could see the two of them, as plain as day, walking hand in hand around the pond on a starry Halloween night.

Then it started to come to me, like a love story that had really happened that I was only now remembering. I watched their love take root and flower as snapshots of their growing devotion scrolled into view like I was turning the pages of their courtship's photo album—Tony forsaking the blues to play Jen love songs on his harmonica; Jen throwing Tony a surprise James Taylor-themed birthday party and learning to play, on his beloved instrument, their signature song, "Your Smiling Face"; Tony's Halloween proposal with a Cracker Jack ring because the real one was not ready on their two-year anniversary. I saw also the climactic event of their engagement's consummation with the real ring—a winsome plot that Tony was scheming, the details of which I could not quite make out. All I knew at that point was that it involved a diamond ring with their birthday gemstones accenting it, and that its unveiling took place during a private picnic at a secluded beach on the coast.

For Jen, birthdays were sacred. So Tony designed an engagement ring that featured their two birth-month gemstones—an amber garnet and a gold-tinged topaz—on either side of a diamond. Then he gathered picnic supplies where every detail—flowers, balloons, blankets, utensils, napkins, glasses, food, and cake candles—was color-coordinated to match the hues of the ring, a festive collage of a meal entirely tinted in various shades of orange and yellow clustered around diamond dashes of white. Tony was so excited about the tailor-made arrangements, only the perfect picnic location would do. The next morning of my scouting trip, the two of us went looking for it.

Leaving early in my truck, I drove north from Santa Rosa, then made my way toward the coast on River Road. Meandering through the shadowed forests that enshrouded the Russian River, I felt the same gleeful anticipation that Tony would have felt as he rode with his unsuspecting girlfriend for a casual afternoon drive along the ocean. The outing seemed so real, Jen could have been in the passenger seat beside me, the picnic supplies hidden beneath blankets in the back of my truck. Both Tony and I grasped what was riding on this. I as the writer, he on the verge of proposing to his beloved, knew that the beach had to be ideal, offering the abundance of splendor and seclusion that would suit our amorous designs. Neither of us knew where it was located, but we could both imagine the scene that was about to play out once we arrived there.

We came into sight of the ocean and turned right on Highway 1 heading toward the rural north. The road ascended a craggy bluff hundreds of feet above the water. The only snatch of beach that we could glimpse was at the foot of eroding cliffs. We continued to drive along the scenic coastline, but no accessible beach was forthcoming. I could imagine Tony's dismay. I felt it too. The picnic that we had planned was too perfect to be denied. Surely some secluded beach would turn up to accommodate it.

But it didn't. The road rambled through sloping hills bordered only by cliffsides and intermittent headlands. Even though our confidence was deteriorating, we continued to drive northward until both of us saw it at once. As the highway arced over a hillock, then curved back toward the coastal cliffs, an aberrant lane, parallel to the shoreline, angled off and ascended a distant bluff. On an impulse, we followed it.

Once it peaked, the road leveled off and continued straight through patches of woods and periodic pasture. Though we couldn't see it, the ocean lay somewhere off to our left. Coming upon a turnout, we got an idea and parked. On the far side of a grassy meadow, a stretch of woods separated us from the coastline. Perhaps an isolated picnic spot could be found on the other side of those trees. Seeing no signs of people or livestock, we slipped through the barbed-wire fence, hiked across the field, and trudged through the woods until we could make out, in the distance, the vast, airy openness beyond the final rim of trees. We trekked toward it and, at its edge, stumbled upon a site that struck us both spellbound.

Stepping out onto a small grassy bluff no larger than a backyard lawn, we stood atop a rugged cliff so high we looked down upon the hawks soaring on the ocean's breeze. The shore was less than a mile away but so far below us we could not hear the waves as they crashed against the rocks. From that craggy height, we could see forever—to the south, all the way to Point Reyes, a full morning's seagull flight downwind; to the north, across miles of evergreens to the far-off threshold of Fort Ross; and before us, an ocean that spanned the full breadth of the horizon.

Tony knew it at once. This majestic ledge was the quintessential location for a romantic picnic at which to pledge his eternal commitment to love. I saw it as well. But I also saw more. On this heath at heaven's horizon, these two young lovers would not only dine on food hued in the ambered colors of their consummated betrothal; they would, while in the midst of their elation, conceive their only child here. The springtime buoyancy of their bliss, however, would crash against the rocks of trauma and tragedy. For untended pain can infest even the most tender of dreams. Within weeks of their marriage, Tony will be stabbed with nightmares and lurid fantasies of abuse so repulsive he will repudiate their factuality and castigate himself for having them. He will recede from Jen. He will be racked with torment. And through no fault of his own, but from the kind of sudden death syndrome that leaves parents forever blaming themselves when not decrying the fates, he will lose a child.

Within a year of their rapturous rendezvous, Tony will be back. This lover's refuge, where bliss and desperation now dwell side by side, will be the stage where Tony faces off with God. In a midnight darkness, he will spew his rage and disgorge his contempt into a tempest that pelts all in its path with callous indiscriminancy. The thunderstorm will yield no theophany. The divine protector, either slain or illusory from the start, will be gone. Tony, now faithless, will be left alone, with a shame that he cannot bear, and a profaning past that he cannot admit.

As I stood in Tony's fictive story, on that cliffside borderland between the infinite and the finite, the real and the imaginary, my story was playing out within his. His longing for love's delight was mine, as was the suspicion that his soiling was too severe to deserve it. His struggle to embrace the suppositions of his past was mine as well. As was the grief at the loss that one's torturedness begets. And both of us were walking away from the impotent God of apathetic desertion. While far below the liminal promontory on which we both were standing—where a life would be conceived, and the divine would die—the ocean merely ebbed and flowed in silence.

MY FACT-FINDING TRIP to Santa Rosa was far more revelatory of my novel's features than I could ever have foreseen. And I headed home with a renewed resolve to weave together my notes and notions into a full draft of my epic tale. I did, however, have a couple of final stops to make—locations with which, while I was up north, I wanted to refresh myself.

My two boyhood homes were on the way back.

Retrieving the address from my dad, I pulled up across the street from my earliest childhood home in South San Francisco. I had not been there since we moved out when I was five years old, but I felt in my belly the recollection of being there. The house looked ordinary and tiny—a mere two-bedroom hovel in a row of them lined along the hill beneath the 280 freeway. Though nondescript, the horror that it had known there radiated like an abandoned domicile—once a crime scene—still haunted by the unavenged victims. I could envision it all: the green camper parked out in front; the monkeys lurking in the bushes; the living room with the couch pulled up against the picture window; my mom's bedroom with the tearless crucifix; and the boy on the bed, naked and disposed of, staring blankly as the chipper music of an ice cream truck faded with his innocence.

As I gazed upon my ghost-house of a home, I imagined the boy now perched on the couch, looking at me parked in my truck. It was as if he had surfaced from the caverns within me, where he had waited long enough for me to come find him, and was now seeking me out in the place that we had both known. His eyes bore the pain that bled from the bedroom. He begged me to see and acknowledge him. And to remember him when I turned away. With my eyes unblinking, I held his gaze. And I promised him. His story, whether symbolic or factual, would be told in my novel in full.

I NEEDED NO assistance in finding the Foster City home in which I had spent my school years. Having dwelt there into the eleventh grade—biking to schools that were miles away in three different directions—I could map the routes to my former residence even if I were half-asleep. It had been over twenty years since I went out of my way to revisit the place. The house looked just as I remembered it—a small one-story dwelling with shake-shingle siding and a pebbled granite walkway that my dad had installed. From the front, all that you could see was the double-car garage door on one side, the curtained sitting room window on the other side, and a recessed entryway in between. The informal family room, adjoined to the kitchen, and the four bedrooms, one of them the master, were buried behind the structural façade.

I did not imagine a small boy staring from the sitting room window. As children, we were never allowed in that room unless company had come over. The wounded ones within me, with the memories that they held so tightly, were hidden in the back of the house, in shadowed recesses far out of sight from anyone's view out on the street. I knew that they were in there. And I let them know that I was waiting for them outside. For now, the house gave the appearance of being empty. And it emitted an eerie cold.

SURROUNDED BY THE bay and a network of lagoons, Foster City has only two roads that lead either in or out. I had taken the more direct route in from the freeway and decided to leave through the less traveled backway that cut through the industrial park then bordered the wetlands before merging with the freeway further north. I had forgotten that Third Avenue, just before the freeway, edged St. Timothy's Roman Catholic Church.

As it was a school day, the chain-link gate at the parochial school's playground was closed. So I drove around to the main entrance on the side street and parked in the visitors' lot. I had not been on the premises since my parents divorced and the priest denied my mother Communion. It felt, now, like I was trespassing. But in the spirit of sifting through my past, I felt compelled to cast about a bit in the place that had once been my spiritual home. Though I had not considered them in decades, the grounds were as familiar as if I were still a child in catechism class there, taking a quick break in the quiet outdoors—the asphalt play-yard, the priest's rectory, the wing where they had their offices, the row of conjoined classrooms, and the church against which the classrooms butted up. Prepared to offer the excuse that I had stopped by to pray, I walked around outside, then ascended the chapel steps to peek into the sanctuary. As the door closed behind me, I was swallowed in darkness, so much so that I sat down in a back pew to let my eyes adjust.

I thought that my heart was pounding because I feared being taken as an intruder. But that was not it. As my sight was slowly restored, it all came back like a long-forgotten horror movie I had once been subjected to being played out before me once more. The life-size Jesus nailed on a cross; the majestic perch of the statued Madonna; the quiet respite I had sought that settled into a swaddling of sacred presence; the door click that snapped me out of it; the priest leering at me from in front of his confessional; his insistence that we study catechism, just the two of us in his office. As if I had been jolted awake from a bad dream, I found that my chest was heaving, my skin was clammy, both rage and wailing were busting to explode checked only by the choking in my throat. But waking up was not an escape. The bad dream was still with me. It is what I had actually lived through. The nightmare, from which there was no waking, was my real life.

Bound to the pew, I was living it again. I was neglecting my lesson in Sister Bernard's classroom, seeing, out the window, my grandfather in his camper, driving the road to my house. I was walking the playground in traumatized distraction, then seeking asylum in the sanctuary from the evil that was coming later that day. And I was unwittingly stepping into the snare of evil that was already in the church awaiting me. I did not imagine that boy slipping into the chapel, through the side door, on his way back to his catechism class. He was too fully inhabiting me. Both of us were sitting there, alone in that church. The grace that space had once offered was now gone. The sense of the sacred had disintegrated. Jesus was dead, his eyes fully closed. Mary was still just a statue, her eyes open but stone. The boy and I had only each other. We were the ones left to see.

I took him with me as I left. I took his story with me as well. He and I were going home. We had work to do. The trip was over. My research was done. It was time, now, to write our novel.

Upland, CA—Age 46

November 2004

UPON MY RETURN from my fact-finding trip, Justin and I moved into a house on a quiet circle in Upland, the town next door to Claremont. The place was perfect for the two of us. With our minimalist taste in furniture, we were able to transform the dining and living rooms into an extended Lego workshop for Justin. And the master bedroom upstairs—the size of a suite with its own fireplace—was large enough to station a writing desk in the corner with views of Mount Baldy to the north and the sunrise to the east. While Justin and his friends built castles and battlefields in their elaborate medieval world, I could work on my novel in peaceful seclusion.

For me, writing was both exhilarating and agonizing. On the one hand, I had never experienced such vocational pleasure as when I was drafting or editing that thinly veiled fictional opus. The sense of purpose, the truthfulness of the tale, and the alchemical process of transforming the filth of my experience into an artistic work literally stoked my reason for living. For the first time in my life, I felt no compulsion to put myself to sleep each night with fantasies of how I would kill myself.

On the other hand, bouts of insecurity and self-ridicule were all but crippling. "What a self-pitying exercise in narcissistic indulgence," a voice would castigate the wordsmith within me. "Who are you to think that you can write a novel—anything beautiful and profound? Your writing is mawkish, shallow, and embarrassingly verbose. Why are you wasting your time? No one is going to publish this. No one is going to read this. If it sees the light of day at all, it will only be panned and disdained." The demon of self-condemnation fires away with live ammunition.

I only found freedom from such debilitating onslaughts when I took them into my meditative practice. Personifying the psychic states and listening to their concerns helped to relax them enough for me to keep trekking forward. One constellation of images proved to be particularly resonant and liberating.

DESCENDING INTO A *grounded stillness, I invite the voice of self-castigation to materialize. It appears as a bouncer—surly and fiercely determined—blocking the entrance to a circus tent. Trusting that he means well in his intrapsychic purpose, I ask him why he is so dogged and disparaging. He says that he is trying to prevent from happening the spectacle inside the tent. I tell him that I can be trusted and ask him if I can enter the tent to see it for myself. He considers me, then lifts the flap.*

In the center ring, I see myself as an adult juggling a dozen clumps of dung. Each one, upon my touch, transfigures into a bouquet of flowers, then is released into the air to be replaced by another clump of dung. Throughout my display, however, my pants are around my ankles, my privates exposed in their prepubescent puerility. I am attempting a feat of advanced magical coordination, but my babyish balls are bared in the process. The spectators packing the stands are laughing hysterically—mocking and scorning the naked shame that I am unable to conceal while performing.

As I walk toward the ring, the adult performer me morphs into a five-year-old. Humiliated, the boy stops juggling, and the clumps of dung fall to the ground all around him. I kneel in front of him and look him in the eye.

"Do not worry," I tell him. "I know why your pants are around your ankles. I know who unbuckled your belt, unfastened your button, unzipped your fly, and slid them down with your briefs. I know that your nakedness is your source of pain. And for you, I am going to write about it."

I pull up his pants and walk him out.

The clumps on the ground have turned into flowers.

THROUGH THE MONTHS—in spite of the perpetual negotiation with the protective self-castigator, and in between the demands of my paying gig directing the narrative-arts project—I put in my hours at my desk and made steady progress on my manuscript. Chapter by chapter, the narrative unfolded, Tony's and Carey's stories at the center. Though always a work of fiction, the parallels with both my adult ordeals and the afflictive fantasies involving my childhood, with details tweaked along the way, are self-evident to those privy to my interior conflicts.

Tony is lost in the sea of his depression—still broken by the deaths of his marriage and child and haunted by obscurities buried in his past whose murky features forebode with dread. Carey, mute with trauma—both of his wrists severely sliced—is placed in the boys' home where Tony works. Tony, instinctively taken with the boy, oversteps his bounds as Carey's therapist and begins to investigate the mystery of Carey's distress. The figures that bedevil Carey's world are gradually revealed—his promiscuous mother, who exudes sexuality without discrimination; the bullish beast of a stepfather, who is stalking the boy in his green camper truck; the priest that oversees Carey's boarding school, who prays in a private chapel with a stained-glass window of a majestic Madonna who gazes upon all that happens there with a cold, sculpted stare.

As Tony pieces Carey's story together, cryptic images of his own past invade with heightening intensity—lurid nightmares and obscene fantasies of him with his mother that repulse him with their sleazy slander. Insisting to himself that the psychic invasions are only unconscious assimilations of Carey's experience, he discounts them and becomes all the more determined to unearth the truth of Carey's trauma. That truth proves to be elusive. Lies are told. Deceptions are exposed. Other lies turn out to be true. As the climax builds, Tony's secrets from himself and Carey's secrets from Tony become entangled. And Tony's inability to face and accept the repressed molestations of his past impairs his capacity to companion Carey as the boy tries to navigate the molestations of his present. As Easter Sunday approaches, their two traumatic trajectories insidiously intersect.

Throughout this process of composing the piece, I found the writing enormously regenerative. Even though the content was emotionally intense—even devastating at times—shaping it into words was neither debilitating nor inordinately depressing. Similar to my image-conjuring meditations, externalizing my felt experience into a fictitious narrative form enabled me to name, ponder, and even honor the psychological dynamics swirling within me in a way that freed me from their possessive clutch and transfigured them creatively. Neither suppressing my psychic reality, nor tossed about in its power, I was able to objectify it into symbols, break it down metabolically, and craft an artistic truth that made meaning out of the residue. In effect, I was taking my hard feelings and making music out of them. Blues, perhaps, but a song all the same.

In this metabolizing reworking of my experience, I turned into imaginative expression all that I had been struggling with—the anguish of being assaulted by sordid fantasies invading one's mind at their will, the self-loathing that accompanies the staining when suspecting oneself as sexually abused, and the unbearability of admitting one's molestation even in the midst of mounting evidence to the contrary. I acknowledged the suffering that one's denial can inflict, even inadvertently, both upon oneself and onto others; the loss of faith in a Supreme Being as he ignores the cries of the victimized when in the hands of their perverted captors; and the ache for a spark of the spirit that can sustain a life worth living in the midst of soul-crushing affliction. As the novel crescendoed toward its ill-fated finale, the creative transmutation cut deeper. The scarred stories of the wounded ones within me were crying out to be heard as well. Tony's and Carey's secrets were set not only to intersect. They would be exposed, in all of their repugnant clarity, both to themselves and to each other.

THE FINAL DAYS of bringing forth that first draft felt like bearing a newborn, ten months in the womb, and now halfway through the birth canal—any further delay at getting it out would have been deleterious. For those last few days, I devoted every spare minute to pushing those culminating chapters into the world. From early morning until late at night—interrupted only to tend to Justin or to pop in at work—I sat at my desk and labored onto the page. As emotionally raw as it was, I told it all.

In a padded-room unburdening, Carey shares with Tony the incident of longing for a treat from an ice cream truck and interrupting his mother with a man where he is molested by her, with the man watching, as the crying eyes of Jesus look on from a crucifix. The bullish beast of a stepfather, who has been bivouacked in the camper that has accommodated his perversions, is caught in the act of abducting Carey. Prompted to visit his own father, and provoked by his father's confessional disclosures, Tony flashes back to his nap with his mother before the *Mary Poppins* premiere and is confronted irrefutably with the truth of his past: his mom satisfied her needs for closeness through sexual intimacy with him, her number one.

Tony is so reeling from the revelations of his molestation and is so certain that Carey's only abuser has been apprehended, he dismisses Carey's enigmatic reticence about going back to the boarding school on the evening of an Easter Sunday recital. Tony takes him back that night and hands him over to the priest. The priest, after the concert, steals Carey away to the Madonna-glassed chapel. Tony belatedly puts it together and races to intervene. Finding the chapel locked, but hearing the two inside, he shatters the stained-glass window with a concrete garden statue.

The priest, already pleasured, is standing over the kneeling boy. Ballistic with rage, Tony attacks, pounding the cleric in all his degeneracy. With the priest beaten down, Tony turns to Carey. Carey, still kneeling, meets Tony's gaze. The boy's eyes bear the despair of being captive in hell's cold center. They stare at Tony uncomprehendingly—the would-be rescuer, the unintended betrayer, Jesus and Judas both. Tony stares back. Victim and accomplice, his eyes have no answer. Without one, the boy is done. Depravity, too defiling, has won. Onto the shard of broken glass held in his hand, Carey falls forward. With a sliver of the shattered Madonna as a brand, Carey refuses this world so vile.

Such is the cruel and bitter truth of childhood sexual abuse. For the victim, no savior descends to stop it from happening. The assault, never ceasing, slays the spirit. The tomb of despair sees no light. And the pain, when denied to oneself and to others, only sharpens—and deepens the cut of the blade. A tragic gospel. Evil unveiled. God's absence unmasked. With only the screams of the condemned survivor piercing the night's cosmic silence.

THE CLIMACTIC LAST scene came out in a fevered rush. I wrote all day, paused to feed and put Justin to bed, then continued into the night. It was three thirty in the morning when the closing words leaked out onto the page and settled into place. The novel that I had envisioned in a middle-of-the-night epiphany was finally completed. I was too emotionally drained, however, to be exultant, too stricken at the story's ending to celebrate. Depleted to the edge of obliviousness, I stepped to the bed, and without bothering to undress, fell flat on top of the covers. Sleep or deadbeat unconsciousness overcame me at once. Outstretched in prostrated collapse, I was gone to the world.

Two hours later, I woke up.

Though still physically spent, I awakened unusually alert. Stillness seemed to pulsate from the dead-of-night quiet. Too fatigued to get up, I turned my gaze toward my desk. By the light of the half moon, I could make out the papers scattered on its surface, my mechanical pencil at rest upon them as if done in after giving its all in service of the cause.

Seeing those last pages of the completed manuscript—the whole story now told, the depths plumbed to the bottom—the enormity of it all hit me. Sobs gushed forth from inside me as if all the unshed tears in the seawaters of my soul now found the freedom to wail and flow. Curled up on my bed, pitching with the waves, I wept for the entirety of it. For all the gut-wrenching pain that was bled onto those pages. For the cleansing release of grief and heartache held in constraint for decades. For the improbable accomplishment, which I still found incredulous, that I had seen it to the end and actually had written my long-dreamt-of novel. And for the sober comprehension, that I had even then, that this work of narrative fiction was the most truthful story that I had ever told, the most truthful self-disclosure that I had ever made. And as the pre-dawn silence received the truth of my tears and absorbed them into the starlit stillness, a sense of presence-infused peace surrounded me and soaked into every cell of my being.

From my project's inception, I had thought that I was crafting a narrative looking glass—a storied version of The Bitter Truth Players' marred mirror of God. I had intended to hammer away the butcher-paper façade of societal disregard and theological abetment and lay bare the brutal reality of child sexual abuse. I wanted readers to gaze unflinchingly into the horror of children's assault. To see the torment that it perpetrates, the death that it inflicts. And to stare into the shattered reflection long enough to perceive their eyes filling up with tears, their hearts opening before the pain and pulsating with engaged compassionate care.

I have since come to see that the mirror that I was creating was more for me than it was for others. As I gave myself to the writing, I was ripping away the masked persona that I had worn in the world for so long. And I was revealing the truth of who I am underneath more to myself than to anyone else. I was stripping away the façade of my own denials and dismissiveness to lay bare a reflection of my own tortured experience so that I could behold and embrace it. In telling Tony's and Carey's stories, I was confessing my own. I was settling into the self-admission that I am Tony. I am Carey. I am an abuse survivor. It is my body that is stained by sexual assault. I have struggled to accept it. The pain and the shame have, at times, been unbearable. And my denials have, unwittingly, contributed to the suffering of the damaged ones within me. They have contributed to others' suffering as well. That, too, is part of the story. That, too, is the truth.

The grace that my writing revealed to me is that the looking glass reflects that as well. I can peer into the polished pages of my novel's narrative and see both my pains and my complicities displayed with neither distortion nor rejection. Those pages are iconic. Like the rippleless waters in the sea of cosmic compassion, the marred mirror of God holds it all. Gazing into the imaginary circumstances unveiling my emotional truth, I was catching a glimpse of the sacred presence that sees every shard of it without blinking nor turning away. In those tear-stained eyes, for the first time I could claim my experience. My heart could open to my own pain. It could pulsate, now resuscitated, as one with the heartbeat of God's restorative care. Lying on my bed, taking in the whole story that was taking me in from my desk, I came to see that the tears in my eyes were reflective of the Divine's.

As the sun rose in the east that morning, its tender reach stretched over both—novel and novelist; the mirror and the marred one mirrored back.

THOUGH THE STORY that Tony had set out to write was now complete, I was still in need of an epilogue. Tony had journeyed to the Hadean center of his suffering—had borne witness to Carey's quite non-redemptive death and faced the truth of his soul's affliction. Where, now, would he find a restorative spark that could bring him back into the land of the living? I had considered the possibility that Tony's descent into the inferno of abuse and betrayal might so crush his spirit that he would, in the end, succumb to taking his own life. To be sure, child sexual violation is devastating enough to spawn such self-destructive despair. Those stories, like Carey's, deserve to be heard and honored. And yet, suicide upon suicide felt spiritually battering and needlessly melodramatic. More to the point, however, it did not feel truthful to either my or to Tony's experience.

I had taken the journey with Tony. With him, I had encountered the demons of self-lacerating desolation. I had stared into the face of our sordid and soiling suffering. I had felt the aloneness of divine abandonment, an All-Powerful Guardian not caring enough to show up and protect his children. And yet, my spirit, in the end, was not vanquished. In the tomb of my pain, a womb of grace emerged—a maternal presence whose power is compassion. She appeared, at times, in moments of oceanic oneness and, at other times, in embodied acts of Shekinah kindness. In every encounter, her presence proved to be restorative. Her sacred care held the pain. It resuscitated the spirit. Resisting the drag into despondency's muteness, it kindled the creative spark that allowed Tony and me to tell our story. The novel itself—as tragic as it is—is testimony to the love and vitality that ever pulsates even in the sordid depths of evil. For Tony's story to be truthful, it would need to reflect that pulsebeat of life.

In the hour or so between dawn and the time to get Justin up for school, I summoned the muses for some possibilities of how a last scene might incarnate this life-giving presence. I got no further than Tony returning to the boarding-school chapel—the cold center of hell's depravity—and glimpsing, perhaps through a child's kindness, the pulse of compassion that still beats even there. As I was driving Justin to school, a little while later, I posed the question to him. If a child were to extend kindness to an adult stranger in some meaningful way, what might that look like?

Justin did not hesitate. With the authority of one who had been there himself, he instantly said, "It's gotta be Tic Tacs. And they gotta be orange."

Once back home, I pulled out the folder in which I had slipped, throughout the five years of living with my novel, random ideas that would come to me about how I could conclude it. As I thumbed through the notes, I came upon a Post-it at the bottom of the heap. It was the very first entry that I had made when I started the folder, shortly after I dreamed of the novel dozens of months before. It merely read, "For the epilogue: like at the hospital, something about orange Tic Tacs."

It all came back—the Shekinah kindness that had come to me. Justin was her emissary. Dispensing them with such care-filled deliberateness, he showed me. Orange Tic Tacs can be medicine for the soul.

They do not take the pain away. But they keep the spirit alive while going through it.

THE MUSE HAVING inspired, the epilogue unfolded on its own. Tony returns to the chapel, seven years after Carey's death, bearing both his grief and a symbolic gift. He pauses before a plaque that commemorates Carey, and the crying eyes of the crucified that Carey once had sought. A young girl emerges from the chapel with her father. Seeing Tony's sorrow, she offers him, with care-filled deliberateness, a single orange Tic Tac. As one who would know, she tells him that it helps you feel better when you are sad. Tony thanks her and assures her that it does.

On the strength of the candied kindness, he enters the chapel. He walks to the altar and sets his offering onto the table. It is the stage-prop sledgehammer that The Bitter Truth Players had used to rip apart the butcher paper God. With that God long gone, Tony's days of railing and raging are over.

He gazes at the floor behind the table. The shards have been swept up, the blood washed away, but in his mind's eye he can still see the broken bodies slumped on the slate. Carey and the priest, abused and abuser, entombed together in their irredeemable horror. Without blinking or turning away, Tony takes them in until colored beams, streaking through stained glass, bathe the floor in their hazy rays.

Tony lifts his gaze to the window that watches all that happens there. The splintered pieces of the majestic Madonna have been gathered up and res-culpted. A Mater Dolorosa now looks on. Mary, a Pietà cast in a lacework of shards, cradles two bodies, one in the crook of each arm. A crown of thorns rings one man's head; a hanging rope circles the other's neck. Jesus and Judas. Two of her boys. Both having died brutal deaths. And unlike Vincent's anti-pietà, both are held in a mother's care.

Staring into the mirror of Mary's compassion, Tony hears the heartbeat. Or at least the trickle that points the way. Tears splatter the hammer's handle like raindrops on stone. In the light of the splintered Pietà, they glisten like stars.

Part VI

Eureka, CA—Age 46

July 2005

—◆—

AFTER AN ENTIRE day on the road, an IPA from the Lost Coast Brewery and homemade chicken enchiladas felt like a eucharistic feast. Justin and I were driving down the coastal highway, after a week in southern Oregon and two weeks in Seattle, and had pulled into Eureka at about seven in the evening. I had called ahead to see if Linda could put us up for the night. She not only had beds made but my favorite local beer on ice and one of her signature dishes warm in the oven. She welcomed us as if our brief stayover made her the wayfaring recipient of grace.

The move to the northwest corner of California had been good for my sister. In the few years that she had been there, she had become a devoted volunteer at her children's schools—elementary, middle, and high. She had established a network of friends through a weekly women's Bible study that doubled as a support group for stay-at-home moms, and she had created a home for her family in one place, then brokered its sale with a profit. In fact, they had just moved into their second Humboldt County residence—a historic Victorian house that she and Kyle had bought at a bargain in the heart of old Eureka.

Once she had slaked our thirst and fed us, she was eager to give us a tour, pointing out all the vintage features and rhapsodizing about the renovations that she was already envisioning. After perusing all three floors—from red-brick cellar to widow's peak—we settled in the parlor where she had us sample a selection of Humboldt Chocolates (that she insisted were better than the family favorite See's) and brought out a deck of cards for us all to play Hearts as we used to do on my returns home from college. It wasn't until the game was over and we had gotten the kids to bed that we had a few moments to talk just the two of us. We took our glasses of wine into a nook off the living room that had a rounded bay window into which Linda was delighted to nestle. Framed against the night sky, her legs wrapped in a comforter, she looked as content as a curled-up kitty-cat.

We chatted about the house—how much bigger it was than her last place and about the work it would require to fix it up. She asked about the retreat that I had led in the mountains of southern Oregon and described the one that she had been on with the women from her church. I remarked on how happy she looked, how she seemed lighter each time that I visited her in the tranquil redwood remoteness, and she affirmed how much she loved it up there—the pace and the distance both. Then I asked about the one person from whom we both had needed to get away for a while.

"So when's the last time you saw Mom?" I inquired.

"She was up with Andy a few weeks ago," she said, Andy being our mom's new husband. "They only stayed a couple of days. You still haven't met Andy, have you?"

"No," I confessed. Still finding it too infuriating to be around my mother, I had declined to attend their marriage ceremony and had yet to be with her in person again since I initiated our separation nearly ten years earlier. "I'm sure he must be wondering who this son is who wouldn't even show up at his mother's wedding."

"No, he's not like that," Linda assured. "He's very laid back. He just lets Mom be Mom. Like the rest of us, I'm sure he figures that it's something between the two of you. Now, Mom, on the other hand—she's beside herself about it all. She can't understand why you still won't talk to her, let alone come to see her on her wedding day."

"I know," I admitted, feeling the familiar pangs of both guilt and dread. "It's getting to be time for the two of us to work some things out. I'm actually thinking of asking her to meet with me and my therapist. I need to talk through some things with her that I have never brought up before. I think that he'll be a good buffer."

"Are you serious?" she asked. "Bringing Mom to your therapy? Do you think that she'll open up and talk about things for real?"

"To be honest," I said, "I don't know. Maybe not. But I need to find out once and for all. And I at least need to say some things for myself—even if she cannot hear them. We'll see what happens and take it from there."

"Well, let me know when you do it," Linda said. "I want to be sure that I'm in another state at the time. I can't imagine what would happen if anyone started talking about things for real with her." She shook her head at the thought. "Hey," she said suddenly. "I haven't shown you my tattoo."

"What? When did you get a tattoo?" I asked. For Linda, a tattoo would have been a bold badge in self-presentation.

"A few months ago. I had been thinking about it for a while, and then, one day, I just said, 'I'm going to do it.'"

She slipped her arm from the sleeve of her sweater and revealed—on her back, just to the side of her shoulder blade—an orange and yellow monarch butterfly.

"That's so cool," I exclaimed. "They did a great job. And what else but a butterfly."

"Yeah," she said. "I always knew that if I was going to get one it would be a butterfly."

"You've liked them forever," I said. "You used to color them as a child. You had drawings of them all over your bedroom."

She stretched her neck to glimpse the one now on her back. Then she asked, "Do you remember the time that a butterfly landed on me when I was a kid?"

"Not really," I admitted. I tried to retrieve such a memory and came up with nothing. "Was I there?"

"Of course you were there," she said, turning back to me. "We were building a fort at Gull Park, remember? Grandpa Harold was watching us once when they were visiting—Mom and the others were out somewhere—and you took me down the street to the park. We decided to make a hiding place in those huge bushes that were clumped together by the lagoon. You could only crawl in on one side, and we made like a tunnel and cleared out a hollow space in the middle. We had bushes all around us. All you could see was a little patch of sky up above. We got a piece of cardboard and covered it with branches and plugged up the entrance so that no one could see how to get in. Then we just sat there until we thought Mom and the rest of them would be back.

"And while we were sitting there, a butterfly flew in from the sky and came down and landed right on my knee. It was amazing. It was so soft and beautiful—all those pretty colors. It stayed super still and it stared right at me, like it had come just for me and wanted to hang out with me in our hiding place for a while. Then it flapped its wings a couple of times and flew back out the top. I remember thinking that I wanted to go with it—that in another life I could be a butterfly, too, and just fly around and land on people's knees all day. Anyway, it was one of those things that you never forget."

It is telling—what we remember and what we forget. To this day, I have no memory of Linda's encounter with the butterfly. I do, however, remember the fort. And the reason that the two of us had fled the house to build it. Linda left out that part of the story. The swinging saloon doors—with me on one side in the family room, she on the other in the back rooms of the house, Harold slipping to and fro between them to terrorize us each in turn—all of that she omitted. Perhaps deep within her, she had already opted for butterflies over brutality.

WITH ANOTHER FULL day of driving ahead of us, Justin and I left early the next morning. Linda was up to see us off. She handed us a grocery bag—a batch of cashew brittle for the road, she said, and some extra pieces of chocolate. We were well on our way through the mountains before it hit me. I asked Justin to open the bag and report on the contents. I was right. No butterflies. Instead, an eight-track tape. Barry Manilow's *This One's For You*. And a note that read, "Happy Early Birthday! And thanks for all of the forts."

She was still fluttering in all of her playful glory.

Claremont, CA—Age 46

September 2005

—— ♦ ——

THE SUMMER AFTER I finished drafting my novel, the funding for my narrative work with teenagers came to an end. Not only had I completed the fictional piece through which I was processing my faith and my trauma, I now had a pressing need for a new source of employment. It seemed too much to hope for that another dream job would come my way that would not only pay the bills but would subsidize the next leg of my quest for psycho-spiritual healing and well-being. I should not have doubted. As if dispatched to validate Goethe's adage that the universe conspires to assist those mobilized in pursuit of their soul work, a patron appeared in the most unlikely of places—the board of the Claremont School of Theology from whose faculty I had resigned several years earlier.

Ralph "Doc" Roberts was an ortho-pediatric physician specializing in reconstructive surgery for children born with cleft palates. Unable to have children of his own with Muriel, his beloved wife of over fifty years, he made it his life's mission to restore smiles in the damaged mouths of young people from impoverished communities. Doc was taken with the work that I was doing, sensing a kindred calling in my use of narrative to restore the spirits of young people damaged by society.

During campus visits for board meetings, he would come to my office and listen to stories about the teenagers in my project and the plays that we produced together. He restored both my smile and my spirit when he announced one day in my office the decision that he had just come to. He was donating a million dollars to the school to fund a faculty position to teach and do grounded research in spiritually regenerative resources for those with childhood wounds. Before my grant funds could be fully depleted, the Muriel Bernice Roberts Chair in Spiritual Formation and Narrative Pedagogy was created and I became its inaugural recipient—finding myself back on the faculty with rank and tenure restored.

Invited to create my own job description, I took the opportunity to recalibrate my vocational explorations. I continued to teach courses in under-resourced neighborhoods that engaged seminary students and young people in the transformative promise of the narrative arts. With those courses already well-developed, however, and in need of rather minimal maintenance, I had both the space and the resources to seek out additional laboratory contexts where I could research psycho-spiritual processes of personal and relational restoration.

In the spring before my return to the faculty, my colleague Andy Dreitcer and I designed a spiritual formation track at the school of theology to commence in the fall with core courses in contemplative practices for personal well-being, creativity as a path of healing and vitality, and compassion-based processes of social transformation. The courses became opportunities to mine the theoretical literature, craft transformative learning activities, and reflect on the experiences of our students and ourselves while we jointly engaged in embodied spiritual practice. Eager to compare notes and synthesize insights, Andy and I co-taught each course in the first two years of that program.

In addition, that summer, I began leading weeklong spiritual retreats in southern Oregon with two colleagues—Doug Frank and Nancy Linton—who, through the years, would become good friends and trusted soul companions. The retreats would meet annually for well over a decade. In them, we immersed ourselves in classic Christian contemplative practices like *lectio divina*, Ignatian contemplation, communal silence, and the awareness examen. Along with those practices, I led meditative experiences crafted from my ongoing experiments engaging the turmoil of my own inner world—praying restoratively with our difficult emotions, using the imagination to self-regulate when passions and impulses engulf us, engaging our shadows both fecal and golden, and cultivating compassion through connecting with the buried stories within ourselves and others. The retreats not only offered an extended space for personal soul excavation, the opportunity to lead others in meditation expanded my insights into the nature of interior experience and honed my skills as a facilitator of contemplative practice.

In that first fall as a spiritual formation professor, I also began, as a student, a three-year certificate program in spiritual direction at the Mercy Center in Burlingame, California. Since I was inviting students and retreatants into contemplative explorations, then processing their experience with them, I felt the need to be trained in the techniques and sensibilities of walking with others on their soul journeys. The daylong gatherings once a month integrated personal retreat time, rigorous study of spiritual experience, and intensive practice in sitting with others discerning together movements of the sacred within the consolations and desolations of their lives. With such seasoned guides as Mary Ann Scofield, Jim Neafsey, and Janice Farrell—and countless hours in triads, process circles, real-plays, and both group and individual supervision—I was immersed in the art of spiritual companionship and sensed the call to listen deeply to others' stories and hold them in the mirror of sacred presence as a fellow sojourner and spiritual director.

With the tumblers of my vocation clicking into place—my roles as a professor of spirituality, a contemplative facilitator, a retreat leader, and a spiritual director coalescing into a complementary whole—I found myself being sought out in various ways as a spiritual teacher. Students, retreatants, and directees were coming to me for guidance in navigating the cacophonies of their inner and outer worlds. Like a child growing into the adult clothes in which they are already draped, the role seemed bigger than my capacities to fill.

For me, the adage was holding true; we teach what we want to know.

Through writing my novel, I had come to accept that I was a survivor of sexual abuse, even though some of the actual memories were still murky. I was able to metabolize some of the pain of my trauma, though hidden behind the veneer of fiction. And in the symbolic mirror of Tony's and Carey's stories, I glimpsed a sacred maternal presence that holds the splinters of a survivor's pain with a compassion that can keep the spirit alive. What I now ached to know, both intellectually but more so experientially, was the process by which those splinters of pain can be mended and made whole.

If the life's work of the feminine divine is *Tikkun Olam*—repairing the world through restorative acts of kindness and compassion while gathering the shards of God's shattered oneness—how do we partner with that presence in repairing the shattered oneness of a survivor's soul? Within the shards of fragmented memories and grotesque recollections hidden in the muck of an abused person's psyche, what is *Tikkun Olam* for the inner world? Beyond the figurative truth of imaginary circumstances, I wanted to know the very real secrets buried in the cesspools of my soul's shadows, and to know them held and restored through a Shekinah-like care.

To unearth this path and to walk it, to truly know what I yearned for and felt called to teach, I would need another spiritual guide. It was a hard lesson to learn: the unlikely people who turn out to be our most transformative spiritual teachers.

WALTER WINK SUGGESTS that there is no way to know God genuinely in our time without going through our enemies. In a world of ever-escalating violence and generational legacies of abuse, learning to love our enemies is not only the truly liberative path of psycho-spiritual transformation, it is essential to our planet's survival. We and those who offend and infuriate us are inextricably linked. Our well-being and the well-being of our world depend upon us living into the implausible reality that our adversaries are, in actuality, our most indispensable spiritual allies.

Amplifying Jungian psychological insights, Wink argues that our enemies offer a uniquely restorative path of spiritual vitality by surfacing aspects of ourselves—essential for our healing and wholeness—that we are not able to access directly. Enemies are those people whose ideologies, attitudes, and behaviors repulse us. Like two positively charged magnets defying contact, they are the people from whom we recoil; connection with them feels abhorrent. We all have such people in our lives. Even our loved ones, at times, can ignite this type of repelling energy.

Instructively, however, we do not have the same ones. The telemarketer that triggers me can evoke tender understanding in another. The family member with whom I am patient one day can incite my irascibility in a heartbeat tomorrow. Our reactivities are unique to ourselves and fluctuate with our emotional states. Wink suggests that this is because the source of our repulsion is not in the one that we are tempted to write off as inherently revolting or egregiously transgressive.

Rather, it is, first of all, within us.

The people who arouse our fury activate some part of us that we have banished to our personal shadows. We all bury splinters of ourselves too difficult to accept and embrace—wounds too painful to hold and let grieve, qualities too shameful to admit and expose, gifts and capacities chronically stifled yet longing to flourish in the light of day. These suppressed aspects of ourselves, in their bid to be known and integrated, project themselves onto people in our lives like images on a movie screen. Essentially, our enemies are mirrors. They reflect back to us that which we have relegated to the darkened chambers of our inner world. Our resistance to holding *them* with compassionate presence is rooted in our resistance to holding *ourselves* with compassionate presence. What we find untouchable in them is tethered to something we find untouchable in ourselves.

Our enemies, then, come bearing us a gift. They have the unparalleled ability to surface whatever is within us that is crying out for healing and wholeness. As Jesus taught with such psychological acumen, the splinters we see in the eyes of our foes are reflections of the logs lodged within our own. He invites us to turn inward and tend to the cry hidden within us—to heal the wound, repair the shame, revitalize the stifled capacities to love and to flourish. As we return to the ground of our truest self, we transform our reactivity into personal restoration.

Along the way, we find that our enemy becomes transformed as well. With our abilities to see clearly renewed, they become human for us. They become people in pain, just as we are. The tether of our repulsion softens into the bond of compassionate connection. Catalysts in securing the well-being for which we and the world both long, and activating an alchemical process that can turn hate into genuine love, our enemies become more than our spiritual allies. They become our potential spiritual teachers.

IF THE PEOPLE who most repel us are our spiritual teachers in disguise, then I was at risk of flunking out of the shadow-work academy where my custom-made guru held residence. As the years of my anguished recovery rolled by, I had grown to despise my mother. I hated myself for feeling such rancor—professor of spirituality and leader of contemplative retreats that I was. But I truly detested the sight and the sound of her. Her voice on my answering machine enflamed me. The thought of being in the same room with her sent me into a rage. Whether tethered as allies or permanently pitched in our entrenched estrangement, it was the shadowy truth: my mom was my enemy. The invitation to love her I found repugnant.

As my initial request for a prolonged separation slid into several years of silence, my mom resorted to leaving me phone messages. They began as perky updates about what she happened to be doing—"Just driving to your brother's for Easter . . ." or "to the beach for brunch . . ." or "to the baseball game with Jim . . . and was thinking of you." They sunk into not-so-subtle swipes at my persistent disregard for reconnecting with her—"I heard from Linda that you stopped by to see her. It must have been nice for her to get some time with you." Then they devolved into guilt-tripping pleas for me to come back to her—"I wish you would find it in your heart to let me back into your life. You have no idea what this is doing to me. I can't even see my own grandson. I don't know what I possibly could have done to deserve this. Why can't you just call me? This is not how I raised you. Please, stop putting me through this."

My mom's messages filled me with rage. The tiny sliver of sympathy that tried to poke through my pounding fury—that she was crying out in the only way that she knew to bridge a breach that was killing her—was swiftly incinerated in the flamethrower of my wrath. My therapist, Mark, witnessed my verbal torching of her during our weekly therapy sessions. The pages of my journal absorbed the scorching as I spewed my ire indecipherably upon them. Even the walls of my bedroom were prey to the blazing as I screamed my venom while pacing to collect myself.

"First, she pretends like nothing is going on, that we are as close as we were when she confided everything to me. Then she resorts to blaming me. Like this is all my fault. That I just have an inexplicably hard heart that won't let her into my life. That our entire estrangement is simply because of an obstinate son's refusal to care about his mother. Like she cares about me—how tortured I've been, how much pain I've been in throughout the years. Not once does she ask about how I am doing. Not once does she inquire about why I remain so distant from her. If she really cared, she'd want to know. She'd want to find out if there is anything at all that she might have done to hurt me. And she'd do everything that she could to repair it. But she doesn't want to go there. Instead it's all a big mystery to her why I stay so far away. And whatever it is, she's sure she doesn't deserve it. So it's on me to soften my heart and find it within myself to pretend it all away so we can be close again and she doesn't have to feel bad that her son doesn't want to have any contact with her. Some mother *she* is."

My rage would be incensed beyond my capacity to appease it. But it had another opponent. As much as it waged war with my mom, it also did battle with my self-rebuke. "Look at yourself," a voice from within me castigated. "You are truly hateful. It's not just that you are a sham as a guide for the spiritual journey. You're also a disgrace as a son. You don't even know for sure that your mom molested you—that she sexually abused you at all. All you've got are vague hunches, fantastical surmisings, and cryptic symptomatic sensations. Your suspicions are speculative. You don't know that she actually violated you. You're accusing her of things without good cause. You're hurting her for nothing. Some son *you* are."

At which point the rage would rise up with rabid indignation, hammering out the evidence like an incensed prosecutor, starting with how she tried to kiss Justin's privates and tried to shower and nap with him nude. Next were the memories that had surfaced as firm as solid ground—her caressing my skin in my bed as a boy, her taking me into her bed after school and at night, her hand under my briefs stroking my butt as I lay on the couch with my head in her lap. It followed up with the incriminating corroboration of the sexualized undercurrent that constantly pervaded our closeness—her incessant flirtatiousness with me, her prancing around me half naked, our nightly bedtime rendezvous with her clad only in a negligee, her constant need to be touching me, and her turning to me as a partner, her number one, her sweetheart, all to satisfy her insatiable needs for erotically charged love. And finally, the circumstantial substantiation of the aftereffects that still plagued me—my terror of romantic intimacy, my phobia about women absorbing me, my repulsion at being touched, my body stinging with sensations of abuse, my fits of fury at every news report of children being fondled by a parent.

"I *know* I was abused by my mom," I insisted to Mark in his office or avowed on the pages of my journal. "I know it in my bones. And she refuses to go there even when her son was suffering to the point of taking his own life. She abandoned me in my pain—my suicidally desperate pain. She deserves every flame of the fury that I have toward her. What kind of a mother is that?"

Still, the self-rebuke was indomitable. It eroded the solid ground of my conviction like a sinkhole swallowing a foundation of sand. "Look at yourself," it would counter, "mired in your hatefulness and uncertain accusation. You gather evidence, but you don't really know. You're trying to convince yourself into believing it. What if your conjectures are based in self-deceptions or distortions of events misremembered? You're tearing into your mother for no good reason. What kind of a son is that?"

Rage and self-rebuke—enemies to each other in a dogged deadlock of fiercely mutual repellence. And enemies to me as well. I wanted to be rid of the both of them. To be free of the toxic venom of the one, and to silence the sabotaging scrutiny of the other. If the way to God is through our adversaries, I had a path to the divine that was heaven-sent. I was fighting a two-front war: one with my mother, the other with myself. One thing was clear. Before I could take on the opponent that bore me, I needed to make peace with the opponents within me.

WALTER WINK'S INVITATION to search for the source of our repulsions within our own soul's shadows resonated with the shifts that I had experienced when I personified the psychic states that overwhelmed me and then meditated on their deeper cries. In an effort to free myself from the possessive clutch of my rage and self-rebuke, perhaps even to tame and transmute them, I turned to contemplative practice once more and used my imagination to engage my contentious inner world. One such attempt brokered an unexpected armistice. The truce proved Wink to be right. Not only are our repulsions pathways to healing. It seems that enemies—both those inside us and those outside—can be held with some measure of genuine love.

SITTING IN MY craftsman chair in my upstairs suite of a bedroom the morning after another voice-mail message from my mom, I close my eyes and sense where in my body I feel the rage. I feel heat pumping from my chest and I cultivate an awareness that rage is racing through my bloodstream. I ground myself as best I can by focusing on my breath and invite the rage to materialize symbolically. After a few more breaths, the image comes of a flamethrower at full throttle blasting my mom with torrents of fire as she lies naked on her bed. Though ablaze, her body remains unharmed, provoking the flamethrower into greater and greater barrages of fire.

As the rage spews its fury, a voice emerges from within me. "Look at yourself. Look at how hateful of a person you have become. And all without knowing for sure whether she actually sexually abused you."

The self-rebuke appears as a mirror the size of a plate-glass window placing itself between the flamethrower and my mom. Seeing its reflection in the mirror, the flamethrower's rage intensifies, the fire gushing into the mirror with escalating fury.

The mirror's derision becomes a mocking chant. "Look at yourself. Look at yourself. Look at yourself."

The fire blasts harder; the chant grows louder, becoming an accumulating reverberation of rage and ridicule, flame and mockery, until the fire and the chant crescendo and the mirror explodes into a heap of shards and the flamethrower, spent of fuel, goes out.

The inner tension relaxes a bit. I breathe into the ensuing reprieve. A grounded openness emerges within me that I extend to the flamethrower and the mirror. I assure them both that I trust that they each serve some positive purpose and I am curious about what that might be. The flamethrower reveals that it aims to remove all threat; it is here to spot a perpetrator, call them out, and keep me safe from their violation at any cost. The mirror reveals that it, too, wants to keep me safe; it wants to protect me from the shame and pain that would come if the rage spews its accusations and is met with denial, chastising, or even disgust. The flamethrower trembles with menace at the insinuation that its accusations may be false.

The mirror responds appeasingly. "No," it maintains, "I am not saying that the accusations are false. I'm saying that when they are shared with another—especially with your mother—that they be spoken from a posture of confidence, a place of solid-ground knowing, not sinking-sand uncertainty."

I ask the mirror, "How do you do that, especially when there is uncertainty?"

As gentle as a benevolent guide, the mirror repeats what it has been saying all along, "Look at yourself."

I still do not catch on. "How?" I ask.

It replies, "Take a shard of broken mirror and look into it."

I pick a piece up and gaze into its surface. I do not see my current-day self. I see, behind me, the network of caverns that I had encountered at the Redwoods Monastery. At the mouth of one, a young boy sits slumped on the floor against the wall, his stare haunted as one broken and abandoned. Somehow I know: he is, all at once, the Munch-like skull from the hospital, the street urchin from the underworld caves, Carey staring at the dry-eyed crucifix, and me as a three-year-old boy staring along with him. And I know that all their pain is real. I turn around to face him directly. He has turned into me as a toddler. And he is now cowering in the darkened living room corner of my boyhood house, naked but for his briefs, shivering in the cold, a line of lipstick stains trailing down from his chest and disappearing inside his underwear. His eyes plead with me to see him.

Compassion wells up within me—both brokenhearted at his pain and protective of his impuissance. I go to him, wrap him in a blanket, and sit down beside him, holding him in my arms as he leans into my embrace.

"It really happened," he says.

"I know," I reply.

"I need you to hear me tell you," he says. "It's time."

"I'm ready," I say. And I am.

He tells me. "She liked to kiss me. Everywhere. Even down there. She liked to eat me up, she said. She liked giving me lots of loving. I didn't like it, though. I still don't."

Somewhere deep inside me, I can feel the weeping—a howl of anguish at the pain that this boy has been carrying. I am not sure where it comes from—some part of me, some part of him, some ancestor moaning a mournful African melody, the nobody who does know the trouble he's seen, the nobody who knows his sorrow. Whatever the source, it feels sacred, as if flowing from the heartbeat of God's trouble and sorrow. I sit still, poised in compassionate presence, and hold the boy in my arms as the wailing rises up through my inner core like a river of tears coursing from the sacred center of the universe and washing over the boy, both giving voice to his suffering and cleansing him of all its soiling. With each breath I take, these rinsing waters spring up and pour through me, absorbing the pain and dissolving it away—the lipstick stains on his body; their sting on his skin; the chill in his bones; his sense of being used and disposed of, left alone in his anguish; even the living room itself and the house that sheltered his violation—all of it washing away until he is left with me back at the cavern, cradled in my arms, safe and secure in a love that will never leave him alone again.

As I hold him, a palpable sense of sacred reality surrounds the boy and me, a divine maternal presence swaddling us both with love. We are sheltered in a sanctuary of infinite care. I am loved and loving, held and holding, safe and offering safety, at one with the heartbeat of compassion that flows from God's being. The boy and I are home—our true home—where the caress of motherly love is a touch that comforts and restores. It is the home that the boy deserves. And one that he never has to leave. We soak in its warm embrace as it saturates our every tissue.

Still steeped in the sanctuary's sacred care, I gaze out at the flamethrower. It is calm now, but it is resolute.

"He's one of the ones that I protect," it tells me. Then it continues in no uncertain terms. "Just so you know, I'll be right here in case anyone tries to abuse him again, or deny his experience, or dismiss his pain in any way. He's hurt enough."

"I understand," I tell him. "I'm here now too. I also will be watching out for him."

"You have a way of not showing up," it counters disbelievingly. "That's where I come in."

"That was before," I answer. "I know his pain now. For real. And I will see that it is never denied or dismissed."

"We'll see," the rage says, far from convinced.

"Fair enough," I accede.

I turn my gaze to the heap of shards from the shattered mirror. Each piece, I now notice, bears a separate image. I glimpse a few of their reflections—me in my *mom's bed after school, me in my bed as my mom strokes me, me as an infant naked for the kissing, me in my grandfather's green camper truck, me in my bedroom's bottom bunk being raped from behind by a beast, me in a priest's office playing his sordid game.*

"This is the path," the shattered mirror shares. "Each shard, over time, needs you to see it, to get it, to wrap it in love, and to dissolve its pain in the wash of compassion."

I assure each shard its full share of care.

I am about to surface from the meditation when I look out beyond the heap of shattered shards. My mom's bed is still there, though she is no longer on it. Hiding behind the bed, a young girl is slumped on the floor against the wall, her stare haunted as one broken and abandoned. It is my mom, as a child, disposed of after her stepfather had preyed upon her. For the first time that I can remember, I feel for my mom, my heart open to the pain that she has known, the pain that is behind the pain that she has brought me.

As I sit holding the young me in the sanctuary of compassion, Shekinah appears and sits holding the young girl of my mom. My mom relaxes into her care, as the boy has relaxed into mine. We are mirrored images of each other—two wounded children receiving care, Shekinah and I the cradling caregivers, the womb of love enveloping one now enfolding the other in a sacred refuge of infinite tenderness. In the restorative safety of that womb, suffering is assuaged, enemies become allies, and mothers and sons are tethered not by repulsion but by compassionate connection—the rage once mirrored now reverberating in care reflected one to the other.

THE GIFT OF such moments of meditative immersion is an intuitive knowing that cuts deeper than any deductive speculation or faith based on dogma. Settled in that contemplative stillness, the truth of my experience resonated with a self-confirming immediacy. Every cell of my soul, every pore of my body, was a receptacle for the really real with such transparent clarity that, in the midst of that mystical alignment, I could say with absolute certainty, "I simply know that what I know is what I know."

I know the pain of my suffering with neither shame nor dismissiveness. I know that my suffering is held by a divine presence, a sacred force field of love that absorbs the pain and restores life with compassion. I know that this sacred force field of love permeates our planet, holding all suffering with compassion and sustaining all life held in its care. And I know that I am one with that sacred reality, that in my essence—when I am most true to myself, when I am back home in who I was created to be—I am a free and flowing vessel of that love, a settled and resilient compassionate presence holding with empathic care both the wounds and the wonders in our world.

In the midst of the swirling windstorms of life—the passions within us and the bustle without that can so often knock us off center—this knowing feels like solid ground. When I am contemplatively connected to the sacred essence of myself and my truth, I feel as if I am standing in such quiet confidence and caring presence that a steel rod of strength and certainty is rooting me into the very core of God's Ground of Being. Like a tree entrenched for centuries, such firm embeddedness in divine certitude can withstand any onslaught. No wind is too strong, no twister too disorienting, to uproot me from the ground of what I know.

In these glimpses of aligned oneness, I experience such a sense of beloved-ness that every shame in me is washed away; such a confidence in my truth that no detractor could ever dislodge me from it; such an infinite and all-in-clusive care that I could love, at least in that moment, any person in our world. My roots went so deep in that sacred soil of empowered clarity that I felt ready to face the most repellent gale that blasted away at my self-possession. It was time to see whether the tether of compassion really could hold true even when taking on the headwinds of Hades. For the first time in some ten years, for the first time since I caught her trying to nap with Justin, I decided to reach out to my mom.

The plan, worked out with Mark, was straightforward. I would not get into any particulars. I would not get hooked by any infuriating dynamics. I was merely inviting her to come to Claremont and to meet with me and my thera-pist to discuss our relationship. Like Odysseus binding himself to his ship's mast to resist being seduced by the Sirens' song, I secured my grounding in the steel-rod certainty of my truth and gave her a call.

We would find out just how seductive a Siren's song can be.

"HEY, MOM. IT'S me."

She gasped as if a lover long since presumed dead had suddenly turned up alive. "Frank, you decided to call your mother."

It didn't take long. The rage within me immediately snapped into full combat mode—as if our lack of contact all these years was simply due to my willful refusal to fulfill my filial duties. Though battle ready, I managed to let it pass.

"Yeah, it's been a long time."

"How are you?" she gushed. "How have you been? You have no idea how much I've missed you. I didn't think that this day would ever come. It's so good to hear from you. Are you feeling better now . . . from all of your emotional problems?"

She may have felt some genuine concern, or she may have been scoping out the danger that my past derangement now posed to her. Either way, I took it as an attack—pinning all our issues on the peculiar instability of my mental health. The rage was pissed. The steel rod of solid confidence was pulled from the ground and poised as a spear. Though tempted, I refrained from hurling it.

"I'm doing fine," I assured her. "Never better."

"Oh, good," she said not needing nor wanting details. "So are you ready to reconcile with your mom—so we can get back together like we used to be?"

This was harder than I thought. Her every word pricked. Was she asking me to make amends? To come with some olive branch of appeasement like you would when wooing back one with whom you had broken up? I refused to get sucked in and stuck with my plan.

"Actually, that's what I wanted to discuss with you. I could be open to having more contact with each other. But first, I need to talk with you about some things."

She retracted as if poised for danger. "What kind of things?" she queried.

"Things about us. About our relationship. Things that happened while I was growing up, for example."

"Frank," she cut off before this went any further. "I never hurt you, if that's what you're talking about. I would never hurt you. I did nothing but love you. You were my number one. Always."

The rage was ready to pounce as the ground was giving way. I steadied my grip on the spear. "That's not going to help us get back together, Mom. I need you to listen to some things—not make denials or defend yourself before I even speak."

"I can listen," she insisted. "But I don't know what there would be to listen to."

I shouldn't have answered. But I did. "Haven't you wondered why your son has been so troubled these years?"

"Of course I wonder," she said. "A mother worries about her son. I know you had some personal problems—a nervous breakdown of some kind. Nobody bothers to tell me about these things. I have to wonder about it all by myself."

I was doing all that I could to keep the rage from going after her through the telephone lines. So this all comes down to me having a nervous condition? And *she's* the one distressed because *I* didn't bother to reach out to *her* when I could barely keep from killing myself?

"My personal problems came from someplace, Mom," I answered. "They didn't just emerge from a vacuum."

"And somehow I'm the one to blame?" she said.

"I'm saying it's complicated, but yes, you're a part of it. You hurt me, Mom. You may not have intended it, but you did."

"You hurt me too," she came back. "Do you know what it's like to have your own son disown you?"

"*And don't you want to know why?*" I exclaimed. This was infuriating. "Instead of insisting that you've never done anything to deserve it, why not be the first person to say, 'My God, I see that you're hurting. You seem to be upset with me. I don't understand why, maybe, but I want to. I want to do whatever I can to help you.' Why don't you say that?"

"Why don't you say that to me?" she parried like a spurned mistress being asked to swallow her snubbing. "I've been hurting all these years too."

"*Because you're the mom!*" I cried out. "*Be the mom!* Be the one who sees their child in pain and would do anything to help him. My God. Don't you care at all about your own son's anguish?" I was ready to scream. Instead, I emitted the steam of my exasperation with sighs from the pressure pot of my belly and reeled the rage back in. My mom, feeling the force of my fury, said nothing.

"Look," I said when I had gathered myself enough. "I don't know what kind of relationship we can have in the future. I'm willing to explore that. But I do need one thing first. I need you to hear what I experienced growing up with you. I don't even need you to respond. Maybe it's better that you don't. But I do need you to hear it. Are you open to that?"

Her silence was so absolute I may have been talking to a dead line.

"Mom," I pushed. "This is a deal-breaker for me. I can't just pretend that some things never happened."

Her silence continued, as if she had vacated her body and crawled inside herself to hide.

"Mom," I pushed harder. "I'm just asking you to listen to my experience. Why is that so much to ask?" Still nothing. "*Mom. I just want to be heard. Why does that have to be so hard for you?*"

Her voice was so soft she seemed frightened to overhear herself. "Because I'm afraid you're going to accuse me of things that I never did."

I felt the gut punch and tightened my grip on the spear. "You don't even know what I'm going to accuse you of. You've never asked. I've never said. You're too busy defending yourself to give a damn."

She whispered, pleading with me to believe her. "Sometimes children imagine things that aren't true. They make up things that didn't happen."

"I'm not making things up, Mom!" I swore. "You hurt me. Whether you know it or not, whether you admit it or not, you did. And I will never be in a relationship with you until you at least own the fact that you may have somehow caused me some pain during the long course of my childhood."

Her voice cracked with desperation. She did not want to lose me, but there was a crypt that could not be unbarred. "I've done some things in my life that I will always be ashamed of. But I never meant to hurt you, Frank. All I did was love you. I never wanted to bring you pain, in any way."

"But you did, Mom. You did. And you need to accept that."

She started to whimper, her words slurred through the sobbing. "I know I've hurt you, Son. I know. And I'm sorry. I've done so many things. I am so sorry. But there are some things that I would never do. Please, you have to believe me."

Her sobs became wails, gasping moans of shame and despair. Though I detested myself for breaking her down to tears, her crying only incensed me. With her maddening denials, her desperate pleading, my own pain now swallowed into the abyss of hers, I wanted to impale her with the rod of my rage. It took all that I had to stab it into the ground instead, and once again regain enough self-possession to get off the phone before I did any more damage to either myself or to her.

"I can't do this anymore, Mom," I said. "I need to go."

"Wait," she implored through her sniffling. "Please, Son, don't leave me again. I'll do anything. Say what you have to say, I'll listen."

"I can't right now," I persisted. "I need some time to figure this out."

"Please, Son," she repeated like a paramour begging not to be scorned.

"I have to go, Mom," I dug in. "I have to. I'll be in touch when I can."

"Son," she gasped a final time. "Please don't forget that I love you. I've always loved you. I always will. Please never forget that."

I hung up.

Even across the miles that separated us, and the wider gulf that estranged us, I could still hear her, in her bedroom by herself, sobbing like a dumped schoolgirl. The mirror of self-rebuke was in place in an instant. "Look at yourself," it scoffed. "What kind of a son would beat his mother down into a weeping heap of shame and sorrow, then abandon her in her pain?"

The rage in the mirror fired back, "What kind of a mother would abandon her son in his pain, then insist on her denials even at the risk of losing her child forever?"

A mother and a son who were enemies to each other—still tethered in an oedipal coupling where hate and desire both are twisted disguises of love.

THOUGH IT WOULD not be until the following spring, my mom and I would have our therapist-mediated tête-à-tête with each other. Painful truths would be told. Truthful pain would be heard. Lies that we had told to ourselves would be exposed and acknowledged.

Yet before I would be ready for such naked self-disclosure, I had more interior work to do. The rage within me needed a more secure grounding. The relentless self-rebuke reminded me that more shattered shards were in need of repairing. With so many pieces of my soul still splintered, and their jagged edges so quick to cut, a season of internal *Tikkun Olam* was necessary before I would be able to face my mom again and maintain an anchored clarity. The wounded ones within me needed, first, to be mothered by a maternal presence capable of a care that my birth mother could never offer.

I turned to Shekinah to be my guide on another extended journey through the underworld of my soul. She brought with her a companion—another spiritual teacher who knew firsthand both suffering and suffering transfigured.

Claremont, CA—Age 46–47

October 2005–May 2006

———◆———

SOME MYSTICS SUGGEST that a sacred music plays at the still center of the universe. The Song of Creation, the Cosmic Dance of the Divine, a Celestial Symphony of Life and Love—whatever we call it, it is a melody of peace and personal power, of grace and resilience, of compassion, coequality, and a reconciled relatedness that extends to all without exception. It flows from the very heartbeat of God and whispers through every sphere of the cosmos inviting each person, each particle of creation, to move in harmony with its restorative rhythms. Each one of our lives is a melody line within this sacred symphony. Each soul is a song—either in tune or not—singing with the celestial song of divine love sounding through all things.

Saint Ignatius of Loyola designed the *Spiritual Exercises*—an extensive series of meditative prayer experiences—as an intensive, transformative process through which the movements within a person's soul become harmonized with the movements of God's spirit in our world. Frequently, our interior movements—the emotions, impulses, attractions, and repulsions that can blare through us with a blustery abandon—are disordered and cacophonous. If God's movement through the world is a life-sustaining melody, our lives often ping discordantly with the din of our emotional distresses and our daily drivenness.

Ignatius's *Exercises* are intended to attune the interior life, to align the noisome vibrations within us into a melodious union with the rhythms of God's presence. When the anxieties, antipathies, and indignations that commonly clang within us are modulated more closely toward serenity, benevolence, and empowered boldness, we are not only more at one with the divine, we are freer to discern ways of being in the world that partner with the divine's regenerative work. The song of our lives sings in tandem with the song of God's presence healing and restoring the world around, with, and through us.

For Ignatius, this is God's deepest desire for us. God creates the universe and its every inhabitant, *out of* love, *within* love, and *for* love. Each one of us is birthed from a sacred care that cradles us with belovedness. Each one of us is ever companioned by a divine presence that is always pulling for our most abundant flourishing. And each one of us is fashioned to be an instrument of God's loving and life-giving presence in the world in ways unique to the particular gifts and capacities that God has bestowed upon us. Like the life-force that infuses all things, God is present within every moment of existence, in every sphere of experience, inviting us and all of creation into ever deeper communion with the sacred reality of infinite love that sustains and restores all things.

Sixteenth-century Catholic that he was, Ignatius encountered this sacred presence through Jesus the Christ. With creedal Christian orthodoxy, he believed that Jesus entered the world as the embodiment of God's eternal being. Through Jesus, God encountered a particular people within the brokenness of their lives, lived in solidarity with their suffering, walked with them as an agent of healing and restoration, and through the mysterious transmutation of the cross and resurrection, absorbed humanity's pain into God's very being and birthed new life out of a brutal and violating death.

This man Jesus endures as the living Christ. And, somewhat akin to his kindred spirit Shekinah, he now journeys like a wandering spirit guide into every nook and cranny of the world, into every hue and shadow of people's lives, and labors continuously to be with us in our suffering, to bring balm to our pain, and to restore a vital and loving connection with the divine that bears new life from whatever tomb we might find ourselves in. This mystical Jesus can be directly encountered by any human being whether lay or religious, whether familied and in the workplace or cloistered in monastic seclusion. Whatever our life circumstances, the purpose of the *Exercises* is to order and align the vibrations of our interior movements—to calibrate the tuning fork of our soul, as it were—so that we can sense more fully the presence of the sacred in our lives, encounter the healing and restorative Christ seeking to companion us, and live in harmony with God's deepest desire for us: that we know ourselves as divinely beloved, and that we flourish as instruments of divine love in the world.

At the heart of these soul-tuning *Exercises* is a meditative immersion into the span of Jesus's life and vocation. Understanding that the imagination is a vehicle through which God encounters us, Ignatius organized the *Exercises* as a series of contemplative prayer experiences in which one enters into the various scenes unfolding throughout the Gospels. From God's initial desire to companion a people within the specific conditions of their world, then following along through the birth of Jesus, his baptism and public life, his taking on the powers that threatened, and his arrest, death, and resurrection, Ignatius invites us to envision ourselves as participants living through these events.

Entering into the symbolic world of the Gospel narratives, we encounter the living Christ for ourselves. We are in the boat on the stormy sea, or at the tomb distressed by its emptiness, and Jesus arrives to meet us. Imaginatively journeying with Jesus as he companions first-century people within the concrete circumstances of their lives, he companions us in the concrete circumstances of our current-day lives. Encountering Christ in the Gospel narratives, we encounter Christ in our personal narratives. Our personal narratives, then, now sites of God's restorative presence, themselves become gospels, "good news" stories of how God enters a world and reunites that world with the life-bestowing movements of the divine. Our story becomes aligned with the cosmic story of God healing and reconciling all things with love.

With my story as broken as it still was—and the interior movements that thrashed within me still capable of such total bedlam—sustained encounters with a sacred presence through the reparative narratives of a gospel seemed uniquely promising in bringing harmony to my inner life and realigning me with the restorative rhythms of the divine. I am not sure that Ignatius ever envisioned the terrain into which I would invite Jesus to meet me. But if God descends into any world that is wounded and, with empathic solidarity, absorbs its suffering and births new life, why not the world of the sexually abused? What would it look like if Jesus's redemptive journey to Jerusalem was in the service of a survivor? In what ways could the soiled and stained narratives of the perversely violated become a salvific story of God's restorative work?

After the season of giving myself to my novel—in which I delved into the experience of abuse through fictional scenes and discovered a God that could mend such pain—this was the desire that drew me to the *Exercises*: that my true story would be discovered and would become a site for divine incarnation.

I hoped that my real-life narrative, all of it, could become "good news"—a gospel according to one molested.

IN THE FALL of 2006, when I returned to the faculty as a professor of spiritual formation, I asked my spiritual director if she would lead me through Ignatius's *Exercises*. Sister Miriam Larkin was a St. Joseph of Carondelet nun that I had heard speak at a workshop on spiritual companioning a couple of years earlier. I was so taken by her wise tenderness that I asked her to be my companion shortly thereafter. A spiritual director for decades, and now well into her seventies, I found that the barometer of her seasoned presence was calibrated both to a sober pathos before suffering's desolations and a heartened savoring of life's consolations. She held joy and sorrow both, each steadied by the other's proximity.

A retired professor of religion and philosophy at Mount St. Mary's University in Los Angeles, Sister Miriam lived on campus with several of her religious sisters on the third floor of the crown jewel in the college's architecture—the Doheny Mansion. The first two floors of the stately manor, the former residence of an oil baron, were restored to their turn-of-the-century museum-piece glory and off-limits to all but paying patrons and guests at gala receptions. Dressed so plainly that she seemed to be a trespasser on the palatial premises, she would meet me at the servants' entrance off to the side and ride with me on the antique domestic elevator to the top-floor flat whose ascetic simplicity was so far from the opulence all around us that we seemed hidden away in quarters reserved for family undesirables or the most lowly of household servants. There, in the isolation of an attic backroom, she would hold with poised poignancy my family's secrets as we searched for the sacred within them. She remained my trusted and treasured soul friend for several years more, meeting me monthly on the mansion's margins until cancer was discovered in her slender frame and took her in a swift three weeks.

Ignatius organized the *Exercises* so that they could be prayed through completely in one of two ways: as an immersive retreat experience of thirty days in secluded withdrawal from one's everyday life, or right in the midst of one's everyday life spread out over the course of some thirty or more weeks. The latter—what the Nineteenth Annotation of the *Exercises* calls a "retreat in daily life"—entails hour-long prayer immersions each day with subsequent journaling, an evening awareness examen or recollection of any grace that the day's prayer may have brought, and weekly sessions with a spiritual director to monitor and guide the process. Sister Miriam, an experienced facilitator of both, agreed to companion me in the extended retreat in daily life. From the Feast Day of Saint Francis in October, through Advent, Christmas, Lent, Easter, and on until the Day of Ascension, I plunged into Gospel narratives each early morning for an imaginative encounter with Jesus—or another spirit guide that might appear—then rode the domestic elevator each Friday at 10:00 a.m. to debrief the experiences with Sister Miriam.

BEFORE EMBARKING UPON the months-long journey, Sister Miriam asked me to identify the deep desires that were prompting me to commit myself to it. My core motivation, as with my entire psycho-spiritual search, revolved around my recovery from childhood sexual abuse. I wanted to align myself with a sacred reality that could help heal the pain that I still carried and animate the well-being that I so sought. I had tasted this spiritual alignment, from time to time, in profound moments of contemplative prayer. But my conversation with my mother revealed to me how tenuous those moments can be. My desire was to know more fully what I had already known more fleetingly. In three ways that I identified for her, I wanted the alignment that I had glimpsed to permeate my being and pervade more of my life.

First, in my meditative experiments personifying my psychic states, I had experienced moments of freedom from the possessive grip that my emotions and impulses had on me. And, through empathic understanding, I was able to engage them as allies and temper them into interior resources. Those interior movements, however, could be tenacious. The distorted affectations so common among abuse survivors—of rage and repulsion, shame and despondency, self-doubt, self-rebuke, and a malicious self-loathing—still clamored at will within me. If the soul is comprised of an inner symphony, then the players in my orchestra kept clashing and clanging. I yearned for the inner freedom where the conductor within me could tame and tune each vibration, and the movements in my soul could play their music in a measured and well-timed harmony.

Second, I ached to know the full extent of my suffering, and to know it held in sacred compassion. My most profound moments of soulful alignment—when I felt most in touch with my truest self and most at one with my sense of the sacred—were moments when I had beheld the faces of the wounded ones within me, saw with certainty their pain, and held them with compassionate care. In those contemplative depths, I mothered the motherless ones crying out alone within me, and my heart coursed with a divine love flowing from the heartbeat of God's maternal essence. While the self-doubt in me dismissed the symbolic images as deceptive fictions—with the absence of actual memories of maternal sexual abuse—I knew that a shattered mirror reflected undeniable pockets of pain still bleeding within me. I yearned to surface those very real remnants of me, buried with their secrets in the shadows, and to hold them with a compassion so fused with love that I could stand in the world, without doubt or shame, knowing my truth and living from its soulful depths.

And third, I yearned to be free of the hate that I felt toward the one person in my life that incensed me like no other—my mom. In rare moments of meditative prayer, I experienced a genuine compassion for my mom's suffering that felt aligned with the sacred and clean from the toxicity of my contempt for her. That compassion vaporized, however, the moment that I sensed her anywhere near me. My repulsion, I knew, would get triggered because it still sensed danger. Her denials and self-deceptions deepened the blade in wounds still gaping within me. I yearned to be so secure in the truth of my experience that her dismissiveness would no longer wield its power over me—to have so tended to my own wounds, bound in the abundance of sacred compassion, that I could perceive her unrelenting disavowal as the desperate cry of her pain and shame.

I yearned to have so divinely mothered myself that I could face my birth mother, honor my pain before her, and in the midst of her inability to acknowledge so much as a thread of culpability, recognize her as the broken human being that she is. And recognize, even if it had to be from a boundaried distance, the compassion with which the sacred surrounds her.

Such was the deep longing that I brought to the *Exercises.* Along the way, I had glimpsed a sacred reality whose heart beat to the pulse of compassion, absorbing my pain and birthing new life as I held what I knew of the suffering within me. Those glimpses, however, were elusive. My day-to-day reality remained more rocked by rage, self-doubt, and resentment. If Jesus enters our worlds to reconcile us with the rhythms of God's being, I yearned to meet him in the sordid wasteland of childhood molestation. I yearned, through him, to unite with the sacred reality that absorbs abuse into its being. I yearned to alchemize the excrement of my antipathies into the soulful radiance of my best and truest self.

In short, I longed for the dirge of my tortured soul to sing, as one, with the divine song of compassion.

As I was to discover—it would take the entire arc of Jesus's gospel journey, from birth, to death, and beyond.

IGNATIUS ORGANIZED THE *Spiritual Exercises* around four "weeks." The word "weeks" can be misleading as the length of time spent in any one "week" can be as long as several months. Better understood as segments, they unfold as four chapters in the overall narrative arc. Week one focuses on the reality of the world's brokenness and God's steadfast love in the midst of it. Week two follows Jesus as he enters this world, companioning him through his birth and public ministry. Week three walks with Jesus through the arrest, trial, and death of his Passion. And week four encounters Jesus in his resurrection appearances. Sister Miriam was trained in the adaptation designed by Joseph Tetlow, SJ, that includes a period of preparation days, the purpose of which is to immerse oneself in God's infinite love as the enduring foundation for the entire journey.

With the voyage laid out, and a navigator to chart it, I set off in search of the sacred encounters that would surface the secrets of my legacy of abuse and bring to some synthesized resolution all that I sought in my quest for recovery.

Preparation Days—Identifying the Lostness in which the Sacred Seeks for Us

For my first meditation, Sister Miriam suggested that I contemplate the story of Jesus, the Good Shepherd, who seeks out the one lost sheep separated from the flock of ninety-nine. She suggested that I consider places where I have felt lost, where Jesus would come looking for me.

As I descend into the imaginal realm, I find myself on the porch of my boyhood home in Foster City. Sensing that my lostness—the truth of my pain—is hidden within that house, I step into it. Everything is covered with sheets—the furniture, the wall hangings, the windows—evoking the feel of a house preserved for years in haunted vacancy. Like a ghost trapped in this time and place, doomed to wander within a site of unceasing violation, I roam the familiar layout—around the family room and kitchen, through the saloon-style doors, down the hall—and make my way to my mom's bedroom. Her bed also is covered in a sheet. I sense two people under it.

All of a sudden, I am under the sheet, now a boy. I am spooned by my mom, both of us naked, my mother touching me in a way that I do not enjoy. My eyes are fixed on a spot on the sheet as if the intensity of my focus could keep me from feeling the tingle of her skin sliding against mine. I wonder, Would Jesus come looking for me in such a despicable wasteland as this?

As if I were a dissociated spirit, I leave the body of the boy and sit in the darkened corner of my mom's bedroom closet. From this vantage point, I can see her bed. Done with me, my mom is gone. The boy lies on the sheets alone. The details from their tryst become vivid. I can see the clothes slipped off to the floor—her lavender nightie, my Batman pajamas, her silk panties, my boy's briefs. I can smell the tangy musk of her scent drifting in the aftermath. I can see my own eyes staring back at me from the boy—my own face imploring me to know how real it is, how long it endures, and how bad it feels.

This is when the Good Shepherd comes. Jesus gets on the bed and cradles the boy. His pained compassion is palpable. I feel it too—coming toward me from Jesus, and from me to the boy.

"This is the journey right now," Jesus tells me with a grief that gets it. "I will take the boy to a pasture far away from here. But for now, he needs you to sit with the truth. He needs you to remember, and to take it in."

For the first time, I do. It comes to me with the force of memory. I was there. That boy is me. This happened to me for real.

The three of us sit there: Jesus, me, and the boy—once lost, now found.

WHEN BACK IN the material world of my everyday consciousness to reflect on the meditation, I worried that my imagination was running away from me. Could this visualization of perversity really be prayer? And yet, as Sister Miriam confirmed in our end-of-the-week debriefing, it led me precisely into the restorative consolation that Ignatius posited as the barometer for discernment. I felt closer to God and closer to myself—God and me at one in facing the truth with power and compassion. As long as these contemplative recollections continued to be consoling, Sister Miriam counseled that I allow them to unfold as they were doing.

With memories of my sordid lostness surfacing in my prayer and longing to be held with sacred compassion, Sister Miriam suggested that I next meditate on a paraphrased passage from the book of Romans.

"What can separate us from the love of Christ? Can distress, persecution, nakedness, or sword? No. In all these things we are more than conquerors through the God who loves us. For I am convinced that nothing in all of creation can separate us from the love of God in Christ Jesus."

Reading it through several times, the word "nakedness" burned like a scarlet letter. I pondered what kind of nakedness might test the limits in separating us from God's love. Could the nakedness that I have known truly be conquered? Could it be proven incapable of severing my connection with the love of God known in Christ Jesus?

Settling into my meditation, I am back in my boyhood house, having just come home from kindergarten. As I enter my mom's bedroom, she is toweling herself off from the shower. Asserting that I need to take a nap, she undresses me. As she pulls down my trousers, we discover that I am still wearing my pajama bottoms. I realize that this is the night that we are going to the movie theater to see "Mary Poppins." In my excitement that morning, I had neglected to take my pajamas off.

My mom laughs at her silly boy, then she removes the rest of my clothes. We nap together in her bed. Neither of us sleeps. She touches me. She has me touch her. She pleasures me. I pleasure her. When she is done, she dresses herself and leaves me to rest before the movie. I lie in the bed soiled in shame—ashamed of what I have done with my mom; ashamed that I am picturing the recollection of it in my prayer.

In the midst of the desolation, I ask forlornly, "Does this kind of nakedness separate me from the love of God revealed in Christ?"

From behind me, I hear Jesus say, "Turn over."

When I do, I find him lying in the bed beside me, his eyes tearful in anguish, his arms outstretched to hold me. I am so moved that he would be with me, even here, that I tear up as well in my prayer. As we lie there, one by one, several women appear—Sister Veronique from the Redwoods Monastery, Sister Miriam my spiritual director, the mother Mary, Shekinah. They look at me and understand how deeply the violation has gone, how stained that I have felt, how tortured my life has been, the miracle that I am even alive. Like a cloud of witnesses testifying to the truth of my trauma, they see what really happened and they surround me with a circle of care—a light of restorative warmth that wraps me as if I were swaddled in love.

"This is my truth," I know as I settle into the sacred wash. "This is who I really am—wounded yet beloved, stained yet held, enveloped in such sacred compassion that not even nakedness can separate me from it."

FOR MY FINAL prayer immersion during the days of preparation, Sister Miriam directed me to meditate on the Foundational Principle that permeates the

Exercises. For Ignatius, it all revolves around a primordial and perdurable reality: that God creates all things out of love; that God's intention is that all things live in harmony with God's everlasting love, knowing their own divine belovedness and flourishing as instruments of divine love in the world; and that God is present in every moment of experience, inviting all things into an ever deeper union with the divine movement of love in the world.

In contemplating this, my intention was to remember and soak in times in which I had experienced the principle to be true—moments of deep connection with this sacred loving presence that could serve as a compass for the rest of the *Exercises.* Instead, as I settled into a meditative space, what came to me were times when I had experienced a disconnection from sacred presence—moments at which God felt profoundly and emphatically absent. One scene, as much an amalgam of experiences as of a single isolated memory, emerged and drew me in.

Descending into my boyhood home, I see the schoolboy me down for the night in his top bunk bed. He is pressed against the wall, curled fetally under the covers, his back to the rest of the room. My mom may have just left after stroking him good night, or she could have sent him to his bed from her room after a few moments of rendezvous. Either way, he feels used and disposed of, left to himself after fulfilling his duties in satisfying her insatiable needs. If God was present in the boy's sense of absence, God's presence was well hidden. The boy's ache pierces me—his simple desire to have a mother, to be cared for by a mother, to be loved by a mother in a way that did not feel dirty.

As I behold him, God appears at my side—in the form of Sister Veronique. I share with her the boy's yearning—for the mother's love that he has never known. Sister Veronique takes the boy in and reveals, "I have always loved him. I have been here the whole time. Every night of his life, I come as he sleeps. I watch him, curled up for protection, and I bathe him with my love."

Her tenderness deepens mine. The two of us gaze upon the boy, our care yoked as one, holding him in a love that he never knew was there. The Foundational Principle felt sound. The sacred surrounds all things.

It was time now for the boy to know it—for God to enter into his world and repair the brokenness that the boy knows better. It cannot stop the bad things from having happened, but it can deliver him from the perpetual pain in which he is imprisoned without a means of escape.

Week 1—The Origins of Sin and the Compassion that Restores It

The focus of the first week of the *Exercises* is the brokenness of the world that Jesus enters to heal and realign. The grace to receive during this segment is a clear-eyed recognition of the wickedness that exists in our world and of God's enduring love within it all. Each of us is enmeshed in the nexus of brokenness that pervades our planet, all of us both capable of hurtful and destructive behavior and victimized by hurtful and destructive behavior. And yet, each of us is ever sustained by a God that sees it all, in the world and in us, yet holds it all with compassionate understanding and restorative love.

For an abuse survivor, it is a delicate dance. Acts that are rightly considered evil are experienced firsthand. How is love extended to a perpetrator while still holding them accountable and deterring any further violation? And the evil that we experience stains us with a soiling that so seeps into our DNA it seems impossible to absolve. How do we acknowledge our very real participation in hurtful and destructive behavior without intensifying the falsehoods of our inherent and irredeemable depravity?

Sister Miriam had me start this week by contemplating the origin story of our ancestors' sin—Adam and Eve. In rereading the narrative, I was struck by the one forbidden thing that brought shame to their nakedness. As I entered the scene meditatively, I pondered: What might I consider that one forbidden thing to be—a transgression so egregious it was capable of rippling through the generations, bearing shame upon shame, in nakedness upon nakedness, onto succeeding and unsuspecting descendants?

Once I have descended, I do not find myself in a garden. As my adult self, I am at the front door of my mom's condo where I had last visited her. Justin is belted in the truck; we are loaded to bolt back home. The one forbidden thing for which I would expel anyone from the garden of my life is sexually assaulting a child, any child. But my God, do not touch Justin. My mom is in the doorway, wrapped in nothing but a satiny night robe, her naked body underneath contoured in the silk.

"Why, Mom?" I demand of her before turning away and fleeing for years. "Why would you do this to a child?"

Her head bowed in shame, she cinches the neckline of her gown, covering the bare skin that betrays her sin.

Like a scene change in a dream sequence, we are suddenly in her childhood house. Her stepfather, Harold, is on the make for my mom's little sister. My mom is only seven or eight years old now. She comes onto Harold, teasingly enough to distract him. He has his way with her instead. When he is through, my mom creeps into the corner and coils in on herself, her arms enfolding her knees to her chest, ashamed in her nakedness.

Seeing her, my heart softens. Somehow I know: sin comes from suffering. Original sin is, more truthfully, the original suffering, passed along through the generations, spanning all time, the web into which we are born where pain and abusiveness are already inextricably interlinked. As I watch, Shekinah appears, wraps the little girl who will be my mom in a blanket, and carries her away, beckoning me to follow. She takes us to the sacred center of the universe where I had been in my meditations at the Redwoods Monastery, to the still pond of water inside the heartbeat of God.

With tears from the One who holds all the world's pain and weeps with everlasting sorrow, Shekinah washes the young girl of my mom, cleansing her of all soiling, then places her in the arms of a Madonna figure sitting at the side of the pool. The young boy me appears—the one from my mom's bed. Shekinah likewise washes him of all soiling and places him in the arms of another Madonna, sitting next to the one who is holding my mom. A young girl appears. Somehow I know, she is my grandmother, my mom's mom, soiled in ways that none of us ever knew. Shekinah washes her as well and places her in the arms of yet another Madonna on the other side of the one holding my mom. As I look, the entire pond is encircled by Madonnas, each one cradling cleansed children stretching back to the beginning of time. Original suffering is held in original compassion, rippling through the generations with the wash of God's tears.

I take my place in the circle next to the Madonna who is holding the young boy me. Another child appears. Shekinah places him in my arms. It is Justin. It is my job to see that the polluted passage of sexual abuse in this generational line stops here. With the ancestral strength of the long lineage of Madonnas, I am determined to barricade him from its seeping approach, even though its leakage, albeit if only secondarily, sullies all in the lacework of our tribe. For now, he and I rest, with all the others, in the heartbeat of compassion whose tears wash all sullying away.

WHILE WE WERE exploring the subject of sin, Sister Miriam and I discussed the fury that I could feel toward a mom who would not acknowledge her sexualized behavior, nor face the impact that it had on her child. She had me meditate on a text lamenting those who get away with evil. Psalm 10 bewails the perpetrators of violence who murder the innocent, pounce on the helpless, violate the vulnerable, then brag that God's eyes are closed, never calling the evildoers to account. The psalmist declares that God sees the victimized and begs for God to protect them from terror.

I no longer believed in a God that has the power to prevent acts of violation from occurring. The infuriation, however, at the lack of account seemed well worth my meditation.

As I settle myself meditatively, I remember the rage that I felt, when on the phone with my mom, as she insisted that she would never do unmentionable things to me as a child. Infuriated that she could so facilely deny it, I imagine her being at the door to her bedroom in my childhood home—me in the hallway outside. She is gesticulating wildly as she swears that she would never do anything to hurt me. Behind her, I can see the schoolboy me on her bed—naked and defiled—his eyes begging me not to believe her.

Knowing the truth, I don't. My mom notices me looking behind her and her denials become more frantic. I look in her eyes; they are begging too—that I believe her in spite of the obvious evidence to the contrary. She sees that I don't and becomes hysterical in her avowals, a screaming, bawling banshee of ashamed denial.

Unswayed, I step past her to tend to the boy. Then I stop in my tracks. Directly behind my mom, cowering on the floor in my mom's shadow, the little girl of my mom is crouched in terror. Naked and defiled as well, her eyes are begging me to believe her suffering. My mom notices me seeing her and stops wailing. Her eyes no longer beg to be believed. They beg for mercy. Despite myself, I feel for her—something akin to what I feel for the little girl.

"I don't hate you, Mom," I tell her directly. "But I need you to know. I will never let you hurt that boy again. I will do whatever is necessary to keep him safe."

The absence of any dissent suggests her understanding. I go to the boy and hold him as he clings to my care. I look back across the room. Shekinah has come and is holding the little girl of my mom as the girl clings to her care. My mom as an adult stands to the side and looks on.

She is welcome to join the loving embrace. All that she has to do is see the wounded children and live true to her own words—to never do anything to hurt them.

THE FINAL INVITATION of the first week was to meditate on our personal sinfulness—to truly understand the pain that we have caused others and to experience God's compassionate love even in the midst of our own transgressiveness. I spent several days bringing my various offenses meditatively to Jesus—my impatience with Justin in his adolescence, my continued rancor toward my ex-wife, miscellaneous misdemeanors of my own adolescence—genuinely hurtful behavior in it all.

Yet I did not find the depths of the consolations that I sought until I prayed with the story of the woman caught in adultery.

As I descend into the scene, I ponder getting caught doing something disgraceful and being exposed to public condemnation. Of what am I most ashamed? What would bring me the greatest abasement if I were discovered in the abhorrent act of it? Sexual abuse with my mother—while saturating me with shame—is not an iniquity for which I feel personally responsible. In what egregious behavior did I participate with some measure of volition?

As it comes to me, the nausea from the gut punch confirms that I have hit a vein that is primal.

The trespass for which I carry the greatest amount of shame is the way that I treated Cathy during the early years of our marriage. Any suggestion by her that I was in any way soiled sent me into a rage. The conjecture that I may have been sexually abused by my mom; the disgust on Cathy's face when I ejaculated obscenities; even the distaste that she displayed when I neglected to pick up my clothes from the floor, would set off a landmine of fury and venom that I would unleash at her without restraint. And one hair trigger in particular was certain to detonate a tantrum of verbal savagery—the hint that I, in actuality, was the responsible party in our getting an abortion. That was blood that I could not accept seeing on my hands, a guilt too crushing to bear.

Yet it was a guilt that was truly on my hands alone.

I had never admitted to myself the truth, and certainly not to Cathy. I not only wanted the abortion, I was brutal to her throughout the ordeal—while coercing her into it, during the procedure itself, and even after it was over as I abandoned her to grieve by herself so that I could maintain the masquerade of spiritual purity and moral uprightness before my professors and grad student colleagues. I was inexcusably cruel to Cathy through the years—and never more coldly so than when we first got pregnant. Fearing the scandal of our sexual activity being on full display, I descended into a transgressiveness that was infinitely more despicable. Concealing my involvement with the woman caught in adultery, I became the first person to stone a young lady whose only sin was longing for her partner's love.

Entering into the scene, I find myself in the lobby of the squalid clinic to which Cathy and I had driven in a seedy neighborhood of Newark. A circle of onlookers surround me, faces that I recognize—mentors and colleagues from Presbyterian Seminary whose derision I fear most. Each of them is casting a scowl of disgust having caught me not only impregnating a woman out of wedlock but cowardly killing the life-to-be for no other reason but to hide the truth of my libidinal desires.

The reality of what actually happened comes over me—the terror that I had felt of public scorning; the hours of conversation bullying Cathy into the decision that, for me, was undebatable; the drive to the clinic with my sense that I was crossing a line, committing an act that was truly staining, yet committing the act anyway. And now I could see the blood on my hands, the procedure performed, and Cathy slumped on a plastic chair like a mother forced to kill her own child. The staining was complete.

When I invite Jesus into the circle, he comes neither accusing nor excusing. He sees the situation for what it is—painful, tragic, with brokenness all around. Remorse overwhelms me.

"I did it," I tell him. "I stopped a life from coming into this world."

"I know," he says.

"And I treated someone with a cruelty that she in no way deserved."

"I know that too," he says.

"And I really am sorry," I say.

"Yes," Jesus consoles. "I know that too." He looks into my eyes with concern for the pain that I had caused another, but understanding at how things could get to this point. "What do you want now?" he asks me.

"I want to be clean," I answer, raising my bloody hands. A fountain appears beside me. With the tenderness of a priest baptizing a newborn, he washes the blood from my hands.

"You are clean," he declares. "You have nothing to fear. You are with me now. No one can take that away."

I am so moved that I have no words for my gratitude. The tenderness in his eyes assures me that he knows anyway. Then he says, "Go to Cathy. She went through this with her body. Wash her as well, and be with her."

I turn to face Cathy. For the first time, I see her—so alone, so crushed, so willing to have had this child to raise with love, so bloody now because I said no. I go to her. She looks up at me like the devastated mother that she is.

"You made me do this," she says, more from pain than from anger. For once, it does not sear. I am genuinely sorrowful—my shame and irascibility both washed clean.

"Yes, I did," I tell her. "And I am so sorry." I wash the mess from her hands, then sit beside her with genuine care.

When I look back at the circle, I see that the scowling colleagues have transfigured into the women and handful of men who have come to the clinic like Cathy and I had. The pain and complexities that have brought them here weigh on each one. As I hold that which brought me and wonder how to grieve, I see Jesus approaching. He had gone to tend to the unwanted souls that had not been born that day. He bore no judgment on the matter—perhaps they were better off not being birthed into a family that could not care for them; perhaps the world would have been better off receiving the gifts that never came to be. Either way, they were discarded souls, the forgotten suffering of lives unlived.

Jesus was carrying one of them to me—a ghost of a girl that he placed in the crook of my arm. Cradling her, I hold the truth with compassion. I was responsible for her death; the cruelty that grew out of that was deadly to another as well. While the staining may be cleansed, the grief remains—that the one in my arms is a ghost, and that Cathy, the one beside me, still bears the bruises of my brutality.

IT TOOK A few years for my prayer to mature, but I eventually shared its fruits with Cathy. Cathy, now married to a Presbyterian minister, joined me in Baltimore to celebrate Justin's graduation from Johns Hopkins. After a meal in Little Italy to laud his accomplishments, we bid goodnight to Justin and I walked Cathy to her hotel. Pausing on the sidewalk out front, I spoke words decades in the coming.

"Cathy," I said. "All of those years at Presbyterian Seminary—in the apartment, the abortion, at Mrs. Colgate's—I was so cruel to you. It was abusive. Verbally. Emotionally. I really was brutal."

She was a tad surprised but not entirely. "You were," she said, merely confirming the truth that we both already knew. "You really were."

"You didn't deserve that," I continued. "Nobody does. And I want you to know that I truly am sorry."

She measured my words, making neither too much of them, nor too little. "Here's the thing," she said. "I stayed. We were so young. I don't know what I was thinking."

"We *were* young," I said. "That doesn't justify how I treated you, though. That was my stuff. It doesn't make it right, but I want you to know that I know that."

She weighed how well I did know it—the allusion to my issues cracking a door open to the perversities that had so tormented me back then. Then she voiced a concern that she had been carrying for all these years. "Then I have a question for you," she ventured. "When she was with us, or when you were with her, do you think that your mother ever sexually abused Justin?"

It was testimony to years of recovery that her mention of my mom's sexual abusiveness evoked neither shame nor defensiveness in me. "No, I don't," I said, taking seriously both her fear and the threat. "When she tried, I wouldn't let her."

She took my words as far as she could knowing my mom as she did. "I hope you're right," she said. "I've always wondered. She's a sick woman. I can't imagine what it was like growing up with her."

Knowing that I had, she knew the scars and malignancies that I had brought to our marriage. It explains a lot, she seemed to be saying. It still does not excuse my behavior.

"I really am sorry, Cathy."

She seemed to know that as well. "Thanks for the apology," she said. "I'll take it."

I hope you can, Cathy. And I hope it offers some balm for the pain.

Week 2—Jesus Enters into Our World from Birth through His Healing Ministry

As my thirty-week sojourn through the *Exercises* entered the holiday season, Sister Miriam invited me to meditate through Week Two. Week Two traces Jesus's life from his birth through his public ministry. The invitation is to become intimate with the way of being that he taught and embodied, experiencing ourselves as one of his disciples during his days to more faithfully be his follower during our days. Ignatius begins this week with a meditation that imagines Christ as a king coming to recruit our allegiance in transforming the world into God's Dominion. Eschewing the patriarchy permeating such a context, Sister Miriam asked me to meditate on an inspiring leader who arrives in my world with a cause that would compel me to leave it all and give myself to the movement.

Descending into the scene, I ponder the disciple Andrew rushing to Peter, his brother, beside himself with enthusiasm at having just met the true Messiah—the Christ who will save their oppressed people. Whose restored hope, I wonder, would move me to drop everything and sprint alongside them so that I could meet the longed-for person for myself? As I imagine various possibilities, I sense someone running toward me from the darkness in my depths. It is the street urchin from the underwater caverns in my soul that I first encountered in the Redwoods Monastery. His Munch-like features transformed into the face of a beaming schoolboy, he is racing with elation to come and get me.

"He's here!" the boy gushes. "The healer. The one who knows the way. He's the real deal. You have to come see for yourself."

His zeal is infectious. I run with him as he leads me to a mental health facility for those who have been sexually abused, one reminiscent of the institution where I had once been interred. Dozens of survivors are scattered about—some caved in on themselves in despair; others picking at scabs from their cutting; still others writhing, beside themselves with rage. Kneeling in their midst, massaging the cracked and swollen feet of a woman staring senselessly into space, is Jesus. His compassion for these people is transparent; his commitment to their cause unshakable.

When he sees us, he stands. The boy who is leading me runs into his arms, delighted to be back with the one who has restored his spirit. Jesus receives him in the tight embrace of a healing love, secure and sustaining. As I approach, he turns to me.

"You are Frank," he says. "I've been looking forward to meeting you. I want to teach you what I know. I want you to be a part of my inner circle." The first-century rush that Peter and Andrew must have felt electrifies me. I want nothing more. He knows. "Come with me," he says. And I do.

We walk through a neighborhood in squalor—a virtual Dachau of incest and assault, each decrepit shack a site of terror and torture. We pause before one. I barely recognize the house as my home from when I was a kindergartner. It is surrounded by barbed wire and blackened by soot from furnaces burning in the distance. I see the kindergartner me sprinting home in his excitement to see "Mary Poppins" that evening. He rushes through the front door and down the hall toward his mom's bedroom.

Knowing what is about to happen, I rush into the house to stop it. I am too late. He is lying on the sheets, naked and alone, all exuberance now bled from his body. He is napped so thoroughly, he will end up suicidal in the years to come and sequestered in an asylum of his own.

From behind me, Jesus walks up and strides to the boy. He cups the boy's head and gazes into his eyes, letting him know how deeply he understands the boy's pain. Then he wraps him in a blanket, lifts him into his arms, and walks us out of the house.

We find ourselves in a cathedral—infinitely safe and palpably sacred. It is a healing space that Jesus has created within the workcamp neighborhood of abuse. I sense, in the wings, survivors of all manner of violation brought here to convalesce in the care of sacred guardians. With the schoolboy me still enfolded in his arms, Jesus takes him to a bed in the heart of the complex. He lays him upon it, swaddles him with a blanket, then kneels down beside him, holding his hand while placing another onto the boy's heart.

Shekinah appears, with a handful of other healing spirits. She lights a paschal candle beside the bed, the kind of candle you see alongside an altar prepared for Eucharist. The air is so still, its flame barely flickers as it reaches up into the hushed darkness. We all form a circle around Jesus, the bed, the candle, and the schoolboy me. Jesus asks us to take in the boy's suffering, all of it—the lost innocence, the buoyancy bled-dry, the spoiling of his skin, the maternal closeness that felt so consumingly lonesome. With our eyes open to the pain, our hearts open to compassion, he has us breathe in the sacred care that restores all things and breathe it out toward this boy, allowing the flow of love's vitality to wash him free of all his affliction and infuse him with the flourishing of life. The sense of divine presence is so profound, I feel as if I am breathing in sync with the breath of life flowing from God, through Jesus's hands, and into this divinely beloved young boy.

As our circle of care bathes him with the breath of sacred compassion, the schoolboy me gently yields to the healing ablution. As if soaking in a spiritual mineral spring, the rigidity in his body relaxes, the aloneness subsides, the beaten-down despondency dissolves, and he drifts into a sleep that promises to restore him with dreams of going to Disney movies still wearing his pajama bottoms underneath his trousers.

The boy now resting, Jesus stands and takes his place in the circle. He reminds us that this boy's suffering is interlaced with all suffering—in that of the violated and of the violating alike. In the sacred nucleus of our circle, he invites us to extend the healing energy of compassion, not just to the boy, but into the entire web of pain in which this boy is entwined. Breathing as one—one with each other, and one with the divine—the band of us comply. We inspire sacred care, then send it out—to the boy on the bed and his kin, to the wounded ones in the wings of the cathedral, to the unseen ones hidden in the workcamp of abuse all around us, and to the planet, beaten and broken, burning to find relief from the pain. As a circle of pulsating love, we are one with the heartbeat of God that holds both a particular boy and an entire cosmos with infinite compassion.

The candle has burned low before I am willing to surface from such a contemplative at-one-ment. Before I finally do, I turn to Jesus. I speak the words of my deepest desire.

"I want to know what you know," I tell him.

He holds my gaze, then simply says, "Follow me."

MY FIRST VENTURE in following the healing path of my inspiring leader involved companioning him at his birth. I entered the story uncertain of where I would be within it. I only knew that I wanted to welcome the baby about to appear.

As I settle into the first-century scene, I empathize with a young couple on the road in search of a place to stay. As I feel what that must have felt like for them, I spontaneously become a young boy from the inn that has no rooms and I am eager to be of help. The scene takes on a life of its own. I escort the two to the manger, clean it of its clutter, and supply it with pillows, blankets, and food. I make a fire for warmth, then fetch a midwife as Mary begins to deliver.

When Jesus is born, I am taken by how tiny he is. They let me hold him. Like Justin at his birth, the baby barely fills my cupped hands. His vulnerability evokes my protectiveness. I will see to it that this baby never gets hurt. When it is time to return him to Mary, I hesitate. Mothers, I realize, are dangerous.

Mary sees my hesitation. Her heart breaks that a child would have reason to distrust a mother's touch. She assures me that Jesus is safe in her hands. I see that she means it and I pass him to her. With Joseph at her side, she radiates in her love for her boy. She looks up at me, tender in her love for me as well, though tempered with compassion for the pain that I know.

With the warmth of her presence, another infant appears, lying in the manger. It is the nude newborn me in the pose of the baby pictures that my mom took of me. The newborn's entire body is covered with lipstick stains—every body part kissed and eaten up for being so delicious. I know what to do. I pick up the boy and cradle him like Mary is cradling Jesus. Then I snuggle up next to her, the two of us wrapping these infants in love. The night around us morphs into the cathedral of compassion, the manger scene now a grotto within that sacred space. Once more, I feel at one with the energetic wash of cosmic love. God has been born into the world, absorbing our pain into God's restorative being.

FOR THE NEXT several weeks, I companioned Jesus through the years leading up to his public ministry. I fled with him and his parents to Egypt—they escaping the massacre of Herod's infanticide, me taking flight from a reign of abuse. I traveled with him to the temple as a boy, where we both are haunted by suffering and dissatisfied with the theological defenses of the ecclesiastical elite. I joined him in his baptism and was immersed with him in the cosmic river of care that courses through the universe and cleanses every blemish that mars our sense of belovedness. I even accompanied him into the wilderness and faced down the temptations that would divert me from the vocation of delivering the captive and healing the wounded in the subjugated world within me. By the time that he was ready to tame demons and cure the sick, I was primed for my apprenticeship to know what Jesus knows—to become a repairer of souls like him.

The first healing narrative that Sister Miriam suggested I contemplate involved the man with a skin disease. Ritually impure and socially a pariah, he comes to Jesus and says, "If you are willing, you can make me clean."

Jesus says, "I am willing." Then he touches the untouchable man. Immediately, his leprosy leaves him. The man is now clean.

As I descend into the scene, I ponder times when I have felt untouchable, when my very skin has seemed diseased and sullied. I find myself back on the porch of my boyhood home in Foster City. The young boy me, who has been haunting this house, is sitting on the front steps.

When he sees me approach, he says, "I've been waiting for you."

"I'm here," I say.

"Are you ready?" he asks.

"I am," I answer. "Show me all of it."

He opens the door and we enter the house. He shows me the table in the family room at which I did homework—my mom standing beside me, with her breasts brushing my back, my shoulders, the side of my head. I see the couch on which we would lie, me wearing nothing but my briefs, my head in her lap as she slips her hand into my underwear and strokes the bare skin of my behind. Last, I see the top bunk in my bedroom where she would come in at night, slip her hand under my pajamas, and stroke my chest, my belly, my privates under the sheets.

"She was always touching me," the boy discloses. "My body wasn't my own. She touched whatever she wanted to touch." He takes me into her bedroom. We stand beside the bed. "This is where I came each night. She liked me to lie down with her to kiss her goodnight. Sometimes she liked to kiss without her clothes on. Her skin would be pressed against mine. Sometimes she touched me. Sometimes she touched herself. It gave her pleasure. So much pleasure, she could not see that it wasn't bringing me any pleasure at all."

He turns to me to be sure that I am understanding it. I am. "Do you see?" he asks. "It is my skin that is defiled. Can it be cleaned?"

"It can," I tell him. "I know a place." I need neither Jesus nor Shekinah. I take him on my own. We sit in the pools until the sacred tears soak into every tissue of his being, rinsing every stain, saturating him with love.

The skin condition leaves him. He is clean.

FOR A SEASON of meditations, I journeyed with Jesus through the healing narratives. As he tended to those paralyzed, possessed, bleeding, and deaf, I tended to the wounded ones within me—the young boy taking showers with his mom before being cupped by her through a nap; the toddler staring at the dry-eyed crucifix after being mouthed by his mom in the midst of a tryst; the schoolboy raped from behind by his grandfather; the catechumen taking turns in a sex game with a priest. I returned to each one, took in each story, and companioned them to a space sacred and safe—like the cathedral of compassion, or the haven of God's heartbeat—where, aligned with divine love, they were cleansed of all staining and wrapped in cosmic care.

It was not a one-time healing. I returned to each boy many times over. I occasionally still do so today. More than a series of single-event restorations, I was internalizing a repeated rhythm of spiritual repair. I would recognize and relax the activated impulses within me, access the tender and wounded parts of me, and reconnect them with a restorative sacred source. In so doing, I was being spiritually realigned with my best self—an energetic essence, fused with cosmic compassion, that faces suffering and tends it with care. Following the Jesus mystically within me, a healer of the soul emerged, healing the very soul that invoked and encased it.

IN THE GOSPEL of Mark, Jesus's final healing before his fateful journey to Jerusalem is of the blind man Bartimaeus. It was the last scene that I engaged during the second week of the *Exercises*. Like Bartimaeus, my eyes were opened in unexpected ways. And also like him, I followed Jesus, through his last days, immediately thereafter.

I enter the meditation wondering about that to which I am blind. Though I have tended a number of the wounded ones within me, I know that other memories are still buried. I descend through the sea depths of my soul until I come to the underwater system of caverns where so many of them have been hiding. I let it be known that I am open to whatever wants to be disclosed.

One cave draws me in. I travel through its darkness, dropping down, until I find myself in the living room of my childhood home in South San Francisco. Ice cream music is playing in the distance. A green camper truck is parked in the street. A pack of monkeys hover menacingly below the window and at the front door.

I am in my earliest memory, my toddler-age nightmare. That camper has cast a sinister shadow throughout my childhood, its very sight able to portend pure evil. I still do not know what happened within it, my impressions obscured in the mists of night terrors and imaginative surmisings. I tell the monkeys that I am ready to know what happened for real. They sense my readiness and transform into allies. I approach the camper. A monkey opens the door. I step in, and the scene shifts.

I am no longer in South San Francisco. I am no longer in my grandfather's camper. I am a schoolboy, maybe eleven or twelve, in the family room of our Foster City home. I am sitting on the floor listening to a Giants baseball game on a transistor radio. My baseball cards are laid out on the braided rug before me, each position player in place as I track the movements of the game. Linda, maybe four or five, is playing house with some dolls by the toy box in the corner. My mom and my brothers,

Jim and Rich, are out. Linda and I are the only ones in the house. The green camper truck is parked outside.

Linda goes to fetch something from her bedroom in the back of the house. The front door opens and footsteps approach. Through the swinging saloon doors, my grandfather Harold walks into the room. I feel the chill of his presence and freeze. Malevolence seems to pulsate from his being. He walks over and sneers derisively at my baseball cards laid out like a diamond.

"Where's your sister?" he demands.

"In her room," I say.

He keeps staring as if studying the players in the game. "Who's your favorite?" he asks.

"Willie Mays," I answer.

"Show me."

I hand him the card that was stationed in center field. He leers at the player staring back at him. Then he rips it in two, then in two again. He drops the pieces to the floor.

"Don't go anywhere," he orders. Then he walks back through the saloon-style doors to the other side of the house.

I am stricken with terror. I am certain that, after telling Linda to stay in her room, he's coming back for me. I can't flee and leave her alone in the house. I can't hide where he won't find me. I can't arm myself with any weapon that could possibly deter him. I am trapped prey. And the truly diabolical is on its way.

It may have been a minute. It may have been a lifetime. I hear his leaden footsteps coming down the hall. Miraculously, they lumber out the front door. A few moments later, Linda comes bounding through the swinging saloon doors. She is dressed in her Easter best. If she knew the peril, she doesn't show it. It doesn't occurr to me that the peril may have known her.

"Linda," I tell her. "Let's go to the park. Now."

We do. We make a fort to hide in.

I had been hiding in it ever since.

WE LIVE IN a world where evil lurks, a world where a brother and a sister can be raped by the same man—their grandfather. How does a person stay alive in the midst of such horror?

Jerusalem will show us.

Not all of us do.

Week 3—The Cross—Jesus Dies with the Sexually Abused

Early in the new year, Justin and I had the opportunity to spend a week in England. I had been asked to give a lecture at a youth symposium in Cambridge on my narrative work with under-resourced teenagers. Justin, an inexplicably emerging Anglophile, was thrilled to visit the motherland. Dressed like a Victorian gentleman in a tie and tweed suit, he threw himself into the part as if reclaiming a forgotten ancestry.

We toured all the London sites: Westminster Cathedral, the Tower Bridge, Windsor Castle, Winston Churchill's WWII bunker. We hopped on and off red double-decker buses letting them take us where they would—one pulling up, to our incredulous delight, in front of 221B Baker Street—and we combed the hallways of the British Museum before sitting at desks in the domed reading room where Darwin, Freud, Marx, and Engel all wrote. Then we rented a car and toured the countryside, motoring through Cornwall, King Arthur's Tintagel Castle, the Roman ruins in Bath, and the rolling hills of the Cotswolds before making our way to the charming town of Cambridge. While I delivered my lectures there, Justin roamed the university grounds as if the school were his alma mater.

Though I continued my early-morning meditations, the trip offered a welcome reprieve from the intensity of the Ignatian journey. It was well timed. Upon our return, Justin would resume his American education and I would resume my immersion in the Gospel narratives—in particular, the decidedly sepulchral journey of Jesus's arrest, torture, and death. Like Justin, I was grateful for the week of sanctuary.

In preparing me for the third week of the *Exercises*, Sister Miriam shared with me her understanding of Christ's death and resurrection. Christ dies "for us" not to take away our sinfulness so that some antiseptic divinity would be willing to accept us. Rather, to the extent that Christ symbolically embodies the sacred, his suffering and torturous death reveal that God experiences complete solidarity with us—is "at-one" with us—in whatever horrors and brutalities we may know.

God enters the places of our pain firsthand, endures intimately the depths of our violation, to disclose to us that we are not alone in them and that even the most debased spheres of existence are occupied by God. In wedding divine nature with our affliction, God demonstrates that even this form of suffering, whatever it might be, even this depth of depravity, no matter how wicked, cannot repel nor vanquish the sacred spirit that infuses every sphere of creation. God is in the tomb with us, in all its lethal forms, enduring death right beside us and giving rise to new life. The mystery of the cross is not some cosmic transaction for humanity's redemption. It is transformational. In saturating all things with restorative presence, God absorbs all manner of suffering into God's being, metabolizes the pain, and births ways of being alive in the world that reflect God's caring and irrepressible essence. Indeed, cradled in the cosmic womb of compassion, even evil can be held and made whole with love.

Sister Miriam's take on the atonement was attractive to me and resonated with the sacred presence that I had been encountering in my prayer excursions. I was uncertain, however, how this drama of divine reparation played out in trauma recovery. How does Christ absorb sexual abuse and metabolize it restoratively? I entered my prayer through Holy Week yearning to experience more deeply this mystery of Jesus's Passion.

As I descend into the scene of the Last Supper, I remember how hidden the meal needed to be—in the upper room of a stranger's dwelling in an unknown section of the city. I wonder what hiding place of mine would be a site for a final meal with Jesus. I find myself in the closet of my boyhood bedroom in Foster City—a place in which I had sometimes concealed myself, buried under a bathrobe and a pile of dirty laundry. Jesus and the disciples are scattered around the room—bunched on the bunk bed, perched on the edge of my desk, and huddled against the walls on the floor. Jesus steps to the center of the room with a piece of bread and a cup. His solemnness stills us all. He tells us that he is going out to confront the powers of death. The ploy is perilous. He may not be back.

He looks at me in the closet. I realize that the power that he is going to encounter somehow includes my mom. He tells me, and the others overhearing, that though the path he is about to take may end in his death, he will be with us, even after he is gone. Anytime that we are nourished by this bread and this wine—anytime that we stand up to evil in power and compassion—we become his body and his blood; we embody his presence in the world. The disciples and I partake of the food. Then they all disappear.

I am alone in my room. My mom enters and sits on the bottom bunk. I come out of my closet and stand before her. I tell her that I will not let her touch me. Those days are over. She understands. She still, however, wants to sit there. I let her—feeling the presence of Jesus rising up within me.

THE NIGHT BEFORE I began a series of meditations on the final days of Holy Week, I watched a video of *Wit* starring Emma Thompson. A scholar of the sixteenth-century English poet John Donne, the main character is dying of ovarian cancer, facing with both sorrow and dignity the death about which Donne wrote such eloquent poetry. Toward the end, as she is rasping through her last breaths and barely conscious through a morphine fog, her mentor and former professor, played by Eileen Atkins, visits her in the hospital. Moved by the ravaged fading of her once star student and protégé, the elderly woman gets onto the bed and cradles the dying colleague in her arms. Like a mother comforting a terror-stricken child back to sleep after a nightmare, she tenderly reads a children's book, an allegory of the soul always found by the sacred love that seeks it. Her care incarnates the story that she reads. The elder is an icon of the maternal divine—a *Runaway Bunny* pietà that carries the languishing scholar into the scene of her passing.

Perhaps it was the buildup of several months of intense meditation in need of some bodily release. Perhaps it was the elegiac effect of the haunting melodic backdrop. Whatever it was, a grief space unexpectantly opened up within me and I wept into the night for the child in me who craved a mother to comfort him with a bedtime story. I imagined him lying naked on my mom's bed, cold and alone, as the music from an ice cream truck faded into the distance. All he wanted was a popsicle to settle him after a monkeyed night terror. Instead, his mother stroked him for her own gratification.

With the backdrop of the movie's soundtrack playing in a melancholic loop, I lay in my bed and howled as wave upon wave of sorrow washed through me. I let that boy weep. I wept with him. This was the pain that Jesus was tending on his pilgrimage to the cross. I promised, both myself and that boy, that through every sleazy scene on the way, I would walk the path with Jesus all the way to the tomb.

As I imaginatively enter the Garden of Gethsemane, I walk past the sleeping disciples and find Jesus praying alone in the moonlight. As I approach, he turns and looks into me. My eyes still bear the eyes of that boy on my mom's bed, and my night of sleepless grief. Jesus sees the pain and tells me that this is the suffering that he will experience for me—for me, and for all those who have known such violation. He wants me to know that even this hell can be endured; that even this tomb can be lived through; that, with Donne, even this death shall be no more, this death, "thou shalt die."

I see the trepidation in his eyes, a cup from which no one should have to drink. Yet, I see his resolve as well—a resolve laden with an unfathomable love. I am stunned beyond comprehension. He is willing to do this—for me.

We hear them approach—a group of soldiers led by my mom.

"Here he is, boys," she tells the centurions provocatively. "The one accusing me of all of those unspeakable things." She sashays up to Jesus with the confidence of a seasoned courtesan—one in bed with all the people in power. Caressing his hair, the sides of his face, the length of his chest, she lets it be known that she could have her way with him. And she just might. Jesus merely stands there in silent dignity. His imperturbability incenses her. She mocks his manhood, spews her derision, and orders the guards to take him away.

His hands now tied behind his back, Jesus walks to his torture and trial.

WHEN I DESCEND into the next scene, I see Jesus in a courtyard tied to a post, awaiting his trial with the Sanhedrin. My mom is with him, and has him to herself. With shameless toying, she strokes his hair, caresses his torso, brushes her breasts against his body. He continues to take it, knowing both his own unassailable self-respect and the sewers of suffering that spawn this woman's perversion. She can do with him what she will. His spirit, though, will not be broken. My mom, sensing this, descends further into her depravity. She does to Jesus what she has done to me. Jesus absorbs it, his eyes filling with tears. He gets the horror. He understands the pain that I have known. His body bearing it intimately, he cries, for real, for me.

Witnessing Jesus taking my suffering into himself is excruciating to watch and inexplicably consoling. With the violation that I have known, the very tissues of my body, the cells of my very being, have felt cosmically and cellularly untouchable. And now, the symbolic essence of the sacred knows the same soiling. In companioning us on the path toward healing and restoration, God is willing to enter into any world in which we live, and to endure with us, in the cells of God's own body, any form of suffering. In the excrement of my world, this is what that looks like.

When my mom is done, she turns on Jesus again. She accuses him of wanting it, of making her do shameful things, of abandoning her when all she ever did was love him with all that she had. He was her number one. Now he can go to hell. She spits at him and stomps away.

THE HUMILIATION AND torture complete, two guards come for Jesus and escort him to his trial. I follow them into a courtyard packed with outraged onlookers. As I stand in the shadows, not far from Jesus, I hear the crowd buzzing with scandalous accusations.

"He says that he slept with his mother."

"He says that his mother came onto him."

"What kind of a son would make up such perversions?"

"I bet he came onto her."

"I bet he enjoyed every minute of it."

The judge studies the charges and scowls, disgusted that a defendant would allege that his mother abused him sexually, repulsed even further by the thought that it might be true.

"It is true," the crowd calls out. "He's defiled."

"He's lying," the crowd responds. "He's a slanderer."

"He slept with his mother."

"He disparages his mother."

"He's vile filth."

"He's a lewd maligner."

"He's excrement to the bone."

"He deserves to die."

The gavel slams. The crowd goes quiet. The judge rises and glares down at Jesus. Spitting words as if defiling himself to say them, he asks the question that all have come to hear.

"Is it true?" the judge excretes. "Did you have inappropriate relations with your mother?"

Jesus turns to me. I step out of the shadows. Looking me in the eye, telling me the truth, telling me that he fully knows the truth, he says, "Yes, we did."

The little boy me appears from where he was watching from the shadows as well. He and I stride toward Jesus. The three of us stand shoulder to shoulder. Facing the crowd, bold in our truth, our dignity in no way on trial for us, we say as one, "Yes, we did."

JESUS IS BROUGHT *before Pontius Pilate. This throne, however, is not occupied by the Roman governor. My grandfather Harold is in his place. Harold sneers at us with contempt. To him, we are pathetic conquests, spoils of his pillaging that he has damaged and discarded. He knows that he has absolute power over us. He can do with us whatever he wills. And he does. Or he doesn't—prey, or not, according to his capricious whims.*

Feeding off the terror that he strikes in his targets, he taunts, "I had you myself. I'll have you again. You're mine. You're nothing to me."

Without saying a word, Jesus stands and stares back. A spirit pulsates through him that cannot be subdued, pumping from a heart that will never stop beating. It dawns on Harold. He has no power over this man.

Harold hurls the omnipotence of his lordship, "I can kill you in a snap." Absolutely no power. His weapon wilting, he wields what is left. "I sentence you to death."

MAKING HIS WAY *through the alleys of Jerusalem, Jesus drags his cross for all to see the pitiless depths to which cruelty can sink. I follow behind, mingled with the throngs that line the streets and take their place in the doleful drift to Golgotha. Bystanders murmur amongst themselves.*

"I heard he was raped by a man."

"I heard he was molested by a priest."

"I heard he had relations with his mother."

"How has he been able to live with himself—he's a walking obscenity."

Jesus trudges on, undeterred by the innuendos whispered all around him. As he nears the outskirts, the lodgings become familiar. He passes before the living room with the camper truck outside, the bedroom with the dry-eyed crucifix, the bunk bed where a child was taken from behind, the bed where a boy napped with his mom. As if exposing to the world the perversity that brought him here, he treads through each scene in my legacy of abuse, his body bearing the marks of the depravities that occurred there.

Just beyond the last scene, he stops at the site of his crucifixion. He is nailed to the cross. A sign is affixed above his head: "This is Jesus. He says he was sexually abused." Then he is hoisted and secured into place.

Wanting to take in what he is doing, I climb a platform and look into his face from a few feet away. It is creased from the agony that he has lived through. His eyes, however, are both tender and determined.

"This is the way," he says. "Your world is my world. What happens to you happens to me. I experience every bit of your pain to show you that even this suffering can be endured. It can be faced and held. It can be absorbed and made new in the power of compassion."

I can see that he is telling the truth. He knows my pain in his very body. He knows it better than I know it myself.

"But why death?" I ask, the sight of his torture so heartrending. "Why do you have to die?"

"Because this too can be held. This too is part of the pain."

As he says this, the little boy me appears in front of Jesus. Facing me as well, he too is hanging on a cross, his body and spirit broken and bled dry. He is me after one assault too many. He was lying in his bed, sodomized into numbness, and all he wanted to do was to die. He is the me that fantasized nightly the taking of his own life; the me that almost did so in the torturous years that followed; the me that so easily could have, and maybe would have, if I had not bottomed out in an emergency room. Recognizing his suicidal despair, I know that this, too, is the truth. Some souls succumb to it; the blade goes too deep. The boy before me is one of them.

He looks at me and aches simply to be seen. He no longer needs rescuing; he does not need fixing. The pit of his despair is too deep; the depth of his defilement is too staining; the hope for a life of love and vitality is dead with the death of his childhood. He just wants someone to get it. Nothing more. To get in their gut the bowels of his pain—an anguish so endless, the only freedom is sinking into a void that forever stops the hurting; an agony so piercing, the only relief is ceasing to be at all.

Jesus is telling me that this too can be held. This boy, also, can be companioned, even into the abyss of his non-being. Jesus is going with him. The boy's pain is so real to me, I want to as well. I find myself on a cross of my own, a mirrored reflection of Jesus on his; the boy is in between us. With Jesus, I hang in outstretched immobility and behold the boy in his desolation. He is lost in forsakenness, descending into nothingness, too drained of life to cry, too drained of dignity to care. Jesus and I have no words. We have no comfort. We have only the solidarity of our sorrow. My eyes locked with the lifeless eyes of the boy, we all three slide into the pit. Yoked in our affliction, the spirit leaks out of us. And the boy, Jesus, and I slip into a darkness as absolute as a heart that stops beating.

Sometimes death wins.

In my prayer, I sit and hold that.

Week 4—Resurrection—New Life for the Sexually Violated

In the fourth and final week of the *Exercises*, Ignatius invites us to encounter the risen Christ, who sends us into the world to continue his restorative work and promises to be our companion as a sustaining and consoling presence. Sister

Miriam suggested that I begin the week contemplating the story of the three women from Mark's Gospel who visited the tomb on Easter morning.

Remembering that Mark's Gospel—more tragic than triumphant—does not include an actual sighting of Jesus, I was not expecting to meet him myself. And certainly not in the way that I did.

I descend imaginatively into the scene recalling the grief-filled intensity of my Good Friday meditation. I had never experienced the crucifixion so acutely before. I find myself at the cross, the bodies now gone. The sorrow is still fresh as I walk toward the tomb.

As I expect, I find it empty, with the stone rolled away. I wonder—who will be the stranger to announce to me Christ's cryptic resurrection? I sense someone behind me. I turn and am stunned. The young boy me—nail marks in his hands—is racing toward me, beaming with delight, as Justin does when he runs, runs, runs into his daddy's arms. I am so moved, tears spring from my eyes for real as I receive and embrace the boy in my imaginative meditation.

"Haven't you heard?" he gushes. "We're alive. We must go and tell the others. I know where they are hiding."

He takes me to the Via Dolorosa that Jesus had walked, to the string of houses in the chaplet of my childhood. We enter the one from Foster City, make for the back bedrooms, cross the room that was mine, and open the closet door. A handful of children are huddled within. Their bodies emaciated, their eyes hollow, they are refugees from a concentration camp. They have not heard. They are still in the depths of the tomb. My heart breaking for them, I know what I must do.

"Do you want to leave this place?" I ask. "Go somewhere safe?"

They nod warily, not daring to believe it truly possible. I gather them in my arms and take them to the cathedral of compassion. Shekinah is there as if awaiting our arrival. The three of us—Shekinah, me, and the young boy—bathe, clothe, and feed each one. When they are nestled in maternal laps to rest and convalesce, I turn to the boy still puzzled.

"Where is Jesus?" I ask him.

"Don't you see?" the boy responds. "He's inside of you. He's inside of me. He is the pulse of compassion that ever beats in our soul's center, in the center of every soul. When we are moved by suffering, ours or another's, and we hold it with care and loving repair, our hearts beat as one with Jesus; we embody Christ in the world. He taught you how. You know how. Follow the path that is within you."

I invite the boy back into my arms. He gladly comes. Our hearts beat as one. I need no other Christly appearance.

IN THE SPRING of 2007, as I was nearing the end of the *Exercises,* I followed through with an invitation for my mom to join me at a therapy session with Mark. After our previous distressing phone conversation, I suggested to her that

Mark could serve as a grounding and supportive presence as we talked through the issues still separating us.

My mom's desire for reconnection outweighed her trepidation. She cautiously agreed, and we set the appointment for a few weeks later. Shortly after the phone call with her, I contemplated the veiled Christ encounter on the road to Emmaus. Perhaps in anticipation, the two storylines became one.

As I enter the scene imaginatively, I wonder what road I could be walking on while I am preoccupied by the unusual events of the day. I find myself on the streets that lead to Mark's office. A stranger appears and walks alongside me. When he asks what I am so absorbed in, I tell him.

"Haven't you heard? I am seeing my mother for the first time in years. I've been so filled with rage and self-berating I never thought it possible. But recently, I have become more sure of myself, more grounded in my truth. I have even started to feel some measure of compassion for her. She's caused me pain, yes, but she's suffered so much herself. I don't know, what do you make of it all?"

"I have heard of a way of compassion," the stranger replies, "that heals the deepest wounds and restores one to themselves. It sounds like you have discovered this path." He pauses before a house—decrepit and shadowed. "Let's go in," he says.

As we enter, I realize that it is my mom's childhood home. Harold, satiated sexually but still seething, is in his recliner, smoking in the gloomy glare of a black-and-white TV. The stranger stares at him, fearless and resolved. Harold, unsure but impassive, stares back. Then chastened in his defiance, he looks down, flicking ash from the end of his cigarette.

We walk to a back room. My seven-year-old mom, still naked, is curled on Harold's bed. The stranger's eyes look poised both to scream and to weep. He walks over, wraps her in a blanket, and lifts her into his arms. In the eucharistic act of his compassion, my eyes are opened. It is Jesus. He walks her over to me and places her in my arms. Then he disappears.

I know what to do. I take her to the cathedral of compassion.

There, I tend to her myself.

FOR MY FINAL imaginative encounter with Christ, Sister Miriam suggested that I journey to Mount Tabor—the site of the Great Commission where Jesus, in their homeland, last sees the disciples and sends them into the world to embody all that he has taught them. She invited me to consider what Jesus has taught me.

What is he calling me to embody in the world?

As I descend into the scene, I ponder what summit in my homeland would serve as a vantage point from which to view Jesus's great commission for me. Like the scene from "Schindler's List," where Oskar and his lady friend peer down from a hilltop at the evacuation of the Warsaw ghetto, I find myself on a ridge overlooking a valley of violation. It is the Dachau neighborhood of abuse and assault to which Jesus had taken me when I first met and followed him as my inspiring leader. I can see the houses of my childhood below, that of my mom's childhood as well, along with acres of other decrepit shacks, hiding within their walls horrors yet unseen and unknown. In the center is the cathedral of compassion, the haven of healing that Jesus has instated. Its wings, I know, are filled with huddled wounded ones held in sacred care.

As we survey the landscape of suffering, Jesus asks me, "What have I taught you?"

I see the ghostly silhouettes of me in my bunk bed, me in my mom's bed, me on the living room couch listening for music from an ice cream truck.

"I know that my suffering is real," I say to them as much as to Jesus. "All of the scenes that we visited—whether literal or symbolic—are truthful to what really happened."

"Yes," Jesus somberly acknowledges. "Each one—they are all truthful."

"I also know," I continue, "that these wounds can be healed. Each one of those boys, each boy within me, can be held—their story can be heard, their pain can be seen, and they can be taken to a sacred site where guardians of compassion can wash them in the tears that restore."

"Yes," he affirms. "They can. You know that." He lets me take in that knowing. "And what else do you know?" he goes on.

"I know that the sacred reality that absorbs their pain, and births in them new life, holds all suffering within its heartbeat. All of creation is sustained by its loving pulse."

"And with that, what else?" Jesus queries, uncovering yet more.

I sense it as soon as he asks. "I know that this includes my mom. Even in her evasions, even in her abusiveness, she is held in compassion. Her evasions and abuses both come from her suffering. That does not legitimate them. And the damage that she can do must be curtailed. But she, too, is held in the heartbeat of God. God's tears are also for her."

He lets that sink in, a hard truth to stay rooted in when relating to her in real life. Then he delves a final layer deeper. "And what else? What more do you know?"

I ponder his question. I feel so aligned with the compassion that he has taught me—so at home with myself and the divine—that I do not know what more there could be. Then it dawns on me. This is the more.

"I know that my heart is one with God's," I reveal. "My heart too beats with compassion. When I am fused with the sacred care that permeates all things, I am restored to myself. This is who I am in my soulful depths. This is who I want to be in the world of my life. Seeing the suffering in me and in others, absorbing it into my being, and bearing the care that heals and restores—this is me when I am most fully being me."

As I say the words, I know that my response pleases him. "Yes," he consecrates. "And this is you being most allied with me."

He turns to me, holding me in eyes that have absorbed every inch of my experience and have been birthed back alive in love. His teaching done, he embraces me. As we hold each other, his body fades and melds into mine. He has disappeared within me.

Like words echoing from my inner depths, I hear him say, "I abide in you. You abide in me. You and I are now one. And lo, I am with you always, even unto the end of the world."

As I receive his words, I find myself in the cathedral of compassion. The schoolboy me is lying on a bed wearing only the pajama bottoms that he had forgotten to take off. I am kneeling down beside him, holding his hand, my other hand placed on his heart. The paschal candle is lit, its flame stretching high into the shadowed stillness. Shekinah and a band of guardians are encircling me and the boy. The spirit guides and I are fused with each other and with the healing breath of the sacred. Restorative care courses through us, from the heartbeat of God to the heartbeat of this boy.

I am at one with the flow of cosmic compassion.

I am standing in the center of who I am.

COMPLETING THE *EXERCISES* on the Feast Day of the Ascension in May, I felt the same emboldened sense of purpose as the eleven disciples deputized by Jesus as he departed this world to take his seat at the right hand of God. In the depths of my contemplative encounters with him, I was grounded in my truth and less prone to doubt it when encountering those who might deny it. I was restored to myself, less reactive and more able to respond to another with clarity and resilience, and I was fused with a compassion that feels for the suffering of friends and adversaries alike. I longed, now, to live from this center consistently within the world of my everyday life.

I did not have long to wait before my spiritual realignment would be put to the test. The week following my final Ignatian meditation, my mom and I were meeting with my therapist.

I HAD WORKED out with Mark my intention for the session. I wanted to share with my mom the pain that I carried from my sexualized childhood in hopes that she could at least hear my experience, even if she could not concede its accuracy. I was prepared that she might not be capable of either, neither of hearing it nor conceding its accuracy. It was entirely possible that her own wounds would be too damaging, her own shame too devastating, for me to pierce her persona of defense and denial. Even so, I owed it to myself to stand up for my truth, and I owed it to her to have the chance to respond before I discerned the limits of any future relationship with her that may be necessary to sustain my newly discovered spiritual grounding.

To my surprise, my mom and I both showed up in unexpected ways.

We met at a park a little before the appointment to reestablish contact and walk over to the session together. In the years since I had seen her, she had aged considerably. Her body puffing out, her asthma clogging her lungs and sinuses, it seemed like the unshed tears from a lifetime of affliction were bloating her from within. I could see how scared she was—a little girl's fear of a loved one's abandonment. She was terrified of losing me—of that even more than of what I might reveal once we started to self-disclose. Seeing her so vulnerable, I was taken aback at how tenderly I felt toward her.

Though I had told myself that I wouldn't, I embraced her, my body stiffening at the touch. We made small talk to ease the awkwardness, then made our way to Mark's office a couple of blocks away. She walked with the dread of one about to receive a terminal diagnosis. Though she kept her composure, she was petrified about what would come up. And yet, on the off chance that our relationship could be repaired, she was putting herself through this anyway. Twisted as it may have become, I sensed her genuine love—that and a resigned resolve forged through a lifetime of forcing herself to do distasteful things.

Mark welcomed her with a sober sincerity and thanked her for coming. She took a seat at the far end of the couch; I sat in a chair across from her. Mark expressed his hope that our time together would help mend our relationship. She said that she wanted nothing more. Since they were meeting for the first time, Mark took a few moments to get acquainted with her. With his queries, my mom shared about her previous marriages, her five children, the man to whom she was currently wedded. She was measured and on task, a far cry from the theatrical irrepressibility with which, when she was on, she could command a room. Mark eased into questions about her childhood, and my mom made mention of her siblings, her mom the registered nurse, the small towns in Oregon where they had picked berries and canned their own fruit.

"And your mom was divorced when you were young," Mark stated, as if double-checking the details of her chronology. "Is that right?"

"Yes," my mom confirmed. "My dad left us when I was three."

"How long was it, then, until your mom remarried?" Mark inquired.

"Not long," my mom said, a little more carefully. "Maybe a year."

"And then your stepfather moved in?" Mark asked.

My mom's hesitation bore witness to a cellar door soldered tight to conceal its secrets.

"That's right," she replied warily.

Mark gazed at her with a depth of understanding that she may never have known before. "I understand that he was not a good man," he said, holding her eyes in his.

The rasp of my mom's reply was barely audible, her features rigid in their freeze response. "Exactly" is all that she said.

Mark held her look as one who knew that very kind of cruelty. "I am so sorry," he said. "It sounds like a nightmare."

My mom looked down. For the little ones within her, the nightmare had yet to stop.

Mark brought her back by shifting his inquiries. "Can I ask what your first marriage was like, to Frank's dad?"

Feeling no need to restrain her divulging, she was remarkably forthcoming. She touched on the rampant infidelities by each of them, the sexual appetites that they both had shared, the shame that she still carried for her unbridled promiscuity, her certainty of God's wrath toward her for it all—that God would demand quite the reckoning from her when she sees him come Judgment Day.

Mark, passing no judgment himself, continued with his curiosity, "Can you tell me what Frank was like as a child?"

Despite all the unpleasantness that she was surfacing, she smiled. "Frank was everything I could have dreamed of for a child. He loved his mom. He helped around the house. He took care of our kids . . ."

"Our kids?" Mark asked to make sure that he had heard right.

"Well, not *our* kids," my mom clarified. "My kids. His brothers and sister. He watched over them for me. Maybe I asked too much of him that way. He was always there for me. He was always my number one."

"Barbara," Mark said more directly. "I want to ask you two things that may be very hard." My mom nodded her readiness. "Did you feel loved in your marriage—by your husband, or by any of the men that you slept with?"

My mom did not hesitate. "Until Andy," she answered, "I have never felt loved by any of the men in my life. Quite the opposite. Men have only been there to use me. When they were done, I was nothing to them."

Mark was gentle but incessant, like a surgeon making the most delicate of incisions. "I have no doubt that that was true," he told her. "I'm sorry for that. And so my second question may be harder." My mom braced for it. "Is it possible—and it would only be natural, after all—that with no men in your life to love you, you may have turned to Frank to meet your intimacy needs, to him as the place where you could feel loved in a way that was special?"

My mom was on that one as well. "It's totally possible," she said. "It's what happened. Frank *was* special. He was my special one. We had that bond that a mother feels for her firstborn. It was the only place that I ever felt love."

"That is totally understandable," Mark reassured, "given everything that you have lived through." Then he segued to me. "I think what Frank would like to share with you is what it felt like for him growing up in such a close relationship with you."

"Okay," my mom said, prepared for the inevitable. "But I know where this is going. And I have one thing that I need to say first. We may have been close. But I never sexually abused Frank. Never. I would never do such a thing."

"I hear you," Mark said appeasingly. "And I hear how much you loved him. I wonder, though, if you would be willing just to hear what it felt like for him. That's all."

She was willing, but with limits. Trying hard to be open, she turned to me and asked, "Okay. What would you like to tell me, Son?"

I gathered my strength, then started. "Mom," I said, "I am learning just to have my feelings—not to judge them, but to honor them and to try to make sense of them. And for whatever reason, I feel like I was used sexually by you. I feel like I was touched in ways that were inappropriate, that we were close in ways that felt bad to me, even invasive."

"Well, those are just feelings," she countered, "and we choose our feelings."

Perhaps it was the *Exercises*, but even with her instinctive dismissal, I was grounded and sure. "No, Mom," I said. "We don't. I would never choose to have these feelings."

She started to rebut, but Mark intervened. "Barbara," he said. "No. We really don't choose our feelings. They come from some place. That's what we're trying to understand."

Coming from a professional authority, my mom was persuaded. She really seemed to be trying to understand as well as she could. "Okay," she consented. "But I have no idea why you would feel such things. Can you give me an example of what I did to make you feel that way?"

"Mom," I said, "it wasn't just one thing. It was everything. Sexuality was everywhere in our house. All that stuff you were just talking about—we kids grew up in it all. It was the air that we breathed. Everything had a sexual element to it. And as close as you and I were, everything about our relationship felt sexual as well—kissing me all over as a baby, eating me up all the time, caressing my skin anytime that you wanted, taking showers together when I was little, taking naps without our clothes on, brushing your breasts against me even when I was older, flirting around in only your underwear, planting big wet ones on me when I came home from college, sexual innuendos even into my adulthood. It felt like sexuality just oozed from you and touched every part of our relationship. I was there for you to enjoy, to feel close to, to make you feel good, in all ways, but sexually too."

"But it was never sex," she said, not understanding what I was saying. "We were just being close. And you loved being close to your mother. Everything we did, you never complained. Not once. You loved it."

"Mom," I said directly. "I did not love it. It was not pleasurable for me. It was for you, but not for me. It only made me feel uncomfortable. It made me feel like a plaything, something there to satisfy you, not me."

She looked at me uncomprehendingly. She and I were living in two categorically different worlds. And in her world, I was making no sense.

Seeing this, Mark interceded. "Barbara," he redirected, "you alluded to some bad things that happened when you were a child. My sense is that you can understand what it feels like to be used—to not be loved for yourself, but as an object for another."

Despite her attempts to stop them, tears came to her eyes. She kept herself contained, however. We had been talking about closeness. Mark was now talking about something else entirely. She spoke through a granite hold on her composure. "What it felt like to be with . . . that man, I would never wish on anyone in this world. Absolutely no one. It was pure horror. No one should ever feel that way. And I would never do that to my son. Not to anyone."

It occurred to me why our two worlds were not converging. "Mom," I said. "What you went through was total hell. What Harold did to you was over-the-top criminal molestation. He was sadistic, deliberate, brutal—an unrelenting rapist; it was what we mean by pure evil. I am not saying that you did anything like that to me. You didn't. When you hear the words 'sexual abuse,' you think of what Harold did, and you rightfully insist that you would never do that. I get that.

"But this is also true—for whatever reason, sex and love got all mixed up together for you, especially when you were young, in your twenties. And I am sure that you did not intend it, and probably you were not even conscious about it, but when you turned to me for love, sexuality got all mixed up in that too. I filled your needs to be close to someone—and that closeness was not just emotional, it was physical too. It involved our skins, our bodies; it was erotically arousing. I was only a child, and that too is a form of sexual abuse. Not in the explicit and malicious way that Harold abused you. But in an equally insidious way from which I have spent a lifetime trying to heal. Our closeness did not feel like love to me. I felt like I was being used for your desires."

"You're saying you didn't like our closeness?" she asked, my world just beginning to break into hers.

"Not that kind of closeness," I said.

"So you felt like I was using you?"

"That's what it felt like for me, Mom. I had no agency over my own body. It was all to make you feel good. You got pleasure from it. I didn't. I felt like your toy."

"Oh my God," she said, our nightmare worlds aligning in a way that she could never have conceived. "Are you saying that I made you feel . . . that you felt like I did when . . . that . . . No . . . Oh God, no . . . Please, no. Please. No."

And she got it. She held her belly and rocked as moaning sobs heaved through her body—some compound of the pain of her own horror coming back to her, the gut ache that her son had felt the same pain, and the chiastic agony that she was the one party to it.

Wheezing through her wailing, she gasped her heartrending remorse, "I am so sorry . . . I am so sorry . . . I did do those things, yes, but . . . I thought you liked it . . . Oh God, I would never . . . I would never . . . God, I am so sorry . . ."

Her anguish was so raw, her comprehension so complete, I had no desire to add to her torment. With Mark, I sat in silence and beheld the truth now exposed to the light—a mom and her son were one in their sorrow.

It took some time for her to collect herself. When she did, she looked at me, repeated her apologies, and asked, "Please, Son, what can I do to make it better?"

In her blood-streaked eyes, I could see the little girl still living in her hell. I could see the guilt-ridden parent desperate to make it right by her child. And I could see, perhaps for the first time, the maternal love of which she would have been capable, if it had not been entombed by the trauma of her rapes.

"Just this," I told her, knowing that she had given her all in this rare moment of authenticity. "You understanding it now, is enough."

And given the limits of her capacities, and of any relationship we would be able to have in the future, it was enough. With her admissions of our sexualized intimacy and her glimpse of what it felt like for me, I did not need anything more from her. We never discussed any of it again. Within a few hours, she had receded into her footloose and fancy-free façade, the awareness of my wounding swallowed into the shadows where her own wounding dwells. I suspect that those spaces are so terrifyingly sordid for her, her only solace is in a self-absorbed nonchalance that pretends that they are not even there. And her only protection is in a self-enclosed world with little ability to perceive her impact upon others. As understandable as it all is, it leaves little room for genuine connection. So we talk by phone occasionally, gather for Thanksgiving, and go out for a meal when I am in town, boundaried by our unspoken agreement to let it all sit in silence. When the pain is so piercing, and the rupture so complete, some relationships can only be repaired so far.

But somewhere in the spirit world—where healing can happen in places too damaged to mend in the material world—a little girl freed from her Oregon captivity and a little boy delivered from his beds of abuse have retrieved the childhoods that they had lost, and they now spend puckish time together. They read to each other picture books like *The Cat in the Hat* and *The Runaway Bunny*. They take delight in Disney movies like *Mary Poppins* on a school night. They eat their fill of home-baked cookies without even bothering to count them. And they consume rocket popsicles with abandon, serenaded by the music from an ice cream truck.

It will not happen in our lifetime. But I look for the day when their adult counterparts are made whole again and similarly reconciled, restored in the unsullied love between a mother and her son.

The flow of tears in a therapist's office, confirming my mom's unintended invasions and carrying my mom's momentary remorse, feed my hope.

Lincoln, OR—Age 50

November 2008

———◆———

MY SISTER KNEW nothing of Jewish allegories, but in the end, she incarnated Shekinah's compassion in ways that were genuinely reparative for women in crisis. Aside from raising her kids, it was the most satisfying work that she ever did. When she shared it with me, she was as enlivened as a chrysalis hatching a swallowtail butterfly.

"HAPPY BIRTHDAY TO you; happy birthday to you; happy birthday, Uncle Frank (you old man); happy birthday to you." As was her annual practice, Linda had gathered Kyle and the kids around the phone to sing for me on the anniversary of my nativity. She followed it up with a characteristic crack, "So how does it feel to be so old? This is a big one—fifty. I'm not old enough to have a fifty-year-old big brother."

"I'm not old enough to be fifty," I went along. "I don't feel a day over forty-nine."

"Ha," she snickered. "So you're feeling it catching up with you?"

"No," I said, and meant it. "I actually feel great. Justin is off to college. I'm as healthy as I've ever been. My work is really coming together. I feel like I am finally coming into my own. This promises to be the best decade ever."

"Plus I hear that you and Mom are speaking again," she said. "Or is it like it's always been—Mom is doing all of the speaking and we're trying to get a word in edgewise?"

"Oh, no," I assured her. "That hasn't changed. It's still like she's talking to herself when she's talking. Do you still put the phone down—when she's lost in her rambling—to get some chores done, picking it up every so often to say, 'Uh-huh'?"

"Are you kidding?" she came back. "I learned that from you. It's the only way to survive sometimes."

"That it is," I concurred. "But hey, she actually sent me a birthday present—a James Taylor CD. With Mom, that's as good as it gets."

"An actual birthday present." Linda understood the significance. "That is something."

"Yeah," I mused. "It makes me wonder what kind of a mom she could have been if she had had a different life."

"It makes me wonder," Linda mused right back, "how we all could have been if we had had a different life." Then I thought that she was changing the subject. "But I've got some news too. Guess what? I got a job."

"Whoa, Linda Lu, doing what?"

"It's only part-time," she explained. "But it's great. I have a friend who volunteers at the Domestic Violence Shelter and she asked me if I would be interested in going with her sometime. As soon as I saw those women, I knew that I wanted to help. They're in such a tough place, and they're trying to get out—many of them with kids. So I started volunteering and it went so well, they offered me an actual job."

"That's so cool," I said. "I can totally see you doing this."

"I know. If I were younger, I'd go back to school and become a counselor or something. I'd love to do this for a career."

"What do you do there?" I asked.

"I'm just an assistant since I only went to high school. But they let me do all kinds of things. I help the women fill out the intake forms, drive them to safe houses, just talk to them really, play with the kids, help them get through it all. That's what they really need—just someone to be with them as they go through it."

"Well, Lu," I said, "they're lucky to have you."

"Yeah, I feel like I'm doing something important. I'm helping them start a better life."

"I'm sure you are," I said with pride. "I am so happy for you."

"Me too," she said. "So, what're you doing to celebrate your big day?"

"I'm actually in Oregon," I told her, "where I lead those retreats each summer. Some friends are throwing me a party tonight."

"Well, don't stay up too late," she teased. "Old people need their sleep."

"I won't," I assured her. "Thanks for calling."

"By the way," she said, "your birthday present's in the mail."

"I am sure that it is," I played along.

"Don't listen to it all at once."

"Believe me, I won't."

BACK AT WORK *and struggling to get up the gumption to complete my novel's revisions and prepare my lectures for teaching, I settle into a meditation. I am aware of the slothfulness that is keeping me from tending to my tasks. It feels so leaden, it is an effort to sustain my prayer. Trusting that it comes as an ally, I invite it to materialize before me. It appears as a two-ton boulder pinning me to the ground. No longer fighting it, nor enmeshed within it, I breathe into a grounded awareness that the boulder is present.*

I ask it, "Why are you here?"

It replies, "I keep you from soaring, from putting yourself out there and becoming noticed."

"And why do you do that?" I ask.

"Being noticed is dangerous," it replies. "It draws attention to you. Then you get sucked into the vortex of other people's needs and agenda."

"If you don't want me to soar," I say, "what do you want me to do?"

"Let me take you down instead of up."

I give into the weight and we descend into the underwater depths of my soul. By the time that we get to the bottom, the boulder has dissolved, its purpose having been fulfilled. I see myself as a young boy, the kindergartner me. He is on stage in a school play, petrified into immobility in the middle of the final scene. He has been cast as the lead in the story of a child asking various animals for advice on a present for his mom. The climax comes when the boy receives an all-enwrapping embrace from a mama bear—a squeezing bear hug being the best gift that a boy could give to his mom. This boy, however, is paralyzed, despite the whispered pleas from directing adults offstage. I freeze the scene and ask the boy why he is afraid to embrace the mama bear.

"Then everybody will see how she hugs," he says.

"How does she hug?" I ask.

"She wraps me into her breasts and rubs herself all over me—like she did when I told her that they made me the lead in this play. Like she does whenever I do something special. Like she does when we are in bed together without any clothes on."

"I am so sorry," I say. "It sounds awful—to be swallowed up like that."

"It's yucky," he says. "I don't want anyone to know. I don't want anyone to see."

"I can get you out of here," I tell him. "Would you like that?"

"Where would we go?"

"Anywhere that you want—someplace safe and sacred, where you can be free just to be you in any way that you want to."

"Can it be just you and me?" he asks.

"It can."

"Can we fly to get there?"

"Of course."

Like an elder eagle and an eaglet, we rise up from the waters and soar through the sky. The wind's lift is sacred enough.

FOR ME, RECOVERY from sexual abuse is never fully completed. I continue to have psychic states that can be reactive or debilitating—flares of anger, bouts of self-doubt, impulses to numb out and escape, even a slothfulness that fights me when I am putting myself out there. And I have tender ones within me still aching for care and deliverance, some of them many times over. The sustaining gift of my psycho-spiritual odyssey, however, is a contemplative practice that can tend to these interior dispositions when I am activated by them and bring me back home to my self-essence.

When the pulse of my inner world is beating discordantly, pounding with agitation or faint with depletion, I have learned to turn inward and pray with whatever dissonance is present. I cultivate a grounded awareness of the emotions, fantasies, or impulses that are activated. I personify them as a symbol or a being and engage them with curiosity, recognizing that every interior movement, in some way, comes as an ally. And I listen for the cry of the deeper concern, then care for any wounded ones that may surface. Sometimes I invite a sacred presence to meet me in that space; other times I journey, with my inner companions, to a healing refuge infused with the divine. However it plays out, I find that this practice settles the interior cacophony within me. It activates my capacities for courage and compassion, and it reconnects me to the currents of life that flow from the source that sustains all things. Forged through my decades of forays into the turbulence of my troubled soul, this process of compassionate self-restoration has become the central recalibrating practice that sustains my ongoing recovery. It steadies my heart and realigns it with the heartbeat of God's loving care.

IN THE MONTHS preceding my fiftieth birthday, this practice was particularly indispensable as I stepped into a future marked less by an absorption in surviving from abuse and more by a survivor's vitality. After years of single-minded dedication to coping with my pain, and through the intense season of tending meditatively to the unhealed wounds within me, a shift had occurred. The flashbacks and fantasized images no longer flooded me with their anguish when they slipped into my awareness. The reactivities and protective impulses, though still present, were milder and more easily calibrated. Making sense of my past and how to live with its legacy no longer consumed me day and night. I was clear about what actually happened to me—my grandfather's rape, the priest's molestation, the ubiquitous sexualized touching from my mom disguised as loving intimacy—and the nightmares and images that did not happen literally but symbolically conveyed my trauma. And I was ready now to craft a life that

I wanted to live, to create a future for myself, and to claim an identity and a vocation that embodied the discoveries that I had made through the course of my healing journey.

Befriending such inner companions as slothfulness, fear, self-doubt, and lingering slivers of shame, I found, in several venues, the capacities to forge ahead as a survivor reentering the world.

I solicited the services of professional editors, completed a revision of my novel, and prepared it for publication as *The God of Shattered Glass*. With a cosmic synchronicity as fitting as it was fortuitous, I came upon a press in Eugene, Oregon, that was inaugurating a literary division. The acquisitions editor was once a reference librarian at the Claremont School of Theology. He had lived in a bungalow on the slopes of Mount Baldy. It turns out that he had been my neighbor—the one who had checked in on me in the middle of the night, many years earlier, when I had thrashed my cabin in a fit of rage.

The spring before my fiftieth birthday, the students at the school of theology asked me to speak at what they had entitled The Last Lecture Series. They wanted to know what my last words would be on the hypothetical occasion of my final public presentation. I told them the story of my breakdown and of my time in the hospital—a man possessed by a legion of demons—and how I encountered a cosmic sea of compassion that can heal and restore even the most wounded. It was the first time that I have ever come out publicly as a sexual-abuse survivor.

That summer, as my spiritual direction training program entered the intern phase of meeting people on our own, I recruited a few volunteers. I crafted a sacred space in my office and awaited the arrival of my first ever directee. When she came, she expressed how eager she was to speak with a spiritual director as she had been struggling with so many hard feelings about God and religion. She was a sexual-abuse survivor, assaulted by a person of faith. She wondered if I could companion her as she sought for the sacred within such forsaken circumstances. The sense came over me: this is what I am called to do—to descend into the caverns of people's suffering and companion them through the darkness, caverns that I know so well having spent so much time in them myself.

And that fall, my friend and colleague Andy Dreitcer bestowed upon me a vocational validation that I had never seen coming. We were leading a contemplative practice when a student asked what he should do if a difficult emotion emerged in the course of the meditation. Andy and I answered in unison. As he said, "Let it go," I said, "Pray that."

Andy looked at me quizzically and asked me what I meant. I told him that our emotions are tenacious—believe me, I know. If we try to let them go, they simply come around right back again. If we push them down, they pop back up like a buoy being pressed underwater. Our emotions, impulses, and interior movements of all kinds are present for a reason. They are the cries of unmet needs or unhealed wounds aching to be heard. When we listen to them with curiosity and tend to them with compassion, they not only relax and realign, they allow us to access our best selves where our greatest spiritual resources are found.

He was so intrigued that he invited me to describe this process in detail during a planning retreat with two of our other friends and colleagues—Mark Yaconelli and Doug Frank. We holed up in an Airbnb beside the bay in Sausalito where we outlined the process that I had discovered of self-restoration through tending to our emotional states with care and resilience. We called this process the Compassion Practice. In those three days, this practice was detailed and diagrammed, and the Center for Engaged Compassion was birthed. We, as a team, with Mark offering himself as a program director, dedicated ourselves to refining this contemplative process and to creating programs and resources to teach it to others.

Who would have known that my relentless introspection throughout my life, assiduously researching the text of my own soul, would turn out to be an asset? And that my decades-long odyssey to find spiritual resources for healing and well-being as an abuse survivor would yield a restorative process transformative for so many? With Andy's insight, Mark's indefatigable dedication, and Doug's unwavering support, my quest merely to stay alive was alchemized into a life's work.

The excrement of my pain became the gold of my vocation.

A survivor's shame became a survivor's mission.

WITH SO MUCH to celebrate—an emerging sense of myself to settle into, and a life's work poised to flourish—I wanted to mark my fiftieth birthday meaningfully. I taught in the morning and took advantage of the occasion to share a few words extemporaneously with my students. Something akin to Martin Luther King's "I have been to the mountaintop, and I have seen the Promised Land," only my words were more to the effect of, "I have been to the depths of hell, and I have seen the cold stare of evil, and I am here to tell you, that it all can be held, that any pain can be companioned, that new life can emerge from any tomb, even the tomb of childhood abuse."

My birthday falling on a Friday, I decided to fly up after class to the mountains of southern Oregon and spend the weekend at the site of the retreats that I was co-facilitating each summer. On Friday evening, a handful of my closest friends gathered down in the valley for a dinner party—Andy and his wife, Steffani, who also flew up from California; Mark Yaconelli and his wife, Jill, at whose house in Ashland we met; Doug Frank and his wife, Marge, who drove down from the mountain retreat site; and Deb Arca, who worked at the spirituality project where the rest of us served as staff or consultants.

With abundant care and good cheer, my friends threw themselves into celebrating the day of my birth. Mark made homemade crab cioppino. Deb brought with her sourdough, fresh from San Francisco. Jill made a devil's food chocolate birthday cake. And Doug made sangria with a recipe from our beloved Cha Cha Cha restaurant in the Haight. After dinner, each of them shared a few words of gratitude for my presence in the world, moving me to tears more than once. And then they offered me gifts. Deb gave me a certificate for the restaurant where a group of us had celebrated the completion of my novel. Andy and Steffani bought me an airline voucher for a retreat in the Oregon mountains. Doug and Marge put together a laminated booklet brilliantly lampooning the Compassion Practice. And Mark followed that with a song that he had written for the occasion. Accompanied by Andy's harmonica, he strummed his guitar and sang for us "The Legion of Demons' Blues."

> I was born in a graveyard, Legion was my name;
> At night you could hear me cryin', and rattlin' my chains.
> The Christ man came over my way, and shared a secret with me;
> He said, 'You got to love your demons, if you want to be free.'
> Now I'm living in my right mind, 2,000 demons at my side;
> Fifty years and countin', and I'm so glad to be alive.
> I'm living like a free man, teaching others the good news;
> But without a good woman, I got the half-century blues.
> Oh yeah, I'd trade this hard-won freedom,
> For a good woman who loves me true.

I may not have had the good woman, but I was freed of my demons. I was in my right mind, and perhaps for the first time in my life, I was truly glad to be alive.

I HAVE DISCOVERED that the demons within us can be loved, that by tending to them with curiosity and compassion, they can be tamed and restored. That being said, they still come occasionally, crying out their pain and rattling their chains.

I woke up the next morning—in the mountain quiet of the bunkhouse in which I was staying—weighed down by a melancholy so heavy I could not get out of my bed. As loving and life-giving as the party from the night before was, it was the image of partnered intimacy that taunted me now as I lay there—the glance that Andy gave Steffani when no one else was looking; Jill resting her hand on Mark's at dinner, and the smooch that they shared in the kitchen while getting the dessert together; the chuckle of recognition that all of us shared as Mark crooned my lack of a good woman.

I had thought that I had made peace with a life of romantic unattachment. And for the most part I had. The rawness of my relational wounds made intimacy terrifying. When it came to women, I walked with a limp. Suspicious of touch, certain to be absorbed, too vigilant in protecting my own space, I had resigned myself that some of us are just too wounded to secure healthy coupling. I had learned to thrive alone, and that was enough. I had a good life ahead of me, apart from the trauma zone of romance. And yet, a primal loneliness could still rip through me, stinging the scraped skin of my singleness. All it takes, sometimes, is a few snapshots of domestic bliss.

As I had learned to do, I invited the loneliness to personify itself. As its features came into view, I recognized them as the Munch-like skull—his eyes and mouth wide and dark, poised in the howl that silently screamed. He bore the same look of horror as the young boy in *The Sixth Sense*, pained to the bone as he shares his terror, "I see dead people." The face of my skull, however, was saying, "I still see suffering. My suffering. And I can't make it stop."

His appearance dislodging another pocket of torment and grief, the sight of him made me want to weep and wail. Feeling his anguish—the anguish that any boy should be haunted by the unatoned dead, that any child should be crippled by unceasing abuse—I shrieked the howl with which his face was frozen. I let the waves come, bellowing and bawling, until the snot was seeping off my chin.

As I sobbed, the skull became a montage of images of me—as an infant, as a boy in a bunk bed, as a boy in my mom's bed—each one bringing with it another wave of sorrow. As gut-wrenching as it was to feel it once more, it felt profoundly consoling—as if the wounded ones within me needed me to cry their pain for real to feel like I was fully getting it. And they needed the trauma that was soaked into my cells to be released through my body. So I obliged, until I had no more mucous to dispel, no more tears to secrete. As the crying subsided, I sensed that Shekinah was with me. She had received each wounded boy in turn as I wept out their sorrow, and she encircled them around me, each one cradled in a maternal sacred care, all of them held in the lap of the cosmic compassion that permeates all things.

Soaking once more in the still pond ocean of divine presence, I recognized two things: that the shattered shards of my brokenness *are* being repaired, and an inner wholeness is reassembling; and yet, the scars remain visible in the cracks, some of them still tender to the touch. Like the Japanese art form Kintsugi—which finds beauty in broken pottery and repairs the fractured with an epoxy of powdered gold—I hold both truths together. A beautiful life is in the making. I will go on to companion others in the caverns of pain in which they are captive, to teach compassion as a means of personal and social restoration, and to craft stories that tell the truth of my experience in solidarity with other survivors of assault and abuse.

But the glittering seams where repair has been necessary remain apparent throughout. Stray nightmares still invade my sleep. An embrace can cause me to stiffen internally. A news story of an abuse scandal can ignite my outrage. A film depicting childhood sexual assault can gut punch me into a spell of gasping tears.

And intimacy with a woman can stir a panic that ripples through my soul into the caves where tender ones still hide.

Those shards, too, yearn for reparation. Their sharp edges ache to be alchemized into a splintered wholeness. This is the Shekinah journey: gathering each piece and restoring it with the glue of healing tenderness. The artistic piece that emerges, though webbed with cracks and held by epoxy, still bears beauty. Both are true—the restoration and the scars, the splendor and the splinters. And truth held in compassionate care is always beautiful. Sometimes soberly so. But still a glimmering fragment of the cosmic mosaic in which all is held and restored with love.

In the limping solitariness of my life as a survivor, that is beauty enough.

THEN THIS.

A little less than a month after my fiftieth birthday, Andy and I were talking in my office when he excused himself for an appointment. A professor from Cal Poly wanted to talk with him about neuroscience and contemplative practice. When I wandered out a little while later, Andy called out from his office next door to mine.

"Frank," he enthused. "You have to meet this person."

I turned and saw a woman in a peasant skirt with a top stenciled in hearts and peace signs. Two thoughts flashed through my mind with absolute clarity. First, *She is so beautiful, she radiates. I could spend the rest of my life with her.* And second, *Is she single?*

"I'm Alane. Remember me?" the woman said as she stepped toward me with an extended hand.

Her question threw me. How could I not remember her from somewhere—her luminescence was unmistakable. She sensed my uncertainty and explained, "You're Justin's dad. Our boys were in debate together at the high school." Apparently, we had both been parent volunteers judging tournaments for our sons the previous year.

"What are you doing here?" I asked.

Andy jumped in, unable to contain his excitement. "She researches the neurophysiology of emotional well-being. She *knows* the body. She can explain all of the physiological reasons why the Compassion Practice works. There's science behind it. It's phenomenal."

As generative as that would turn out to be, in that moment, I was interested in neither science nor the Compassion Practice. I was interested in the woman right in front of me. I left them to their conversation, then hustled into Andy's office the moment that she left.

"Isn't that amazing?" Andy was still gushing. "She gave me her book. She explains it all."

"That's great, Andy," I said. "But what I want to know is—is she single?"

"Is she single?" Andy echoed, bewildered at the question. "Why?"

"Are you kidding?" I said. "She shines. If I had the guts, I'd ask her out."

Andy, not surprisingly, had no idea about her relational status. And soon thereafter, he returned to his home in San Francisco, taking her book with him. Unable to shake my attraction to her, I phoned Andy up and asked if I could borrow the book once he was done reading it. He sent it down to me a few days before Christmas, and I devoted myself to studying it from cover to cover. At that moment, I had no interest in the content. I only wanted to determine whether she was romantically available. The clues were promising: the book was dedicated to her two sons, and the acknowledgments, likewise, made no mention of a husband or a boyfriend. I skimmed through the pages, teasing out biographical indicators, until I got to page 164. In describing the emotional regulation practices that she had developed, she underscored the value that they had had for her and her partner.

So, that's it, I thought. *She's a lesbian. That's great for her partner but not for me.* I called up Andy and told him. He commiserated, then asked me to send him the book back—he wanted to reread it. Before dropping it off with UPS, I took a red pen, circled the word "partner" on the page, then wrote on an index card, "P. 164. Bummer."

It was two days before Christmas. Justin, home for the holidays from college, was with me running a few errands. After sending the book off at the UPS Store, we drove to Sprouts, the local farmer's market grocery store. I was still absorbed in my ruminations of her when it occurred to me that she had written the book a couple of years earlier. Perhaps she was no longer partnered. Pulling into the supermarket parking lot, the slim hope prompted me to do something that I never do. I put out a fleece to the universe. *If she happens to be in this grocery store right now*, I pledged to whoever was listening, *I will ask her out.*

Justin and I walked in. Across the store, at the end of aisle number two, Alane was standing with her two boys. I was so stunned, my phobia around romance temporarily receded.

I walked over and greeted her. Then I nonchalantly added, "Say, Andy really likes your book. That's high praise." As she received the compliment, I followed through with my promise. "How would you like to get coffee some time and talk about your work?" She said that she would love to, that she was going up north for the holidays, and she would be back a couple of days after Christmas. I told her that I would email her.

Two days after Christmas, I did. Then I checked my messages every hour for her reply for the rest of the week. She wrote back just after New Year's, having stayed with relatives longer than she had originally anticipated. We set a coffee date for an evening that week.

When we met at the Coffee Bean & Tea Leaf, I had only one objective—to find out if she was single. We hit it off immediately, the conversation swiftly veering far from academic research. We had so much in common, I could already envision her as a soulmate, a playmate, and a workmate all at once. But still, she revealed nothing about her relational availability.

An hour into the conversation, her cell phone rang. Her junior-high-school-aged son was not feeling well and she felt the need to be home with him. She wanted to keep talking, though, so she invited me to her house where we could continue the conversation in her meditation room. *My God*, I thought, *she even has a meditation room.* As we walked through her house to get to it, I searched for signs of a partner—photographs of the two of them, a pair of toothbrushes in the bathroom, anything. But it had all the appearance of a single mom raising two boys.

And then she brought up Laurie. Laurie helped shape her practices. Laurie used them with her students. Laurie went to the Bay Area with her on Heart-Math projects.

Finally, I had to ask, "So, who is Laurie?"

Alane looked at me as if it was already clear. "Laurie is my partner," she said definitively.

Damn, I thought. *So she really is partnered. And here it was going so well.*

She walked me to the door when we were done and assured me of how much she enjoyed our time together. Once more, I was taken with how warm and inviting she was. Too bad—for me—she was a lesbian.

When I got home, I called Andy again and told him that Alane's partner was named Laurie. He asked me if she had elaborated on what kind of a partner Laurie was, and I told him that we all know what "partner" means in today's world. He offered the comfort that her research was going to enhance the Compassion Practice. It did not help in making me feel any more compassionate just then.

Alane emailed me soon after, thanking me again for our conversation. We wrote back and forth, following up on various threads already connecting us. Then figuring that it would not happen unless she took the initiative, she put it out there.

"I was thinking, Frank," she wrote. "You mentioned that you and Justin like to hike by the ocean in Malibu. I'd love to do that with you one day . . . that is, if your relational life would allow for that."

I was so excited, I yipped around my house. "Absolutely, my relational life would allow for it," I wrote back. "How about this Saturday?"

Saturday could not come soon enough. Fortunately, I could preoccupy myself with helping Justin prepare for his college trip to India that Friday. Alane was giddy with anticipation as well. She was also, though, hounded by a nagging sense of unplaced recognition. She was certain that she had known me from someplace besides high school debate tournaments. But for the life of her, she could not put her finger on it. On through the week it bugged her, until it was Friday evening and, as she walked through her house looking forward to our hike, it hit her.

"Oh my God," she exclaimed to herself. "Could it really be?"

To find out, she made a phone call.

The significance of the phone call requires some context.

Some four years earlier, I was bemoaning to my friends that I would never find a woman truly compatible with me—I had too many disparate passions and interests. Tired of hearing it, they challenged me to place a profile on Match.com. I had no faith in an internet dating site surfacing my soulmate, but I acquiesced. I warned them, however, that I would describe myself in all of my heterogenous complexity. I was a professor with a PhD who dressed in jeans and had long hair. I researched, both intellectually and experientially, spirituality and emotional well-being. I was a post-Vatican II Roman Catholic that admired both the mysticism of Merton and the peace work of the Berrigans. I was committed to contemplative practice and to politics that were extremely progressive. I had a boy and a dog. I was a long-distance runner and an avid baseball fan. I loved hiking, snorkeling, meditation retreats, and road trips. My favorite book was *Sophie's Choice*. My favorite movie was *Schindler's List*. My favorite TV show was *M*A*S*H*. And the music that I most listened to was James Taylor and Bruce Springsteen. The woman for me would have to run the table. I dared the internet universe to find her.

Within a month, I had pulled the plug on Match.com. The few women that I did meet were all good people, but the chemistry was missing. And the survival shelter harboring me from the red-alert dangers of romance was still in lockdown mode. It was time to resign myself to a lifetime of singleness.

Alane, at the time, was still recovering from a recent divorce. For Thanksgiving, she drove to her sister's in Chico—a thousand miles away. Late in the evening, after the other family members were in bed, Alane was bemoaning to Joan that she would never find a man compatible with her given all her disparate passions and interests. Joan suggested, just for fun, that they troll through Match.com to see what men were out there. Alane, though skeptical, agreed. They did a thousand-mile search, scrolled through dozens of dating profiles, and I came up.

Joan gasped. "Oh my God, Alane, he's perfect for you. He *is* you—a professor with a hippie vibe, spirituality and emotional well-being, a Vatican II Catholic, contemplative, politically progressive, has a boy and a dog, baseball, road trips, Springsteen, *Sophie's Choice*, *M*A*S*H* for God's sake—this is crazy . . . And he lives in Claremont!"

Alane was taken aback too. But it being so soon after her divorce, she was not ready to reach out quite yet. Joan, however, was. She wrote me to introduce me to Alane. It was a note that I never received. My subscription had already been canceled. And though Match.com would send me emails saying that someone was interested in my profile, I ignored their request for the $19.99 needed to find out who it might be. Alane, though, kept working it over. When she returned to Chico for Christmas, a few weeks later, she told her sister that she wanted to write me after all. Her sister said that she had already written me and it looked like I had canceled my subscription.

Alane then printed out my picture and, when she returned to Claremont, she inquired with colleagues at various colleges to see if they happened to recognize me. No one did. So she put the picture in a drawer and, a few months later, tossed it out while cleaning. And now, the Friday night before our first date, it all came back to her.

She called up her sister in Chico. "Do you remember that guy on Match.com that we found a few years ago at Thanksgiving?"

"Yeah," Joan replied. "He seemed perfect for you."

"Do you still have his picture in your archives?"

"Sure, let me pull it up."

"Now," Alane requested, "Google Frank Rogers at the Claremont School of Theology. Then tell me if that is the same guy."

Her sister Googled the school, clicked on the faculty link, and opened up my profile.

"Oh my God," her sister said. "It's not only the same guy. It's the same picture."

"Guess who I'm going on a date with tomorrow?"

WE WEREN'T AN hour into our first date before Alane told me the story. We both knew that the universe had conspired to bring us together—and did so at the right time. A few years earlier, I would not have been far enough into my recovery to bring myself fully into a romantic relationship. I also now knew that for our intimacy to be real, I would have to be open with Alane about the truth of me, and trust her love to hold it. The time for secrets was over. We were deep into the hike when I took the leap.

"Alane," I said. "I need to tell you something about myself. I walk with a limp. You see, I have this mom . . ."

She was the first person, apart from my therapist, to whom I told the entire story.

A FEW WEEKS later, we celebrated our first Valentine's Day together. Alane made me a banner filled with symbols of all the disparate elements that make me "me"—images that depict her and me, Justin, my friends, my novel, the Compassion Practice, contemplative prayer, hiking, running, even baseball and blues harmonica. The banner is affixed to a tree branch. Her card explains the symbolism.

"My gift comes from the place where my love for you most deeply took root. When you trusted me with your story, hiking on that trail, I knew that I would hold you in love forever. I went back to that trail and found this branch. It is a walking stick. It serves as my pledge. I see all of it, your beauty and your pain. And my love will bear any limp with which you walk through life."

We've been walking ever since.

AS I DESCEND *into the underwater depths, I am aware of my resistance to share with Alane the last of my shame. I come upon the boy hiding in the sewer, his body stained with excrement.*

"Why are you still hiding here?" I ask him.

"I am dirtier than the others," he says. "I am too soiled to be cleaned."

"Why do you think that?" I ask him. He looks down, too ashamed to say. "I really want to know," I assure him.

"I should not have been late for catechism class," he says. "I should not have been in that church. I didn't belong there."

"What happened to you that day was not your fault," I tell him. "Not even a little bit."

He is not convinced. "The game we played," he says, "that was bad. That was really bad."

"It was," I affirm. "But the bad is on that priest, not on you. Nothing about that was your responsibility."

He takes that in, wanting to believe it. Then he asks, "What I felt there, in the church, before, with Mary . . . was that real?"

"It was," I tell him. "As real as the other. Even more." He ponders the possibility; he knows the other so well. "I can take you away from all of this, if you want."

He looks up. "I do," he says. And I take him.

We go to a beach near Half Moon Bay, across the coastal hills from where I grew up. I wash him in the ocean waters; I wash away every stain. His sense of play coming back to him, he kneels in the sand and starts to build a sandcastle. A little girl shows up. It is Alane, five or six years old. The two of them build the castle together.

When it is time for me to leave, the boy comes to me in terror.

"Please," he begs. "Don't make me go back to that place, to where that office is."

I assure him that he never has to go back there again—that he can stay and play on this beach forever. He is still afraid. "I don't want that little girl to know why," he says. "If she finds out the truth, she'll think that I am disgusting and repulsive."

I assure him that the little girl is not like that. He turns to her. She is still kneeling over the sandcastle. Her tears are dripping onto the sand. She does not want to leave either. She knows. And she wants to stay and play with the boy on this beach forever. The boy wipes her tears away. She wipes away his. Together, they build their sandcastle.

It is time for my meditation to end. Before I ascend, I sense the presence. A womb-like warmth swells and saturates us. From the cosmic sea of compassion, a Madonna's love sees and embraces each one of us.

In the lap of her tender care, all may not be well. But it all will be held.

Part VII

South San Francisco, CA—Age 57

November 26, 2015

———◆———

THE LAST TIME that I saw Linda—before the ravaging of her spirit rendered her unrecognizable—she was draining the remains of an agave margarita straight from the plastic pitcher. Though seldom a serious drinker, she was a little looped that afternoon. Then again, she had a good reason. We were fortifying ourselves for a Thanksgiving evening with our mom.

Never really one for the kitchen, my mom had sworn off all holiday cooking and had started an alternative tradition to turkey at her house a few years earlier. For any family members so inclined, Thanksgiving would be celebrated as a Dutch-treat dinner at the Italian restaurant, Bertolucci's, in the working-class neighborhood of South San Francisco. The siblings countered with a tradition of our own—drinks in a cantina around the corner a couple of hours before. Not only could we catch up a bit before the high-pitched bedlam to come, but a couple of belts, in sibling solidarity, dulled the pain of being with a parent too pained herself to be there much for her children.

Linda was in particularly high spirits that day. Her son, Matt, had flown in that morning from the Marine base in Okinawa to surprise her with a holiday visit. After dinner, their immediate family was driving back up to Eureka in their van to enjoy his weeklong leave together. They had no way of knowing that it would be the last time Matt would ever be with his mom.

Thanksgiving dinner was loud and flamboyant. The restaurant had long since learned to sit us in a back room out of earshot from the other patrons. With Andy and his two adult children, my mom with all five of hers, an array of grown grandchildren, and a smattering of partners, some twenty of us from the Rogers, Ovalle, Kuttler & Klase clan kept the bar busy shouting out toasts and yelling over each other as if the one that could command the most attention would win the round of the most valued relation. Rich hovered all around, directing everyone to speak into the camera in his commitment—for ten years, now, and running—to film every minute in which he was awake. My mom, even in her seventies, worked the table—doling out smooches and talking dish on this person's unemployment and that one's still single status. Michelle, Linda, Jim, and I took turns distracting her from intruding herself on the grandchildren, angling to steal from them love-squeezes while bemoaning how seldom they stayed in touch with her. Then we imposed upon the long-suffering server to take for us a family picture—my mom in the center, Linda and me in the far back, Richard down in front getting it all recorded on his handheld.

Before we could disperse from our pose, my mom wanted hugs. When she gave me mine, she pulled back just enough to whisper into my ear, "Do you still love your mother, Son?" The frightened little girl was in her voice. The adult was hard to be around, but I could not help feeling for the little one.

"Sure, Mom," I said. "I do." And I meant it. Even as I pulled myself free from her embrace.

Linda was the first to take her leave—the long drive still ahead of her and her family. All three sheets to the wind, and more if she had had them, we laid her on a bed, converted from a seat, and bid her goodbye. She grinned in the Cheshire glory of getting through dinner unscathed and making a clean break north once more.

"So, we'll see you at Dad's for Christmas?" I asked, assuming our usual pattern in parental visitation.

"Nah," she slurred. "We're goin' away. We'll be in Bend for the holidays, at Kristina's new place."

"If I had known that," I kidded, "I would have brought you your Christmas present. I guess I'll have to put it in the mail."

Even soused to a sleepy oblivion, she was on it. "Ah, you better hang on to that," she said. "I know how much you love it."

I let her have that one; she was in too good a mood to tease her anymore. "Then, we'll see you in the new year," I said.

"When're you comin' up?" she quipped, remembering her line from our routine.

Instead of responding with mine, I simply said, "We'll see. We'll talk soon." I turned to Kyle behind the wheel. "Drive safe," I admonished. With Matt as his copilot, he assured me that he would. We closed the door and waved them off.

It was the last time that I ever saw her as herself; the last time that the others ever saw her at all. The next time that I would be "comin' up" would be to retrieve her from an insane asylum. Two months after that, she would take her own life—downing pills in her car, alone in a cul-de-sac.

I never did send her that eight-track tape. I still have it to this day. I cannot say that I love it, perched by her picture in my study.

I'd much rather, each holiday, be sending it off to my sister.

Claremont, CA—Age 57

June–November 2016

—————◆—————

IN THE MONTHS after Linda's suicide, I was gripped by a grief that was piercing. The simplest things could stab with her absence and precipitate the tears—the sight of a butterfly or a bouquet of daisies, hearing "Mandy" on a supermarket soundtrack, an advertisement for "Barry Manilow Live in Las Vegas," "Moon River" sung at a concert in the park. Sometimes I gave into it and let it cascade, bawling inconsolably while watching *Breakfast at Tiffany's* or playing Eva Cassidy standards while driving through the foothills. Other times, I sat, staring numbly into the distance, the loss so overwhelming I could not let myself feel it.

The blade that cut deep was always the same, the sight of her in her last hours. The image would fix itself into my mind's eye and slay me—her, alone in her car, swallowing as many pills as her body would allow, waiting for obliviousness to take her away. I knew what that was like, to sit in a vehicle so desperate that death seems the only escape. Nobody should know such anguish. That my sister did—and that the desolation devoured her—was devastating enough to plunge me into an abyss of sorrow. I knew her agony. My sister's pain had once been mine.

The sorrow was so consuming, I solicited the aid of two professional companions. Their skilled and consoling support saw me through my months of mourning. Jim Neafsey had agreed to be my spiritual director after Sister Miriam had passed away. Jesuit trained and a seasoned contemplative, he knew intimately the restorative power of imaginative meditation. He encouraged me to continue, and processed with me, the soul excursions on which I embarked as a way of working through my grief. And he planted in me the seed that, when the time was right, I might dialogue with Linda in the spirit world. It may not bring closure. But it might mend some of my torment around the way that she had passed. With Mark, my psychologist, now retired, I sought the expertise of an Internal Family Systems therapist, Cathy Curtis, a consummate facilitator and teacher of the healing modality remarkably similar to the Compassion Practice. She led me on a number of psychic journeys that treated all the dimensions of my grief as allies and tended to my sorrow from my self-essence, the ground of compassionate resilience that I had discovered in my recovery.

Aided by the expertise of them both, I resumed my meditative immersions. I engaged my grief in the way that I had already learned to engage my trauma. After the crushing loss of my sister, the journeys helped restore me back to myself.

In the end, they may have helped Linda as well.

As I descend into an interior space, I am aware of a fortress surrounding me. The thick granite walls protect me in a haven of unfeeling invulnerability. The fortress, however, is built on sinking sand. Around the outer edges, the ground underneath is swiftly eroding. In desperation, the fortress is getting smaller and smaller, grasping for solidity while squeezing me into an increasingly confined seclusion. I freeze the scene and ask the fortress what it fears will happen if the ground gives way altogether. It says that we will be swallowed into an abyss of infinite suffering. I sense from the sinking ground that it wants me to see the suffering—that healing lies somewhere in its depths. I ask the fortress to go with me and we descend into the darkness.

We sink into an ocean of misery. Countless spirits are swimming around, moaning in their agony. All of it is here: my mom's pain, her siblings', Linda's suicide, the suicides of three cousins and counting, and all those damaged by the legacies of abuse and the despair that it spawns. It is too much to take in all at once. As I settle onto the solid ground at the bottom of the sea, I seek a single face on which to focus. Hidden in the shadows, I see the Munch-like skull of my own trauma. He is howling with the rest of them. As I gaze at him, he turns into the little boy me, alone again, and wailing once more in his mournfulness. My heart opens to him. I let him know that I am here. He is stunned with relief and races into my arms. The two of us sob in our sadness.

As the boy trusts that he is now held in my care, the sobbing subsides. I tell him that I can take him away from here. He does not want to leave; these are the people that he loves. Instead, the fortress that we are in transforms into a chapel. A candlelit reverence fills the space. A sacred presence swells and surrounds us like a womb of infinite love. Through the walls, now translucent, we can see the suffering all around, while staying safe and grounded in the midst of it. From this restorative center, care can be extended—one at a time—to the spirits out there drowning in their misery.

Though I do not see her, I know that Linda is one of them. I send my promise into the shadows wherever she is hidden. When she is ready to come, I will be here to hold her.

EVEN THOUGH I found occasional respite in a sacred solace within the sea of my sorrow, the distress of Linda's death still shattered me. Nightmares once again invaded my sleep, forcing into my awareness that which ached to be faced and restored. One nightmare in particular encapsulated this season of grief. It took place in Linda's car. It was so vivid, I could have been in that car with her for real.

I am sitting in the passenger seat. It is deep into the middle of the night. Linda is passed out beside me. An uncapped bottle of Tylenol PM rests in her slackened hand. Dozens of capsules are spilled onto the floor. In the shadows outside the window, a rapacious beast is stalking in the darkness. I cannot see him, but I know that he is Harold. I feel Linda's terror. He is coming after her.

Linda stirs and opens her eyes. She is lost in a drugged-out stupor. She doesn't notice me in the seat beside her. She senses only the presence outside. She fumbles around for another handful of pills and slurps them down, water from the bottle dribbling from her chin. She closes her eyes and sinks back into oblivion.

The reality of it overwhelms me—she really is taking her own life. I try to revive her, but my hand passes through her as if I were a ghost. The beast draws nearer. Linda fades deeper. There is nothing that I can do. I am at her side, but my presence is of no avail. I am merely the big brother unable to save her from either the pills or the beast.

AS MUCH AS the scene of Linda's last night haunted me, the pang that exacerbated the heartache came from a regret that could be castigating. I was the one to whom Linda had turned when in the horrors of her despair. I was the big brother that she looked up to, the one that she called when she needed assistance, especially in times of crisis. That was my job—to keep her safe, even from an assault that seems impossible to live with. And to help her find a way through when the impossible comes back, to help her discover what I had come to know—that the truth of our past could be faced; that our bodies could be trusted in surfacing our trauma; that our pain could be met, not with shame and revulsion, but with resilience and compassion. She thought that I could deliver. Instead, I built her a fort and went home, this time not taking her with me. I should have been there with her. I had failed her once. I now failed her again.

As counterintuitive as it seems, I discovered that my relentless regret was not only an ally, it led me to the one place where I could attend to that which, surrounding her death, was still unresolved for me.

As I descend meditatively, I find myself on the cul-de-sac where Linda died. A few feet in front of me, I see her car. She is inside, slumped against the door, already dead. The sight of her so forsaken still stings, triggering another jag of tears. The familiar voice cuts in.

"You should have been there," it scolds. "She called you. She looked to you to help her. You went back to your life. You should have stayed with her."

I start to debate the voice, to insist that I really did do all that I could. Then I check myself. The voice needs to be heard, not debated.

"I trust that you are here for a reason," I address the voice. "How are you trying to help me?"

It tells me. "I keep you from feeling too much pain. If I scold you, you get lost in that instead."

"That doesn't sound much better," I reply.

"It isn't," the voice admits. "But if I weren't here, you would drown in the sorrow."

"I understand how immobilizing that would be," I say. "What if there were another way?"

"There is," the voice says. "You can remember her pain, but not be overcome by it. You can see it for what it is, and simply understand it."

"How would you have me do that?" I ask.

More gently this time, as an invitation instead of a chastisement, the voice repeats the words with which it has been castigating me. "You should be with her," it encourages. "Just be with her where she is."

As the voice says this, I know it is right. And I know that I can do it.

I take my place in the passenger seat of my sister's car. Linda is leaning against her door. I take in her death. And how it happened. She spent the night utterly alone. Feeling forsaken by God and her loved ones alike—void of hope, captive to terror—she ditched a world that was decidedly unlivable.

I cannot make her world more bearable, but I can sit with her within it. I can be the presence in the absence that she knows. I can face her forsakenness and feel for it. This is her truth. In a world of divine abandonment, death wins. I see it in the lifeless sleep of my sister.

THOUGH THE MONTHS of bereavement felt perpetually shadowed, shimmers of a Shekinah compassion found their way into the crevices of my grief. Her presence appeared in the most unexpected of places, her emissaries as varied as they were kindhearted.

When I arrived back home after the week of arranging Linda's funeral and speaking at her memorial, it was several days before I had the spark to stop by my office at school. When I did, I found a framed picture on my desk. It was a snapshot of outer space taken by the official star registry. My dean, Dr. Sheryl Kujawa-Holbrook, on behalf of the faculty, had had a star named after Linda. She may have passed away, the caption suggested, but the light with which she touched her loved ones continues to shine in the night's sky.

The publisher of my two books on the Compassion Practice sent me a lamenting shawl and a card hand-signed by the entire staff. One of them, my editor, Jeannie Crawford-Lee, also passed along a legacy. John Mogabgab, one-time research assistant to Henri Nouwen and a widely hailed spiritual teacher at the Upper Room for decades, had recently passed away as well. He wanted me to have his prized copy of one of Nouwen's early books—the hard-covered copy that Henri had personally given to him in appreciation for John's help in writing it. The first-edition reflections on the Christian life was appropriately entitled *Compassion*.

Another package from a surprising source appeared on my doorstep in the weeks after Linda's passing, this one from the San Francisco Giants. My dear friend Tim Feak had written them from Wales, sharing with them my loss and my lifelong devotion to the team as a fan. Little did any of them know, Giants baseball was more than a pastime for me; it was my sustaining refuge through a childhood of abuse. The team sent me a handwritten letter with their condolences and a box of memorabilia from their championship season in 2014. A few months later, they would win another championship.

For my birthday that November, Alane surprised me with a photo album with various pictures of Linda shining in her glory—dressed in her Easter best as a child, walking the beach with her children, cheering with her brothers at a Giants baseball game, singing karaoke at our wedding. The cover showcased her reveling in her butterfly tattoo, the monarch spirit animal that she had aspired to be. Tucked into the sleeve of the album's back cover were two concert tickets. "A Very Barry Christmas" was coming to Los Angeles. Linda's prophecy would come true. Though with tears streaming from my eyes, Barry Manilow would receive my spirited standing ovation.

And a nonprofit in Salem, Oregon, in a moment of cosmic synchronicity, became for me a serendipitous icon of sacred solidarity in sorrow. I had flown up for a weekend meeting and left the hotel early to squeeze in a Saturday morning run. Visiting Salem was always tender for me. Harold had lived with my mom and her sisters in a hovel on the edge of town. The abuse that bled through the generations began but a few blocks away.

Needing the exercise to ground myself, I passed through Riverfront Park, then made my way along the web of trails weaving through the Willamette wetlands. As I made my way back, I could see that the park was now hosting an event. A crowd, filling the grassy field, faced a makeshift amphitheater. I could hear a voice from the sound system, but I could not make out the words.

As I got closer, I heard the emcee say, "Now. All of you who have lost a sibling to suicide, raise high the purple beads."

The tears were coming before I fully registered what was happening. Here in the city of my mom's molestation, the Salem chapter of the American Foundation for Suicide Prevention was staging a rally in support of those with loved ones who had taken their own lives. I was moved for Linda and for the heritage we inherited. I was not the only one. A sea of people were crying along with me, each with their own legacy of pain. A strand of purple beads now graces my office desk.

It was Sister Veronique who, for me, first gave voice to the observation years before at the Redwoods Monastery. She incarnated it so movingly, she appeared in my prayer. When Shekinah came a short while later, the spirit guide not only confirmed it, she made the sacred credible for me again. Gathering the splintered shards within me one by one, she companioned me through my meditative recovery from abuse. Now she was present once more, mending the shattered pieces of my grief.

Sister Veronique's hard-won wisdom held firm.

"Acts of kindness and care—they do not take the pain away, but they keep the spirit alive while going through it."

Claremont, CA—Age 58

August 2017

---•---

KINDNESS, THOUGH SUSTAINING, cannot keep the nightmares away. As the months passed, the nocturnal terrors continued. One even came with a visitation. Linda, it seems, was reaching out to me from the other side.

I am in a forest at night. I sense a malevolent presence in the shadows: a pure sociopath, a Hannibal Lecter hell-bent on slaying every soul in his path. I have brought a few police officers, but they do not take me seriously. I plead with them to apprehend the killer. Halfheartedly, they do.

The cops and I are now in a holding cell; the sociopath is hidden out of sight. The police are playing cards and laughing amongst themselves. I insist to them that the monster will escape. I beg them to lock him away more securely. They titter their derision.

Another officer rushes in. The sociopath has escaped. The cops scramble and go in search of him. I am alone in the holding cell. The sociopath appears. He is a bullish beast of a man, reminiscent of Harold. From his hands, he emits a black smoke at any creature that he sees. The vapor is evil and malignant. If you breathe it in, it will turn you insane. He sees me and fills the cell with smoke. I hold my breath determined not to inhale it. I cannot hold out. Gasping, I breathe it in.

The second that I do, the cell goes dark, lit only by an eerie incandescence. A pack of savage animals surrounds me—a menacing assemblage of rottweilers, pit bulls, panthers, and boars. Their teeth bared, their eyes sadistic, they snarl as they approach, taking their time in circling toward their prey. As they near, I realize with a despairing certainty. This is not a dream. I cannot wake myself up. I cannot leave this room. As if trapped in a dungeon in Dante's Inferno, *I will be fully conscious as these beasts, for eternity, rip my body and gnaw on my bowels with abandon. I am stuck here forever, unable to escape, unable to die, unable to deaden even an iota the pain of unending torture.*

The thought comes to me with a self-confirming immediacy. This is what genuine psychosis is like. This is the living hell of ineludible traumatic terror. This is precisely what Linda experienced.

I bolt awake.

As sure as if her ghost is whispering into my ear, I hear Linda say to me, "Frank, please. Don't be mad at me."

THE LINDA OF my nightmares may not have been certain, but I was far from being mad at my sister. On the contrary, inextricably yoked to her, I understand her experience all too well. And I am committed to honoring it in its entirety. Perhaps it is the eldest brother in me, awash in my grief-filled care for her. Perhaps it is the uncanny co-occurrence of our two paths toward the same suicidal design—one taken, the other no longer needed. Or maybe it is the depth to which I do comprehend her pain, she trapped in the psychosis of her trauma, prey to the beast that had raped us both. Whatever the combination of sympathies and resemblances, I find myself determined to keeping her memory alive. All of it. The beauty of her living, and the brutality of her dying.

On the first anniversary of her passing, I organized a family gathering to bury her ashes, along with symbols of the gift that her life had been for us. Then we released a hundred monarchs into the winds above her gravesite. Alane and I, on a trip to New York City, made a pilgrimage to Tiffany's and toasted Linda in the glitter of the jewels that, once upon a time, made her shine so brightly. On her birthday, we buy drinks for strangers who share the same birthday as her. On the date of her suicide, we light candles and hold vigil, not wanting her to be alone in the solitude of her death. And we constructed an altar in our meditation room, with sacred objects that celebrate her—a picture of Holly Golightly; a copy of *The Cat in the Hat;* the trowels with which we maintain her roadside memorial; the cabbie hats that we wore to the Manilow concert; rocks from her favorite beach; the photograph of her star; another of her butterfly tattoo; and looming over it all, a poster-sized Barry, flashy in red sequins, hands outstretched as he prepares to take his final bow.

She may have died alone, but my sister will always be remembered with love.

AS THE MONTHS passed by, the family understandably got on with their lives. Linda's daughters had their babies, her son had his wedding, and Kyle began dating the woman that would become his second wife. Something in me, how-ever, could not refrain from brooding over my sister's suicide. I would drive north, occasionally, to the site where it had happened and freshen up her road-side memorial. I would muse on the scene of her death as I ran, listening to mournful music on my headphones. And, at times in my prayer, I would sit contemplatively in the seat beside her on that cul-de-sac.

It was as if Linda's spirit, for me, was still entombed in that car and I could not abandon her there. I could not find comfort in the notion that she was now somewhere else, in some blissful paradise where happiness replaces all the pain that one has known. Suffering is real. Her suffering was real. And exiling her to a heavenly rapture, as if it all had never happened in the first place, felt as if it minimized the severity of her pain and covered up the unatoned horror of her death. Her self-immolation—166 sleeping pills so she could be sure of it—is part of her story. Its very brutality is testimony to the pain that she had experienced.

I found it equally disturbing, however, that her spirit would be eternally held captive in the prison of her suicide, that she was now a forgotten ghost, haunting the site of her cessation, tossed in the cold winds off the ocean to which she never quite made it. Her death felt unresolved to me. Moving on as if she were resting in peace was as unsatisfying as dooming her to an unre-deemed demise. She needed to be released somehow. Or perhaps I was the one still hanging on. Either way, her pain felt unappeased. The abuse that she had known remained unrecognized. And her story, with all its secrets, was still not heard. It was simply wasting away in the forgetfulness of life moving on with itself.

So I stayed in the car with her—or kept her there with me—refusing to forget the tragedy that had happened there, nor dismissing the atrocities that had given rise to it. In tearful meditation and somber rumination, I sat beside her broken body.

Until I sat, not only with her, but with the me that felt compelled to keep her in that car. In embracing us both, the two of us would be freed. It was time both to hold her and to let her go.

I descend into a meditative space and settle into Linda's car. My sister is slumped against the door across from me. I have been here so much, I know right when it is. She has just taken her last handful of pills. She is moments away from death. I am aware of the resistance within me never to forget the way in which she dies and the suffering that provoked it. When I invite the resistance to mate-rialize as an image, it appears as an aged shaman whose spirit journeys have taken him to the most gnarly of depths.

Trusting that he is present for a reason, I ask the shaman, "Why do you hang on so tightly to my sister's suicide?"

He replies, *"Because this is critically important. Both for you and for her."*

"How so?" I ask. "What do you want from me?"

He answers, *"I want you to be with her."*

I am confused. *"But I am with her. I've been in the car with her ever since it happened."*

"No," the shaman says. *"You sit beside her. You see her pain. But she does not feel your presence. She needs to know that you are with her for real."*

"How can she know that?" I ask. "She's already unconscious. She will be dead in minutes. In the real world, she's already dead."

"You can hold her in her death," he says. *"Absorb her pain and saturate her with compassion until new life is birthed. You know how to do this. You've done it to yourself."*

"But this is different," I say. "This is somebody else—a real person."

"In the spirit world," he says, *"it is all the same."*

I look at my sister. She is collapsed against the door. The last sliver of life is about to leave her body. I realize that I cannot keep it from happening, but I can hold her through it. I reach out and pull her into my arms.

I feel the tepid warmth of her body, the faint and infrequent beat of her heart, her breath intermittently gasping for air. Enfolding her into my chest, I know her pain. I know her despair. And I know that it all can be held.

And I do.

I press her close as the last of her life leaves her. Her breath rasps and goes quiet. Her heart stops beating. Her body goes cold. She is dead. I hold her in her death as well. A sacred care swells up within me, fused with the pulse of presence that holds all things with compassion. It holds my sister, and also me holding her. We are enfolded in infinite love. As we settle into that love, Linda's spirit drifts out from her body. Alive, but no less suffering, she gazes at me with wounded eyes. She needs me to see. I do.

"What you lived through was hell," I tell her. "Truly a living nightmare."

"It was," she says, imploring me to know it fully.

"All of it," I affirm. "The times just now, and the times long ago."

"Yes," she says. "It was. We never talked about it. But it was. For you too."

"Yes," I say. "For me too."

"It hurts so bad," she says. *"The pain goes so deep."*

"It does," I say. "I know."

She searches me. *"You do know,"* she recognizes. *"And you found a way out of the despair."*

"I did," I say.

She notices me still embracing her dead body. *"And you can be here with me in mine? You can hold me even in the midst of it all?"*

"I can," I say. "And I will."

She studies the two figures before her—the living one cradling the dead one. "I want to know what you know," she says.

"I have a feeling that you already do," I tell her.

She ponders this. It dawns on her that she does. As the realization washes over her, her haunted woundedness transforms into a sober pathos. She strokes the hair of the one in my arms. In the sacred care of being held in her pain, she is able to see her suffering for what it is, and to hold it herself with a tender compassion. This is Linda restored to her essence. In the likeness of Shekinah, fused with the sacred that repairs and regenerates. As she comes back home to herself, her healing work comes to her.

"I have something that I need to do," she says.

"I know," I say, already knowing what it is. "And then what?" I ask. "Where will you go after that?"

"I'm not sure," she says. "There is still so much pain in this world. Maybe that is what comes next."

"What?" I ask.

She smiles at the possibility. "Becoming what our souls have always been," she says cryptically.

"And what is that?" I ask.

"What I've told you before," she shares. "In another life, I could be a butterfly."

I mirror her eyes' glimmer with my own. "You'll make a great one," I tell her.

"And what about you?" she asks. "What will you do now?"

"I'm staying right here," I say. "I have something that I need to do as well." I have the sense that she, too, already knows what it is.

"You really won't forget me, will you?" she says with pleasure.

"No, I won't," I avow.

She takes in the truth, and the love behind it. "Thank you," she says. "Thank you for being there. Through all of it."

"Of course," I say. "I'm your big brother. And I always will be."

She gazes at me as if she were leaving for good. Then she dissipates. Not into a butterfly. She simply dissolves into the ether, at one with the presence that permeates all with compassion.

I sit and hold both—her body and the butterfly spirit that emanated from it. I am holding them to this day.

Half Moon Bay, CA—Age 60

March 17, 2019

———•———

A YEAR LATER, I am at a conference in Los Angeles. Asleep in the hotel room, I have a dream.

I am in Half Moon Bay. I am sitting on the beach where I have brought children to play—me as a boy, Alane as a girl, even my mom finding refuge from the house of her childhood. I am holding the Munch-like skull that I carved from a piece of driftwood I had found once on this beach. I keep it in my pocket to remind the wounded ones within me that I hold them all with care. Now, I gaze into the hollowed eyes and fissured face with gratitude for the journey that we have been on together, and for where that journey has taken us.

To my surprise, the face transfigures into a butterfly. It flutters about in the ocean breeze, then flies up the coast to Linda's car in Eureka. As it lands on Linda's slumped-over body, a butterfly emerges from within her as well. The two flitter with the wind, then wing their way back to Half Moon Bay.

As they approach the beach, the butterfly that is Linda notices that a young man has hidden himself amongst the trees and is sitting near the edge of a precipitous bluff. The man is engulfed in despair, drained of all hope, and is contemplating a leap from the cliffside. Linda sees his desperation and flies over. She lands on his knee, stays super still, and stares right into him, like she gets it, and she has come just to be with him in his hiding place for a while. Then she flaps her wings a couple of times and flies away.

To the young man, it is a miracle—a connection that you never forget. He gets up and goes home. Linda flits around the beach, just being herself, ready to land on any knee that might happen to need her.

WHEN KYLE FIRST called with the news of Linda's death—the grief crashing down on me like a tidal wave—Alane sat with me as I sobbed. When I had wept myself dry, at least for the time being, I sank into a speechlessness that struggled to accept the calamitous truth. My little sister had just taken her own life. I was still struggling when Alane shared a consolation that was coming to her in the moment.

"I know that this is excruciating," she told me. "And I don't mean to minimize the tragedy one bit. But I think that you should know. I feel Linda's presence with us right now."

Alane's connection to the spirit world was too preternatural to dispute. The premonitions that she would have, and the visitations from the other side, defied any earthly explanation. At the time, however, I was still too upset to receive any consolation for myself. Alane, though, was perceiving more.

"She wants you to know," Alane continued, "that she is okay. That she's free from all of the pain now." Alane paused. My silent reticence was more defeated than skeptical. "She doesn't think that you believe me," Alane relayed further. "So she told me to tell you this. I have no idea what it means. But she wants you to know that she is by the swinging doors."

I had never told Alane about the saloon-style doors that brokered any passage between the family room and the back of the house in our childhood home in Foster City. I barely made reference to that house at all and offered only the scantiest of details the very few times that I did. Even so, as Alane conveyed Linda's words, I felt their truthfulness.

For some reason, Linda had gone back to our old house. It took another year before I understood why. She had something that she needed to do. In her Shekinah-like restoration, Linda was there to retrieve a young girl still trapped in her back bedroom. Healing work, it seems, can continue from this world to the next.

I DO NOT know, for certain, where Linda's spirit now resides. Perhaps her healing work is done and she has moved on to another place. Perhaps, with some of her story now told, she has found her way to rest—her pain assuaged, at least enough; her death, if not atoned, held in a cocoon of love. In the imaginal landscape of my inner world, I envision her as the spirit animal that she always knew herself to be. She flutters into the houses of the abused and the violated and onto the bluffs of the fraught and forlorn, offering a moment of care and understanding, a miracle of connection that can, even in suffering, keep the spirit alive. Maybe, in the mysterious magic of the mystical realm, she is the butterfly that once flew down into a fort made of bushes and landed on the knee of a little girl dressed in her best to disguise her shame while hiding out with her big brother.

What I do know, for certain, is where my spirit now resides. Like Linda, I too have been mired in a lethal despair. I have been trapped in those houses, haunted into hopelessness by the assaults that had happened within them. I have been poised on the edge of cliffsides, desperate enough to drive off to my death. I have sat in the desolation of my car, longing to escape with a bottle of sleeping pills. My life has been a continuous quest to survive and live with the psychic devastation of childhood sexual violation.

And yet, along the way, I have discovered a path in which the pulse of my spirit has been resuscitated. A sacred presence has held me in the womb of its restorative care. In sanctuaries and insane asylums, at retreat centers and on suicidal cul-de-sacs, in meditative prayer and crafting a novel, companioned in a therapist's office and letting loose on a stage, I have soaked in its healing presence. It has held my suffering, metabolized my pain, taught me to do the same for myself, and transformed the shame of my abuse into the compassionate resilience that can hold not only my own woundedness but the broken body of my sister's as well.

The heartbeat of such sacred care births new life out of any tomb. Enfolded in its cosmic love, abused children become able to build castles at the beach. Mothers and sons share moments of truth with each other. Butterflies materialize from deceased spirits.

And big brothers generate the resources to answer their sister's question. Sitting beside the sea, staring into the psychosis of her trauma, my little sister posed this one to me.

"You were like this once," she said, her eyes pleading for a roadmap to sanity. "What did you do? What did you do to get better?"

My spirit has found its home in the source that sustains all things. When fused with that presence, my heart beats robustly with the pulse of its care. Restored into life, I can find it within me to hold Linda in her death and tell the truth of my story.

This is what I did.

Cradled in the arms of boundless compassion, I became my sister's pietà.

AFTERWORD:
SYNTHESIZING THE JOURNEY

"What Did You Do to Get Better?"

———◆———

IT IS A sober truth—healing from sexual abuse is an odyssey, a long and wandering journey with many upheavals along the way. Each person's voyage to a Promised Land of emotional stability, sustained freedom from the triggers of trauma, and a life lived with contentment, connection, and purpose is utterly distinctive. The winds that whip then dissipate into a dead-sea calm, the storms that strand us in desolate shores, the routes that we navigate, and the ports of call that replenish us are as unique for each survivor as the circumstances surrounding the horrors from which we are recovering.

For all the idiosyncrasies, however, several things are true for each voyage. The journey is lengthy—spanning across years if not a decade or two. The journey circles and spirals, stalls and speeds up, gains ground and regresses, ever defying any linear progression. And the journey is hard—it demands resilience, determination, confidence, and courage. It is truly a hero's and shero's epic quest.

To adequately delineate all that I have learned about recovering from sexual abuse, I needed to tell the entire story—with all its sordidness, and all its dead-ends and misdirections, in the midst of all its discoveries. On this side of the telling, though, I can distill a few of the measures that helped me, over time, to get better.

Judith Herman, in her landmark book *Trauma and Recovery*, suggests that recovery from trauma happens in three stages—three legs in the epic journey to the homeland of healing. The first stage is *Safety and Stabilization*. Trauma dysregulates us. Furies, flashbacks, nightmares, and instinctive reactivities typically overwhelm the survivor and perpetuate a chronic sense that the world is unsafe. In this first stage of recovery, supports need to be put into place to sustain a season of healing, and skills need to be developed to navigate difficult emotions and regulate the body's fight, flight, and freeze impulses.

The second stage is *Remembrance and Mourning*. This is the season of deep and therapeutic healing. Traumatic memories need to be processed and metabolized. The losses that one has experienced—of innocence, connection, trust, and self-worth—need to be acknowledged and grieved. And the resilient spirit of a survivor—as opposed to a passive victim—needs to be discovered and internalized.

The third stage is *Reconnection and Integration*. On the far end of recovery, trauma no longer defines who one is. The horrors that one has lived through are integrated as but a single chapter in one's overall ongoing story. A life of agency and vitality can now be claimed. Meaningful relationships with others can be cultivated, work that is intrinsically fulfilling can be pursued, and a heightened meaning can be given to the trauma—perhaps by companioning other survivors, sharing one's story and wisdom, writing about it, speaking publicly, volunteering for support organizations, or even engaging in political advocacy work. That which could have defeated someone now inspires a life well-lived.

As I look back on my journey, I recognize this threefold arc. I loosely followed its trajectory, although, for me, each stage circled back multiple times and interlaced with the others. Throughout this meandering journey, I found the following coordinates most helpful in continually pointing me back in the right direction and keeping me on the course toward healing:

1) *Circles of Support:* It was indispensable for me to find people in whom I could confide about my abuse and its tortured aftermath. Be they friends, confidants, support groups, or professionals, I needed people like my therapists and spiritual directors who would say repeatedly and unequivocally, "I believe you; something happened to you that was horrific and wrong. You are not crazy; you feel what you feel for a reason. You are not alone; others have been through this too. And yes, the way is hard, but you can get through it."

2) *Setting Boundaries:* I needed to suspend contact with the still-living person that abused me as her presence only triggered me into a state of chronic agitation. A prolonged period of separation not only removed me from physical proximity with the external source of my activation, it reassured my inner world—the wounded ones within me and the defensive impulses that protected them—that I would keep them all safe from any further violation.

3) *A Season of Recovery:* Mike Lew suggests that survivors leave a shingle for a spell on the door front of their lives that says, "Temporarily Closed for Repairs." I needed to give myself a season dedicated to my recovery—both minimizing the demands on my life as much as possible and mobilizing myself with the determination that it takes for the hard work of recovery.

4) *Learning about Sexual Abuse:* I went through a spell of devouring works depicting sexual abuse—everything from self-help books to novels, films, and documentaries. For me, this was not a masochistic wallowing. It was profoundly consoling. I recognized myself in the portrayals, thus validating my experience. I learned how trauma impacts the body and soul,

which normalized my own crazy-making symptoms. And with the vast number of accounts available, I felt like I was not alone—others knew the horrors of assault as well and had discovered resources for overcoming it.

5) *Trauma Therapy:* Finding skilled counseling with people trained in working with trauma was essential for me. Trauma work is more than talk therapy. Memories need to be surfaced and shared; neural circuits of reactivity need to be rewired; physiological symptomology needs to be released. And the trauma does not need to be re-experienced—which only re-traumatizes and further entrenches protective systems—but it does need to be reimagined and metabolized. I found such therapeutic modalities as Internal Family Systems Therapy (IFS), Eye Movement Desensitization and Reprocessing Therapy (EMDR), BioSpiritual Focusing, and Jungian Active Imagination particularly suited to healing the trauma that I had endured. In explaining why such therapies are necessary for trauma recovery and summarizing the most promising among them, I find Bessel van der Kolk's book, *The Body Keeps the Score*, both brilliant and definitive.

6) *Trusting My Body:* Foundational for cultivating the stability necessary to plunge into the deep work of therapy, I needed to stop fighting my body and to learn to trust it. It was a hard-won recognition—the body does not lie. The rages, reactivities, and revulsions to touch; the instinctive stone walls of unyielding invulnerability; the sordid images that invade one's mind both night and day—it all comes from some place. We were not born that way. Something gave rise to it. Instead of minimizing my body's maladies, battling to subdue them, or lacerating myself in self-condemnation, it helped when I learned to listen to what my body was telling me, and to trust it to lead me to the truth of my anguish.

7) *Giving Expression to My Emotions:* The passions and impulses that warred within me needed an outlet. Simply smoldering in their possessive energy did not help. Nor did trying to suppress them, judge them, or find a way to manage them. I needed to honor and validate them by giving them a safe space to express themselves. For me, this came through incessant journaling, drawing them with colored pencils, working them out with clay, emoting them on a stage, howling in the woods, and venting them to my therapists. The energy was seared into my cells. Giving my chaotic emotions expression discharged their intensity and dissipated the power with which they were wreaking havoc within me.

8) *Befriending and Restoring My Psychic States:* Perhaps the single most restorative game-changer for me on my journey of recovery was the discovery that every one of our interior movements—the emotions, impulses,

fantasies, and self-talk that whip through our psyches—all serve some life-promoting purpose. To be sure, in their cry to get our attention, they usually overwhelm us with their force, prompting us to try to suppress, numb, or manage these interior psychic states. My recovery took a radically restorative turn when I learned the process that came to be known as the Compassion Practice. This involved cultivating a grounded, mindful awareness of the presence of these interior states within me. It then required listening to the deep cry or need hidden within them, extending a loving care to the wounded parts of me buried underneath my reactivities, and accessing a sacred source of compassion—sometimes personified in divine figures or ancestors, sometimes experienced as a spiritual energy of care and vitality—that restored me to my best self. I engaged this process most consistently through meditation that evoked my imagination. I also discovered that this process could be engaged in other ways—writing it out in both fictive and non-fictive narratives, acting it out on stage, working it out with externalized figures drawn on a page or symbolized with objects, and talking it through with spiritual directors and confidants. The mode is multiple; the liberation, revolutionary.

9) *Physical Activity:* Frequently, my body merely needed to discharge energy. I had to move, and to move vigorously. When I was physiologically flooded and emotionally overwhelmed, I tended to power-walk through the hills or run for miles, though cycling, swimming, dancing, and yoga would all have been equally effective. Sometimes, it was necessary just to exert myself mindlessly to get away from the barrage of my inner torment. Other times, I ruminated over memories while pushing myself physically, which helped metabolize the pain without being consumed by it. And sometimes, I simply needed to tire myself out to at least approach a good night's sleep.

10) *Transforming Trauma into Art:* Art takes human experience and crafts it into objects of beauty. The art form can be many—composing music, painting, poetry, pottery. For me it was story—giving shape to my experience through playwriting, writing a novel, and molding accounts of abuse, my own and others', into short stories that I could share at speaking events. Whatever the form, art is more than simply sharing one's experience. Art takes the raw material of experience, reflects upon it, and fashions it with meaning and purpose—to provoke the mind and pierce the heart. In doing so, creating art resists the passivity of despair and births life out of the death-dealing tomb of trauma. In the midst of the horror, the human spirit endures. A creative life-spark is uncovered. Power and agency are reclaimed. And the ugly is transformed into something sublime. The music may be blues; the poetry may be bleak; the sculpture may be replete

with jagged edges and barbed hooks. But the truth is told, and told with emboldened vitality. In the end, I wrote a spiritual autobiography—dedicated to my sister. I told my truth unveiled from fiction. And with it I share the hope of all art that is born from the crucible of trauma. If this story inspires a single other survivor to claim the truth of their experience, to know that they are not alone, and to launch—even with trepidation—a journey toward healing, then my odyssey would be complete.

AUTHOR'S APOLOGY

———— ✦ ————

THIS SPIRITUAL MEMOIR recounts events that are usually consigned to the shadows. Consumed with shame and terrified of social disdain, childhood sexual abuse survivors most often keep their stories secret. Secrets, however, can kill. The nightmares in my family's shadows ended up taking my sister's life. A fundamental commitment in writing this book is that such stories need to be brought into the light of day. Keeping abuse a secret only perpetuates suffering. The harsh truth needs to be told. Only then can it be healed.

That being said, in the legacy of sexual abuse, the survivor is not the only one who knows affliction. Sometimes, a survivor afflicts others. Wounded people wound people. Such is certainly true of me. In my inability to face the truth of my pain, and with my resistance to embracing a path of recovery, I severely mistreated several women with whom I was intimately involved. That is part of the story too. That is part of the truth that needs to be told.

Disclosing details, however, about another's suffering demands careful consideration. On the one hand, denying my abusive behavior, and omitting it altogether from the narrative, would not only be untruthful, it would violate the imperative to no longer keep secret painful and lethal realities. For me, an honest recounting of recovery from trauma must include a reckoning with the abuse that a survivor can also perpetrate. To deny this *pedestalizes* a survivor as one incapable of misconduct and minimizes the pain wrought when the abused becomes an abuser. True recovery includes repentance when warranted, and repair to the extent that it is possible.

On the other hand, the women that I mistreated have every right to agency over their own story and freedom to follow their own survivor's path however that unfolds. Their story is theirs to disclose—or not. Their trauma does not need re-wounding by exposing it to public scrutiny and robbing them of the privacy required to heal on their own. They have suffered enough. They deserve anonymity if they so desire it. And the safe space that confidentiality can provide.

Toward that end, I have created a composite fictitious character, Cathy, that conflates several of my intimate relationships into a single persona. To obscure the identities of the actual women involved, I have altered such identifying particulars as names, hometowns, locales, professions, and leisurely pursuits; and I have modified plot points in the scenes that unfold, consolidating events that played out over several different relationships into a single character's story. To attribute every dimension of Cathy's narrative to any one individual would be inaccurate; it would also be an invasion of the privacy of those actually involved. To be sure, the tenor of the abuse portrayed in my relationship with Cathy is absolutely truthful. The details, though, are obscured to protect those who were abused.

In this way, I hope both to hold myself accountable for my afflictive behavior and to preserve the anonymity of those who endured it. The only ones who know what happened to them specifically are the women themselves. And as for them, I hope that this recounting, as painful as it is, offers some measure of validation. Each of you—I really did treat you brutally. I know that no words can repair the damage. I can only acknowledge it, and acknowledge that wounds I shed continue to bleed. May it be some consolation to know that I know it was all on me. And for what it is worth, to know that I am sorry. So sorry, I am breaking the silence of how I hurt you.

ACKNOWLEDGMENTS

———◆———

A NETWORK OF support—incarnating a Shekinah-like care—sustained me through my recovery from abuse. I would not have a book to write—nor the resources to write it—if not for the friends, companions, and therapeutic professionals named throughout this work. Your care kept me alive.

A similar network sustained me through the writing and publication. President Kah-Jin Jeffrey Kuan, Dean Sheryl Kujawa-Holbrook, and the Claremont School of Theology Board of Trustees granted me a research leave to craft the manuscript. Ulrike Guthrie—the editor extraordinaire who reads everything that I write—offered invaluable feedback and unfaltering encouragement along the way. A number of beloved friends read the entire manuscript and gifted me with their empathy and insight: Alane Daugherty, Andy Dreitcer, Robert Falconer, Doug Frank, Nancy Linton, Jim Neafsey, and Daniel Judah Sklar. Dudley Delffs provided a professional assessment for the first full draft with his customary insight and precision. David Morris of Lake Drive Books—with his extensive publishing savvy, his cheerleading care for books and authors, and his soulful commitment to books that make a difference—honored me with his unwavering efforts to bring this book into the world. And my family—Alane, Justin, Michael, and Sammy—knew what this book meant to me and granted me, as we were hunkered down during Covid, grace and understanding while I stole away to work on it.

Finally, my wife, Alane, was the ground that held it all. Babe, it is truly your nature: You can turn the world on with your smile and make nothing days suddenly seem worthwhile. I won the lottery when you wed your smile to me. You are my soulmate and my playmate. You are my confidante and my best friend. You are my eternal "partner" in both love and work. In truth, you are my pietà.

ABOUT THE AUTHOR

———— ◆ ————

FRANK ROGERS JR., PhD, is the Muriel Bernice Roberts Professor of Spiritual Formation and Narrative Pedagogy at Claremont School of Theology. He's a spiritual director, speaker, retreat leader, and the author of *Practicing Compassion, Compassion in Practice: The Way of Jesus*, and *The God of Shattered Glass: A Novel*. He focuses on spirituality that is contemplative, creative, and socially liberative. He is the cofounder of the Center for Engaged Compassion (centerforengagedcompassion.com) and lives in Southern California with his wife, Dr. Alane Daugherty, with whom he shares three sons.

ABOUT LAKE DRIVE BOOKS

———◆———

LAKE DRIVE BOOKS is an independent publishing company offering books that help you heal, grow, and discover.

We offer books about values and strategies, not ideologies; authors that are spiritually rich, contextually intelligent, and focused on human flourishing; and we want to help readers feel seen.

If you like this book, or any of our other books at lakedrivebooks.com, we could use your help: please follow our authors on social media or join their email newsletters, and please especially tell others about these remarkable books and their authors.